HARCOURT
Science

Harcourt School Publishers

Orlando • Boston • Dallas • Chicago • San Diego

www.harcourtschool.com

The **North American Porcupine** can be found throughout the western United States and Canada. They live mostly in woods and woodlands. When porcupines are born, their quills are soft, but they become hard within an hour after birth. The quills of a porcupine are found on its back and tail. There can be up to 30,000 of them. The inside covers of this book show a closeup of porcupine quills.

Printed in the United States of America
ISBN 0-15-322920-9

12 13 14 15 048 10 09 08 07 06 05

Authors

Marjorie Slavick Frank
Former Adjunct Faculty Member
Hunter, Brooklyn, and
    Manhattan Colleges
New York, New York

Robert M. Jones
Professor of Education
University of Houston–
    Clear Lake
Houston, Texas

Gerald H. Krockover
*Professor of Earth and Atmospheric
    Science Education*
School Mathematics and
    Science Center
Purdue University
West Lafayette, Indiana

Mozell P. Lang
Science Education Consultant
Michigan Department
    of Education
Lansing, Michigan

Joyce C. McLeod
Visiting Professor
Rollins College
Winter Park, Florida

Carol J. Valenta
*Vice President—Education, Exhibits,
    and Programs*
St. Louis Science Center
St. Louis, Missouri

Barry A. Van Deman
*Program Director, Informal Science
    Education*
Arlington, Virginia

UNIT A LIFE SCIENCE
Plants and Animals

UNIT B

LIFE SCIENCE

Plants and Animals Interact

UNIT C

EARTH SCIENCE
Earth's Land

Cycles on Earth and in Space

UNIT E · PHYSICAL SCIENCE
Investigating Matter

UNIT F PHYSICAL SCIENCE
Exploring Energy and Forces

Planning an Investigation

How do scientists answer a question or solve a problem they have identified? They use organized ways called **scientific methods** to plan and conduct a study. Scientists use science process skills to help them gather, organize, analyze, and present their information.

Lerin is using this scientific method for experimenting to find an answer to her question. You can use these steps, too.

STEP 1 Observe, and ask questions.

- Use your senses to make observations.
- Record **one** question that you would like to answer.
- Write down what you already know about the topic of your question.
- Decide what other information you need.
- Do research to find more information about your topic.

Which food does my hamster like best?

STEP 2 **Form a hypothesis.**

• Write a possible answer to your question. A possible answer to a question is a **hypothesis**. A hypothesis can be tested to see if it is correct.

• Write your hypothesis in a complete sentence.

My hypothesis is: My hamster likes sunflower seeds best.

STEP 3 **Plan an experiment.**

• Decide how to conduct a fair test of your hypothesis by controlling variables. **Variables** are factors that can affect the outcome of the investigation.

• Write down the steps you will follow to do your test.

• List the equipment you will need.

• Decide how you will gather and record your data.

I'll give my hamster equal amounts of three kinds of food and then observe what she eats. The food she eats the most of is the one she likes best.

STEP 4 **Conduct the experiment.**

• Follow the steps you wrote.

• Observe and measure carefully.

• Record everything that happens.

• Organize your data so you can study it carefully.

I'll repeat this experiment for four days. I'll measure how much food is left each time.

STEP 5 Draw conclusions and communicate results.

• Analyze the data you gathered.

• Make charts, tables, or graphs to show your data.

• Write a conclusion. Describe the evidence you used to determine whether your test supported your hypothesis.

• Decide whether your hypothesis was correct.

> My hypothesis was correct. My hamster ate more of the sunflower seeds than she ate of the other kinds of foods.

INVESTIGATE FURTHER

If your hypothesis was correct...

You may want to ask another question about your topic that you can test.

If your hypothesis was incorrect...

You may want to form another hypothesis and do a test of a different variable.

> I think my hamster likes sunflower seeds better with water.

Do you think Lerin's new hypothesis is correct? Plan and conduct an experiment to find out!

Using Science Process Skills

When scientists try to find an answer to a question or do an experiment, they use thinking tools called **process skills.** You use many of the process skills whenever you think, speak, listen, read, or write. Think about how these students use process skills to help them answer questions, do experiments, and investigate the world around them.

What Maria plans to investigate

Maria is interested in birds. She carefully observes the birds she finds. Then she uses her book to identify the birds and learn more about them.

How Maria uses process skills

She **observes** each bird by using her eyes and her ears. She pays careful attention to the colors of the bird's feathers and the sounds that it makes.

Process Skills

Observe—use your senses to learn about objects and events

What Charles plans to investigate

Charles finds rocks for a rock collection. He observes the rocks he finds. He compares their colors, shapes, sizes, and textures. He classifies the rocks into groups according to their textures.

How Charles uses process skills

He collects many rocks. He **compares** the rocks to find out how they are alike and how they are different. Then he **classifies** the rocks by their textures.

Compare—identify characteristics of things or events to find out how they are alike and different

Classify—group or organize objects or events in categories based on specific characteristics

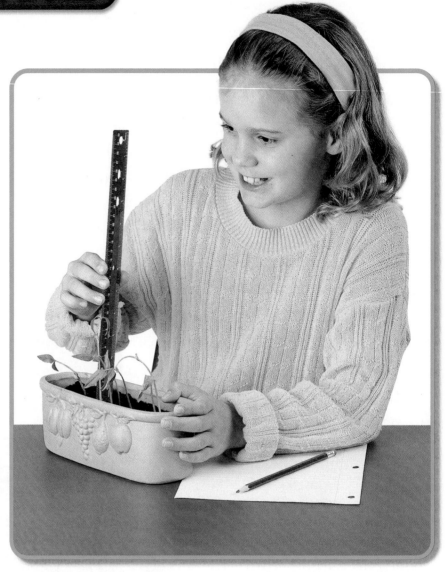

Process Skills

Measure— compare mass, length, or capacity of an object to a unit, such as gram, centimeter, or liter

Record Data— write down observations

Display Data— make tables, charts, or graphs

What Katie plans to investigate

Katie measures her plants to see how they grow from day to day. Each day, after she **measures**, she **records the data**. Recording the data will let her work with it later. She **displays the data** in a graph.

How Katie uses process skills

She uses a ruler to measure the height of her plants every day. She writes down the measurements and shows them on a graph.

What Carlos plans to investigate

Carlos wants to know if low-fat potato chips really have less fat than regular potato chips.

How Carlos uses process skills

Carlos chooses regular and low-fat potato chips of the same brand. Carlos **hypothesizes** that regular potato chips have more oil. He **plans and conducts an experiment** to test his hypothesis, using the following steps:

- Choose two potato chips of each type. The chips must be about the same size.
- Label a paper bag *Regular* and *Low-fat*. Put the chips in the right places on the bag and crush the chips.
- Allow the chips to sit for one hour.
- Measure the size of the oil mark for each chip.

   Carlos **controls variables** by making sure the chips were the same size and by timing his experiment exactly.

Process Skills

Hypothesize— make a statement about an expected outcome

Plan and Conduct an Experiment— identify and perform the steps necessary to test a hypothesis, using appropriate tools and recording and analyzing the data collected

Control Variables—identify and control factors that affect the outcome of an experiment so that only one variable is changed in a test

Reading to Learn

Scientists use reading, writing, and numbers in their work. They **read** to find out everything they can about a topic they are investigating. So it is important that scientists know the meanings of science vocabulary and that they understand what they read. Use the following strategies to help you become a good science reader!

Before Reading

- Read the **Find Out** statements to help you know what to look for as you read. Think: I need to find out what resources are and how people use them.

- Look at the **Vocabulary** word.
- Be sure you can pronounce the word.
- Look up each word in the **Glossary**.
- Say the definition to yourself. Use the word in a sentence to show its meaning.

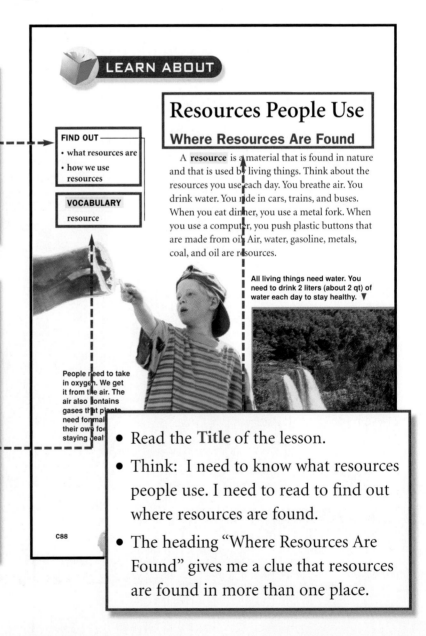

LEARN ABOUT

Resources People Use

Where Resources Are Found

A **resource** is a material that is found in nature and that is used by living things. Think about the resources you use each day. You breathe air. You drink water. You ride in cars, trains, and buses. When you eat dinner, you use a metal fork. When you use a computer, you push plastic buttons that are made from oil. Air, water, gasoline, metals, coal, and oil are resources.

All living things need water. You need to drink 2 liters (about 2 qt) of water each day to stay healthy. ▼

FIND OUT
- what resources are
- how we use resources

VOCABULARY
resource

People need to take in oxygen. We get it from the air. The air also contains gases that plants need for making their own food and staying healthy.

C88

- Read the **Title** of the lesson.
- Think: I need to know what resources people use. I need to read to find out where resources are found.
- The heading "Where Resources Are Found" gives me a clue that resources are found in more than one place.

During Reading

Find the **Main Idea** in the first paragraph.

- A resource is found in nature and is used by living things.

Find the **Details** in the next paragraph that support the main idea.

- Air, water, and metals are resources.
- People use these things.
- Resources are below, on, and above Earth's surface.

Check Your Understanding of what you have read.

- Answer the question at the end of the section.
- If you're not sure of the answer, reread the section and look for the answer to the question.

LEARN ABOUT

Resources People Use

Where Resources Are Found

FIND OUT
- what resources are
- how we use resources

VOCABULARY
resource

A **resource** is a material that is found in nature and that is used by living things. Think about the resources you use each day. You breathe air. You drink water. You ride in cars, trains, and buses. When you eat dinner, you use a metal fork. When you use a computer, you push plastic buttons that are made from oil. Air, water, gasoline, metals, coal, and oil are resources.

All living things need water. You need to drink 2 liters (about 2 qt) of water each day to stay healthy. ▼

People need to take in oxygen. We get it from the air. The air also contains gases that plants need for making their own food staying hea...

C88

In the investigation you learned that some resources are found below Earth's surface. Some examples are oil, coal, and diamonds.

Some resources are on Earth's surface. Water and soil are important resources on Earth's surface. Water is so important that without it, there would be no life on Earth.

Air is a resource that is above Earth's surface. Air has many gases that living things need. One of these is oxygen, a gas you take in when you breathe.

✔ **Where do resources come from?**

Forests cover one-third of the land on Earth. People get wood, paper, food, and other resources from the plants and animals in these forests. ▼

C89

After Reading

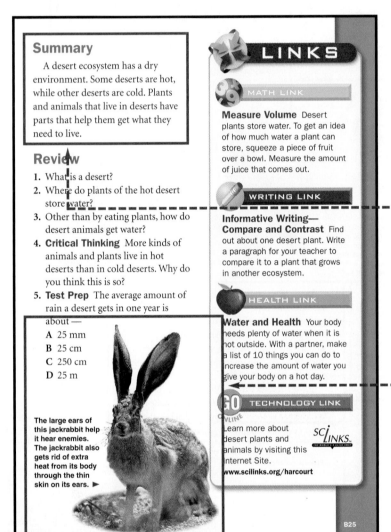

Summary

A desert ecosystem has a dry environment. Some deserts are hot, while other deserts are cold. Plants and animals that live in deserts have parts that help them get what they need to live.

Review

1. What is a desert?
2. Where do plants of the hot desert store water?
3. Other than by eating plants, how do desert animals get water?
4. **Critical Thinking** More kinds of animals and plants live in hot deserts than in cold deserts. Why do you think this is so?
5. **Test Prep** The average amount of rain a desert gets in one year is about —

   A 25 mm
   B 25 cm
   C 250 cm
   D 25 m

The large ears of this jackrabbit help it hear enemies. The jackrabbit also gets rid of extra heat from its body through the thin skin on its ears. ▶

LINKS

MATH LINK

Measure Volume Desert plants store water. To get an idea of how much water a plant can store, squeeze a piece of fruit over a bowl. Measure the amount of juice that comes out.

WRITING LINK

Informative Writing— Compare and Contrast Find out about one desert plant. Write a paragraph for your teacher to compare it to a plant that grows in another ecosystem.

HEALTH LINK

Water and Health Your body needs plenty of water when it is hot outside. With a partner, make a list of 10 things you can do to increase the amount of water you give your body on a hot day.

GO **TECHNOLOGY LINK**

Learn more about desert plants and animals by visiting this Internet Site.
www.scilinks.org/harcourt

SC LINKS

B25

Summarize what you have read.

- Think about what you have already learned about desert ecosystems.
- Ask yourself: What are the characteristics of the plants and animals in the desert?

Study the photographs.

- Read the caption for each photograph.
- Think: What characteristics of desert animals are shown in the photograph?

For more reading strategies and tips, see pages R42–R53.

Reading about science helps you understand the conclusions you have made based on your investigations.

Writing to Communicate

Writing about what you are learning helps you connect new ideas to what you already know. Scientists **write** about what they learn in their research and investigations, to explain their work to others. Like a scientist, you will use the following kinds of writing to explain your own work.

In **informative writing**, you may

- describe your observations, inferences, and conclusions.
- tell how to do an experiment.

In **narrative writing**, you may

- describe something, give examples, or tell a story.

In **expressive writing**, you may

- write letters, poems, or songs.

In **persuasive writing**, you may

- write letters about important issues in science.
- write essays expressing your opinions about science issues.

Writing about what you have learned about science helps others understand your thinking.

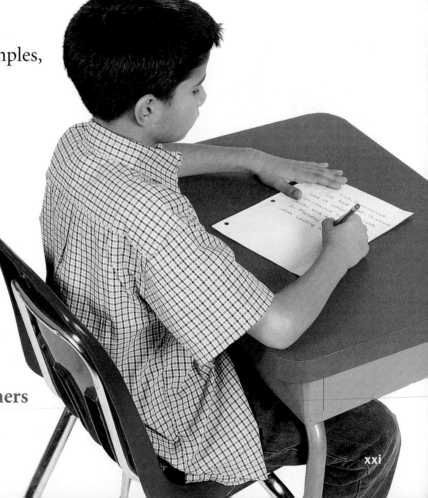

Using Numbers

Scientists **use numbers** when they collect and display their data. Understanding numbers and using them to show the results of investigations are important skills that a scientist must have. As you work like a scientist, you will use numbers in the following ways:

Measuring

Scientists make accurate measurements as they gather data. They use measuring instruments such as thermometers, clocks and timers, rulers, spring scales, and balances, and they use beakers and other containers to measure liquids.

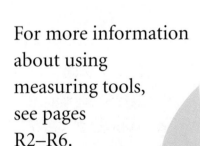

For more information about using measuring tools, see pages R2–R6.

THE INSIDE STORY

Sizes of Seeds

Corn seed

Apple seed

Butter bean seed

Coconut seed

Avocado seed

Seed Lengths

Apple	7 mm ($\frac{5}{16}$ in.)
Corn	10 mm ($\frac{3}{8}$ in.)
Butter bean	18 mm ($\frac{3}{4}$ in.)
Avocado	38 mm ($1\frac{1}{2}$ in.)
Coconut	300 mm (12 in.)

0   10   20   30   40   300
millimeters

Interpreting Data

Scientists collect, organize, display, and interpret data as they do investigations. Scientists choose a way to display data that helps others understand what they have learned. Tables, charts, and graphs are good ways to display data so that it can be interpreted by others.

Using Number Sense

Scientists must understand what the numbers they use stand for. They compare and order numbers, compute with numbers, read and understand the numbers shown on graphs, and read the scales on thermometers, measuring cups, beakers, and other tools.

Good scientists apply their math skills to help them display and interpret the data they collect.

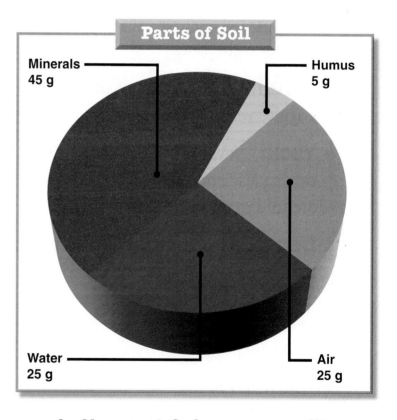

Parts of Soil

Minerals
45 g

Humus
5 g

Water
25 g

Air
25 g

In Harcourt Science, you will have many opportunities to work like a scientist. An exciting year of discovery lies ahead!

Safety in Science

Here are some safety rules to follow.

1 **Think ahead.** Study the steps and safety symbols of the investigation so you know what to expect. If you have any questions, ask your teacher.

2 **Be neat.** Keep your work area clean. If you have long hair, pull it back so it doesn't get in the way. Roll up long sleeves. If you should spill or break something, or get cut, tell your teacher right away.

3 **Watch your eyes.** Wear safety goggles when told to do so.

4 **Yuck!** Never eat or drink anything during a science activity unless you are told to do so by your teacher.

5 **Don't get shocked.** Be sure that electric cords are in a safe place where you can't trip over them. Don't ever pull a plug out of an outlet by pulling on the cord.

6 **Keep it clean.** Always clean up when you have finished. Put everything away and wash your hands.

In some activities you will see these symbols. They are signs for what you need to do to be safe.

CAUTION

Be especially careful.

CAUTION

Wear safety goggles.

CAUTION

Be careful with sharp objects.

CAUTION

Don't get burned.

CAUTION

Protect your clothes.

CAUTION

Protect your hands with mitts.

CAUTION

Be careful with electricity.

Plants and Animals

Plants and Animals

UNIT EXPERIMENT

Liquids and Plant Growth

Plants need water to grow and be healthy. While you study this unit, you can conduct a long-term experiment to find out how other liquids affect plant growth. Here are some questions to think about. Will plants grow if they are given liquids other than water? Will plants grow if other liquids are mixed with water? Plan and conduct an experiment to find answers to these or other questions you may have about plants and water. See pages x–xii for help in designing your experiment.

1

Types of Plants

Plants grow almost everywhere on Earth. Plants come in many sizes. Some are tall, like oak trees. Others are smaller, like rosebushes. But each plant has the same basic needs. These needs must be met in order for the plant to live and grow.

Vocabulary Preview

root
stem
leaf
cell
simple plant
seed
germinate
seedling
photosynthesis
chlorophyll

Fast Fact

Duckweed floats on the tops of ponds and quiet streams. It is the smallest flowering plant in the world.

Sizes of Plants	
Plant	**Height**
Duckweed	0.6 mm (0.02 in.)
Saguaro	15 m (50 ft)
Bamboo	30 m (100 ft)
Redwood	113 m (370 ft)

Frog in duckweed

Fast Fact

The largest cactus is the saguaro. It can be 50 feet tall and can weigh 14,000 pounds! In fact, it would take about 200 8-year-olds to match the weight of one giant saguaro.

What Is a Plant?

In this lesson, you can . . .

 INVESTIGATE plant needs.

 LEARN ABOUT how plants meet their needs.

 LINK to math, writing, art, and technology.

INVESTIGATE

Needs of Plants

Activity Purpose Plants need certain things to live and grow. In this investigation you will **observe** changes in plants. Then you will **compare** your observations to find out some of the things plants need to grow.

Materials

- 6 young plants
- 6 paper cups
- potting soil
- marker
- brown paper bag
- water
- ruler

Activity Procedure

1 Put the plants in the paper cups and add soil. Make sure all six plants have the same amount of soil. Label two of the plants *No Water*. (Picture A) Put these plants in a sunny window.

◀ **The radishes you eat are roots.**

Plants	Day 1	Day 3	Day 5	Day 7	Day 9	Day 11
No Water						
No Light						
Water and Light						

2 Label two plants *No Light*. Place these plants on a table away from a window. Water the plants. Then cover them with a paper bag.

3 Label the last two plants *Water and Light*. Water these plants. Put them in a sunny window.

Picture A

4 Every other day for two weeks, **observe** the plants. Check to make sure the plants labeled *No Light* and *Water and Light* have moist soil. Add enough water to keep the soil moist.

5 Make a chart like the one shown. On the chart, **record** any changes you **observe** in the plants. Look for changes in the color and height of each plant. (Picture B)

Picture B

Draw Conclusions

1. Which plants looked the healthiest after two weeks? Why do you think so?

2. Which plants looked the least healthy after two weeks? What was different for these plants?

3. **Scientists at Work** Scientists often **compare** observations to reach their conclusions. Compare your observations of the plants to tell what things plants need to grow. Make a list.

Process Skill Tip

When you **compare**, you tell how things are the same and how they are different. You may compare objects, events, or observations.

What Plants Need

FIND OUT

- four needs of plants
- how roots, stems, and leaves help plants live
- some different shapes and sizes of leaves

VOCABULARY

root
stem
leaf
cell

These bluebonnets and Indian paintbrush flowers get what they need to live from nature. ▼

Plant Needs

Plants are living things. They live in places all over the world. Plants grow in deserts, in rain forests, and in your back yard. But no matter where they grow, all plants need the same things to live. As you learned in the investigation, these things include water and light. Plants also need soil and air.

Most plants live and grow without human care. They get what they need from the sun, the air, the rain, and the soil. Different kinds of plants need different amounts of these things. For example, a cactus needs very little water. Other plants, such as water lilies, need a lot of water. This is why the kinds of plants in one place may be very different from those in another place.

✔ **What four things do all plants need?**

The sun provides plants with light. ▼

Rain gives plants the water they need. ▼

Plant Parts

A tall oak tree looks very different from a daisy. A rosebush looks different from a dandelion. Yet all these plants have the same parts.

The **roots** of a plant are underground, where you often don't see them. A **stem** connects the roots with the leaves of a plant and supports the plant above ground. You may have seen a thin green stem on a flower. The thick, woody trunk of a tree is also a stem.

Leaves are plant parts that grow out of the stem. Most plants have many leaves.

✔ **How does water in the soil get to a plant's leaves?**

Soil contains the nutrients plants need. ▼

Roots, stems, and leaves are parts of a plant. They help the plant get what it needs to live.

The stem carries water and nutrients from the roots to other parts of the plant.

Leaves take in the air and light a plant needs.

Roots hold a plant in the ground. They take in water and nutrients from the soil.

Plant Cells

All living things are made up of small units called **cells**. Every kind of cell does a special job. A leaf cell helps a plant make food. A root cell helps a plant absorb water and nutrients from the soil. All the cells in a living thing work together to keep the organism healthy.

Most cells cannot be seen without a microscope. The microscope was invented in 1609. Cells were first seen using a microscope in 1665. It took scientists another 170 years to realize that all plants and animals are made of cells.

The first cells to be observed were from a piece of cork. Since cork is made of dead cells from a tree, the cells looked empty. However, living cells are not empty at all. They are full of very important structures. Every plant cell has structures inside it that help it do certain jobs. To find out more about these structures, look carefully at The Inside Story on page A9.

✔ **What is a cell?**

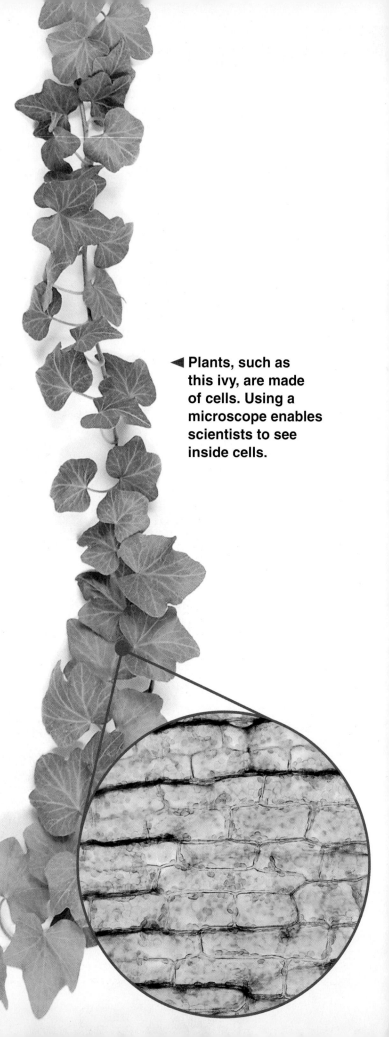

◀ Plants, such as this ivy, are made of cells. Using a microscope enables scientists to see inside cells.

A Plant Cell

Plant cells have different shapes and sizes, but they have the same parts inside. This diagram shows you what a plant cell could look like.

2 CELL MEMBRANE Around the cell is the cell membrane, which is similar to your skin. The cell membrane controls what goes into and out of the cell.

3 CELL WALL Plant cells have another layer around the outside called the cell wall. It is much thicker than the cell membrane and gives the cell shape.

1 NUCLEUS The nucleus of a cell can be compared to your brain. The nucleus has all the instructions the cell needs to do its job.

4 VACUOLE The vacuole contains water and waste materials.

5 CHLOROPLAST Another important part of a plant cell is the chloroplast. The chloroplast contains the chlorophyll that allows the plant to make food.

6 CYTOPLASM The inside of the cell is filled with cytoplasm. This substance is liquidlike and helps hold the other parts of the cell in place.

A9

Leaf Shapes

Leaves help plants get the light and air they need. You may know that most leaves are green. But did you know that leaves have many shapes and sizes?

Many leaves, such as those from maple and oak trees, are wide and flat. Others, such as those from the jade plant, are small and thick. A leaf may have smooth or rough edges. Some leaf shapes may remind you of other things you have seen in nature. The way a leaf looks can help you tell what plant the leaf came from.

✔ **When you observe a leaf, what can help you tell what plant the leaf is from?**

▲ **The black oak leaf is long and wide, with rough edges.**

◄ **The leaf of the beech tree is oval and has rough edges.**

The leaf of the sweet-gum tree is star-shaped. Its edges are rough. ▼

The jade plant has leaves that are small and thick. The edges are smooth. ►

The ginkgo leaf is fan-shaped with smooth edges. ▶

Summary

Plants are made of cells. Plants need water, light, soil, and air to live and grow. Roots, stems, and leaves help a plant get what it needs to live. Roots take in water and nutrients from the soil. Stems carry the water and nutrients to other parts of the plant. Leaves help the plant use light and air. Leaves have different shapes and sizes.

Review

1. Name four things a plant needs to live.
2. What are three parts of a plant cell?
3. What plant part supports the leaves and branches of a tree?
4. **Critical Thinking** How might you care for an indoor plant?
5. **Test Prep** The plant parts that take in water and nutrients from the soil are the —

   A flowers   C leaves

   B roots   D stems

LINKS

 MATH LINK

Make a Graph Gather five to ten kinds of leaves. Use a ruler to measure the length of each leaf. Make a bar graph to show the lengths of the leaves.

 WRITING LINK

Informative Writing— Description Most states have a state tree and a state flower. What are these plants in your state? Write a description for your teacher of each.

 ART LINK

Leaf Album Make drawings or crayon rubbings of your favorite kinds of leaves. Show the different shapes, sizes, and colors of the leaves. Label each drawing, and put it into a booklet.

 TECHNOLOGY LINK
ONLINE

Learn more about plants and what they need by visiting the National Museum of Natural History Internet site.
www.si.edu/harcourt/science

 Smithsonian Institution®

What Is a Simple Plant?

In this lesson, you can . . .

INVESTIGATE the parts of a simple plant.

LEARN ABOUT how simple plants meet their needs.

LINK to math, writing, social studies, and technology.

INVESTIGATE

The Parts of a Simple Plant

Activity Purpose Have you ever felt a soft carpet of moss on a forest floor? A carpet of moss is made up of many moss plants growing closely together. In this activity you will take a close look at a single moss plant and **observe** its parts.

Materials

- moss
- hand lens
- white paper
- colored pencils or crayons
- ruler

Activity Procedure

1 Feel a clump of moss. Describe how it feels. **Observe** it closely with a hand lens. Notice that it is made up of many tiny moss plants growing very close together. (Picture A)

2 Separate a single moss plant from the clump. Place it on a sheet of white paper. (Picture B)

◄ This liverwort is one kind of simple plant.

3 **Observe** the stalk with the hand lens. Use colored pencils or crayons to make a drawing of the stalk. Label your drawing *stemlike part*.

4 **Observe** the tiny hairs growing from the bottom of the stemlike part. Add these parts to your drawing. Label them *rootlike parts*.

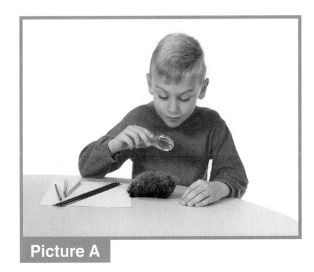
Picture A

5 **Observe** the tiny green leaflike parts growing around the stem. Feel their texture and thickness. Add these parts to your drawing. Label them *leaflike parts*.

6 Use the ruler to **measure** the height of the moss plant in millimeters. **Record** this height on your drawing.

Draw Conclusions

Picture B

1. How is a moss plant like plants you have seen?

2. How is a moss plant different from plants you have seen?

3. **Scientists at Work** Scientists use tools such as hand lenses to **observe** living things more closely. What could you see with a hand lens that you could not see with your eyes alone?

Investigate Further Get a cup of dry peat moss and a cup of potting soil. **Record** the mass of each. **Form a hypothesis** about how much water each material can soak up. **Design and conduct an experiment** to test your hypothesis. **Infer** why peat moss is often added to garden soil.

Process Skill Tip

You can use your senses of touch and sight to **observe** the parts of a moss plant. Tools can help you make more accurate observations.

FIND OUT

- what parts simple plants have
- how simple plants meet their needs
- where simple plants usually live

VOCABULARY

simple plant

Simple Plants

Mosses and Liverworts

In the activity, you observed the parts of a moss plant. A moss is a simple plant. A **simple plant** has no roots, stems, or leaves. In most of the plants you know, such as trees and flowers, the roots, stems, and leaves have tubes that carry water to all parts of the plant. Simple plants do not have tubes to move water and nutrients through their parts. Instead, their parts take in directly from the environment, the water and nutrients that the plant needs. Because there are no tubes in the plant, the water taken in cannot move very far. For this reason most simple plants, such as mosses and liverworts, are not very big.

✔ **How is a simple plant different from a tree?**

This is a hair-cap moss. The parts that look like roots, stems, and leaves help the plant meet its needs. Like all other plants, simple plants need water, light, soil, and air to live. ▼

At the tip of the stalk is a capsule. Inside the capsule are spores. Spores do the same thing as seeds do. They grow into new plants.

The leaflike parts take in air, light, water, and nutrients that the plant needs to live and grow.

The stemlike part supports the green, leafy parts.

The rootlike parts hold the plant in the soil.

These rocks are covered with moss plants. The plants can easily take in the water they need from the damp, shady environment near the waterfall. ▼

Summary

Simple plants have parts that look like roots, stems, and leaves. These parts do not have tubes to take in and move water and nutrients. Instead, all parts of simple plants take in water and nutrients directly from the environment.

Review

1. How do the leaflike parts of a moss plant get water and nutrients?

2. How are mosses different from daisies?

3. Why are most simple plants small?

4. **Critical Thinking** If you find a plant growing in a shady spot, how can you tell whether it is a simple plant?

5. **Test Prep** Where do most simple plants grow?

   A in water   **C** in damp places

   B in full sun   **D** in the desert

LINKS

 MATH LINK

Divide When you drew the moss in the activity, you probably drew it bigger than it really was. How much bigger is your drawing than the real moss? Measure the length of both the moss and your drawing.

WRITING LINK

Informative Writing— Explanation Suppose you are a nature writer. Write a paragraph that describes places where mosses might live in your area.

 SOCIAL STUDIES LINK

The History of Sphagnum Moss During World War I, sphagnum moss was used to wrap wounds because it contains a natural disinfectant. Find out other uses of sphagnum moss in history.

 GO TECHNOLOGY LINK
ONLINE

Visit the Harcourt Learning Site for related links, activities, and resources.

www.harcourtschool.com

A15

What Kinds of Plants Have Seeds?

In this lesson, you can . . .

 INVESTIGATE what seeds need to sprout.

LEARN ABOUT why seeds are important.

 LINK to math, writing, technology, and other areas.

◄ **These corn seedlings have roots, stems, and leaves.**

 INVESTIGATE

Sprouting Seeds

Activity Purpose Cucumbers, carrots, and apples come from very different kinds of plants. But as different as these plants are, they all started as seeds. Seeds need certain things to sprout and grow. In this investigation, you will **observe** seeds to find out what they need to grow into new plants.

Materials

- 3 kinds of seeds
- paper towels
- 3 small zip-top bags
- scissors
- water
- tape
- hand lens

Activity Procedure

1 Start with a small amount of mixed seeds. Use size and shape to sort the seeds into three groups.

Seeds	Days				
	1	2	3	4	5
Group 1					
Group 2					
Group 3					

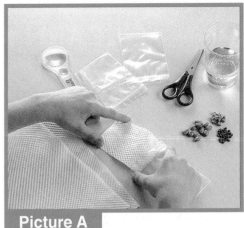
Picture A

2 Cut two paper towels in half. Fold the towels to fit into the plastic bags. (Picture A) Add water to make the towels damp. Do not use too much water or you will drown the seeds.

3 Put one group of seeds into each bag, and seal the bags. Label the bags *1*, *2*, and *3*. Tape the bags to the inside of a window.

Picture B

4 Use a hand lens to **observe** the seeds every school day for 10 days. (Picture B) Use a chart like the one shown to **record** your observations.

Draw Conclusions

1. What changes did you **observe** in the seeds?

2. How quickly did the changes take place in the different kinds of seeds?

3. **Scientists at Work** Scientists **observe** their investigations closely to get new information. How did observing the seeds help you understand more about seeds?

Investigate Further Repeat the investigation steps, but place the bags in a dark closet instead of in a window. **Predict** what will happen. **Record** your observations.

Process Skill Tip

When you **observe,** you use your senses to gather information. Observing seeds as they grow will help you understand more about plants.

Plants and Seeds

FIND OUT

- how plants reproduce

- what seeds need to germinate and grow

- four ways seeds are spread from one place to another

VOCABULARY

seed
germinate
seedling

Plants Without Seeds

You have read that some simple plants don't have roots, stems, or leaves. These simple plants don't have seeds either. They reproduce by spores.

The **seed** is the first stage of growth in many plants that have roots, stems, and leaves. However, not all of these plants produce seeds. Ferns are examples of this type of plant. Ferns, like simpler plants, reproduce by spores. These spores are found on the bottom of the fern leaves, or fronds.

✔ **What is a seed?**

Plants, such as this fern, reproduce by spores. The spores shown in the magnified photo are in small dots. There are hundreds of spores in each dot. ▼

Some Plants Make Seeds

Plants that reproduce by seeds usually form more than one seed at a time. These seeds carry the information needed to grow into plants that look very much like the adult plant they came from.

Two groups of plants form seeds. In one group are the plants that have flowers. You may have seen flowers growing on bushes, on trees, or on small plants.

In the other group of seed-forming plants are plants that have cones. Some evergreen trees, such as pine trees, have cones. The cones have hard scales that protect the seeds under them.

Some plants can be grown from other plant parts. For example, if you place a leaf or a piece of a stem in water, it may form roots. Once roots form, you can put the plant part in soil, and it will grow into a new plant. The leaf or piece of stem used to grow the new plant is called a cutting. Underground plant parts such as bulbs can also be used to grow new plants.

✔ **Name five plants that form seeds.**

Many flowers, such as this tulip, grow from bulbs.

◄ **Dandelions form many seeds that are easily blown by the wind.**

The seeds in a watermelon are protected by its fruit. ►

A19

What Seeds Are

Have you ever found seeds inside an orange or apple you were eating? Many plants reproduce, or make more plants like themselves, by forming seeds.

Seeds may be large or small. They may be round, oval, flat, or pointed. Seeds may be many colors, too—they may even be striped. A seed looks very different from the plant that grows from it. But all seeds become plants that look like the plants they came from.

✔ **What does a seed do?**

▲ After a sunflower seed germinates, a new sunflower plant will grow.

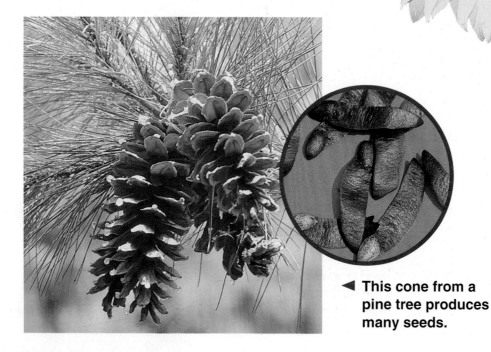

◄ This cone from a pine tree produces many seeds.

What Seeds Need

In the investigation, you observed that seeds began to grow into new plants when you gave them water and warmth. When the small plant breaks out of the seed, we say the seed **germinates**.

As a seed begins to sprout, a root grows from it. Next, the seed breaks open and a young plant, or **seedling**, appears. The seedling begins to form the parts it will need as an adult plant. The roots and the stem grow longer. Soon the seedling breaks through the soil. As the plant grows larger, more leaves begin to form.

✔ **What do both seeds and plants need to grow?**

This summer squash is ready to eat. It is filled with seeds that could grow into new plants. ▼

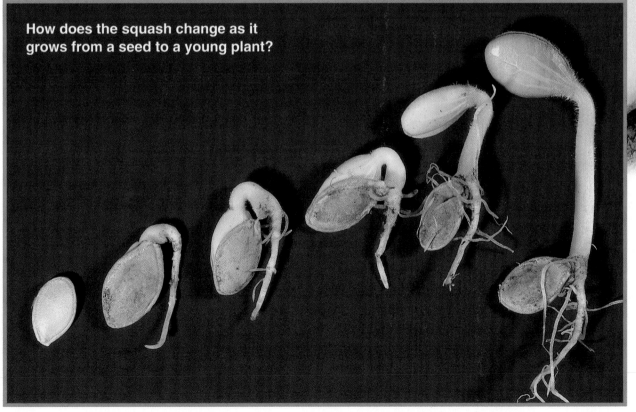

How does the squash change as it grows from a seed to a young plant?

Seed Parts

Seeds may be many different shapes, sizes, and colors. But all seeds have the same parts. Seeds are like packages with tiny plants inside. The "package" is wrapped by the seed coat. Inside the seed coat is a seedling and food for the seedling.

✔ **What are the parts of a seed?**

Seedling: A seedling lives inside every seed.

Seed coat: The seed coat protects the young plant inside the seed.

Stored food: Most of the inside of a seed is stored food. The young plant uses the food to grow when the seed sprouts.

THE INSIDE STORY

Sizes of Seeds

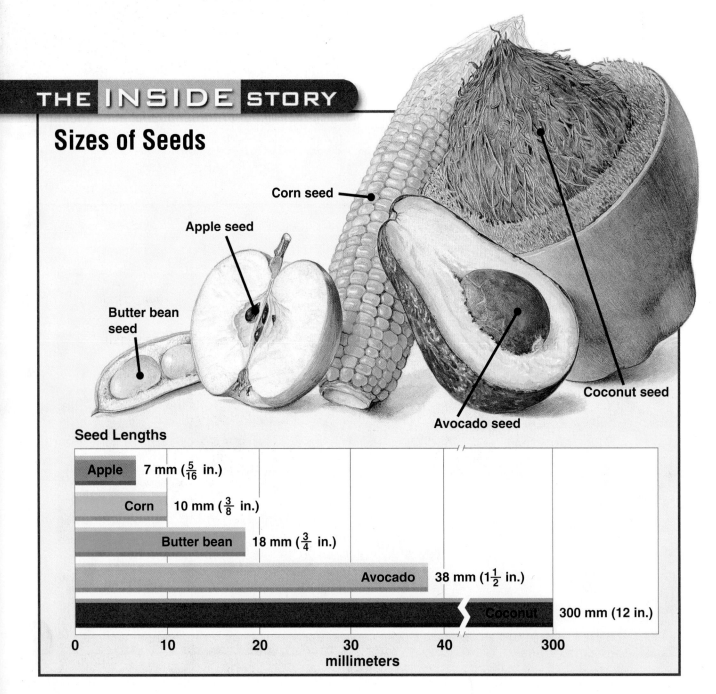

Corn seed

Apple seed

Butter bean seed

Coconut seed

Avocado seed

Seed Lengths

Seed	Length			
Apple	7 mm ($\frac{5}{16}$ in.)			
Corn	10 mm ($\frac{3}{8}$ in.)			
Butter bean	18 mm ($\frac{3}{4}$ in.)			
Avocado	38 mm ($1\frac{1}{2}$ in.)			
Coconut	300 mm (12 in.)			

0   10   20   30   40   300
millimeters

Where Seeds Form

Have you ever looked closely at a pine tree? If you have, you may have noticed that it has two kinds of cones. The small cone is male and the large cone is female. The seeds form inside the female cone. When the seeds are ready to grow into new pine trees, the cone opens and the seeds fall out.

Seeds also form in flowers. Look at the diagram of the flower below. The male part of the flower is called the stamen. The female part of the flower is called the pistil. Seeds form in the bottom part of the pistil. As the seeds grow, the bottom part of the pistil swells around them to form a fruit.

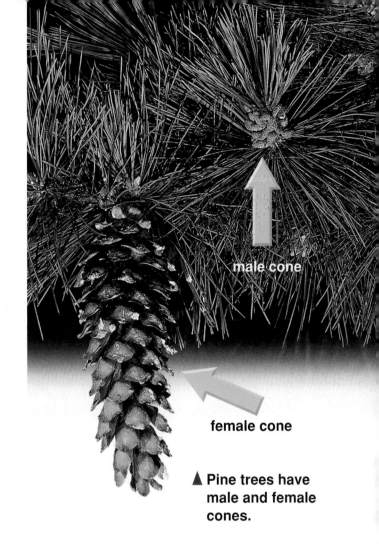

male cone

female cone

▲ Pine trees have male and female cones.

✔ **Where do seeds form?**

Inside a Flower

anther

filament

STAMEN

petal

stigma

style

Seeds form here.

PISTIL

How Seeds Are Spread

Many seeds do not simply fall off the adult plants and sprout in the soil. Instead, they are scattered and moved to new places. Seeds are spread to new places in many ways. Some seeds are shot out of the adult plant like cannonballs from a cannon! Other seeds are spread by air, water, and animals.

✔ **What are some ways seeds are spread from one place to another?**

The fluffy parts of these milkweed seeds help them float away on the wind. ▶

▲
Many berries contain seeds. When birds and other animals eat the berries, the seeds pass through their digestive systems unharmed. These seeds are later dropped onto the ground far away from the plant they came from.

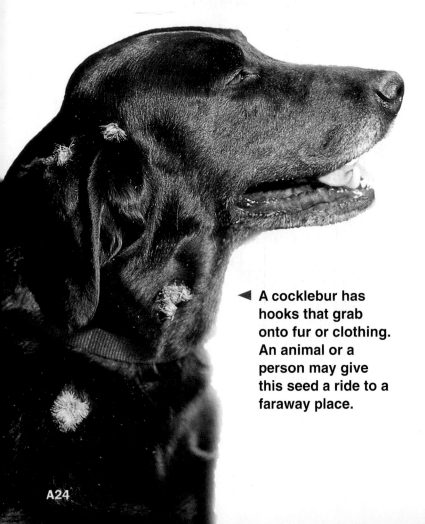

◀ A cocklebur has hooks that grab onto fur or clothing. An animal or a person may give this seed a ride to a faraway place.

Water carries these mangrove seeds to new places. ▶

▲ Witch hazel plants shoot their seeds to spread them. This is called bolting.

Summary

Some plants form seeds to make new plants. Some plants also can be grown from plant parts. Seeds grow to look like the adult plants they came from. Although they may look different from one another, all seeds have the same parts and need water to sprout. Seeds are often spread to new places by air, water, and animals.

Review

1. What is a seedling?

2. What are some ways plants make new plants?

3. Describe some ways an animal can carry a seed from one place to another.

4. **Critical Thinking** If two seeds look alike, will they always grow into plants that look the same?

5. **Test Prep** What happens when a seed germinates?

   A The seed breaks open and a seedling appears.

   B The seedling breaks through the soil.

   C Leaves begin to form.

   D A root grows from the seed.

LINKS

MATH LINK

Solve a Problem Working with a partner, cut open an apple. Count the seeds inside. How many seeds in the whole class? Group the seeds by tens.

WRITING LINK

Narrative Writing—Story Write a creative story for a younger child about the life of a seed.

SOCIAL STUDIES LINK

Seeds Are Food Research the kinds of seeds people eat. Share with the class what you learn.

ART LINK

Fruity Posters Collect seeds from your favorite fruits. Use them to make a poster that tells about each fruit and its seeds.

TECHNOLOGY LINK

Visit the Harcourt Learning Site for related links, activities, and resources.

WELCOME TO **THE LEARNING SITE**

www.harcourtschool.com

LESSON 4

How Do Plants Make Food?

In this lesson, you can . . .

INVESTIGATE what plants need to make their own food.

LEARN ABOUT photosynthesis.

LINK to math, writing, language arts, and technology.

Food Factories

Activity Purpose How do plants get food? They make it! To make food, plants must use the things around them. In this investigation, you will **observe** a plant making food. Then you will **infer** what plants need to make their food.

Materials

- scissors
- elodea
- dowel or pencil
- twist tie
- empty 0.5-L plastic bottle
- water
- brown paper bag
- watch or clock

Activity Procedure

CAUTION

1 **CAUTION** **Be careful when using scissors.** Use scissors to cut a piece of the elodea (el•oh•DEE•uh) as long as the bottle.

2 Wrap the elodea around the dowel. Use a twist tie to attach it to the dowel. (Picture A)

◀ **Lemon trees make their own food.**

3 Put the elodea into the bottle, and fill the bottle with water. (Picture B)

4 Put the bottle in a place away from any windows. Cover the bottle with the brown paper bag. After 10 minutes, remove the bag. **Record** any changes you **observe.**

5 This time, place the bottle in bright sunlight and don't cover it with the brown paper bag. After 10 minutes, **observe** the bottle. **Record** any changes you observe.

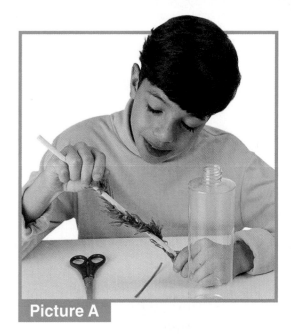
Picture A

Draw Conclusions

1. Did the elodea and water in the bottle look different after Steps 4 and 5? If they did, tell how they were different.

2. What did you change between Steps 4 and 5? What remained the same in Steps 4 and 5?

3. **Scientists at Work** From what you **observed,** what can you **infer** about the bubbles you saw?

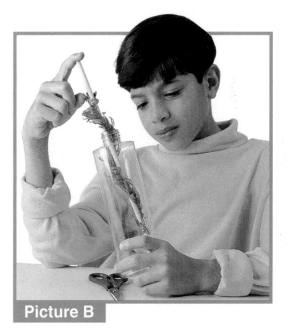
Picture B

Investigate Further Scientists often **measure** what happens in experiments. One way to measure what is happening in this experiment is to count the number of bubbles that appear. Put the bottle with the elodea in bright sunlight, and count the number of bubbles that appear in one minute. Then move the bottle out of the direct sun. Again count the number of bubbles that appear in one minute. How are the two measurements different? **Infer** why they are different.

> **Process Skill Tip**
>
> When you **infer,** you use what you have **observed** to form an opinion. That opinion is called an inference.

How Plants Make Food

FIND OUT

- how plants make their own food
- why plants need chlorophyll to make their food

VOCABULARY

photosynthesis
chlorophyll

Making Food

Like other animals, you cannot make food in your body. You must get your food by eating. Plants, however, can make their own food. This food-making process is called **photosynthesis** (foht•oh•SIN•thuh•sis). A process is a way of doing something.

The leaves of most plants are green. Plants get their green color from **chlorophyll** (KLAWR•uh•fil). Chlorophyll helps the plant use energy from the sun to make food. Plants need light to make food. They also need water and carbon dioxide. Carbon dioxide is a gas in the air.

◀ A plant that gets enough light (and soil and water) grows into a healthy plant.

The sun provides light energy to plants.

▲ A plant that does not get enough light does not grow well, even though it has soil and water. It may die.

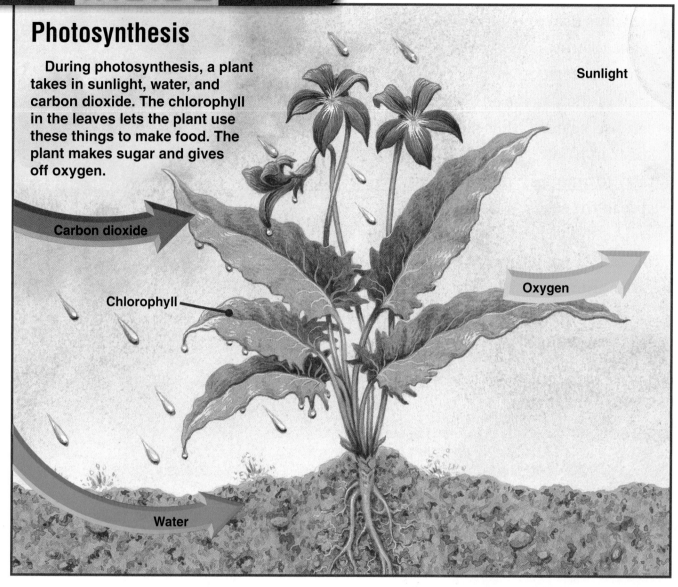

Photosynthesis

During photosynthesis, a plant takes in sunlight, water, and carbon dioxide. The chlorophyll in the leaves lets the plant use these things to make food. The plant makes sugar and gives off oxygen.

Sunlight

Carbon dioxide

Oxygen

Chlorophyll

Water

During photosynthesis, water and carbon dioxide are used by the plant to make food. Sunlight provides the energy needed for this to happen. The food the plant makes is a kind of sugar. The plant uses some of the sugar right away and stores the rest.

During photosynthesis, plants also make oxygen. The oxygen is given off into the air through the plant's leaves. The bubbles you observed in the investigation were oxygen given off by the leaves into the water.

✔ **Name four things plants need for photosynthesis.**

How Plants Use Food

Plants use some of the food they make to grow larger. They also use it to make seeds. Some plants store food in their stems and roots so they can use it later. Other plants store sugar in fruits. This makes the fruit tasty to animals, who eat it and spread the seeds.

The stems, leaves, roots, seeds, fruits, and even flowers of plants are used as food by people and other animals.

✔ **What are three ways plants use the food they make?**

▲ **Bananas grow in bunches called hands.**

◀ **People eat the red fruit of the strawberry plant.**

◀ **The stalks of celery plants contain fiber and water.**

A potato is an underground stem that stores food made by the potato plant. ▼

▲ When you break open a pea pod you can see the pea seeds inside.

Summary

Photosynthesis is the process plants use to make their own food. Plants need chlorophyll, light, carbon dioxide, and water for photosynthesis. The sun provides the light energy that plants need to make food. Plants use the food they make to grow bigger and to make seeds. They store some of their food in roots, stems, and fruits. People and other animals eat many different plant parts.

Review

1. Describe what happens during photosynthesis.
2. Why are plants green?
3. How does chlorophyll help in photosynthesis?
4. **Critical Thinking** How does photosynthesis help make the food people and other animals eat?
5. **Test Prep** What do plants give off during photosynthesis?
   - **A** carbon dioxide
   - **B** water
   - **C** oxygen
   - **D** light

LINKS

MATH LINK

Make a Graph Make a list of 20 foods you eat that come from plants. Identify how many of these foods come from roots, stems, leaves, fruits, seeds, and flowers. Make a bar graph from your list.

WRITING LINK

Informative Writing— Explanation Plants are like food factories. Use what you know about photosynthesis to write a paragraph for your teacher that explains how a plant is like a factory.

LANGUAGE ARTS LINK

Putting It Together The word *photosynthesis* is made up of the words *photo* and *synthesis*. Use a dictionary to find out what these words mean.

TECHNOLOGY LINK

To learn more about how people use the food that plants store, watch *Grocery Garden* on the **Harcourt Science Newsroom Video.**

A31

DROUGHT-RESISTANT Plants

Different kinds of plants live in different kinds of places. Water plants need lots of water. Plants that live in the desert need very little water. Plants that need little water are called drought-resistant plants.

What Makes Plants Drought-Resistant?

Drought-resistant plants have traits that allow them to live successfully with little water. One trait is gray or white leaves or bark. Their light color reflects the heat of the sun rather than absorbing it. This keeps the plant cooler, so it doesn't dry out as much. Another trait these plants have is narrow leaves, which help the plant keep moisture in.

Many drought-resistant plants bloom early in the spring, when there is plenty of water. They develop seeds before the hot, dry months. Some plants have underground bulbs or enlarged root systems that store food. When dry weather arrives, the plant has plenty of food it can use.

Who Needs Drought-Resistant Plants?

Some parts of the United States get little rain. Many of these places are warm and get lots of sun. More and more people are deciding to live in these warm, sunny places. These people often try to grow gardens with the kinds of plants they had where they came from. These plants need more water than they get naturally in dry areas, so people have to water them a lot. But this uses water that is needed for other things, such as farms, animals, and people.

One way to have pretty plants without using much water is to use a process called Xeriscaping (ZIR•uh•skayp•ing). Xeriscaping is the use of water-saving methods and drought-resistant plants in gardens and yards.

How Does Xeriscaping Work?

First the gardener analyzes the soil and the amount of water in the garden area. Then the gardener chooses plants that can grow well in those conditions. Often the gardener chooses plants that are native to the area because they have adapted to the local climate. The gardener puts a layer of mulch, such as leaves or wood chips, around each plant to help hold water in the ground. Xeriscaping saves water costs for the gardener and conserves water for the whole community.

THINK ABOUT IT

1. How can planting drought-resistant plants help the environment?
2. What are some native plants in your area?

CAREERS

AGRICULTURAL EXTENSION AGENT

What They Do Extension agents often work for state or local governments. These people offer help and information to farmers, gardeners, and teachers. They often travel to different areas to teach and train people in new technology used in agriculture.

Education and Training An extension agent must study agriculture and animal science. Training in computers and agricultural technology will be required for the agents of the future.

WEB LINK
For Science and Technology updates, visit the Harcourt Internet site.
www.harcourtschool.com

George Washington Carver

AGRICULTURAL CHEMIST

How many ways can you think of to use a peanut? George Washington Carver found more than 300!

After completing college, Carver was invited to teach at the Tuskegee Institute in Alabama. For almost 50 years, he taught there and conducted experiments with plants. He experimented to solve many problems of farming. The problems included poor soil, amounts of sunlight and moisture, plant diseases, and ways of reproducing plants.

Carver persuaded farmers to rotate their crops so the soil would not lose all its nutrients. One year the farmers could plant cotton or tobacco, but the next year they planted peanuts or sweet potatoes. The land produced so many crops that Carver had to find new uses for them. Besides his work with peanuts, he found more than 100 uses for sweet potatoes and 75 for pecans.

THINK ABOUT IT

1. From boyhood George Washington Carver was interested in plants. Think about the things that interest you now. Which ones do you think will interest you when you grow up?

2. What qualities do you think a plant scientist ought to have?

WHAT STEMS DO

How does water move through a stem?

Materials

- 3 1-L plastic bottles
- water
- food coloring
- 3 freshly cut white carnations
- scissors

Procedure

❶ Fill the plastic bottles with water. Add a few drops of food coloring. Put a different color in each bottle.

❷ **CAUTION** **Be careful when using scissors.** Trim the end off the stem of each flower. Place one flower in each bottle.

❸ Keep the flowers in the bottles overnight. Then observe the flowers.

Draw Conclusions

Explain your observations. Make a bouquet of flowers with the colors you like best.

GROWING PLANTS

Can plant parts be used to grow a new plant?

Materials

- 1 plant with many stems and leaves
- scissors
- 1-L plastic bottle
- water
- ruler

Procedure

❶ **CAUTION** **Be careful when using scissors.** Cut off a 15-cm piece of the plant.

❷ Fill the plastic bottle with water. Place the cut part of the plant in the bottle.

❸ Place the plant in bright sunlight.

Draw Conclusions

Observe the plant for ten days. Record any changes you observe.

Vocabulary Review

Use the terms below to complete the sentences 1 through 10. The page numbers in ( ) tell you where to look in the chapter if you need help.

roots (A7) seeds (A18)

stem (A7) germinate (A21)

leaves (A7) seedling (A21)

cells (A8) photosynthesis (A28)

simple plant (A14) chlorophyll (A28)

1. Many new plants grow from ____.

2. The plant parts that grow out of stems are ____.

3. All plants are made of ____.

4. ____ gives plants their green color.

5. A seed needs water to ____.

6. A young plant is a ____.

7. The underground parts of a plant that take in water and nutrients from the soil are the ____.

8. The food-making process of plants is ____.

9. A ____ connects the roots and leaves of a plant.

10. A plant with no roots, stems, or leaves is a ____.

Connect Concepts

Use the terms from the Word Bank to complete the concept map.

wind   chlorophyll   water   oxygen   animals

How Plants Grow		
What Plants Need	**What Seeds Do**	**How Plants Make Food**
Roots help a plant take in water and nutrients from the soil.	Many plants can form seeds. Seeds need air and water to sprout. Seeds are spread in many ways.	Plants make their own food by a process called photosynthesis.
Leaves take in carbon dioxide from the air. They give off 11. ____.	Three ways seeds are spread are by 12. ____, 13. ____, and 14. ____.	15. ____ in plants helps take in light.

Check Understanding

Write the letter of the best choice.

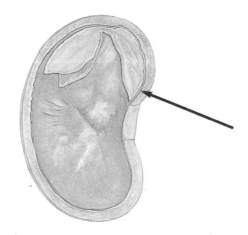

16. Look at the picture. Which part of the seed is the arrow pointing to?
    A stored food   C seed coat
    B young plant   D stem

17. Simple plants have —
    F roots   H stems
    G spores   J leaves

Critical Thinking

18. What would happen to a farmer's crop if there were little or no rain for a long period of time?

19. How can a dandelion growing in the schoolyard be a parent to young dandelion plants growing miles from school?

20. If a plant reproduces by bulbs, does it make seeds, too? Explain.

Process Skills Review

21. You are growing two plants. You want to test one plant to find out how sunlight affects its growth. You will provide the other plant with everything it needs for growth. Explain how you will **observe** the plants and **compare** your results.

22. What can **observing** tree leaves help you learn?

Performance Assessment

Design a Garden

With a partner, design a garden to grow your favorite kinds of plants. Make a list of all the things you will need for your garden.

Types of Animals

How many different kinds of animals can you name? You probably listed animals such as cats, dogs, cows, and fish. But there are many more. Even though there are many kinds of animals, they all need the same types of things to live and grow.

Vocabulary Preview

inherit
trait
mammal
bird
amphibian
gills
fish
scale
reptile
instinct
hibernate
migrate
camouflage
mimicry
extinct
species
endangered
threatened
fossil

Fast Fact

It's a trick! These butterfly fish have spots on their tails that look like eyes. The "eyes" scare away larger fish that might eat them.

**Types of Animals
on Earth**

75% insects

25% all other animals

Swat! Slap! Mosquitoes bite.
Bees sting. Of every 100
types of animals in the world,
75 are insects.

LESSON 1

What Is an Animal?

In this lesson, you can . . .

 INVESTIGATE animal homes.

 LEARN ABOUT how animals meet their needs.

 LINK to math, writing, literature, and technology.

Animal Homes

Activity Purpose Everyone needs a place to live—including animals. Animals live in many kinds of places that give them the things they need. In this investigation you will **observe** animal homes and use the homes to **classify** the animals.

Materials

■ Animal Picture Cards

◀ Ladybugs eat other insects on this bluebonnet.

Activity Procedure

1 Select six Animal Picture Cards or use the pictures on page A40. As you **observe** the cards, pay close attention to the types of homes the animals live in. (Picture A)

2 Describe each animal home you **observe**. **Record** your descriptions.

3 With a partner, discuss the different types of animal homes shown. Talk about the ways the animal homes are alike and the ways they are different. Then **classify** the animals by the types of homes they live in.

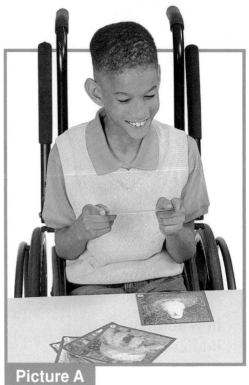

Picture A

Draw Conclusions

1. **Compare** two of the animal homes you observed. Tell how each home helps protect the animal that lives there.

2. What did you **observe** about the home of a Canada goose and the home of an albatross?

3. **Scientists at Work** Scientists **classify** animals into groups based on what the animals have in common. How many groups did you classify the animals into? What were the groups?

Investigate Further Study the Animal Picture Cards again. This time, look at the body covering of each animal. Describe each covering. How can you use body coverings to **classify** the animals?

Process Skill Tip

When you **classify** things, you put them into groups. You put things into a group because they have something in common. For example, you could put into one group the animals that build nests.

Animals and Their Needs

FIND OUT

- what animals need so they can live
- how animals' bodies help them meet their needs
- how animals get their traits

VOCABULARY

inherit
trait

What Animals Need

Have you ever cared for a pet? If so, you know that a pet needs food and water. A pet also needs shelter, or a place to live. Wild animals have the same needs as pets. The difference is that wild animals must meet their needs on their own.

As you learned in the investigation, different animals make their homes in different surroundings. From their surroundings, they get all the things they need. This is something all animals have in common.

✔ **Name three things animals need.**

This reef is made up of tiny living animals called corals. Other animals, such as the dolphin shown here, look for food in the reef and use the reef for shelter. ▼

Animals Need Air

Have you ever thought about the air around you? Air contains a gas called oxygen. Animals need oxygen to live.

Animals that live on land, such as giraffes, have lungs that get oxygen from the air. Insects get oxygen from the air through tiny holes in their bodies. Many water animals, such as fish, get their oxygen from water. Other water animals, such as whales, must come to the surface and breathe air to get oxygen.

✔ **Name two ways animals get oxygen.**

▲ **An alligator comes to the water's surface to breathe the air it needs.**

Animals Need Water

The bodies of all animals contain water. Every day some of this water leaves the animals' bodies. For example, when an animal pants or sweats, it loses some water from its body. The animal must replace this water to stay alive.

Most animals get the water they need by drinking. The water they drink may come from puddles, streams, rivers, ponds, or lakes. Other animals get most of their water in the foods they eat.

✔ **How do animals get the water they need?**

At this water hole on the African plains, animals drink the water they need. ▼

Animals Need Food

All animals need food. Food gives animals the materials they need so they can grow and stay healthy. Animals also get energy from food.

Unlike plants, animals cannot make their own food. Instead, they get their food by eating plants or other animals. Some animals eat only plants. Some eat only animals. Some eat both.

How do animals get the food they need? Many of them have body parts that help them get their food. For example, an elephant uses its trunk to grab leaves from trees. A hawk can use its sharp claws to catch a mouse.

✔ **What do animals eat?**

▲ **This chameleon uses its tongue to catch insects.**

Brown bears live in forests, where they eat many kinds of plants and animals. They often eat fish they catch in streams. They also eat grass and other plants.

A panda eats only bamboo plants. ▼

Beavers Build Shelters

1 Beavers cut down trees to build a dam in a stream.

2 The dam makes a pond. In the pond, the beavers build their home, called a lodge.

3 To build their lodges, beavers use trees they have cut down and rocks that they cover with mud.

4 Young beavers, called kits, stay warm and dry inside the lodge.

Animals Need Shelter

Most animals need shelter, or a place to live. Shelters protect animals from other animals and from the weather. Some birds build shelters called nests high in tree branches. They build their nests out of twigs, grass, and mud. Other animals, such as deer mice, build their homes in hollow logs or in spaces under rocks. Turtles use their own hard shells as their homes. Many other animals dig tunnels and make their homes in the ground.

✔ **Why do animals need shelter?**

Animal Cells

You may remember that all living things are made of small units called cells. Every kind of cell has a special function. A skin cell protects the animal from its environment. A muscle cell helps an animal move. All the cells in a living thing work together to keep the organism healthy.

Most cells cannot be seen without a microscope. However, there is one animal cell that you can see easily—an egg. The egg of any animal is a single cell. In a bird's egg, the yolk, or yellow part, of the egg is food for the cell.

Look at the diagram on A47 to learn more about the parts inside animal cells. Notice that animal cells do not have cell walls or chloroplasts. These are just two of the ways that animal cells and plant cells are different.

✔ **How are plant cells and animal cells different?**

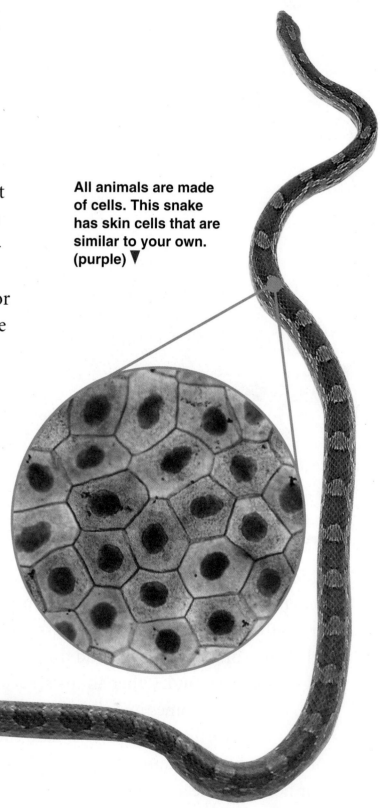

All animals are made of cells. This snake has skin cells that are similar to your own. (purple) ▼

An Animal Cell

Animal cells have different shapes and sizes, but they have the same parts inside. This diagram shows you what an animal cell could look like.

1 NUCLEUS The nucleus of a cell can be compared to your brain. The nucleus has all the instructions the cell needs to do its job.

2 CELL MEMBRANE Around the cell is the cell membrane, which is similar to your skin. The cell membrane controls what goes into and out of the cell.

3 VACUOLES The vacuoles store the water that the cell needs to stay healthy, as well as waste products.

4 CYTOPLASM The inside of the cell is filled with cytoplasm. This substance is liquidlike and helps hold the other parts of the cell in place.

Animal Traits

Jellyfish, polar bears, and snakes don't look much alike, but they are all animals. Different animals have many different shapes and sizes. They also have many different body parts. For example, a bird has wings and feathers. A lion has paws and fur. All these features are important to the way an animal lives.

How do animals get their features? Young animals inherit their features from their parents. **Inherit** (in•HAIR•it) means "to receive from parents." The body features an animal inherits are called **traits**. Traits also include some things that animals do.

✔ **What are traits?**

▲ A sea horse is a type of fish. This male sea horse has the trait of carrying its young inside a pouch.

These young cheetah cubs will grow to look like their parents. They will stay with their mother for several years and will learn to hunt for their food. ▼

▲ A mother duck watches her young ducklings carefully.

▲ These young snakes will grow to look very much like the adult snake.

Summary

Animals need air, water, food, and shelter. Different animals have many different shapes and sizes and many different body parts. These traits help the animals get the things they need. All animals inherit their traits from their parents.

Review

1. How do animals that live in water get air?

2. Describe how beavers change their surroundings to meet their needs.

3. What are four things that animals need?

4. **Critical Thinking** Why will a young lion cub grow to look like an adult lion and not like a sea horse?

5. **Test Prep** Which of the following is **NOT** a need of all animals?

   A food   C air

   B water   D soil

LINKS

MATH LINK

Multiply Whole Numbers
Suppose that there are 15 duck families that live at a pond. If each of the families has 8 ducklings, how many ducks would live at the pond?

WRITING LINK

Informative Writing—Compare and Contrast Birds make many sounds. Listen to birds that live in your area. If possible, record their sounds with a sound recorder. Write a paragraph for your teacher that compares and contrasts the bird songs.

LITERATURE LINK

A Wolf Pup Diary You can learn about the life of a young wolf by reading *Look to the North: A Wolf Pup Diary* by Jean Craighead George.

GO ONLINE

TECHNOLOGY LINK

Learn more about animals by visiting the Smithsonian Internet Site.

www.si.edu/harcourt/science

 Smithsonian Institution®

A49

2

What Are Mammals and Birds?

In this lesson, you can . . .

 INVESTIGATE how fur helps animals.

 LEARN ABOUT the traits of mammals and birds.

 LINK to math, writing, art, and technology.

◄ The fur on this deer keeps him warm all winter long.

 INVESTIGATE

Fur Helps Animals

Activity Purpose When it's cold outside, you might put on a jacket or a sweater to keep warm. Animals can't do that. In this investigation you will **use a model** to find out how fur helps keep animals warm.

Materials

- glue
- 2 metal cans
- cotton batting
- hot water
- 2 thermometers
- classroom clock

CAUTION

Activity Procedure

1 Make a chart like the one shown.

2 Spread glue around the outside of one can. Then put a thick layer of cotton around the can. Wait for the glue to dry. Then use your fingers to fluff the cotton. (Picture A)

3 **CAUTION** **Be careful with the hot water. It can burn you.** Your teacher will fill both cans with hot water.

Time	Water Temperature in Can with Cotton	Water Temperature in Can Without Cotton
Start		
10 min		
20 min		
30 min		

4 Place a thermometer in each can, and **record** the temperature of the water. (Picture B)

5 Check the temperature of the water in each can every 10 minutes for a period of 30 minutes. **Record** the temperatures on the chart.

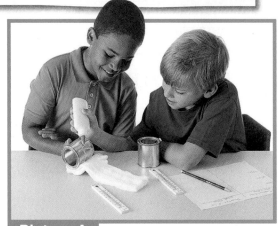
Picture A

Draw Conclusions

1. In which can did the water stay hot longer? Why?

2. How is having fur like wearing a jacket?

3. **Scientists at Work** Scientists often **use a model** to study things they can't observe easily. In this investigation, you made a model of an animal with fur. Why was using a model easier than observing an animal?

Picture B

Investigate Further How do you think your results would be different if you used ice-cold water instead of hot water? Write a **hypothesis** and **conduct an experiment** to find out.

Process Skill Tip

It would be hard to measure the temperature of a real animal to find out how fur helps it stay warm. **Using a model** helps you learn about animal fur.

A51

Mammals and Birds

FIND OUT

- four traits of mammals
- five traits of birds

VOCABULARY

mammal
bird

Mammals

In the investigation you learned that fur can help an animal stay warm. Animals that have fur or hair are called **mammals** (MAM•uhlz). Horses, cows, and dogs are all mammals.

Mammals use lungs to breathe. Mammals that live in water, such as whales, also breathe with lungs. But these mammals must come to the surface of the water to breathe the air they need.

Most mammals give birth to live young. A cat gives birth to many kittens at one time. Before the kittens

THE INSIDE STORY

Keeping Warm

A polar bear's fur looks white, but it is really clear. The fur looks white because it reflects sunlight.

hair

fat

The skin of a polar bear is black. The black skin takes in the heat from the sun. Polar bears have a thick layer of fat under their skin. This fat helps keep a polar bear warm.

are born, the mother cat carries them inside her. After the kittens are born, they feed on milk made by their mother's body. Feeding their young with milk from the mother's body is another trait of all mammals.

When a mammal is born, it cannot care for itself. It must be sheltered and fed by its mother. The milk gives it what it needs to grow and stay healthy.

Most mammals learn from their parents how to care for themselves. The parents often teach their young how to find food. In time a young mammal learns what it needs to know to live on its own.

✔ **What are four traits mammals inherit from their parents?**

▲ These puppies drink milk from their mother to get the food they need.

◀ Gorillas often live in large families. All the adults help care for the young.

A53

Types of Mammals

There are many types of mammals. Most of them have the four traits you read about. Some also have other traits, such as trunks, pouches, or wings. Mammals are often placed into groups based on traits they share. Some of these groups and their traits are shown on this page.

✔ **Name three traits used to place mammals in groups.**

▲ Bats are the only mammals that fly.

This orangutan (oh•RANG•oo•tan) is a primate. Primates are mammals that can use their hands to grasp objects. ▼

A koala is one of a few mammals that carry their young in a pouch. ▼

▲ This spiny echidna (ee•KID•nuh), an anteater, has fur and lungs. It is a mammal, but it does not give birth to live young. It lays eggs.

Whales are mammals that live in water. They have very little hair. This helps them glide easily through the water. ▶

Birds

Birds are animals that have feathers, two legs, and wings. Most birds use their wings for flying. Some birds, such as penguins, cannot fly. But like other birds, they still have feathers and wings.

Like mammals, birds have lungs for breathing air. Many birds also care for their young for a while after the young are born. Unlike most young mammals, young birds hatch from eggs.

Feathers cover most of a bird's body. But not all feathers are the same. Some feathers help keep a bird warm. Other feathers help birds fly. For example, the wing feathers of many birds have a shape that helps them fly.

✔ **What are five traits of birds?**

▲ **A weaverbird uses leaves and grass to make a hanging nest. The mother bird lays her eggs on soft grass placed inside the nest.**

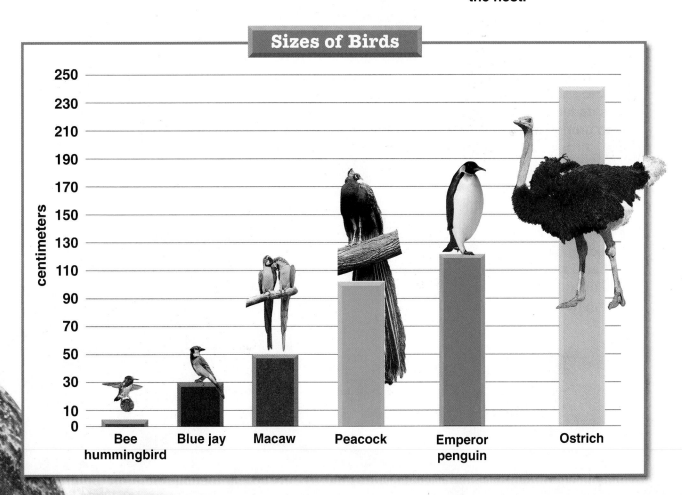

Sizes of Birds

centimeters

250
230
210
190
170
150
130
110
90
70
50
30
10
0

Bee hummingbird | Blue jay | Macaw | Peacock | Emperor penguin | Ostrich

Types of Birds

There are many types of birds. Like mammals, birds are grouped together because of traits they share. The most common traits used for grouping birds are beak shape and foot shape.

Beak shape can be used to tell what kind of food a bird eats. For example, wading birds have long beaks that help them catch fish and dig small animals from the mud.

Foot shape can be used to tell where a bird lives. For example, wading birds have long toes that keep them from sinking into the mud. For some birds foot shape is also important in getting food.

✔ **What can you tell about a bird from the shape of its beak or feet?**

▲
A barn owl catches other animals for food. The feet of a barn owl are useful for catching animals such as mice.

A cardinal uses its beak to eat seeds. It uses its feet to hold on to branches. ▶

The purple gallinule (GAL·ih·nool) lives in marshes and swamps. It has long, thin toes that help it walk on lily pads and other plants in the water. ▼

The great blue heron is a wading bird. Its beak has a shape that is useful for catching fish. ▶

Summary

Mammals are animals that have fur or hair and breathe with lungs. Most mammals also give birth to live young and feed their young with milk from the mother's body. Birds are animals that have feathers, two legs, and wings. Like mammals, birds breathe with lungs. Unlike most mammals, birds lay eggs from which their young are hatched.

Review

1. Name a mammal that lives in the water. How does it breathe?

2. How does the spiny echidna differ from most other mammals?

3. What two features of birds are most often used to classify them? Why?

4. **Critical Thinking** A bat can fly, but a bat is a mammal. What traits do you think bats have that make them mammals instead of birds?

5. **Test Prep** Which trait is shared by birds and mammals?

    A have feathers

    B have fur

    C breathe with lungs

    D give birth to live young

LINKS

MATH LINK

Interpret Graphs Look at the graph on page A55. Which birds have the longest tails? If the length of the tails were added to the length of the bodies in the graph, which bird would be the longest?

WRITING LINK

Informative Writing— Classification Go bird-watching in your schoolyard, a park, or in your back yard. If possible, use binoculars. Write a description of each bird to share with your classmates. Identify as many birds as you can.

ART LINK

Animal Tracks You can identify many animals by the tracks they make with their feet. Make a collage of tracks. Label each track with the animal's name.

TECHNOLOGY LINK

Learn more about mammals and birds by investigating *Whose Tracks Are These?* on **Harcourt Science Explorations CD-ROM.**

What Are Amphibians, Fish, and Reptiles?

In this lesson, you can . . .

INVESTIGATE how frogs change as they grow.

LEARN ABOUT amphibians, fish, and reptiles.

LINK to math, writing, technology, and other areas.

INVESTIGATE

From Egg to Frog

Activity Purpose Frogs lay eggs in the water. When a young frog hatches, it can live only in water. But as the young frog grows, its body changes. The changes get it ready to live on land. In this investigation you will **observe** these changes in real frogs.

Materials

- gravel
- aquarium
- water
- ruler
- water plants
- rock
- tadpoles
- dried fish food

◄ These frog eggs were laid underwater. They will hatch into tadpoles.

◄ Unlike frogs you may know about, this red-eyed tree frog makes its home in trees.

Activity Procedure

1 Put a layer of gravel on the bottom of the aquarium. Add 12 cm to 15 cm of water.

2 Float some water plants on top of the water, and stick others into the gravel. Add the rock. It should be big enough so that frogs can sit on it later and be out of the water. (Picture A)

Picture A

3 Put two or three tadpoles, or young frogs, in the water. Put the aquarium where there is some light but no direct sunlight.

4 Feed the tadpoles a small amount of dried fish food once a day. Add fresh water to the aquarium once a week.

5 **Observe** the tadpoles every day. Once a week, make a drawing of what they look like.

Draw Conclusions

1. What changes did you see as the tadpoles grew?

2. When the tadpoles began to climb out of the water, what did their bodies look like?

3. **Scientists at Work** Scientists **record** what they **observe.** How did recording your observations help you learn about the growing tadpoles?

Investigate Further How important were the water plants to the growth of the tadpoles? **Form a hypothesis** about this question, and **plan an experiment** to test your hypothesis.

Process Skill Tip

When you **observe,** you use your senses of sight, hearing, smell, and touch. Then you **record,** or write down, your observations.

Amphibians, Fish, and Reptiles

Amphibians

FIND OUT

- four traits of amphibians
- four traits of fish
- three traits of reptiles

VOCABULARY

amphibian
gills
fish
scales
reptile

In the investigation, you observed that a tadpole lives in water. But as the tadpole grows into a frog, it spends more time out of the water. Frogs are amphibians. **Amphibians** (am•FIB•ee•uhnz) are animals that begin life in the water and move onto land as adults.

Amphibians lay eggs in the water. The eggs stay there until they hatch. Young amphibians live in the water, just as tadpoles do. Most adult amphibians live on land.

Amphibians have moist skin. But most amphibians still stay close to water.

✔ **Name three traits of an amphibian.**

◀ A salamander moves its body from side to side to help its legs move forward.

Newts live in water for part of the year. Then they live on land. ▼

▲ Toads live most of their adult lives on land. Unlike some other amphibians, toads have rough, bumpy skin.

A60

Frog Metamorphosis

A frog changes as it grows from an egg to an adult. The changes it goes through are called *metamorphosis* (met·uh·MAWR·fuh·sis).

Frogs Grow and Change

As you saw in the investigation, young frogs look very different from adult frogs. Young frogs hatch from eggs and begin life in the water. They breathe with gills. **Gills** are body parts that take in oxygen from the water.

As they grow, young frogs change. In time, they form lungs. Once they have lungs, their gills begin to disappear. Then they develop other body parts that help them live on land. Adult frogs spend most of the year on land near water.

✔ **What body parts do young frogs have that adult frogs do not have?**

1 A frog lays many eggs at one time. The eggs are covered by a jellylike coating.

2 Hatched tadpoles have gills for breathing in water. They also have a tail but no legs.

3 As a tadpole grows, lungs begin to form. Back and front legs begin to grow. These parts allow an adult frog to live on land.

4 Once the lungs work, the gills and the tail disappear. The adult frog is now ready to live on land.

Fish

Fish are animals that live their whole lives in water. Like young amphibians, fish have gills. The gills are on the sides of a fish's head. The gills take in oxygen as water moves over them.

Most fish are covered with scales. **Scales** are small, thin, flat plates that help protect the fish.

Different fish have many different shapes and sizes. Like other animals, some fish eat plants and others eat animals. Most fish lay eggs, but some fish give birth to live young.

✔ **What are two traits of fish?**

▲ **This Guadeloupe bass has a skeleton made of bone.**

▲ **This ray has a cartilage skeleton just like a shark, but its body is flat.**

Sharks do not have bones. Instead, their skeletons are made of a softer material called cartilage (KAR•tuh•lij). ▼

Reptiles

Reptiles (REP•tylz) are land animals that have dry skin covered by scales. Because they live mostly on land, reptiles use lungs to breathe air. Reptiles that spend a lot of time in water must come to the surface to breathe air. A crocodile, for instance, often stays in water. But it stays near the surface so its nose and eyes are above the water. This allows the crocodile to breathe and see.

Many reptiles hatch from eggs laid on land. The eggs have a tough, leathery shell. Other reptiles are born live. Either way, most of the young are able to meet their needs as soon as they are born.

Reptiles are found almost everywhere on Earth except for the coldest places. Many live in warm, wet tropical rain forests or in hot, dry deserts.

▲ **The Eastern box turtle hatches from eggs laid on land.**

✔ **What are three traits of reptiles?**

The turtle has a hard shell that protects most of its body. The turtle has scales on its body. ▼

Types of Reptiles

There are three main groups of reptiles. Lizards and snakes are in one group. Their bodies have rows of scales that overlap. Most lizards live in very warm places. They have four legs and long tails. Snakes don't have legs. They move by pushing their bodies against the ground.

Alligators and crocodiles are another reptile group. They live in water a lot of the time. They come out of the water to sun themselves.

Tortoises and turtles make up the third group of reptiles. They are the only reptiles that have shells. Tortoises live on land. Turtles live in water.

✔ **What are the three groups of reptiles?**

▲ The boa is a large snake. Like other snakes, it sheds its scaly skin and grows new skin.

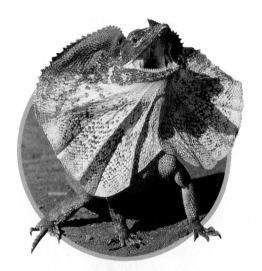

▲ The Australian frilled lizard uses a fan-shaped body part to scare away enemies.

This is an American crocodile. A crocodile can lie very still in the water, with only its eyes and nose above the water. This helps the crocodile catch animals that can't see it. ▼

▲ This is a Galápagos tortoise. Like turtles, tortoises have hard shells that protect them from enemies.

Summary

Amphibians are animals that begin life in water, change in form, and then live on land. Fish live in the water, use gills for breathing, and have body parts that help them swim. Reptiles are animals that are covered with scales.

Review

1. What happens during the metamorphosis of a frog?
2. List three features that help fish live and move in water.
3. What do gills do?
4. **Critical Thinking** Why do many amphibians stay near the water for their whole lives?
5. **Test Prep** Which trait is shared by most fish, amphibians, and reptiles?
   A fins   C eggs
   B scales   D legs

  # LINKS

 MATH LINK

Using Graphs Take a survey of the kinds of amphibians, fish, and reptiles that people keep as pets. Use a computer graphing program such as *Graph Links* to make a bar graph to show your results.

 WRITING LINK

Narrative Writing—Story What if you were a frog? Write a story for a younger child telling how you change from an egg into an adult.

 LITERATURE LINK

Verdi To learn more about a snake called a python, read *Verdi* by Janell Cannon.

 ART LINK

Collage Make a collage that shows adult animals with their young.

GO ONLINE **TECHNOLOGY LINK**

Visit the Harcourt Learning Site for related links, activities, and resources.

WELCOME TO THE LEARNING SITE

www.harcourtschool.com

How Do Animals Behave?

In this lesson, you can . . .

INVESTIGATE how some animals blend in with the environment.

LEARN ABOUT animal behaviors.

LINK to math, writing, technology, and other areas.

INVESTIGATE

How Animals Hide

Activity Purpose Did you ever walk past an animal without seeing it? Some animals can be very hard to see because they blend in with their environment. In this activity you will **make a model** of an insect that is the same color as its environment.

Materials

- construction paper
- crayons or markers
- chenille stems
- scissors
- ruler
- tape
- watch or clock

Activity Procedure

1 Choose a place in the room to put your insect. Note the color and shape of the objects in that place. Decide what color and shape your insect should be to blend in.

2 Your insect should be at least 5 cm long and 3 cm wide. Use a ruler to draw a rectangle this size. Draw the shape of your insect inside the rectangle. (Picture A)

◀ Can you find the insect in this picture? It is hard to see among the leaves because of its color.

3 Color your insect. Use colors and patterns that blend in with the place you chose to put it.

4 Place your insect. It should be in full view and not be hidden behind anything. If necessary, use tape to hold it in place. (Picture B)

5 When all the insects are placed, ask someone from another class to be a bird. Tell the "bird" to find as many insects as he or she can in one minute. Record in the chart the number found.

6 Give the bird another minute to find more insects. Record the number found. Continue until all the insects have been found.

Picture A

Picture B

Draw Conclusions

1. Which insects were found first? How could they have been harder to find?

2. Which insects were found last? Why were they so hard to see?

3. **Scientists at Work** Scientists **observe** animals closely to see how they blend in with their environment. How did observing help you understand how animals' shapes and colors help them to do this?

Process Skill Tip

Before scientists **make a model** of something in nature, they **observe** the object. They use their observations to make their model as accurate as possible.

A67

Animal Behavior

FIND OUT

- **different kinds of animal behavior**
- **ways animals escape from harsh winters**
- **how animals use colors and shapes to protect themselves**

VOCABULARY

instinct
hibernate
migrate
camouflage
mimicry

Types of Animal Behavior

Birds build nests and lay eggs. They keep the eggs warm. When the eggs hatch, the parents feed and defend their chicks. Birds know how to do these things without being taught. Behaviors an animal knows how to do are called **instincts**. Instincts help animals attract a mate and care for young. They help animals defend themselves and find food and shelter.

Animals can also learn behaviors. When a bird eats a bad-tasting insect, it learns not to eat that insect again. A bird that catches a good-tasting insect will try to catch the same kind of insect again.

Many animals learn behaviors from others of their own kind. Lions teach their cubs how to hunt. Birds learn their songs by listening to others of their kind sing.

✔**Give an example of a learned behavior and an instinct.**

A dog will learn a new trick very quickly if it is rewarded for the behavior. ▶

Hibernation

In the fall the days get shorter and cooler. In cold climates, these changes tell some animals to eat a lot of food. These animals get very fat. Then they go into a deep sleep, or **hibernate**. They do not stir again until spring. When animals hibernate, they are not just sleeping. Their life activities slow down. The animal's body temperature falls. Its heartbeat rate drops, and its breathing slows down.

Why do animals hibernate? In cold weather, animals lose a lot of body heat. They need to eat a lot to stay warm, but food is hard to find in winter. Hibernating is a way of saving energy. It allows an animal to survive on its body fat for months.

✔ **Why do animals hibernate?**

▲ Some bats eat insects, especially mosquitoes, during the warm months of the year. In winter their food disappears. To survive without food, they go into hibernation.

This chipmunk curls ▶ into a ball when it hibernates. Its breathing and heartbeat go way down so it can survive on energy stored in its body.

▲ In spring people who live in the northeastern United States await the return of robins from the south.

▲ Arctic terns are champions at long-distance migration. In summer they nest in the North American Arctic. In fall they fly across the Atlantic and down the coasts of Europe and Africa, all the way to Antarctica. At the end of the Antarctic summer, they fly back to the Arctic.

Migration

Many birds fly south in the fall to spend the winter in warmer places. They return north in the spring to raise their young. These birds **migrate**, or travel from one place to another and back again.

Many kinds of animals migrate. Gray whales spend the winter in warm waters off the California coast. There the mothers give birth to their young. In spring the whales return to the waters off Alaska. Food is plentiful there at that time of year. In fall they swim south again.

Even some butterflies migrate. Monarch butterflies travel from the Eastern United States to warm places in Mexico. There, millions of butterflies rest on trees. When spring comes, they fly north again to lay their eggs.

✔ **Why do animals migrate?**

Caribou

ALASKA

Caribou (CAR•uh•boo) migrate long distances between their summer and winter homes. Their summer range provides a great deal of grass. Here the caribou grow healthy and fat before winter. But the summer range becomes very cold and windy in the winter. Deep snow covers all the food. So in the fall, the caribou migrate to their winter range. Here, there is more food and the weather is milder.

Each caribou herd follows its own migration route. Their routes change from year to year. ▶

PACIFIC OCEAN

CANADA

UNITED STATES

ATLANTIC OCEAN

◀ Caribou spend their summers on the Arctic tundra. They migrate farther south in winter.

Large herds, such as the one shown here, leave clear trails as they migrate between their summer and winter ranges. ▼

monarch

viceroy

◄ The monarch butterfly tastes bad to birds. The viceroy butterfly looks like the monarch. This keeps birds from eating it, even though it does not taste bad.

Octopods use camouflage to catch their meals and to hide from their enemies. The octopus must stay perfectly still, or the effect is spoiled. So behavior is also important to good camouflage. ▼

Animal Hide and Seek

Animals have many ways to avoid becoming someone else's dinner. As you found in the activity, some animals can hide in the open. Their colors, patterns, and shapes disguise them from predators or prey. This disguise is called **camouflage**. Camouflage helps animals blend in with their surroundings.

Some animals have warning features that help protect them. Their colorful markings tell others that they are not good to eat. They may have a poisonous sting, or they may taste terrible. Other animals with similar warning colors are not poisonous or bad-tasting. The colors and patterns on their bodies mimic, or look like, the patterns of dangerous or bad-tasting animals. This makes their enemies stay away from them. Imitating something else is called **mimicry**.

✔ **What are two ways in which some animals' colors and shapes protect them?**

Summary

There are two kinds of animal behavior—instinct and learned behavior. Hibernating and migrating are instincts. A bird learning its song or a dog learning to sit are learned behaviors. Some animals hide from enemies or their prey by using camouflage. Other animals are protected by mimicry.

Review

1. List two examples of instinct and two examples of learned behavior.

2. What happens to an animal's body when it hibernates?

3. Describe two behaviors that animals have that enable them to survive cold winters.

4. **Critical Thinking** A butterfly fish has spots near its tail that look like big eyes. Is this an example of camouflage or mimicry? Explain.

5. **Test Prep** An example of a learned behavior is –

   A a spider making a web

   B a dog sitting when you say "Sit."

   C a bird building a nest

   D a marmot hibernating

LINKS

MATH LINK

Make a Graph Find out how far four different animals migrate each year. Draw a graph to compare these distances.

WRITING LINK

Narrative Writing – Story Choose an animal that migrates. Write a story about its yearly journey between its summer and winter ranges.

ART LINK

Camouflage Art Draw a woodland or meadow scene. Add some animals that are camouflaged in the scene.

LITERATURE LINK

Amphibian Behavior To find out about all kinds of amphibian behaviors, read *Amphibians* by Stephen Savage.

TECHNOLOGY LINK

Visit the Harcourt Learning Site for related links, activities, and resources.

www.harcourtschool.com

INVESTIGATE

LESSON 5

What Is Extinction?

In this lesson, you can . . .

INVESTIGATE
endangered animals.

LEARN ABOUT
living things that are threatened, endangered, or extinct.

LINK to math,
writing, social studies, and technology.

Endangered Animals

Activity Purpose Over time, the numbers of some animals can become so low that they are in danger of disappearing forever. These animals are called endangered. In this investigation, you will **use numbers** to **predict** what might happen to some endangered animals.

Materials
- reference books
- graph paper
- ruler

Activity Procedure

1 Find lists of endangered species in reference books or on the Internet. (Picture A)

◄ Zebras are one type of endangered animal.

2 Choose five endangered animals from the lists. Look for information about how the numbers of these animals have changed over time. Find out how many of each animal are living now.

3 Make a bar graph for your animals. For each animal, draw one bar to show how many were alive 10 years ago. Use a second bar to show how many are alive now. (Picture B)

4 **Infer** what will happen in the future to the animals on your graph. Explain your inferences, and share them with the class.

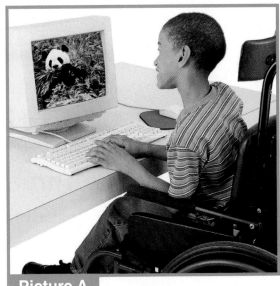

Picture A

Draw Conclusions

1. How did **using numbers** help you **organize your data** in this activity?

2. What could happen that would change your prediction? **Record** your ideas.

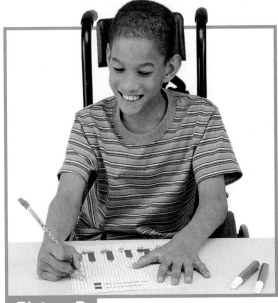

Picture B

3. **Scientists at Work** Scientists **use numbers** to help them **organize their data**. They then use their data to make inferences. How did making a bar graph help you make your prediction about the future of the animals?

Investigate Further Animals are not the only kinds of organisms that can become endangered. Find information on five kinds of plants that are endangered, and make a bar graph as you did for the animals.

Process Skill Tip

When you **infer**, you are using what you have observed to explain something that has happened. You can **use numbers** to help you organize data that supports your inference.

Extinction

FIND OUT

- how different species are threatened with extinction

- why animals become extinct

- how some animals are protected from becoming extinct

VOCABULARY

extinct
species
endangered
threatened
fossil

Threatened, Endangered, Extinct

Last time you were outside, did you see any robins or ladybugs? How about oak trees or grass? These animals and plants may be easy to find. Other kinds of organisms are less common.

Although there are billions of ladybugs in the world, some kinds of organisms have only a few hundred members left. When there are only a few hundred individuals of one kind of organism, there is a chance that all of the individuals will die and the organism will become **extinct**. When a plant or animal becomes extinct, it is gone forever.

Each living organism that scientists have identified has its own name. This name identifies a **species** (SPEE•sheez) of organism. The desert tortoise is a species of animal. The prickly pear cactus is a species of plant. Species that are in danger of becoming extinct are called **endangered**. Scientists add the names of these species to the endangered species list.

◄ The desert tortoise lives in Mexico and the southern United States. It is listed as a threatened species.

Before a species becomes endangered, there may be a reduction in its numbers. When scientists notice that the number of organisms is steadily going down, they say that the species is **threatened**. A threatened species is on its way to becoming endangered or extinct.

The desert tortoise is a threatened species. To protect the tortoise, scientists have put it on the threatened species list.

The whooping crane is a bird that lives in wet, swampy areas where it eats snakes and frogs. It is on the endangered species list because only about 150 of the birds are left in the world.

The saber-toothed cat roamed the forests of the world more than a million years ago. It hunted mastodons—giant elephant-like animals. When the mastodons died out, the saber-toothed cat had nothing to eat. Eventually, the cats

▲ The bald eagle was once an endangered species. In many places, it has been taken off the endangered species list.

became extinct. We know they existed because scientists have found their bones buried in the ground. Evidence of an animal or plant that lived a long time ago on Earth is called a **fossil**.

✔ **What does *endangered* mean?**

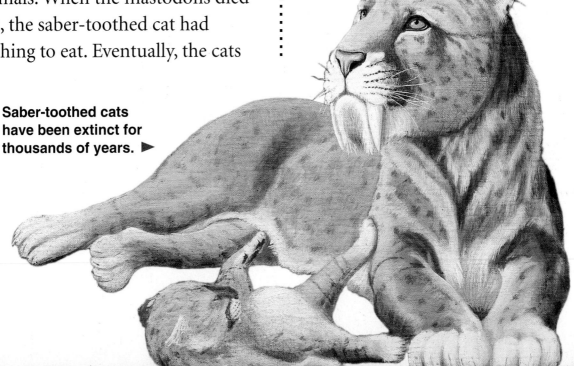

Saber-toothed cats have been extinct for thousands of years. ▶

How Animals Become Extinct

Many kinds of animals that once lived on Earth have become extinct. Extinction is a natural process. Over time, some species live while others die out.

Suppose a certain species' environment suddenly changes. Maybe it becomes colder or wetter. Or maybe a new predator moves in or the animal's main food source disappears. How does the species react? It adapts to the new environment, moves to a different environment, or dies.

Although extinction can be natural, often people cause a species to become extinct. Most animals today become extinct because their *habitat*, or the area they live in, is destroyed. When trees and grasslands are cut down to make room for houses and roads, animals that live on the land have to go somewhere else. Sometimes there is nowhere for them to go, and they die.

Most animals know how to avoid predators in their habitats. But when a new predator appears, the animals may not know how to avoid it. In this case, the predator can easily kill many of the animals and may cause their extinction.

◄ The dusky seaside sparrow used to live along the Florida coast. As people started to build houses there, the sparrow's habitat was destroyed. The animal became extinct just a few years ago when the last bird died.

◀ The Caribbean monk seal was hunted to extinction by fishers who thought the seals were eating too many valuable fish.

This is exactly what happened in Africa's Lake Victoria. People took a kind of large fish from another part of the continent and put it in the lake. Soon most of the smaller species of fish had been eaten by the new predator. In total, over 200 species of local fish became extinct.

Many animals in the wild are hunted for food or sport. Today, we have laws that tell us which animals can be hunted and which cannot be hunted. But a few hundred years ago, these laws didn't exist and people hunted some animals until they were extinct or nearly extinct.

The Caribbean monk seal is an animal that became extinct this way. Because the seals ate fish, fishers saw them as competition. So they killed thousands of the seals. The last monk seal was killed near the coast of Florida in 1922.

Some species become extinct for only one reason. But usually extinction has more than one cause. For example, loss of habitat might reduce a population to very few individuals. This small population could then be easily wiped out by a new predator.

✔ **What are the causes of extinction today?**

Species Watch

Animals on the endangered and threatened species lists are protected by different laws. Some of the laws prevent the animals from being hunted. Others protect the habitats they live in from being used by humans.

In some cases, the animals do better under the protection of these laws. They are able to reproduce, and their numbers increase until they are no longer endangered.

✓ **How do laws protect endangered animals?**

▲ The Key deer is the smallest deer in North America. It lives on the southern islands of Florida, known as the Keys. As more people move to the Keys, less habitat is available for the deer. Key deer were put on the Endangered Species list in 1967. The deer cannot be hunted and they have land set aside for them to live on.

The grizzly bear is on the threatened species list. The bears live mostly in Canada and Alaska now, where there are fewer people to disturb them. Because of the bears' enormous size, people used to hunt them as trophies. Today, loss of habitat is the main reason for their decline. ▼

▲ Red wolves were killed by people who were afraid of them and by people who didn't want the wolves to eat their sheep. The wolves lived in the woods of the southeastern United States. As time passed, much of their habitat was cleared to make room for houses. The wolves were put on the Endangered Species list in 1967. Then scientists began breeding them and then releasing the young wolves into their natural habitat again.

Summary

Sometimes species of animals become extinct. Fossils show us that animals that are not on Earth today existed thousands or even millions of years ago. Extinction is sometimes caused by natural changes in habitat. Other times it is caused by people. Some species living today are in danger of becoming extinct. These animals are protected by laws and watched by scientists.

Review

1. How are threatened species different from endangered species?
2. How can people cause animals to become extinct?
3. What can we learn about how animals became extinct by looking at fossils?
4. **Critical Thinking** How can we better protect animals that are threatened or endangered?
5. **Test Prep** What is the main cause of animal extinction today?
   A fossils
   B hunting
   C habitat loss
   D weather

LINKS

MATH LINK

Compare Heights Moas, an extinct species, grew to a height of about 4 meters. Today's ostriches are about $2\frac{1}{2}$ meters tall. How much taller was the moa than the ostrich? How much taller is the ostrich than you are?

WRITING LINK

Informative Writing—Report Find out about an endangered or threatened species that interests you. Write a report for your teacher explaining the factors that are causing its numbers to decline. What laws has the government set up to protect the animal?

SOCIAL STUDIES LINK

The Law Use your media center to find out when the Endangered Species Act became a law.

TECHNOLOGY LINK

To learn more about endangered animals, watch *Endangered Animals* on the **Harcourt Science Newsroom Video** in your classroom video library.

Discovering Animals

No one knows how many kinds of animals there are. New kinds are found every year. There are more than one and one-half million kinds of animals! More than one million kinds of animals are insects. Some scientists think there could be as many as 50 million kinds of animals!

Grouping Animals

People have been observing animals for centuries. New animals are discovered as scientists and explorers go to new places. One of the first people to observe animals and to write about them was Aristotle. He lived about 350 B.C.

He divided animals into two groups. One was made up of animals with a backbone and red blood. This group included horses, cats, dogs, and oxen. The other group did not have a backbone or red blood.

Since then, scientists have discovered that most animals do not have backbones. Clams, spiders, ants, sponges, worms, jellyfish, and squids are all part of this group.

Your senses can mislead you when you study animals. A whale looks like a fish, and it lives in the water. Not until the 1600s did an English scientist, John Ray, observe whales closely. He learned that they are mammals, just as humans are.

The History of Animal Discovery

about 350 B.C.
Aristotle develops a classification system for animals.

1600s
John Ray discovers that whales are mammals.

| 350 B.C. | 1400 | 1500 | 1600 |

1400–1600
Age of exploration—many animals are discovered.

1590
The microscope is invented.

Discovering New Animals

The microscope was invented during the late 1500s. Using this tool, scientists began to discover living things made up of only one cell. In 1665 Robert Hooke published a book of drawings of biological specimens viewed through a microscope. Scientists today use microscopes to study all kinds of cells. These studies help scientists understand how animals are related to one another.

When explorers during the 1400s through the 1600s traveled to new places, they returned home with animals that had never been seen before. They brought parrots and other brightly colored birds from tropical areas such as South America. They also brought many different kinds of monkeys from those areas. A giraffe from East Africa was sent to China. All of these animals were studied carefully by scientists.

People continue to find and study new animals. Modern explorers search the oceans for unknown species. We still know very little about animals living at the bottom of the ocean. Thermal vents are places where heat comes from the ocean floor. Many strange creatures live near these thermal vents.

Scientists will continue to explore unfamiliar places, such as rain forests, ocean floors, and volcanoes. Each new place will probably have animals we have never seen before.

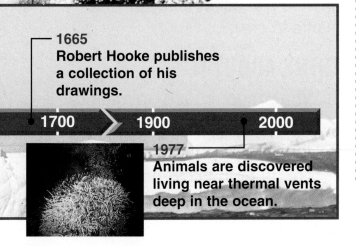

1665
Robert Hooke publishes a collection of his drawings.

| 1700 | 1900 | 2000 |

1977
Animals are discovered living near thermal vents deep in the ocean.

THINK ABOUT IT

- How have microscopes helped scientists learn about animals?

Rodolfo Dirzo
TROPICAL ECOLOGIST

Growing up in Mexico, Rodolfo Dirzo used to watch bugs. That early interest led him to study snails and slugs far away in Wales. After completing his education, he returned to Mexico. He has taught for many years at the Organization for Tropical Studies. He does research on tropical forests. Teaching is one of Dirzo's main interests. He especially wants to interest Latin American students in ecology.

Besides teaching, Dirzo studies two different forests in Mexico. In one, the forest has not been disturbed. There are many kinds of plants and animals. In the other, some of the forest has been cut down. As a result, many of the animals that would be expected to live there are no longer there. Dirzo compares the two places. He uses his imagination and his training in science to describe what happens to a habitat that has changed. Without animals to help spread seeds and to trample down the vegetation, the forest plants may change. Dirzo expects that there will be fewer kinds of trees without the animals to help provide places for many different plants to grow.

THINK ABOUT IT

1. What might cause animals to leave a forest?
2. How does comparing the two forests help Dirzo analyze his data?

SHELL STUDY

Why is a spiral shell larger at one end?

Materials

- safety goggles
- gloves
- spiral shell from an animal such as a whelk, conch, or sea snail
- coarse sandpaper
- hand lens

Procedure

❶ **CAUTION** **Put on the safety goggles and gloves.** Observe the outside of the shell. Rub the tip of the shell with sandpaper until you have a hole about 5 millimeters (about $\frac{1}{4}$ in.) wide.

❷ Use the hand lens to observe the inside of the shell. What do you see?

Draw Conclusions

Animals that live in spiral shells usually keep their shells for their whole lives. When they begin their lives, they are very small. Their shells are very small too.

Think about the shell you observed. Why do you think the spiral is small at one end and gets bigger at the other end?

FEATHER STUDY

What are the parts of feathers?

Materials

- 1 or 2 types of feathers from a bird
- hand lens

Procedure

❶ Study the feathers. Use the hand lens to look at their parts. Record what you observe.

❷ Touch the feathers as you look at them. Record what you feel.

Draw Conclusions

Discuss what you know about birds. Think of ways the feathers help birds fly.

Vocabulary Review

Use the terms below to complete sentences 1 through 19. The page numbers in ( ) tell you where to look in the chapter if you need help.

inherit (A48)   **hibernate** (A69)
traits (A48)   **migrate** (A70)
mammals (A52)   **camouflage** (A72)
birds (A55)   **mimicry** (A72)
amphibians (A60)   **extinct** (A76)
gills (A61)   **species** (A76)
fish (A62)   **endangered** (A76)
scales (A62)   **threatened** (A77)
reptiles (A63)   **fossil** (A77)
instinct (A68)

1. One trait of ____ is a body covering called fur.
2. The features a young animal gets from its parents are called ____.
3. Animals ____ their traits from their parents.
4. Animals that begin life in water and later live on land are ____.
5. Animals ____ to the south to escape the cold winter.
6. ____ have bodies covered with feathers.
7. Reptiles and fish have ____.
8. When one animal looks like another it is called ____.
9. Scales make it easy for ____ to glide through the water.
10. Young amphibians and fish use ____ to take in oxygen.
11. Behaviors that animals know without being taught are called ____.
12. ____ have dry, scaly skin.
13. Evidence of a plant or animal that lived long ago is a ____.
14. An animal that has a color similar to its environment has ____.
15. When all of one kind of organism dies, the organism is ____.
16. If the numbers of an organism are going down, the organism is ____.
17. Animals that sleep through the winter ____.
18. A specific scientific name identifies a ____ of an organism.
19. An ____ species may become extinct.

Connect Concepts

Write the terms that belong in the concept map.

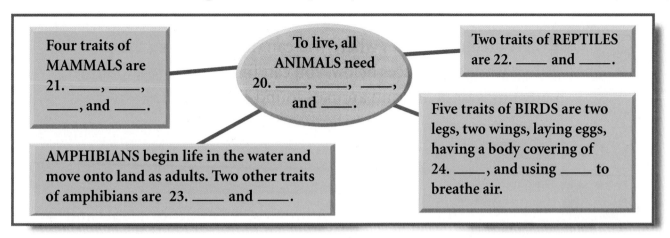

Four traits of MAMMALS are 21. ____, ____, ____, and ____.

To live, all ANIMALS need 20. ____, ____, ____, and ____.

Two traits of REPTILES are 22. ____ and ____.

Five traits of BIRDS are two legs, two wings, laying eggs, having a body covering of 24. ____, and using ____ to breathe air.

AMPHIBIANS begin life in the water and move onto land as adults. Two other traits of amphibians are 23. ____ and ____.

Check Understanding

Write the letter of the best choice.

25. What kind of shelter do beavers build?
    - **A** dam
    - **B** lodge
    - **C** den
    - **D** nest

26. Which kind of animal feeds its young with milk from its body?
    - **F** fish
    - **G** mammal
    - **H** amphibian
    - **J** bird

27. All animals are made of—
    - **A** fur
    - **B** skin
    - **C** scales
    - **D** cells

28. Which kind of animal is a salamander?
    - **F** reptile
    - **G** mammal
    - **H** fish
    - **J** amphibian

Critical Thinking

29. Describe how an animal could become extinct.

30. How are polar bears and bats alike?

Process Skills Review

31. Use what you have learned about animals to **classify** these animals into groups: snake, robin, dog, lizard, cow, goose, whale. Explain why you grouped the animals as you did.

32. Explain how making and **using a model** of a bird's nest can help you learn about birds.

33. How can you use your senses to **observe** birds?

Performance Assessment

Grouping Animals

Use the animal cards from the Investigate in Lesson 1. Group them by using what you have learned about animals. Are there any animals that don't belong in a group? What traits did these animals have?

There are many places where you can discover living things. By visiting the places below, you can find out more about the many kinds of plants and animals found on Earth.

The State Botanical Garden of Georgia

WHAT A preserve set aside for plants and nature by The University of Georgia

WHERE Athens, Georgia

WHAT CAN YOU DO THERE? See the Visitor Center. Explore the gardens, tour each of the garden collections, and learn more about Georgia's endangered plants.

St. Louis Zoo

WHAT A collection of many living animals from around the world

WHERE St. Louis, Missouri

WHAT CAN YOU DO THERE? Explore different exhibits and discover the many animals at the zoo. See mammals, birds, amphibians, reptiles, and more.

GO ONLINE Plan Your Own Expeditions

If you can't visit The State Botanical Garden of Georgia or the St. Louis Zoo, visit a garden or zoo near you. Or log on to The Learning Site at www.harcourtschool.com to visit these science sites and other places to observe plants and animals.

Plants and Animals Interact

UNIT B — LIFE SCIENCE

Plants and Animals Interact

UNIT EXPERIMENT

Acid Rain

Plants get most of the water they need from rain.
While you study this unit, you can conduct a long-term
experiment to find out how acid rain affects plant growth. Here are some
questions to think about. Will plants grow if they are watered with acid rain?
Will they be as healthy as plants that receive regular water? Plan and conduct
an experiment to find answers to these or other questions you may have
about plants and acid rain. See pages x–xii for help in designing your
experiment.

CHAPTER 1

Where Living Things Are Found

Vocabulary Preview

environment
ecosystem
population
community
habitat
forest
deciduous forest
tropical rain forest
coastal forest
coniferous forest
desert
grassland
salt water
fresh water

Living things are all around us— in the air, on the land, and in the water. In this chapter you'll explore where living things are found and how their bodies and behaviors help them live in their environments.

Fast Fact

One of the most unusual wildflowers of the southwest United States is the ground cone. It looks like a pine cone sitting on the ground. Since most animals don't eat pine cones, this is a great way of hiding!

Fast Fact

There are about 2,500 black rhinoceroses left in the wild. Because of their small numbers, they are endangered.

Endangered Animals

Animal	Number Alive
Giant Pandas	1,000
Manatees	1,900
Black Rhinoceroses	2,500
Cheetahs	11,000

LESSON 1

What Are Ecosystems?

In this lesson, you can . . .

INVESTIGATE what makes up an environment.

LEARN ABOUT parts of an environment.

LINK to math, writing, literature, and technology.

◄ These bees live and raise their young in the hive. They make honey to feed the young.

Observing an Environment

Activity Purpose You may have seen trees, insects, and mammals near your home. You may also have seen grass, flowers, worms, and birds. All these things get what they need to live from their *environment,* or everything around them.

In this investigation you will **observe** an environment to find out what kinds of things live there. You will also observe the nonliving things that are part of the environment.

Materials

■ wire clothes hanger

Activity Procedure

1 Bend your hanger to make a square. Go outside and place the hanger on the ground. Inside this square is the environment you will **observe.** (Picture A)

2 Make a list of all the things you **observe.** Next to each thing on your list, **record** whether it is living or nonliving. Write *L* for living and *N* for nonliving.

3 Ask a classmate to share his or her list with you. **Compare** the environments each of you observed.

4 Choose a living thing you **observed** in your hanger environment. Talk with a classmate about which things in the environment help the living thing survive.

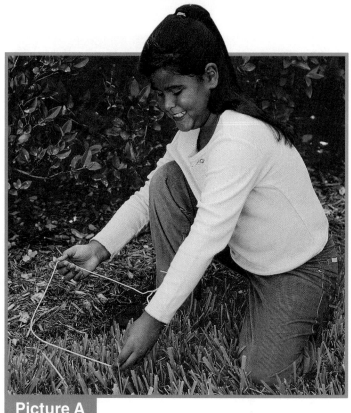
Picture A

Draw Conclusions

1. Describe the environment you **observed**.

2. How can you use **observation** to find out how an animal lives?

3. **Scientists at Work** Scientists learn by **observing** and by **gathering data.** They also learn from the data gathered by others. What did you learn about an environment from your classmate's data?

Investigate Further **Observe** a sample of soil in which an earthworm lives. Describe the environment. **Predict** what would happen if all the earthworms disappeared.

Process Skill Tip

When you **observe** living things in their environments, you can **gather data** about the organisms and the environment. The data can help you learn about the environment and about the things that live there.

Living Things and Their Environments

FIND OUT

- how an environment affects a living thing
- what makes up an ecosystem

VOCABULARY

environment
ecosystem
population
community
habitat

A raccoon in a city may find food in trash cans. Many animals can live in more than one environment. ▼

Where Things Live

Think about where different kinds of plants and animals live. Some kinds of plants and animals live in hot, dry places. Others live in cool, shady forests. Fish live in water. Some insects live in the ground. Others live on plants. In the investigation you observed an environment. An **environment** (en•VY•ruhn•muhnt) is everything around a living thing.

Living things get what they need to live from their environments. They need things such as air, water, food, and shelter. When many kinds of living things share an environment, they must also share the things they need. For example, the plants and animals in a pond all use the air, water, and food from that pond.

✔ **What do living things get from an environment?**

A raccoon in a forest may catch fish to eat. ▶

The Parts of an Ecosystem

In an environment the living and nonliving things that affect each other, or interact, form an **ecosystem** (EK•oh•sis•tuhm). An ecosystem, such as the pond shown on this page, has many parts.

Frogs live in the pond. All of the frogs, as a group, are called a population. A **population** (pahp•yoo•LAY•shuhn) is a group of the same kind of living things that live in the same place at the same time.

Populations of insects, waterlilies, and cattails live in the pond, too. Together these populations form a community. A **community** (kuh•MYOO•nuh•tee) is all the populations that live in an ecosystem.

Within the pond ecosystem, each population lives in a **habitat** (HAB•ih•tat). A habitat provides a population with all its needs and includes nonliving things and living things. There are many habitats in an ecosystem. For example, the cattails live on the edge of the pond. That is their habitat.

✔ **What makes up an ecosystem?**

The frog population, the cattail population, and all the other populations in this pond form a community.

The pond is the habitat, or home, of all the living things that make up the community.

Nonliving things, such as air, sunlight, water, rocks, and soil, are also part of an ecosystem. The community of living things needs the nonliving things to survive.

The ecosystem of this pond is made up of all the living and nonliving things that interact in and around the pond.

◄ Fires in 1988 destroyed the large trees of this ecosystem. Before 1988 these large trees in Yellowstone National Park were the habitat of many living things.

▲ Ten years after the fire, these wildflowers showed that life had returned to Yellowstone.

How Ecosystems Change

Ecosystems can change. Some changes to ecosystems are caused by nature. For example, floods or fires can kill many living things and destroy habitats. But some living things survive when an ecosystem is damaged. A fire doesn't destroy all the seeds in the ground. The seeds that survive grow into new plants. As the plants grow, animals that feed on them return to the area.

A flood can also harm an ecosystem. But a flood brings a new layer of rich soil to a riverbank. New plants grow in the soil.

Ecosystems are also changed by living things. Some changes help the living things meet their needs. For example, beavers cut down trees to build dams and lodges in streams. The other animals that lived in the trees must find new homes. Sometimes, the animals move to a nearby part of the ecosystem. But sometimes the ecosystem is changed so much that the plants and animals can no longer live there.

Many spiders spin webs to use as homes and to help capture food. ▼

✔ **Why do ecosystems change?**

People Change Ecosystems

Whenever people move into a new area, the ecosystem is changed. People cut down trees to build houses, roads, and businesses. They use water that was used only by plants and animals before the people arrived.

Sometimes the changes people make in ecosystems are good ones. They may add irrigation to dry areas to grow crops. They may plant new forests where old ones have burned down. Other times the changes people make harm the ecosystem. Removing trees can cause erosion. Destroying habitats can cause animals to leave an area and plants that grow there to disappear. Polluting the water and air can also harm plants and animals.

In places where people like to live, such as islands, the land may have so many roads and buildings that there is hardly any room for wildlife. Large numbers of people also increase the amount of traffic, and their cars and trucks pollute the air. On some islands, to protect these natural areas, people are not allowed to build anything at all. This is one way to preserve ecosystems.

Some islands, such as the one below, are preserved in their natural state. Others, such as the one at the right, are used by people as places to live and play. ▼

▲ Strip mines such as this one destroy the land.

▲ After the deep holes are filled, new plants begin to grow.

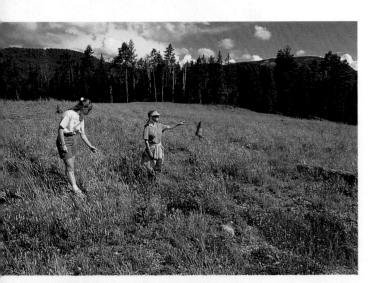

▲ This beautiful meadow is on the land where the strip mine (above) was. The land has been reclaimed.

Some human activities destroy ecosystems. Strip mines, for example, leave huge holes in the ground with no plants to prevent erosion. If left alone, these areas would never recover. Today, mining companies must *reclaim* the land they have destroyed. This means that they must fill in the holes and replant the area. They cannot always make the land just as it was before, but they do make it usable again.

✔ **Name two ways people change ecosystems.**

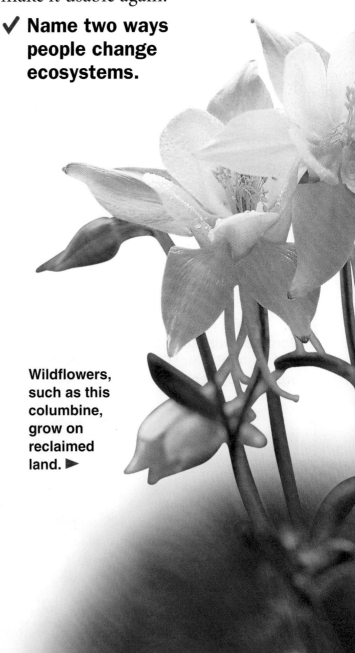

Wildflowers, such as this columbine, grow on reclaimed land. ▶

Summary

An environment is everything that surrounds a living thing. The living and nonliving things that interact in an environment make up an ecosystem. An ecosystem is made up of smaller parts that include populations, communities, and habitats, as well as nonliving things, such as air, sunlight, and soil. Nature and living things can change ecosystems.

Review

1. What is an environment?
2. What nonliving things are found in an ecosystem?
3. What is a population?
4. **Critical Thinking** How can building a new road change an ecosystem?
5. **Test Prep** A pond that contains waterlilies, frogs, fish, insects, and cattails is an example of —
   A   a population
   B   an island
   C   a habitat
   D   a community

LINKS

MATH LINK

Solve a Problem Suppose an ecosystem has 54 squirrels, 12 rabbits, 15 trees, and 100 grasshoppers. How many animals are in the community? How many populations are there?

WRITING LINK

Informative Writing—Report What if a flood destroyed part of an ecosystem near your home? Write a newspaper report for your class telling what happened to an animal because of the flood.

LITERATURE LINK

Read About Fire To learn more about how fire can affect an ecosystem, read *Wildfires* by Ann Armbruster.

TECHNOLOGY LINK

Learn more about how changes in an ecosystem can affect the living things there by watching *Tainted Water* on the **Harcourt Science Newsroom Video.**

CNN
Turner
Le@rning®

What Are Forest Ecosystems?

In this lesson, you can . . .

INVESTIGATE trees in forests.

LEARN ABOUT different types of forests.

LINK to math, writing, art, and technology.

INVESTIGATE

Variety in Forests

Activity Purpose Forests have trees. But did you know that there are several types of forests? In this investigation you will **use numbers** to **interpret data** about trees in two kinds of forests.

Materials

- tray of beans, labeled *Tray 1*
- tray of beans, labeled *Tray 2*
- 2 paper cups

Activity Procedure

1. Make a data table like the one shown. Tray 1 stands for the trees in a tropical rain forest. Tray 2 stands for the trees in a deciduous forest. Each kind of bean stands for a different kind of tree.

2. Scoop a cupful of beans from each tray. Carefully pour each cup of beans into its own pile.

◀ **Moose like this one live in coniferous forests.**

Tropical Rain Forest (Tray 1)		Deciduous Forest (Tray 2)	
Kind of Bean	Number of Beans	Kind of Bean	Number of Beans

3️⃣ Work with a partner. One partner should work with the beans from Tray 1. The other partner should work with the beans from Tray 2. (Picture A)

4️⃣ Sort the beans into groups so that each group contains only one kind of bean.

5️⃣ **Record** a description of each type of bean in the data table. Count the number of beans in each small pile. Record these numbers in the data table.

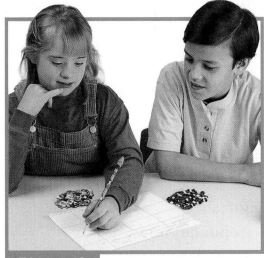
Picture A

Draw Conclusions

1. How many kinds of "trees" were in each "forest"?

2. Which forest had the most trees of one kind? Why do you think this was so?

3. **Scientists at Work** Scientists learn by **gathering, recording,** and **interpreting data.** What did you learn from your data about variety in forests?

Investigate Further Suppose you want to find out what kinds of trees are most common in your community. Explain how you could **use numbers** to find out.

Forest Ecosystems

Types of Forests

FIND OUT

- about four kinds of forests
- about living things in different kinds of forests

VOCABULARY

forest
deciduous forest
tropical rain forest
coastal forest
coniferous forest

You probably know that a **forest** is an area in which the main plants are trees. But many other kinds of plants and animals also live in forests.

Forests grow in many parts of the world. Some forests are named for the types of trees that grow in them. Other forests are named for the area in which they grow.

Each type of forest needs a certain amount of rainfall and sunshine. Each also has certain temperatures that let it grow best. If any of these things change, the kinds of plants that grow in the forest may also change.

✔ **What is a forest?**

This graph shows how much rain falls each year in each kind of forest. ▼

This graph shows the average yearly temperature in each kind of forest. ▼

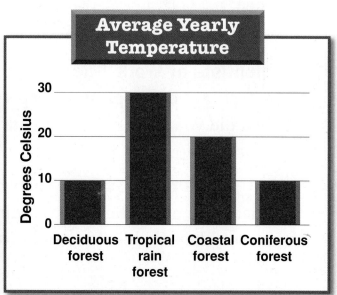

Deciduous Forests

Some trees, such as maples and oaks, have large, flat leaves that drop off each fall. New leaves grow back in the spring. Trees that lose and regrow their leaves each year are called deciduous (dee•SIJ•oo•uhs) trees. Forests made up mostly of these trees are **deciduous forests**. They grow in places that have warm, wet summers and cold winters.

Deciduous leaves change color before they drop in the fall. When a deciduous tree drops its leaves, it needs less water. This helps the tree live through the winter, when water may be frozen.

The deciduous forest is a habitat for many kinds of living things, such as ferns, shrubs, and mosses. Animals such as insects, spiders, snakes, frogs, birds, rabbits, deer, and bears also live here.

✔ **Where do deciduous forests grow?**

The leaves of deciduous trees change color just before they drop from the trees in the fall. ▼

▲ During the winter deciduous trees have no leaves.

Deciduous trees grow new leaves in the spring. ▼

In the summer a deciduous forest looks healthy and green. ▼

Tropical Rain Forests

Tropical rain forests grow in places such as Hawaiʻi and Costa Rica. These places are hot and wet all year. The trees grow very tall, and their leaves stay green all year.

More types of living things live in rain forests than anywhere else on Earth. Plants and animals make their homes in all the layers of the forest, from the tops of the trees to the ground.

✔ **Where do tropical rain forests grow?**

◄ This moth lives in the tropical rain forest. It feeds on the plants that grow beneath the trees.

THE INSIDE STORY

Layers of the Rain Forest

A tropical rain forest has three main layers. The top layer is called the *canopy.* It is formed by the branches and leaves of the tallest trees. Below the canopy is the *understory.* The understory is formed by plants that don't grow as tall as trees. The *forest floor* is the lowest layer. Many kinds of plants and animals make their homes in each layer of a tropical rain forest.

Coastal Forests

Coastal forests grow where there is a lot of rain. Unlike a tropical rain forest, a coastal forest grows where it does not get too warm or too cold. But like tropical rain forests, coastal forests are thick with many kinds of tall trees. Coastal forests have the same kinds of layers as tropical rain forests.

✔ **Describe a coastal forest environment.**

▲ The northern spotted owl thrives in the moist, cool environment of the coastal forest.

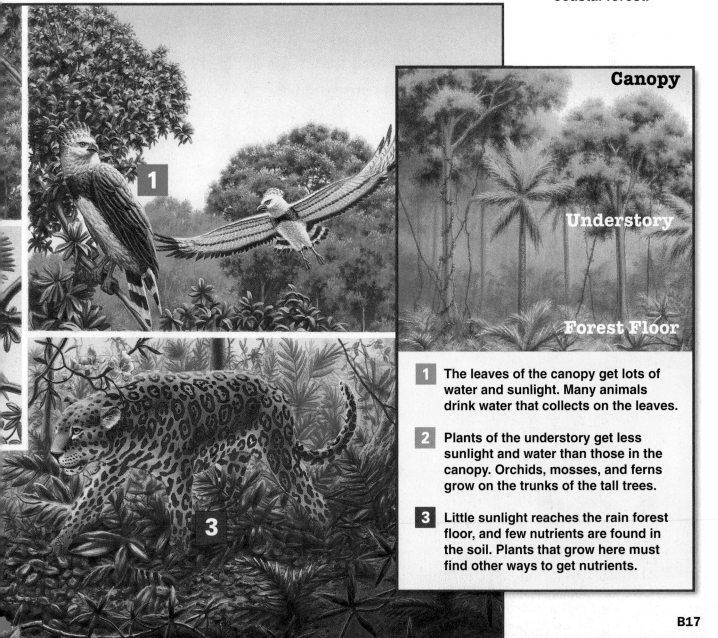

Canopy

Understory

Forest Floor

1   The leaves of the canopy get lots of water and sunlight. Many animals drink water that collects on the leaves.

2   Plants of the understory get less sunlight and water than those in the canopy. Orchids, mosses, and ferns grow on the trunks of the tall trees.

3   Little sunlight reaches the rain forest floor, and few nutrients are found in the soil. Plants that grow here must find other ways to get nutrients.

Coniferous Forests

What kind of trees would you find where there are very cold winters and cool summers? Mostly, you would find *conifers* (KAHN•uh•ferz)—trees that form seeds in cones. Conifers have needle-like leaves. Pines, spruces, and firs are common conifers. Conifers don't lose their needles in the fall. They stay green all year. This is why conifers are often called *evergreens*. Forests that contain mostly these kinds of trees are **coniferous** (koh•NIF•er•uhs) **forests**.

Conifers grow in areas that get less rain than other types of forests. The needle-shaped leaves of these trees help keep the trees from losing too much water.

Many conifers are shaped like triangles. This shape helps keep heavy snow from piling up on a tree's larger branches in winter, which might cause them to break.

Coniferous forests often have many lakes and streams. The trees, lakes, and streams provide habitats for many animals. Squirrels, moose, and wolves are common. Insects such as mosquitoes and flies also live in coniferous forests.

✔ **What kinds of trees grow in a coniferous forest?**

Coniferous forests are homes for animals such as moose, bears, and wolves. ▼

Summary

There are different types of forest ecosystems. The main types of forests are deciduous forests, tropical rain forests, coastal forests, and coniferous forests. These forests provide habitats for many kinds of plants and animals.

Review

1. What is a forest?
2. Which kind of forest has trees that lose their leaves in the fall?
3. What are the layers of a tropical rain forest?
4. **Critical Thinking** What is the main difference between a tropical rain forest and a coastal forest?
5. **Test Prep** A deciduous forest has —
   - A cool summers and warm winters
   - B warm, wet summers and dry winters
   - C warm, wet summers and cold winters
   - D warm, dry summers and dry winters

LINKS

MATH LINK

Interpret a Graph Look back at the first graph on page B14. What is the difference in yearly rainfall between the tropical rain forest and the deciduous forest? Which gets more rain each year?

WRITING LINK

Expressive Writing—Friendly Letter Pick a forest from this lesson. Imagine that you live there. Write a letter to a classmate telling what you like most about your forest.

ART LINK

Leaf Prints Gather leaves from the trees that grow in your area. Dip the leaves into paint, and make leaf prints on paper. Label each print.

TECHNOLOGY LINK

Explore forests as you complete the activity *Backpacking Through Forests* on **Harcourt Science Explorations CD-ROM.**

What Is a Desert Ecosystem?

In this lesson, you can . . .

INVESTIGATE a desert ecosystem.

LEARN ABOUT desert ecosystems.

LINK to math, writing, health, and technology.

◄ This scorpion is one type of animal that lives in the desert.

Make a Desert Ecosystem

Activity Purpose
A desert is a very dry place. But this ecosystem is home to many kinds of living things. In this investigation you will **make a model** of a desert ecosystem.

Materials
- shoe box
- plastic wrap
- sandy soil
- 2 or 3 desert plants
- small rocks

Activity Procedure

1 **Make a model** of a desert ecosystem. Start by lining the shoe box with plastic wrap. Place sandy soil in the shoe box. Make sure the soil is deep enough for the plants.

2 Place the plants in the soil, and place the rocks around them. Lightly sprinkle the soil with water. (Picture A)

3 Place your desert ecosystem in a sunny location. (Picture B)

4 Every two or three days, use your finger to **observe** how dry the soil is. If the soil is *very* dry, add a small amount of water. If the soil is damp, do not add water. Be careful not to water the plants too much.

5 Continue to **observe** and care for your desert ecosystem. **Record** what you observe.

Picture A

Draw Conclusions

1. What kind of environment does your desert ecosystem model?

2. How does **making a model** help you learn about a desert?

3. **Scientists at Work** Scientists often learn by **making models**. What other types of ecosystems can you make models of?

Picture B

Investigate Further How would getting rain every day change a desert ecosystem? **Plan an experiment** in which you could **use a model** to find out.

Process Skill Tip

Observing a desert would be difficult to do in the classroom. To learn more about the real thing, you can **make a model** of a desert.

B21

Desert Ecosystems

FIND OUT

• about two kinds of deserts

• how plants and animals get what they need in a desert ecosystem

VOCABULARY

desert

Types of Deserts

A **desert** is an ecosystem found where there is very little rainfall. Most deserts get less than 25 centimeters (about 10 in.) of rain each year. Desert plants and animals need very little water to live.

In the investigation you made a model of a hot desert. In summer, hot deserts can have temperatures over 43°C (about 110°F) during the day. At night, the temperatures drop to around 7°C (about 45°F). Most hot deserts have mild winters in which the temperature usually stays above freezing.

Besides the hot deserts you probably know about, there are cold deserts. These deserts have freezing temperatures and blizzards in the winter. But in the hottest months, they are as hot as hot deserts.

✔ **What are the two kinds of deserts?**

The Taklimakan Desert is a cold desert located in western China. ▼

This hot desert is located in the southwestern part of the United States. ▼

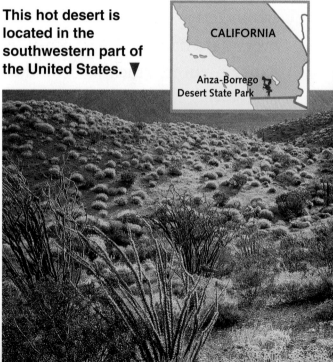

CALIFORNIA

Anza-Borrego Desert State Park

Taklimakan Desert

CHINA

Parts of a Cactus

The parts of the barrel cactus allow it to live in hot deserts. These parts are common to many other desert plants.

1 A barrel cactus has a thick stem that stores water taken in by the roots. The water is stored in the center part of the stem.

2 Like most cacti, the barrel cactus has a thick skin that is covered with spines. The skin and spines help keep the plant from losing water. The spines also protect the plant from being eaten by animals.

3 The barrel cactus has shallow roots that spread out near the soil's surface. When it rains, these roots quickly soak up the water.

Desert Plants

Deserts are dry places. Plants that grow in deserts have parts that help them save water. Many desert plants grow low to the ground, where it is coolest. Most desert plants have long, shallow roots that spread out near the top of the soil. Here the roots can easily soak up water when it does rain.

Many desert plants have thick stems that store water. Some animals eat these stems to get the water they need to live.

Some desert plants, such as the barrel cactus, have spiny leaves. Spiny leaves help keep the plant from losing water.

✔ **How do desert plants get water?**

Desert Animals

Many animals live in the desert. Desert animals get most of their water by eating plants that store water or by eating other animals.

Reptiles such as snakes and lizards live well in the desert. They stay in the shade during the hot days. During the cold nights they keep warm near rocks, which the sun made hot during the day.

Small mammals such as bats, rabbits, and squirrels also live in deserts. These animals are active at night, when it is cooler. During the day they sleep in their shelters, which shade them from the sun. Some animals burrow into the soil to stay out of the sun.

Scorpions and insects are other desert animals. These animals have hard body coverings that keep them from losing much water.

✓ **How do desert animals get water?**

This sidewinder has dry, scaly skin that helps keep water inside its body. ▼

The shape of this bird's beak helps it get water from the stems of the saguaro cactus. It also uses the saguaro as a home. ▼

◄ Saguaro cactus

Summary

A desert ecosystem has a dry environment. Some deserts are hot, while other deserts are cold. Plants and animals that live in deserts have parts that help them get what they need to live.

Review

1. What is a desert?
2. Where do plants of the hot desert store water?
3. Other than by eating plants, how do desert animals get water?
4. **Critical Thinking** More kinds of animals and plants live in hot deserts than in cold deserts. Why do you think this is so?
5. **Test Prep** The average amount of rain a desert gets in one year is about —
   A 25 mm
   B 25 cm
   C 250 cm
   D 25 m

The large ears of this jackrabbit help it hear enemies. The jackrabbit also gets rid of extra heat from its body through the thin skin on its ears. ▶

LINKS

MATH LINK

Measure Volume Desert plants store water. To get an idea of how much water a plant can store, squeeze a piece of fruit over a bowl. Measure the amount of juice that comes out.

WRITING LINK

Informative Writing— Compare and Contrast Find out about one desert plant. Write a paragraph for your teacher to compare it to a plant that grows in another ecosystem.

HEALTH LINK

Water and Health Your body needs plenty of water when it is hot outside. With a partner, make a list of 10 things you can do to increase the amount of water you give your body on a hot day.

TECHNOLOGY LINK

Learn more about desert plants and animals by visiting this Internet Site.

www.scilinks.org/harcourt

What Is a Grassland Ecosystem?

In this lesson, you can . . .

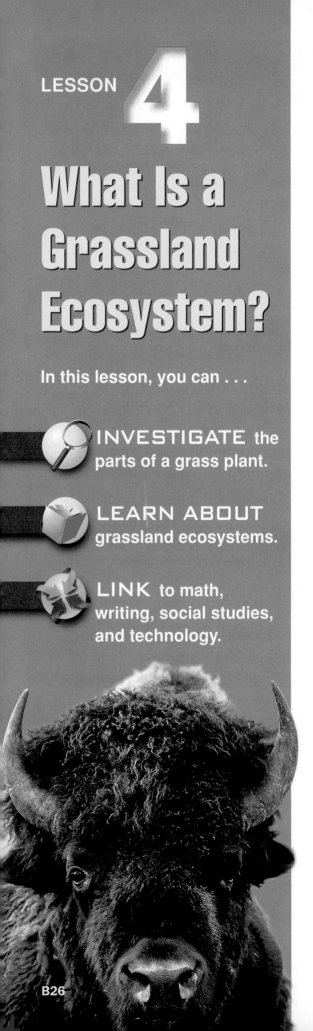

INVESTIGATE the parts of a grass plant.

LEARN ABOUT grassland ecosystems.

LINK to math, writing, social studies, and technology.

INVESTIGATE

Grass Roots

Activity Purpose   You know what grass looks like. It grows around many homes, in parks, and on playgrounds. But have you ever looked closely at a grass plant? In this investigation you will **observe** all the parts of a grass plant.

Materials
- trowel
- 2 sheets of paper
- hand lens

Activity Procedure

1. **CAUTION** **Make sure you have permission to dig in the spot you choose.** Dig out a small clump of grass, about the size of your palm. Be sure to include the roots. (Picture A)

2. Hold up the clump of grass. **Observe** what happens to the soil around the roots. Gently shake the grass, and again **observe** the soil around the roots.

◀ You might think of grasslands as empty places. In fact, many plants and animals, including the American bison, make grasslands their homes.

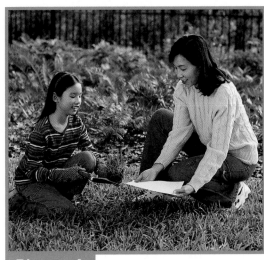
Picture A

3 Carefully remove the soil from the roots, and separate one grass plant from the rest.

4 Put the grass plant on a clean sheet of paper. **Observe** it with the hand lens. The leaves of a grass plant are called blades. Notice how the roots and blades are shaped. (Picture B)

5 Draw and label your grass plant.

Draw Conclusions

1. Describe the roots of grass plants. How might they help hold soil in place?

2. Think about the leaves of other plants. How do grass blades compare with the leaves of other plants?

3. **Scientists at Work** Scientists make inferences about plants by closely **observing** them. The blades of grass plants do not lose much water to the air around them. Grass roots can absorb water from large areas of soil. From these facts, **infer** the kinds of places in which many grasses live.

Investigate Further Take a walk in the neighborhood. Look for places where the soil has been washed away. **Observe** the slope of the land and the plants growing in those places. **Form a hypothesis** about how to prevent more soil from washing away.

Picture B

Process Skill Tip

When you **observe** living things closely, you can learn about their structures. A plant's structure can help you **infer** the type of ecosystem in which it is found.

B27

Grassland Ecosystems

Rainfall and Temperature

In the investigation you observed a grass plant. Grasses do not need a lot of water to grow. Their branching roots soak up water from a wide area of soil. Their long, thin leaves do not lose much water to the air around them.

In some places, there is not enough rain for most trees to grow but too much rain for a desert to form. In these places there is just the right amount of rain for grasses. A **grassland** is an ecosystem

The grasses grow tall and thick in most grasslands. Wildflowers and a few trees and bushes can also grow there. In drier grasslands, grasses are shorter and do not grow as thick. ▼

Temperature and Rainfall in the Nebraska Prairie

This graph shows temperatures and rainfall amounts for grasslands in Nebraska. Spring and summer have more rain than the dry fall and winter seasons. Winters are cold and summers are hot.

Pampa is the Spanish word for *plain*. The pampas stretch across central Argentina.

Grasslands are found on every continent except Antarctica.

Steppe is the Russian word for plain. The steppes stretch across Ukraine. They look like the North American Great Plains.

made up of large, flat areas of land that are covered with grass.

The graph shows seasonal temperature and rainfall for a grassland in the central United States. As in many grasslands, it is hot in summer and cold in winter. Grasslands average 30 to 60 centimeters (12 to 24 in.) of rain each year. However, rain does not fall evenly all year long in a grassland. More rain falls in spring and summer than in fall and winter.

✔ **Where are grasslands found?**

Grasslands of the World

Grasslands are found all over the world. In North America the grasslands are called *prairies*. Prairies stretch from the Midwest to the Rocky Mountains. In central Argentina the grasslands are called *pampas* (PAHM•pahs). In Ukraine the grasslands are called *steppes* (STEPS). No matter what they are called, all grasslands look similar. They are large, flat areas of land covered with grass. They all have the right temperature and rainfall for grasses to grow well.

Once the grasslands were wild. Picture a meadow that stretches as far as you can see. There are no buildings, crops, or cities. That is what the grasslands once looked like. Today many grasslands have become farms, ranches, and towns.

✔ **How are all grasslands alike?**

Animals of the Grasslands

Many animals live in grassland ecosystems. Pronghorn antelope, rabbits, deer, mice, and prairie dogs all eat the grasses of the North American prairies. These animals are hunted by foxes, coyotes, badgers, and rattlesnakes. The smaller animals are also prey for hawks and owls. Grasshoppers provide food for birds and some snakes.

In the open prairie, there is no place to hide. Many small prairie animals, such as burrowing owls, rattlesnakes, and black-footed ferrets, live in underground burrows. Burrows make good hiding places. In winter the air in the burrow is warmer than the outside air. In summer it is cooler. Burrows also protect the animals that live in them from dry winds and grass fires.

Many large prairie animals are good runners. The pronghorn antelope is the fastest animal in North America. It runs to get away from predators. Coyotes and foxes run fast to catch their prey.

✔ **Name three animals that live in the grasslands.**

Prairie dogs live in burrows that stretch for miles under the prairie. ▼

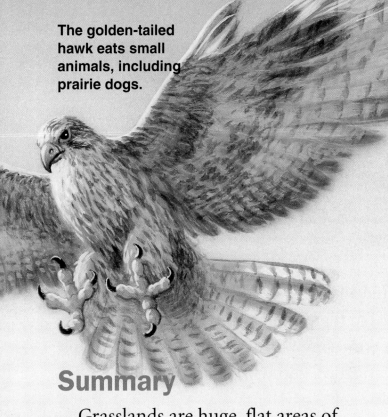

The golden-tailed hawk eats small animals, including prairie dogs.

Construct a Graph Make a graph comparing the average amounts of rain a desert, a grassland, and a deciduous forest get in one year.

WRITING LINK

Informative Writing— Compare and Contrast Find out about the animals that live on the pampas. Write a paragraph that compares them with the animals that live on the North American prairies.

SOCIAL STUDIES LINK

Native Americans of the Prairies Find out about one of the Native American tribes that lived on the prairies around 1800. How did the tribe adapt to the grassland ecosystem? What did the people eat? Make a poster showing how the people lived.

Summary

   Grasslands are huge, flat areas of land covered with grass. Grasslands are found wherever there is not enough water for most trees to grow, but too much water for a desert to form. Many kinds of animals live in the grasslands.

Review

1. What is the rainfall like in a grassland?
2. How is grass adapted for growing in grasslands?
3. How are prairie dogs adapted for living in grasslands?
4. **Critical Thinking** Corn, wheat, and rye are grasses. Why do you think many grasslands have been plowed up to make farms that grow these plants?
5. **Test Prep** Which animal does **NOT** live in grasslands?

   A mouse   **C** coyote

   B rattlesnake   **D** shark

GO ONLINE   TECHNOLOGY LINK

Visit the Harcourt Learning Site for related links, activities, and resources.

WELCOME TO THE LEARNING SITE

www.harcourtschool.com

B31

LESSON 5

What Are Water Ecosystems?

In this lesson, you can . . .

INVESTIGATE freshwater ecosystems.

LEARN ABOUT two types of water ecosystems.

LINK to math, writing, social studies, and technology.

Make a Freshwater Ecosystem

Activity Purpose If you have ever visited a lake, you may know that many kinds of plants and animals live there. Lakes and ponds are freshwater ecosystems. In this investigation you will **make a model** of a freshwater ecosystem.

Materials

- aquarium or other large, clear plastic container
- gravel
- sand
- sheet of paper
- fresh water
- freshwater plants
- rocks
- fish and snails

Activity Procedure

1 Put a layer of gravel at the bottom of the aquarium. Add a layer of sand on top of the gravel.

◀ Dolphins live, swim, and play in saltwater ecosystems.

2 Set the aquarium in a place where it isn't too sunny. Place a sheet of paper over the sand. Slowly add the water to the tank. Make sure you pour the water onto the paper so the sand will stay in place. (Picture A)

3 Remove the paper, and put the plants and rocks into the tank. Let the tank sit for about one week. After one week, add the fish and snails. (Picture B)

4 **Observe** and care for your freshwater ecosystem.

Picture A

Picture B

Draw Conclusions

1. What are some things you **observed** in your freshwater ecosystem?

2. Why do you think you waited to add the fish to the tank?

3. **Scientists at Work** Scientists often **make a model** of an ecosystem so they can **observe** it in a laboratory. How did making a model help you observe a freshwater ecosystem? How is your model different from a real pond?

Investigate Further What other kinds of plants and animals might live in a freshwater ecosystem? To find out, visit a pet shop that sells fish. Make a list of the freshwater plants and animals you find there.

Process Skill Tip

It can be difficult to **observe** all the living things in a freshwater pond or lake. You can learn about the real thing by **making a model** of a freshwater ecosystem.

Water Ecosystems

FIND OUT

- about freshwater and saltwater ecosystems
- what plants and animals live in water ecosystems

VOCABULARY

salt water
fresh water

The blue parts of this map show the major water ecosystems of the world. ▼

Types of Water Ecosystems

Water covers more than 70 percent of Earth's surface. When you look at a globe, you can see that most of this water is in oceans and seas. Oceans and seas contain **salt water**, or water that has a lot of salt in it. Marshes and a few lakes also have salt water in them. These ecosystems are called *saltwater ecosystems*.

In the investigation you made a model of a freshwater ecosystem. **Fresh water** is water that has very little salt in it. Lakes, rivers, ponds, streams, and some marshes are *freshwater ecosystems*.

✔ **What are two types of water ecosystems?**

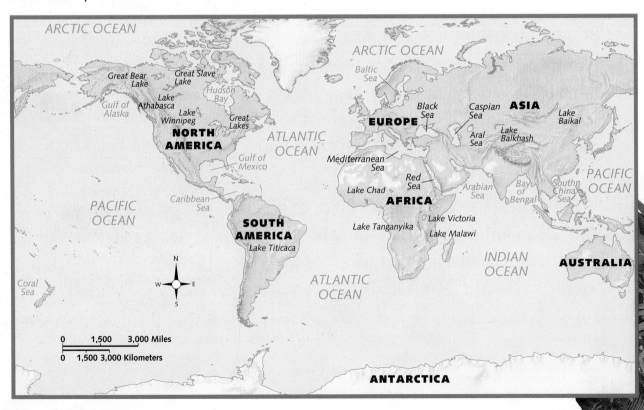

Saltwater Ecosystems

There are many different saltwater ecosystems because salt water is not the same everywhere. The amount of salt in ocean water is different in different places. Near the surface, rain can make the water less salty. Water is also less salty near shores where fresh water from rivers and streams flows into oceans. But no matter where you are in the ocean, the water has more salt in it than fresh water has.

Ocean water that is near shore or at the surface is often warmer than water deep in the ocean. This is because the sun warms the water in these areas. At the shoreline, salt water may collect in tide pools. Many plants and animals live in this warm, shallow water.

✔ **Why might salt water be less salty near shore?**

Barnacles (BAR•nuh•kulz) are small animals that live out their lives stuck to rocks and other objects. ▼

A tide pool is a saltwater ecosystem that forms at a shoreline. ▼

◀ **Some anemones (uh•NEM•uh•neez) live in the warm, shallow waters of tide pools.**

Ocean Ecosystems

The oceans are Earth's largest ecosystems. Because they are so large, many kinds of plants and animals live in them. All these living things are suited to life in salt water.

Not all parts of the ocean are the same. The saltiness of the water can be different. Water is deeper in some places than in others. The water temperature also changes from place to place. All these differences, along with how deep into the water the sunlight can reach, affect the kinds of living things that are found in different parts of the ocean.

✔ **What do all ocean plants and animals have in common?**

Ocean Zones

The ocean can be divided into zones. Each zone is defined by how much sunlight it gets. Areas that get the most sunlight usually have the warmest temperatures and more plant and animal life. Areas that receive little sunlight are dark and have few animals and very few plants. They also have very cold water.

This underwater kelp forest grows in shallow water. It provides food and shelter for many different fish and other ocean animals.

◀ These tropical fish live in areas of warm water.

Where water is shallow, sunlight reaches the ocean bottom. The sunlight allows many plants to grow in this zone. Animals that feed on these plants also live here.

Farther from shore, sunlight cannot reach the ocean bottom. Plants in this part of the ocean float near the surface, where they can get sunlight. Many swimming animals come to the surface to feed. Others feed on the animals that eat the plants.

This angler fish lives in the deep part of the ocean. ▼

Sunlight cannot reach the floor of the deep ocean. This part of the ocean has almost no plants. Water is very cold here. Because there are very few plants (if there are any at all), the deep ocean also has the fewest animals.

Freshwater Ecosystems

Not all freshwater ecosystems are the same. The main kinds of freshwater ecosystems include rivers, streams, lakes, and ponds.

Many plants and animals live in or around rivers and streams. Rivers and streams have moving fresh water. The water may move quickly or slowly. How fast the water moves helps determine what living things can survive in the water.

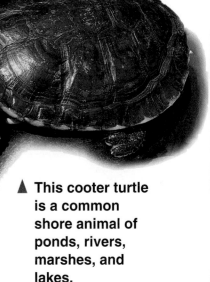

▲ This cooter turtle is a common shore animal of ponds, rivers, marshes, and lakes.

The water in lakes and ponds is still. Lakes are usually larger and have deeper water than ponds. Water temperature depends on where the lake or pond is and how deep the water is.

As in an ocean, most plants and animals in a lake or pond live in the shallow water. The fewest plants and animals live where the water is too deep for sunlight to reach the bottom.

✔ **What are two kinds of freshwater ecosystems?**

The American egret is a wading bird that lives near freshwater ecosystems such as lakes. ▼

A young mayfly can stick to a rock or a plant so fast-moving water won't wash it away. ▼

The bullhead catfish makes its home in a lake. ▼

Summary

Water ecosystems may have salt water or fresh water. An ocean is a saltwater ecosystem. Rivers, streams, lakes, and ponds are freshwater ecosystems. Different kinds of plants and animals live in and around these water ecosystems.

Review

1. What are the two kinds of water ecosystems? Name two ways they are different.

2. In a pond, where do most of the animals live?

3. Which zone of the ocean gets the least amount of sunlight?

4. **Critical Thinking** What would happen to the animals and plants in a saltwater ecosystem if it were flooded by fresh water? Explain your answer.

5. **Test Prep** Which is **NOT** a freshwater ecosystem?

    A river   **C** pond
    B lake   **D** tide pool

LINKS

MATH LINK

Construct a Graph Use a computer graphing program such as *Graph Links* to make a bar graph of the following water depths: river, 1 meter; lake, 6 meters; ocean, 122 meters. How much deeper is the ocean than the lake?

WRITING LINK

Informative Writing— Narration Suppose you are a tour guide on a submarine in the deep ocean. Write a narration that describes to your passengers the kinds of plants and animals you would expect to find living there.

SOCIAL STUDIES LINK

Mapping Water Ecosystems Make an outline map of your state. Draw the major bodies of water. Label them as fresh or salt water.

TECHNOLOGY LINK

Visit the Harcourt Learning Site for related links, activities, and resources.

www.harcourtschool.com

Prairie Restoration

Fire can have a powerful effect on an ecosystem. Because of that, some scientists occasionally set fires to help an ecosystem. Scientists at the Konza Prairie Biological Station in Kansas have learned that carefully controlled burning can help restore a prairie. Once a prairie is restored, scientists can study the interactions within it.

Prairies and Restoration

Long ago, droughts and high winds combined to start fires that burned entire prairies. These fires affected both the prairie soil and the plants and animals that depended on the prairie for their survival. But grassland plants with underground stems from which new plants could grow were protected from the fires and continued growing.

Over time, prairie lands changed as farmers began planting crops, such as wheat and corn, on them. Today many scientists are working to restore prairies to the way they used to be. But in order to restore a prairie, plants and animals must be brought back to it slowly and carefully.

How Is Fire Used?

In the fall, prairie tallgrass turns brown and dies. The dead grasses cover the prairie like a blanket. If left alone, the dead grasses could prevent new plants from growing. Controlled burning, however, removes these dead grasses so that sunlight, water, and other nutrients can reach the soil.

At the Konza Prairie Biological Station, some lands are burned every year. Other areas are burned every two to 20 years. To better control the fires, scientists carefully plan each burn. They use strips of cleared land, called firebreaks, to stop fire from spreading. They also use weather stations at the Konza Prairie Biological Station to help them learn how strong the wind is and in which direction it is blowing. These are important things to know for controlling fires.

THINK ABOUT IT

1. How do prairie grasses survive a fire?

2. How has controlled burning helped the prairie near Konza Prairie Biological Station?

CAREERS

ECOLOGIST

What They Do
Ecologists study how living things interact with the environment. They use many kinds of scientific equipment and other tools to help them learn.

Education and Training Most ecologists have college degrees. Because there are many areas of study in ecology, ecologists need to know different types of science, including biology and physics. Ecologists work at places such as research centers and universities, where they also teach classes.

WEB LINK
For Science and Technology updates, visit the Harcourt Internet site.
www.harcourtschool.com

Margaret Morse Nice
ORNITHOLOGIST

Ornithologists are people who study birds. Perhaps, like Margaret Morse Nice, you have watched birds in your back yard. By the age of 12, she was recording her observations about birds. What began as fun became her lifework.

After college, Morse married Leonard Nice, whom she had met there. Each time the family moved, Margaret Nice studied the birds around her home.

Nice was one of the first to use colored bands to identify birds. To follow birds over time, she would first capture a bird. Then she would place a colored band of plastic on the bird's leg and let the bird go. In this way, Nice studied how birds mated, built nests, and raised their young.

Nice and her husband wrote a book together on the birds of Oklahoma. Nice later published a two-part study of song sparrows. She wrote more than 250 articles for magazines during her lifetime. She also translated into English many of the articles that people from other countries had written about birds.

THINK ABOUT IT

1. Why is it helpful to have someone translate articles written by scientists in other countries?

2. What birds can you observe from your home?

EARTHWORM HABITAT

What is the habitat of an earthworm?

Materials

- clear plastic container
- garden soil (not potting soil)
- 2 to 3 earthworms
- small rocks, sticks, and leaves
- wax paper
- water

Procedure

❶ Loosely spread the soil on the wax paper. Add the rocks, sticks, and leaves. Add a small amount of water so the soil is moist but not wet. Mix these materials together.

❷ Add the soil mixture to the plastic container. Carefully add the earthworms to the loose soil. Place your earthworm habitat in a warm, dark place. Keep the soil moist.

Draw Conclusions

After observing your earthworm habitat for a week, make a list of the things you think the habitat you provided gave your earthworms that they needed to live.

SALT WATER AND FRESH WATER

How are salt water and fresh water different?

Materials

- small jar
- small spoon
- water
- salt
- egg in the shell

Procedure

❶ Half fill the jar with water. Put the egg in the jar. Record what happens to the egg.

❷ Remove the egg, and stir a spoonful of salt into the water. Put the egg back into the water, and record what happens to the egg.

❸ Continue adding salt to the water until you observe a change.

Draw Conclusions

How do you think salt in the water affects the animals living in the ocean?

Vocabulary Review

Use the terms below to complete sentences 1 through 13. The page numbers in ( ) tell you where to look in the chapter if you need help.

environment (B6)
ecosystem (B7)
population (B7)
community (B7)
habitat (B7)
forest (B14)
deciduous
  forest (B15)
tropical rain
  forest (B16)
coastal
  forest (B17)
coniferous
  forest (B18)
desert (B22)
grassland (B28)
salt water (B34)
fresh water (B34)

1. An area where the main plants are trees is called a ____.

2. All the living things of the same kind that live in the same area at the same time make up a ____.

3. Populations that live in the same place make up a ____.

4. An ecosystem that is very dry is a ____.

5. The interactions between the living and nonliving parts of the environment make up an ____.

6. To a population of frogs living near a pond, the pond is its ____.

7. Rivers and most lakes are ____ ecosystems.

8. A ____ has warm summers and cool winters. The trees drop their leaves in the fall.

9. Two types of forests that get a lot of rain are a ____ and a ____.

10. An ____ is everything that surrounds a living thing.

11. The winters are cold in a ____, and the trees have needle-shaped leaves.

12. The water in the ocean is ____.

13. A ____ has hot summers and cold winters.

Connect Concepts

Write the terms from the Word Bank where they belong in the concept map.

tropical rain   **coastal**   **forests**
coniferous   **deciduous**

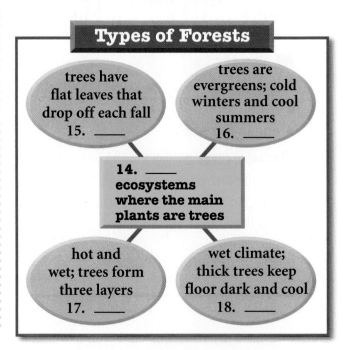

Types of Forests

trees have flat leaves that drop off each fall
15. ____

trees are evergreens; cold winters and cool summers
16. ____

14. ____ ecosystems where the main plants are trees

hot and wet; trees form three layers
17. ____

wet climate; thick trees keep floor dark and cool
18. ____

Check Understanding

Write the letter of the best choice.

19. What might happen to a forest that is damaged by fire?

    A It will grow back.

    B It is destroyed forever.

    C It will stay the same.

    D It will fill up with water and become a marsh.

20. Why do grasslands have few large trees? They are too—

    F flat

    G cold

    H dry

    J wet

21. What are the two types of desert?

    A dry and wet

    B hot and cold

    C fresh and salt

    D tropical and coastal

22. What are the two types of water ecosystems?

    F fresh and salt

    G hot and cold

    H hot and dry

    J deciduous and coniferous

Critical Thinking

23. Why might a raccoon hunt for food in a trash can instead of in a forest?

24. How can the building of new homes and roads by humans affect the plants and animals in an area?

Process Skills Review

25. In Lesson 1 you used your **observations** to **gather data** about organisms in their environment. What are some of the ways that you gathered data?

26. Find three examples in the chapter where you could **use numbers** to **record data**. Why is this a good way to **interpret data**?

27. In Lessons 3 and 5 you **made a model** of two ecosystems—a desert and a pond. How did either model help you learn about the features of these ecosystems?

Performance Assessment

Diagram a Rain Forest

Work with two or three other students. On a large sheet of paper, draw a rain-forest ecosystem. Show the three layers, and label each. Then draw or describe two or more animals that live in each layer.

Living Things Depend on One Another

Vocabulary Preview

interact
producer
consumer
herbivore
carnivore
omnivore
decomposer
food chain
energy pyramid
food web
predator
prey

Like all living things, you depend on plants and animals around you to meet your needs. You eat plants and animal products. You may live in a building made from wood. You wear clothes made from plant fibers. Plants and animals depend on one another to help them meet their needs.

Fast Fact

Hippopotamuses live in the rivers of central Africa. They eat grasses and other plants that grow in the water. The wastes they produce are rich in nutrients, which help the plants to grow.

Tropical rain forest

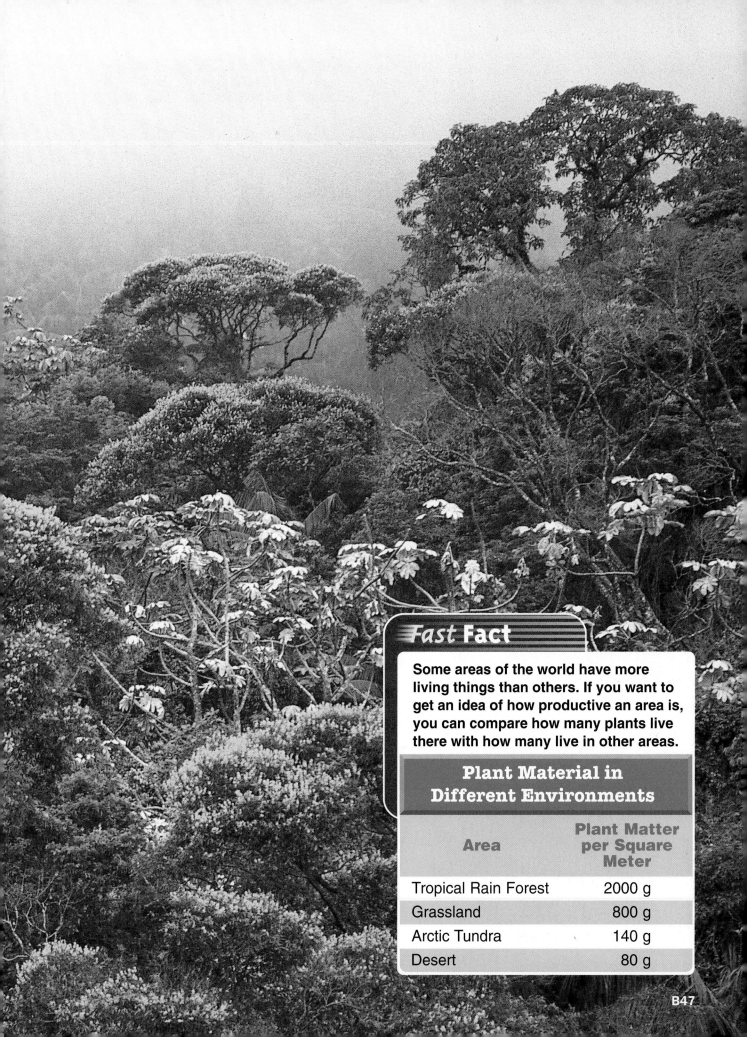

Fast Fact

Some areas of the world have more living things than others. If you want to get an idea of how productive an area is, you can compare how many plants live there with how many live in other areas.

Plant Material in Different Environments

Area	Plant Matter per Square Meter
Tropical Rain Forest	2000 g
Grassland	800 g
Arctic Tundra	140 g
Desert	80 g

How Do Animals Get Food?

In this lesson, you can . . .

INVESTIGATE how animals use their teeth to help them get food.

LEARN ABOUT how living things get food.

LINK to math, writing, health, and technology.

INVESTIGATE

Animal Teeth

Activity Purpose Bite into an apple. Which teeth do you use? Which teeth do you use to chew the apple? In this investigation you will **observe** the shapes of teeth of different animals.

Materials
- blank index cards
- books about animals

Activity Procedure

1. **Observe** the pictures of the animals. Look closely at the shape of each animal's teeth.

2. Use one index card for each animal. **Record** the animal's name, and draw the shape of its teeth.

◀ Animals that are pets get their food from people. But animals that are wild must find their own food.

Shark ▼

Bobcat ▼

3 With a partner, make a list of words that describe the teeth. **Record** these words next to the drawings on the index cards. (Picture A)

4 Think about the things each animal eats. Use books about animals if you need help. On the back of each index card, make a list of the things the animal eats.

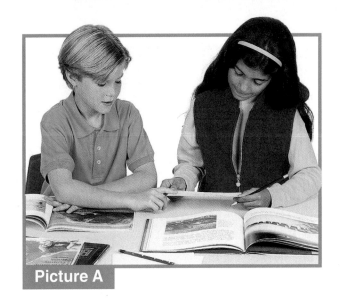
Picture A

Draw Conclusions

1. Which animals might use their teeth to catch other animals? Which animals might use their teeth to eat plants? Explain.

2. Some animals use their teeth to help them do other things, too. **Observe** the beaver's teeth. How do its teeth help it cut down trees?

3. **Scientists at Work** Scientists learn by **observing**. Scientists can learn how animals use their teeth by watching how and what the animals eat. From what you observed in this investigation, what can you **infer** about the shapes of animals' teeth?

Process Skill Tip

Observing and inferring are not the same. When you **observe**, you use your senses. When you **infer**, you form an opinion using your observations.

Wolf ▼

Horse ▼

Beaver ▼

B49

Living Things and Food

Making and Getting Food

FIND OUT

- **how living things get food**
- **how plants and animals interact with the environment**

VOCABULARY

interact
producer
consumer
herbivore
carnivore
omnivore
decomposer

All living things need food. In the investigation you saw that an animal's teeth match the food it eats. But not all living things have teeth. Some living things get their food in other ways. For example, a bird uses its beak to get food. Plants make their own food.

Plants and animals work together, or **interact** (in•ter•AKT), with the environment to get what they need. Plants interact with sunlight, air, and water to make food. Animals interact with plants or other animals to get their food. Animals also interact with nonliving things in their environment, such as water, sunlight, soil, and rocks. For example, a snake lies in the sun for warmth and drinks water. The same snake may make its home in the soil or under a rock.

✔ **Why do plants and animals interact with the environment?**

This strawberry plant uses energy from the sun to make its own food. ▼

This strawberry provides a chipmunk with some of the energy it needs to live. ▼

The chipmunk provides energy for a snake that catches and eats it. ▼

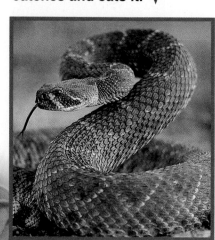

Producers

Plants are producers. A **producer** (proh•DOOS•er) is a living thing that makes its own food. Producers use the food they make to live and to grow.

Plants make more food than they need. This extra food is stored in roots, leaves, seeds, and fruit. People and other animals then eat this stored food as their own food.

✔ **What is a producer?**

▲ These foods come from plants. Plants are producers that make their own food. Animals then eat plants as food.

Consumers

Animals cannot make their own food. They must eat plants or other animals. An animal is a **consumer** (kuhn•SOOM•er). A consumer is a living thing that eats other living things as food.

Consumers can be grouped by the kinds of food they eat. Some consumers eat only plants. These animals are **herbivores**. Sheep, like this bighorn sheep, are herbivores.

A few consumers eat only one kind of plant. Giant pandas eat only bamboo. To survive, they must live where bamboo grows.

Animals that eat only plants may have body parts that help them eat. For example, the giant panda has an extra bone in its hand that helps it hold bamboo as it eats.

The bighorn sheep is a consumer that eats plants. ▼

Some animals get food by eating other animals. These animals are **carnivores**. Often they must hunt and kill their food. Animals that get food in this way have body parts that help them catch and eat their food. For example, an owl has strong claws that it uses to catch animals. Its sharp beak helps it tear meat.

Some animals, called **omnivores**, eat both plants and other animals. A box turtle eats both berries and insects. The meats you eat come from animals and the vegetables you eat come from plants.

✔ **What is a consumer?**

This owl catches small animals for its food. ▼

Decomposers

A **decomposer** (dee•kuhm•POHZ•er) is a living thing that breaks down dead things for food. Decomposers also break down the wastes of living things. As decomposers feed, they help clean the environment. Two decomposers you may know of are fungi, such as mushrooms, and earthworms.

✔ **What is a decomposer?**

The fungi growing on this log are decomposers. The fungi are using the dead log as food. ▼

▲ **Many bacteria are decomposers.**

Summary

Plants and animals interact. They depend on their environments and on one another to get the food they need. Plants are producers. Animals are consumers. Decomposers get food by breaking down wastes or dead things.

Review

1. How do producers get their food?
2. How do consumers get their food?
3. What are the three groups of consumers?
4. **Critical Thinking** How do decomposers help keep the environment clean?
5. **Test Prep** Which of the following is **NOT** a consumer?

   A bird   C squirrel
   B tree   D human

LINKS

MATH LINK

Solve a Problem Scientists studied 60 moose on an island. They found that during the summer, each moose eats the fruit of 25 blackberry bushes. What is the minimum number of blackberry bushes on the island?

WRITING LINK

Informative Writing— Explanation Suppose that the bushes on the island in the Math Link all die. Write a paragraph for your teacher explaining what you think might happen to the moose population.

HEALTH LINK

Teeth Think about how you use your teeth to eat. Which teeth do the cutting? The chewing? How are the teeth different?

TECHNOLOGY LINK

Learn how scientists help injured animals get food by visiting the Smithsonian Institution Internet Site.

www.si.edu/harcourt/science

Smithsonian Institution®

LESSON 2

What Are Food Chains?

In this lesson, you can . . .

 INVESTIGATE a food-chain model.

 LEARN ABOUT food chains and energy pyramids.

 LINK to math, writing, literature, and technology.

Make a Food-Chain Model

Activity Purpose You get energy from the food you eat. All living things get energy from the food they eat. In this investigation you will **make a model** to show how living things interact to get their energy from food.

Materials

- index cards
- marker
- 4 pieces of yarn or string
- tape

Activity Procedure

1 In the bottom right-hand corners, number the index cards 1 through 5.

2 On Card 1, draw and label grass. On Card 2, draw and label a cricket. On Card 3, draw and label a frog. On Card 4, draw and label a snake. On Card 5, draw and label a hawk. (Picture A)

◀ **A puffin eats different kinds of sea animals. It can catch as many as ten small fish at one time in its beak.**

Picture A

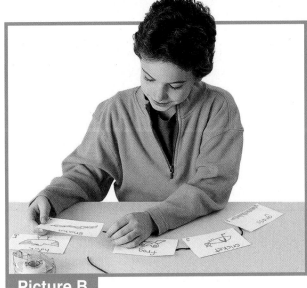

Picture B

3 Order the cards in a line with Card 1 first and Card 5 last. Use yarn and tape to connect the cards. (Picture B)

4 Stretch the connected cards out on a table. The cards form a model called a food chain.

5 Discuss with a classmate how each living thing in the food chain gets its food. Tell which things in your model show producers. Tell which things show consumers.

Draw Conclusions

1. In your model, which living thing is last in the food chain? Why do you think it is in this place?

2. In which part of the food chain is the producer found? Why do you think it is there?

3. **Scientists at Work** Scientists **use models** to help them study things in nature. How does using a model of a food chain help you understand living things and the food they eat?

Process Skill Tip

It is hard to **observe** a real-life food chain. **Using a model** of a food chain helps you learn about the real thing.

Food and Energy

Food Chains

FIND OUT

- **how living things get energy**
- **how energy moves through a food chain**

VOCABULARY

food chain
energy pyramid

All living things need energy to live. Producers get energy from sunlight. They store the energy in the food they make. Consumers can't make their own food. They get their food by eating other living things. In this way, the consumers get the energy they need.

In the investigation you saw that the path of food from one living thing to another forms a **food chain**. A food chain also shows how energy moves through the environment. For example, grass uses the energy in sunlight to make its food. A cricket that eats the grass gets the energy stored in the grass. If a frog eats the cricket, it gets energy that is stored in the cricket. In this way, the energy that started with the sun is passed from the grass to the cricket to the frog.

✔ **What is a food chain?**

This turtle eats slugs that eat leaves. ▶

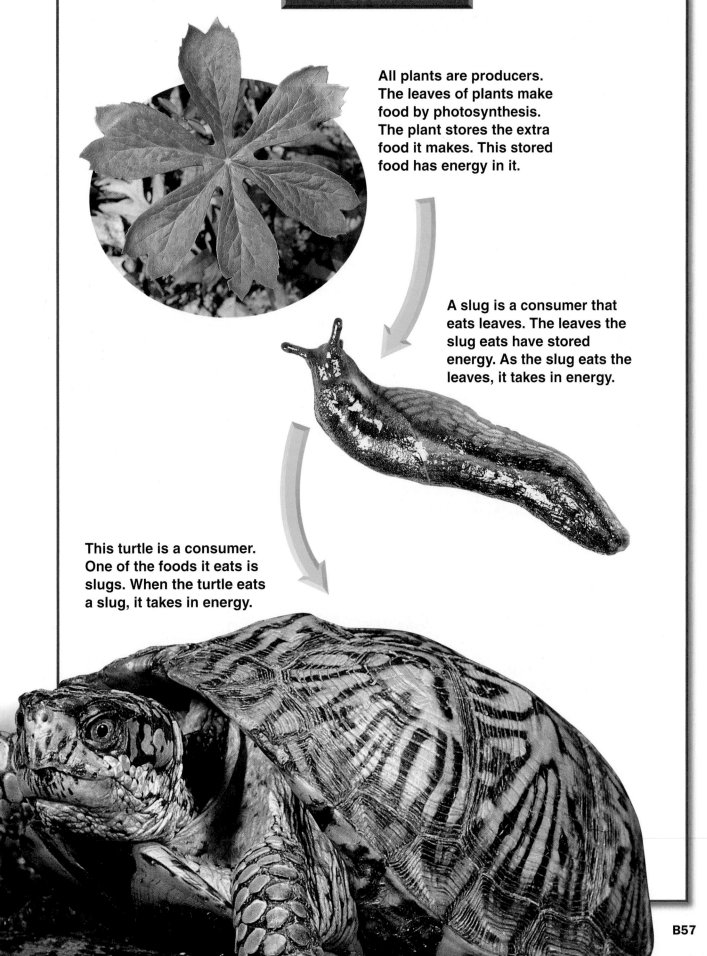

A Food Chain

All plants are producers. The leaves of plants make food by photosynthesis. The plant stores the extra food it makes. This stored food has energy in it.

A slug is a consumer that eats leaves. The leaves the slug eats have stored energy. As the slug eats the leaves, it takes in energy.

This turtle is a consumer. One of the foods it eats is slugs. When the turtle eats a slug, it takes in energy.

Energy from Food

Every living thing uses energy to live and to grow. The energy that a living thing uses cannot be passed along through the food chain. Because of this, the higher on the food chain a living thing is, the less energy there is.

An **energy pyramid** shows that the amount of usable energy in an ecosystem is less for each higher animal in the food chain.

In an energy pyramid, there are more producers than any other kind of living thing. Most of the energy in an ecosystem is found in plants. Animals that eat plants make up the next level. The upper parts of the pyramid are made up of animals that eat other animals. The higher in the pyramid an animal is, the fewer of that animal there are. This is because there is less energy available to them.

✔ **What is an energy pyramid?**

1 Energy from the sun is taken in by plants and other producers. This energy is used by plants for growth and to make fruits and seeds. Energy that is not used by the plant is stored.

2 Animals that eat plants are called first-level consumers. These animals must eat many plants to get the energy they need. Energy not used by the animal is stored in its body.

3 Animals that eat other animals are called second-level consumers. There are fewer of these animals. Some of the energy that is stored in first-level consumers can be passed on to these animals.

4 There are very few animals at the top of the pyramid. The energy these top-level consumers get has been passed through all the other parts of the food chain.

THE INSIDE STORY

An Energy Pyramid

4 Animals that are not usually eaten by other animals

3 Animals that eat other animals

2 Plant-eating animals

1 Plants

▲ A hyena is a *scavenger,* an animal that feeds on dead animals.

Summary

Living things get their energy from food. Animals cannot make their own food, so they eat other living things to get energy. A food chain is the flow of food in an ecosystem from one living thing to another. An energy pyramid shows that the amount of usable energy in an ecosystem is less for each higher animal in the food chain.

Review

1. How does energy get from a producer to a meat-eating consumer?
2. What kind of living thing is at the top of a food chain?
3. Where is the most food energy in an energy pyramid found?
4. **Critical Thinking** What is the source of all the energy on Earth?
5. **Test Prep** Which is passed in a food chain from one living thing to another?

   A producers   C sunlight
   B animals   D energy

LINKS

MATH LINK

Name Fractions One food chain is made up of a producer, a consumer that eats plants, a consumer that eats both plants and animals, and a consumer that eats only animals. What fraction of living things in this food chain eats plants?

WRITING LINK

Expressive Writing—Poem
You are part of many food chains. Pick your favorite dinner. Write a poem for your family about how the different foods fit into food chains.

LITERATURE LINK

Underwater Food Chains
Plants and animals that live in water are parts of food chains, too. In the book *Mangrove Wilderness*, Bianca Lavies tells about food chains in an estuary.

TECHNOLOGY LINK

To learn more about food chains, watch the video *Poisoned Eagles* on the **Harcourt Science Newsroom Video.**

What Are Food Webs?

In this lesson, you can . . .

INVESTIGATE food webs.

LEARN ABOUT how food chains overlap to form food webs.

LINK to math, writing, literature, and technology.

INVESTIGATE

Make a Food Web

Activity Purpose Most animals eat more than one kind of food. Because of this, one living thing can be a part of more than one food chain. Food chains in an ecosystem overlap to form *food webs.* In this investigation you will **make a model** of a food web.

Materials

- index cards, cut into fourths
- poster board
- tape or glue
- crayons

Activity Procedure

1 Write the name of each living thing from the chart on its own card.

2 Glue the cards onto a sheet of poster board so they form a circle. Leave room for writing. (Picture A)

◄ A sea otter is part of an ocean food web. It feeds on abalone and other shellfish. As the otter floats on its back, it cracks open the shellfish by banging it against a rock it carries on its chest.

Living Thing	What It Eats
clover	uses the sun to make its own food
grasshopper	clover
frog	grasshopper
snake	frog, mouse
owl	snake, mouse
mouse	clover

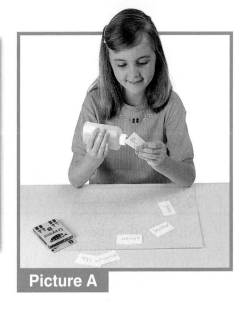

Picture A

3 Look at the chart again. List two different food chains you could make.

4 Draw arrows between the parts of each food chain. Use a different color for each food chain. You have now made a food web. (Picture B)

5 **Observe** your model to see how the food chains overlap. What other living things could you add to your food web?

Picture B

Draw Conclusions

1. What is the producer in this food web?

2. What does your food web tell you about producers and consumers?

3. **Scientists at Work** Scientists sometimes **make models** to help them learn about things. How did drawing a food web help you learn about animals in a real ecosystem?

Investigate Further Cut out magazine pictures of different plants and animals. Work with a partner to make a food web that includes these plants and animals.

Process Skill Tip

It is hard to observe a real-life food web. **Using a model** of a food web helps you learn about the real thing.

Food Webs

FIND OUT

- about food webs
- how living things interact in food webs

VOCABULARY

food web
predator
prey

Predator and Prey

There are many food chains in an ecosystem. Sometimes these food chains overlap. A model that shows how food chains overlap is called a **food web**. A food web contains producers and consumers that are used as food by more than one living thing.

Food webs contain animals that eat other animals. An animal that hunts another animal for food is called a **predator** (PRED•uh•ter). The animal that is hunted is called **prey** (PRAY). Some animals can be both predator and prey. For example, when a snake eats a mole, the snake is the predator. The mole is the prey. If the snake is eaten by a hawk, the snake becomes the prey. The hawk is the predator.

✔ **What is a food web?**

This marsh ecosystem has many kinds of animals. These animals may be predators, prey, or both. ▼

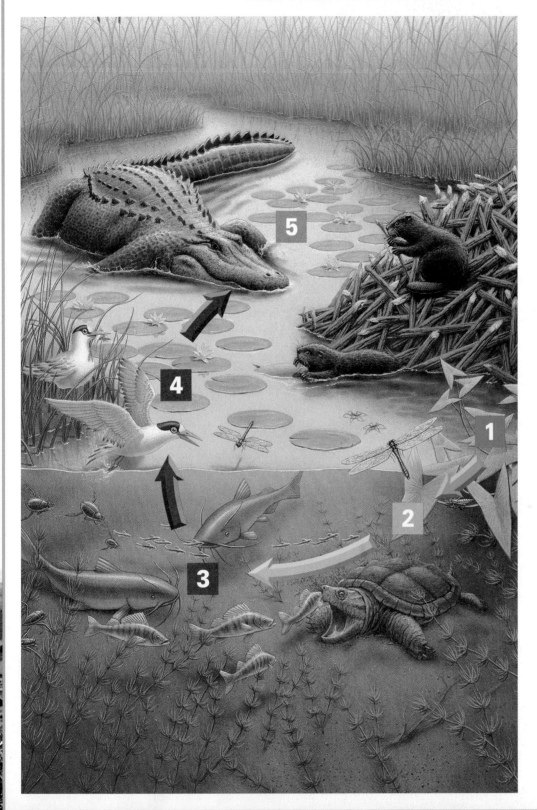

Many overlapping food chains make up the food web for this marsh ecosystem.

1 The plants in the marsh use the energy of the sun to make food.

2 Insects eat the plants that grow in the marsh.

3 Fish eat the insects. Some fish also eat the plants. Smaller fish are eaten by larger fish.

4 Birds eat the fish in the marsh. Some birds also eat the insects and the plants that grow in the marsh.

5 Alligators eat both fish and birds. Alligators are top-level consumers. They are not eaten by other animals in the marsh.

What other food chains can you identify in this food web?

Animals Defend Themselves

Animals defend themselves from predators in many ways.

Sometimes they run away or fly away very fast. One of the fastest runners is the gazelle. It can run as fast as 100 kilometers per hour (62 miles per hour).

Some animals have body parts that help protect them. Sharp quills keep animals away from this porcupine.

Being in a group is safer than being alone. Zebras stay in groups to confuse predators. The striped patterns on their bodies make it very hard for a predator to pick one animal out of the group.

Skunks have a special way of defending themselves. When a predator gets close, the skunk will stomp its feet. If the predator ignores the warning, the skunk turns, lifts its tail, and sprays the predator. The spray smells awful, and it also burns the predator's eyes.

Summary

Most ecosystems have many food chains. These food chains overlap and link together to make food webs. An animal in a food web may be a predator, prey, or both.

Review

1. How are food webs and food chains alike? How are they different?

2. How can an animal be both predator and prey?

3. How does an alligator get energy?

4. **Critical Thinking** In the following food chain, name the predators and the prey.

   insect → frog → snake

5. **Test Prep** Which of the following is **not** a way animals defend themselves?

   A running away   **C** fur

   B staying in   **D** protective
   a group   body parts

Other animals prey on shrimp. Just like animals that live on land, many ocean predators have body parts that help them catch and eat their prey. ▼

LINKS

MATH LINK

Organize Data Choose a food web from this lesson. Count the different food chains in that web. How many animals in the web are predators, and how many are prey? Record your findings in a table.

WRITING LINK

Informative Writing— Explanation Study the Inside Story on page B64. Pick one of the animals and write a paragraph for your classmates that explains how the animal defends itself.

LITERATURE LINK

Read About Predators Learn about some amazing predators, such as a fishing spider or a vampire bat. Read *Extremely Weird Hunters* by Sarah Lovett.

GO ONLINE   TECHNOLOGY LINK

Visit the Harcourt Learning Site for related links, activities, and resources.

WELCOME TO
THE LEARNING SITE

www.harcourtschool.com

People and Animals—
A Long Relationship

Animals and humans have had a long relationship. People learned many thousands of years ago to domesticate, or tame, animals. Animals have also been hunted for food and clothing for thousands of years.

Uses of Animals

Animals are part of the web of life. They are consumers, living off plants and smaller animals. But people use animals and animal products as food. Some people choose not to eat

The History of People and Animals

15,000 B.C.
Horses are drawn in cave paintings in France.

15,000 B.C.   7500 B.C.   B.C./A.D.   1500   1600   1700

8000 B.C.
People begin to tame animals.

1400 B.C.
Hittites who live in Turkey train horses.

1519
Spanish explorers bring horses to North America.

animals. Many of those people do eat products that come from animals, such as milk, eggs, or honey. All of us depend on animals to pollinate the flowers of many fruits and vegetables.

Animal fur or skins may be used for clothing. Perhaps some of the clothing you are wearing today came from an animal. We get wool from sheep. Silkworms make silk.

Over the centuries, people have used animals to work. Large animals like oxen can be used to plow fields. Horses, camels, and elephants are good for carrying people and goods. Some dogs can guard, rescue, hunt, herd, or guide. Cats catch mice.

For some of us, domestic animals are best friends. You may have a cat or a dog as a family pet. Some people have more unusual pets, such as small reptiles or birds from foreign countries.

The Camel—A Very Useful Animal

The camel is one animal that is very useful to humans. Most camels now live in the deserts of Asia and Africa. But scientists have evidence that camels lived in North America before the Ice Age. They died out before Europeans came to the continent. But the U.S. Army brought camels back to North America to carry cargo from Texas to California during the mid-1800s. The railroad was faster than camels, though. After the railroad across the country was finished, most camels went to live in zoos and circuses.

People in Asia still use camels to carry heavy loads, especially in desert areas. One camel can carry more than 136 kilograms (300 lb). A working camel travels about 40 kilometers (25 mi) a day at about 5 kilometers per hour (3 mph). Also, camels can go for a long time without water.

Camels provide meat and milk. People make cheese and butter from their milk. Camel hair makes warm blankets, clothes, and tents.

As you can see, the relationship of animals and humans is complicated. Think of all the types of animals you have studied—fish, reptiles, birds, amphibians, and mammals. Then look around at home and at school. What should you thank an animal for today?

1850
Camels arrive in the United States.

1800   1900   2000

1973
The United States passes the Endangered Species Act to protect animals.

THINK ABOUT IT

- Why do you think people train animals to do specific jobs?

Akira Akubo
OCEANOGRAPHER

Growing up in Japan, a country surrounded by water, Akira Akubo became interested in the ocean. His interest led him to study oceanography.

Questions Akubo has studied include why and how fish live in schools. Fish gather in schools for protection. A school may break up at night to feed, but the fish gather again the next morning. A school may have as few as two dozen fish or as many as several million. All the fish in a school are about the same size. Adult fish and young fish are never in the same school. Some fish form schools when they are young and stay together all their lives. Other species of fish form schools for only a few weeks after hatching.

Akubo has also studied plankton—tiny animal-like and plantlike living things that float near the water's surface. Most plankton are so small that they can be seen only with a microscope. Plankton is food for many other living things in the sea. Animal-like plankton eat the plantlike plankton. A lot of plankton is eaten by fish. Some whales eat nothing but tons of plankton!

Akubo is interested in land animals, too. He believes that studying land animals can help him learn more about animals in the water. He hopes that comparing ocean animals with land animals will help him predict animal behavior.

THINK ABOUT IT

1. Why is plankton important?
2. What is the advantage for fish of traveling in schools?

FOOD CHAINS

How do animals get their food?

Materials
- name tags
- colored game markers
- small plastic bags

Procedure
Play this game with ten or more people.

1 Have each player wear a tag that names him or her as a grasshopper, a snake, or a hawk. Scatter the game markers over a large area. The game markers are food.

2 Each round of the game is 30 seconds. In the first round, only grasshoppers play. They collect as many markers as they can and put them in their bags.

3 In the next round, only snakes play.

4 In the final round, only hawks play.

Draw Conclusions
Which animals had the most food after three rounds? Talk about your answer.

ENERGY FLOW

How does energy flow through a food chain?

Materials
- index cards
- crayons
- pushpins
- yarn

Procedure
1 Divide the class into five groups: producers, plant eaters, plant and animal eaters, animal eaters, and decomposers.

2 Have each person in your group draw on an index card and label a kind of plant or animal that is from your group.

3 Form teams made up of one member from each group. Each team should make a food chain with the pictures. Use yarn and pushpins to connect the parts on a bulletin board.

Draw Conclusions
How does energy flow through the food chain?

Vocabulary Review

Use the terms below to complete sentences 1 through 12. The page numbers in ( ) tell you where to look in the chapter if you need help.

interact (B50) **food chain** (B56)
producer (B51) **energy**
consumer (B51)   **pyramid** (B58)
herbivore (B51) **food web** (B62)
carnivore (B52) **predator** (B62)
omnivore (B52) **prey** (B62)
decomposer (B52)

1. A ____ feeds on the wastes of other living things.

2. A fish that is hunted and eaten by another consumer is called ____.

3. The path of food in an ecosystem can be shown as a ____.

4. A ____ makes its own food.

5. A living thing that eats other living things is called a ____.

6. Consumers that eat both plants and animals are ____.

7. The living things in a community ____ with each other and with nonliving things.

8. Several linked food chains make up a ____.

9. Consumers that eat only plants are ____.

10. A shark is a ____ because it hunts its food.

11. A model of how energy moves through a food web is called an ____.

12. Consumers that eat only animals are ____.

Connect Concepts

Use the words listed below to complete the concept map.

consumer   horse
decomposer   mushroom
grass   producer

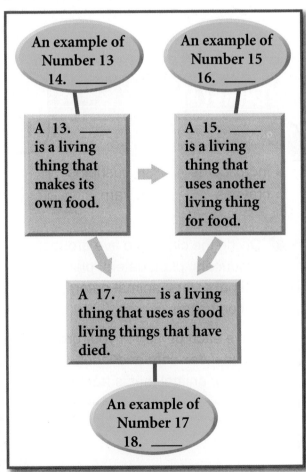

An example of Number 13
14. ____

A 13. ____ is a living thing that makes its own food.

An example of Number 15
16. ____

A 15. ____ is a living thing that uses another living thing for food.

A 17. ____ is a living thing that uses as food living things that have died.

An example of Number 17
18. ____

Check Understanding

Write the letter of the best choice.

19. Which is **NOT** a producer?

   A tree   **C** grass

   B flower   **D** bird

20. A model that shows how energy moves through a food chain is —

   F a decomposer

   G an ecosystem

   H an energy pyramid

   J a food web

21. A spider hunts and kills other animals for food. It is —

   A prey

   B a decomposer

   C a predator

   D a producer

22. Producers get their energy from —

   F other living things

   G the soil

   H an energy pyramid

   J the sun

Critical Thinking

23. A bear lives in the woods near a river. How might the bear interact with its environment to get food?

24. A cat and a dog meet. How does each animal defend itself?

Process Skills Review

25. How can you use **observation** to find out what a goat eats? How might you **infer** what the goat eats?

26. Use what you know about **models** to draw a food web that includes a bear, a water plant, berries, a big fish, a small fish, and a mouse.

Performance Assessment

Diagram a Food Web

Work with a partner. Choose an animal with which you are familiar. Draw a food web that includes the animal. Identify the producers and the consumers in each food chain. Identify predators and prey in as many food chains as you can.

There are many places where you can learn more about how living things interact. Nature centers and wildlife refuges are two places where you can see plants and animals interact.

Louisiana Nature Center

WHAT An educational facility designed for the study of life through nature

WHERE New Orleans, Louisiana

WHAT CAN YOU DO THERE? Learn about plants and animals while touring the Interpretive Center, or explore the wetlands and forest.

Mississippi Sandhill Crane National Wildlife Refuge

WHAT A protected habitat where the endangered Mississippi sandhill cranes can live safely

WHERE Gautier, Mississippi

WHAT CAN YOU DO THERE? Hike the refuge nature trail, observe the cranes, and see other birds and animals.

GO ONLINE Plan Your Own Expeditions

If you can't visit the Louisiana Nature Center or the Mississippi Sandhill Crane National Wildlife Refuge, visit a nature center or wildlife refuge near you. Or log on to The Learning Site at **www.harcourtschool.com** to visit these sites.

Earth's Land

Earth's Land

UNIT EXPERIMENT

Landfills

The materials we throw away often end up in landfills. While you study this unit, you can conduct a long-term experiment to find out how materials decompose in landfills. Here are some questions to think about. Do all materials decompose when they are buried in a landfill? Do some materials decompose faster than others? Plan and conduct an experiment to find answers to these or other questions you may have about landfills. See pages x–xii for help in designing your experiment.

Minerals, Rocks, and Fossils

Take a look around at rocks. Some may be on the ground. Others may have been used to build homes and office buildings. Some rocks are shiny. Others may have different-colored pieces in them. You may even be able to see traces of once-living animals or plants in some rocks.

Vocabulary Preview

mineral
rock
crust
mantle
core
igneous rock
sedimentary rock
metamorphic rock
rock cycle
fossil

Fast Fact

If lightning strikes a beach, a new kind of rock may form. The heat from the lightning melts sand to make a glassy rock called fulgurite (FUHL·gyuh·ryt).

Fast Fact

Lava can destroy everything in its path. How hot is lava? Its color can give you a clue. The brighter the color, the hotter the lava.

Lava Temperatures

Color	Degrees C
Yellow-white	1250
Orange	1075
Bright red	900
Dark red	725
Brown-red	575

1

What Are Minerals and Rocks?

In this lesson, you can . . .

INVESTIGATE the hardness of minerals.

LEARN ABOUT how people identify and use minerals and rocks.

LINK to math, writing, literature, and technology.

INVESTIGATE

Testing Minerals

Activity Purpose How do scientists tell minerals apart? They test them for specific properties. A property is a feature that identifies something. In this investigation you will test seven minerals for the property of hardness. Then you will **order** the minerals from softest to hardest.

Materials

- minerals labeled *A* through *G*

Activity Procedure

1 Make a chart like the one shown.

2 A harder mineral scratches a softer mineral. Try to scratch each of the other minerals with Sample A. **Record** which minerals Sample A scratches. (Picture A)

3 A softer mineral is scratched by a harder mineral. Try to scratch Sample A with each of the other minerals. **Record** which minerals scratch Sample A.

◄ A geode is a hollow rounded rock with mineral crystals inside.

Mineral to Test	Minerals It Scratches	Minerals That Scratch It
Sample A		
Sample B		
Sample C		
Sample D		
Sample E		
Sample F		
Sample G		

④ Repeat Steps 2 and 3 for each mineral.

⑤ Using the information in your chart, **order** the minerals from softest to hardest. Give each mineral a number, starting with 1 for the softest mineral.

Picture A

Draw Conclusions

1. Which mineral was the hardest? Which was the softest? How do you know?

2. How did you decide the **order** of the minerals?

3. **Scientists at Work** Scientists often put objects in **order.** How can putting minerals in order of hardness help you identify them?

Investigate Further To test for hardness, scientists sometimes scratch an unknown mineral with common objects. That's because they don't always have other minerals with them. But to use common objects, scientists need to know how hard the objects are. Using the minerals from this investigation, find out the hardness of glass, a copper penny, and your fingernail. Put them in **order** with the minerals you tested.

Process Skill Tip

In a scratch test, you **observe** the results and **record** them on a chart. You use the chart to put the objects in **order.**

Minerals and Rocks

FIND OUT

- what minerals are and how they are used
- what is under the surface of the Earth

VOCABULARY

mineral
rock
crust
mantle
core

What Minerals Are

If an object is a solid, was formed in nature, and has never been alive, it's likely to be a **mineral** (MIN•er•uhl). There are many kinds of minerals. No two are exactly alike. For example, gold is metallic and shiny. Graphite is dark and dull. Diamonds are hard enough to cut steel. Chalk is so soft that you can write with it.

In the investigation you saw that hardness is one property of minerals. Other properties of minerals are color and shape. Almost all minerals can be identified by their properties.

✔ **Name three properties of minerals.**

▲ Diamond is the hardest mineral.

▲ Corundum, the second hardest mineral, may be many colors. This sapphire is a corundum. It has a beautiful deep blue color.

▲ The ruby shown here is a red corundum.

▲ Quartz is a common mineral. It is almost as hard as diamond.

▲ An emerald is a mineral called beryl. It is among the most valuable minerals.

How Minerals Are Used

You use a mineral whenever you pick up a glass or put salt on your food. You use a mineral when you write with a pencil. The "lead" in the pencil is the mineral graphite.

Your body needs small amounts of minerals such as iron and zinc to stay healthy. You get these minerals from the foods you eat.

Minerals are in many of the things around you. For example, iron comes from the mineral hematite. Iron is used to make steel for airplanes, buildings, and washing machines.

Minerals such as gold and diamond are used to make jewelry. The pennies in your pocket contain copper. Copper comes from minerals, too.

✔ **Name three ways that minerals are used.**

▲ **Aluminum comes from the mineral bauxite. Aluminum is molded into many products, such as baseball bats, cooking pots, and airplanes.**

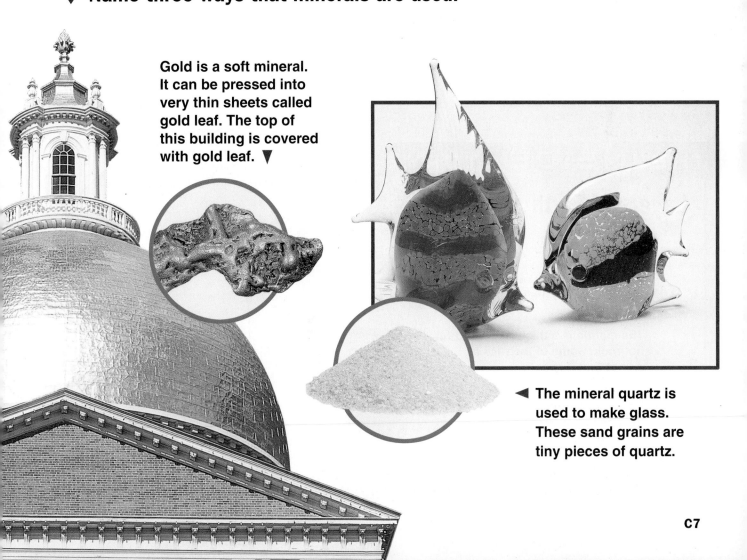

Gold is a soft mineral. It can be pressed into very thin sheets called gold leaf. The top of this building is covered with gold leaf. ▼

◄ **The mineral quartz is used to make glass. These sand grains are tiny pieces of quartz.**

What Rocks Are

The Earth is made mostly of rocks. A **rock** is made of minerals. Some rocks are made of just one mineral. Other rocks are made of many minerals.

If you could cut the Earth open, you would see three different layers of rocks. At the surface of the Earth is the solid outside layer, called the **crust**. The crust is the part of the Earth you have seen.

The crust sits on the **mantle**, the middle layer. The mantle is so hot that some of the rocks have nearly melted. They are soft like taffy.

Below the mantle, at the center of the Earth, is the **core**. It is even hotter than the mantle. The core is made of iron. The outer part of the core is so hot that it is liquid. The inner part of the core is much hotter than the mantle, but it is solid. Because the weight of the whole planet presses in on the core, the inner part stays solid.

✔ **Name the three layers of the Earth.**

Biotite

Feldspar

Quartz

Muscovite

Layers of Earth

The crust is a thin outer layer. The rocks here are solid.

The mantle is a thick layer of hot rock. Some of the rock is so hot that it is soft.

The core is the center of the Earth. It is made of very hot iron. Part of it is liquid and part is solid.

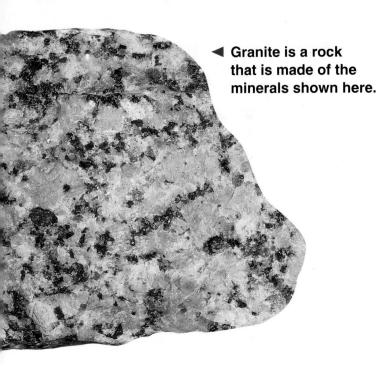

◄ Granite is a rock that is made of the minerals shown here.

Summary

A mineral is a solid natural material that has never been alive. Rocks are made of minerals. The Earth has three layers.

Review

1. What is a mineral? List three uses of minerals.
2. What is a rock?
3. Describe the layers of the Earth.
4. **Critical Thinking** How is the mantle of the Earth different from the crust? How are the mantle and crust alike?
5. **Test Prep** Which of these minerals is the hardest?
   A quartz
   B diamond
   C hematite
   D corundum

LINKS

MATH LINK

Analyze Solid Figures The particles in minerals form patterns called crystals. There are seven types of crystal shapes. Gather information on crystal shapes. How are they alike, and how are they different?

WRITING LINK

Informative Writing— Description Look for rocks where you live. Choose one that looks interesting. For a family member, make a list of words that describe it.

LITERATURE LINK

Magic School Bus Take a ride on the Magic School Bus to explore the center of the Earth. Read *Inside the Earth* by Joanna Cole. List three new things you learn about the Earth's layers.

GO ONLINE **TECHNOLOGY LINK**

Learn more about rocks by visiting the Smithsonian Institution Internet site.

www.si.edu/harcourt/science

 Smithsonian Institution®

LESSON 2

How Do Rocks Form?

In this lesson, you can . . .

 INVESTIGATE different types of rock.

 LEARN ABOUT how rocks form.

 LINK to math, writing, literature, and technology.

Types of Rocks

Activity Purpose In this investigation you will **observe** six different rocks and **compare** their properties. Then you will use your observations to group the rocks.

Materials

- 3 rocks labeled *I*, *S*, and *M*
- hand lens
- 3 unknown rocks labeled *1*, *2*, and *3*

Activity Procedure

1 Make a chart like the one shown.

2 Rocks *I*, *S*, and *M* are three different types of rocks. Look at them with and without the hand lens. **Record** your observations in the chart.

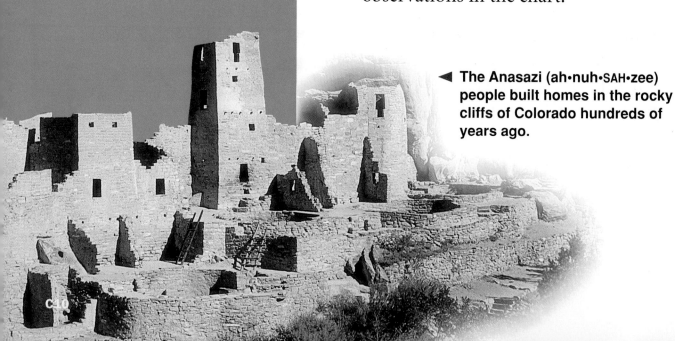

◀ The Anasazi (ah·nuh·SAH·zee) people built homes in the rocky cliffs of Colorado hundreds of years ago.

Rock	Observations
I	
S	
M	
1	
2	
3	

Picture A

3 Look at each of the numbered rocks with and without the hand lens. **Record** your observations in the chart. (Picture A)

4 **Compare** the properties of the lettered rocks with the properties of the numbered rocks. Think about how the rocks are alike and how they are different.

Draw Conclusions

1. What properties did you use to **compare** the rocks?

2. Which numbered rock is most like Rock *I*? Which numbered rock is most like Rock *S*? Which numbered rock is most like Rock *M*? Explain your answers.

3. **Scientists at Work** Scientists learn about new objects when they **compare** them with objects they have already studied. What did you learn about the rocks when you compared them?

Investigate Further Look near your school or home for small rocks. **Compare** them with Rocks *I*, *S*, and *M*. Try to **classify** the rocks as *I*, *S*, or *M*.

Process Skill Tip

When you **compare** objects, you **observe** their properties to find out how the objects are alike and how they are different. Comparing can help you put things into groups.

How Rocks Form

FIND OUT

- how rocks form
- ways people use rocks to make things

VOCABULARY

igneous rock
sedimentary rock
metamorphic rock
rock cycle

Three Types of Rocks

Exploding volcanoes, flowing water, and heat and pressure inside the Earth all form rocks. Rocks are grouped by how they form. There are three groups of rocks.

Igneous rock (IG•nee•uhs RAHK) is rock that was once melted but has cooled and hardened.

Sedimentary rock (sed•uh•MEN•ter•ee RAHK) forms from material that has settled into layers. The layers are squeezed together until they harden into rock.

Metamorphic rock (met•uh•MAWR•fik RAHK) is igneous, sedimentary, or other metamorphic rock that has been changed by heat and pressure.

✔ **What did the *I*, *S*, and *M* stand for in the investigation?**

◄ Rivers carry *sediment*, or pieces of rocks and soil. When a river slows down, it drops the sediment. Sediment builds up in layers at the bottom of rivers, lakes, seas, and oceans. These layers are pressed and stuck together to form sedimentary rocks.

Igneous rocks form from melted rock that has cooled and hardened. Some igneous rocks come from volcanoes. ▼

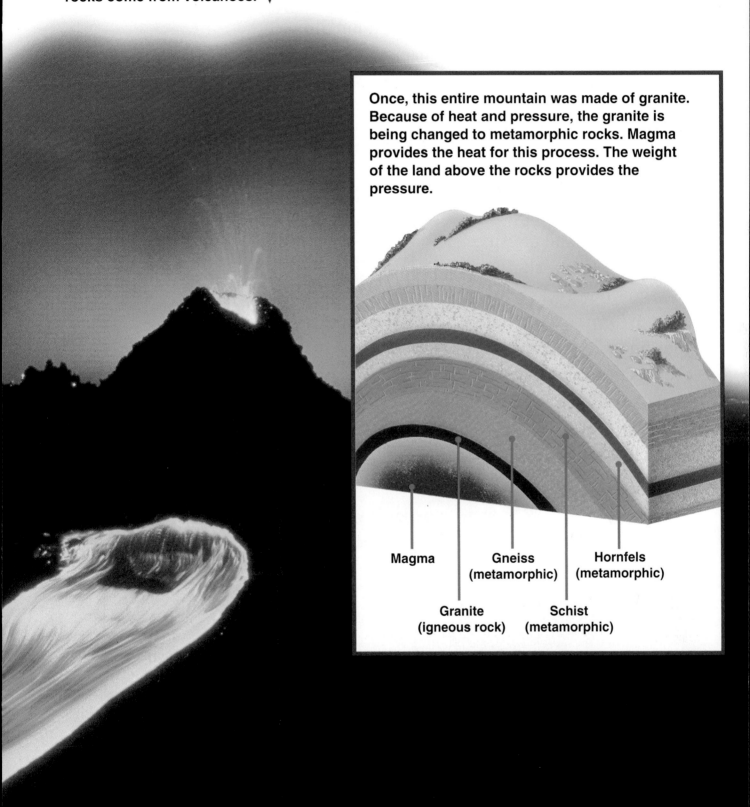

Once, this entire mountain was made of granite. Because of heat and pressure, the granite is being changed to metamorphic rocks. Magma provides the heat for this process. The weight of the land above the rocks provides the pressure.

Magma

Gneiss
(metamorphic)

Hornfels
(metamorphic)

Granite
(igneous rock)

Schist
(metamorphic)

How Rocks Form and Change

You know that there are three types of rocks—igneous, metamorphic, and sedimentary. But did you know that each type can be changed into the other types? This process of changing is called the **rock cycle** (RAHK SY•kuhl).

The diagram shows how rocks can change. The arrows show what is happening to make the rocks change. They tell about heat and pressure being applied to rocks. They also show how rocks break apart to form sediments. Use your finger to trace the changes that can happen to each type of rock.

✔ **What is the rock cycle?**

Metamorphic

Quartzite

Marble

Slate

Heat and pressure can change metamorphic rocks into other metamorphic rocks.

Sedimentary

Red sandstone

Limestone   Breccia (BRESH·uh)

Wind and water can break up sedimentary rocks to form other sedimentary rocks.

Wind and water can break up metamorphic rocks to form sedimentary rocks.

When sedimentary rocks are put under heat and pressure, metamorphic rocks can form.

Wind and water can break up igneous rocks to form sedimentary rocks.

Sedimentary rocks melt to form igneous rocks.

Igneous

When metamorphic rocks melt, they form igneous rocks.

Heat and pressure can change igneous rocks into metamorphic rocks.

Obsidian

Snowflake porphyry (POR·fuh·ree)

Pumice

Igneous rocks can melt to form new igneous rocks.

How People Use Rocks

Rocks are all around you. You see them all the time. But rocks are also in places you might not think of. Did you know that rocks help you play video games? The games use silicon chips, and silicon comes from rocks. Computers, satellites, and microwave ovens also use silicon chips.

Colorful rocks are worn as jewelry. Roads are paved with rocks, and many buildings and statues are made of rocks.

✔ **What are two uses of rocks?**

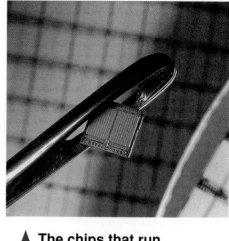

▲ The chips that run computers are made of silicon. Silicon comes from quartz, a very common mineral. Quartz is found in igneous, metamorphic, and sedimentary rocks.

◄ Metamorphic rocks such as marble are used to make statues.

Summary

There are three types of rocks. Igneous rocks form from melted rock that has cooled and hardened. Sedimentary rocks form from layers of sediment. Metamorphic rocks have been changed by heat and pressure. The rock cycle shows how one type of rock can be changed into another type of rock.

Review

1. Where do igneous rocks come from?

2. How can igneous rocks become sedimentary rocks?

3. How can metamorphic rocks become igneous rocks?

4. **Critical Thinking** Choose a rock, and tell about some things that are made from it.

5. **Test Prep** Which type of rock forms in layers?

   A igneous

   B metamorphic

   C sedimentary

   D All rocks form in layers.

◀ The Jefferson Memorial in Washington, D.C., is made of marble, a metamorphic rock.

LINKS

MATH LINK

Solve a Problem Suppose you were asked to make a model of the rock cycle. You were told to include 3 types of each kind of rock in your model. How many rocks are in the model?

WRITING LINK

Informative Writing—Report Interview someone who works with minerals and rocks. Find out how he or she uses them at work. Write a report for your teacher about what you learn. Share it with your class.

LITERATURE LINK

Rock On Want to find out more about rocks? Read *The Rock* by Peter Parnall. Tell how the rock changed over time.

TECHNOLOGY LINK

Learn more about the rock cycle by observing rocks as they change. Try *Rock Processor* on **Harcourt Science Explorations CD-ROM**.

LESSON 3

What Are Fossils?

In this lesson, you can . . .

INVESTIGATE how fossils form.

LEARN ABOUT different types of fossils.

LINK to math, writing, literature, and technology.

Fossil Layers

Activity Purpose You have never seen a live dinosaur. But you may know a lot about dinosaurs because of fossils (FAHS•uhlz). A *fossil* is what's left of a plant or animal that lived long ago. In this investigation you will **make a model** of rock layers and fossils.

Materials
- 5 colors of modeling clay
- 5 sheets of wax paper
- 5 different seashells labeled *A* through *E*

Activity Procedure

1. Make a chart like the one shown.

2. Use clay of one color to make a layer about the size and shape of a hamburger. Put the layer of clay on a sheet of wax paper.

3. Press a shell into the clay to make a print. Remove the shell. **Record** the clay color and the shell letter in your chart. (Picture A)

◀ **Fossil bones show how dinosaurs looked. This fossil is of a Tyrannosaurus rex.**

Rock Layer	Clay Color	Shell Letter
1 (bottom layer)		
2		
3		
4		
5 (top layer)		

4 Place a sheet of wax paper over the clay layer.

5 Repeat Steps 2, 3, and 4 until you have made new layers with each color of clay and each shell.

6 Trade your group's clay layers and shells with another group's. Make a second chart. Remove each layer of clay, and **observe** it. Do not change the order of the layers. Match each shell to its print. Fill in the second chart. Check your answers with the group that made the model.

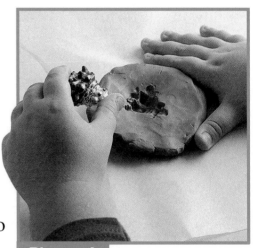

Picture A

Draw Conclusions

1. How did you know the correct layer for each shell?

2. Pretend the shell prints are fossils and the clay is sedimentary rock. List the shell letters from the oldest to the newest. Do this by using what you know about sedimentary rock layers.

3. **Scientists at Work** Scientists **use models** to understand how things happen. How did **using a model** help you understand how fossils are left in layers in time order?

Process Skill Tip

In class you can't see how real rock layers and fossils form. So **using a model** is helpful. It shows what the layers can tell you about the order in which the fossils were formed.

What Fossils Are

FIND OUT

• how fossils form

• how fossils show that life on Earth has changed

VOCABULARY

fossil

How Fossils Form

Some places are better for fossil hunting than others. Sedimentary rocks have more fossils than other kinds of rocks. That's because what's left of a plant or animal is sometimes trapped in the sediments that form the layers of the rock. The heat and pressure that form metamorphic and igneous rocks often destroy fossils.

Every **fossil** is something that has lasted from a living thing that died long ago. But there are different types of fossils. Some are body parts, such as bones or teeth, that have turned into stone. Other fossils are only marks, such as animal tracks.

The fossils of the shells in the picture on C21 show two ways fossils can form. The fossil shell on the top is a mold. You made a mold in the investigation.

Fossils often form in sedimentary rocks, such as limestone and shale.

1 The soft parts of an animal decompose.

2 Hard parts of the animal, such as shells or bones, are slowly buried under layers of sediment.

A *mold* is the shape of a plant or animal left in sediments when the rock formed. The shell that made the mold in the picture dissolved.

The other fossil shell is a cast. A *cast* forms when mud or minerals fill a mold. The cast has the exact shape of the animal that made the mold.

Fossil *imprints* are molds of leaves or other thin objects. Some imprints are of animal parts such as wings or feathers. The leaves or animal parts decomposed long ago.

✔ **What are fossils?**

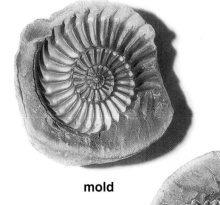

mold

Here are a mold fossil and a cast fossil. They were made by ancient sea animals called *ammonites.* Ammonites died out millions of years ago. ▶

cast

▲ This is a fossil of a dragonfly.

Plant fossils are much less common than animal fossils. This is because plant parts are more easily destroyed as rocks form. ▶

3 Over a long time, the sediment turns into rock.

4 Movement of the Earth's crust brings the rock and fossils closer to the surface. Wind and rain wear away the rock on top of the fossils.

How Fossils Help Us Learn About Dinosaurs

Dinosaurs became extinct long before there were any scientists to study them. But scientists today can use fossils to learn how dinosaurs looked and how they lived.

Using fossil bones, scientists can put together skeletons of dinosaurs. The skeletons show how large the dinosaur was and whether it walked on two legs or four.

Fossil dinosaur teeth show the kinds of foods dinosaurs ate. The shapes of the teeth are suited to eating plants or other animals. Some dinosaurs ate other dinosaurs. How do we know that?

▲ This dinosaur fossil was recently discovered. Look at its teeth and you will see that it ate other animals.

This paleontologist (a scientist who studies fossils) is digging up fossil dinosaur bones. ▼

Scientists have found fossil dinosaur bones with the teeth of other dinosaurs broken off in them!

New dinosaur fossils are being discovered all the time. Each new discovery increases what we know about dinosaurs.

✔ **How do scientists learn about dinosaurs?**

Summary

A fossil is something that has lasted from a living thing that died long ago. Fossils are found mostly in sedimentary rocks. Scientists can use fossils to understand how dinosaurs looked and lived.

Review

1. Why are most fossils found in sedimentary rocks?
2. Name two types of fossils, and tell how they formed.
3. What dinosaur fossils have scientists used to learn how dinosaurs looked?
4. **Critical Thinking** Would you find fossils in igneous rock? Why?
5. **Test Prep** Which of the following rocks would be most likely to have a fossil in it?
   A granite
   B limestone
   C marble
   D quartz

LINKS

MATH LINK

Describe Number Relationships Find the sizes of the largest and smallest dinosaurs. Make a model to show the difference in their sizes. Subtract to find the difference in their sizes.

WRITING LINK

Informative Writing— Description Choose a type of dinosaur, and make a card that describes it. At the top of the card, draw the dinosaur. Then write information about it under your drawing. Share your card with your classmates.

LITERATURE LINK

Would you like to know more about fossils? Read *Dinosaurs Walked Here* by Patricia Lauber. Choose a fossil described in the book. Then make a model showing how the fossil formed.

TECHNOLOGY LINK

Learn more about finding dinosaur fossils by watching *Dinosaur Discovery* on the **Harcourt Science Newsroom Video.**

CNN.
Turner
Le@rning®

Discovering Dinosaurs

As early as the third century, people in China wrote about dragon teeth and dragon bones. But what those people described weren't dragons. They were dinosaurs.

Dinosaur Discoveries

No one knew what dinosaur fossils were before the 1800s. One early scientist thought the thighbone he had found was from a giant human. In 1824 William Buckland gave the name Megalosaurus ("great lizard") to the animal whose jaw and teeth he had been studying. The next year, Mary Ann Mantell found a large tooth partly buried in a rock in England. She didn't know what it was. Her husband, Gideon Mantell, was a doctor who collected fossils. He thought the tooth came from a large reptile like an iguana. So he called it Iguanodon, which means "iguana tooth."

During the next few years, many remains were found. In 1842 Richard Owen, an English scientist, gave the name Dinosauria to the whole group of

Dinosaur model

fossil remains. Dinosaur means "terrible lizard."

The first dinosaur craze was in the 1850s in England. There was an exhibit at the Crystal Palace in London in 1853. Sir Richard Owen and Waterhouse Hawkins, an artist, made some life-size dinosaur models. The models have errors, but they are still on view at the Crystal Palace Park.

Studying Dinosaur Fossils

Dinosaur fossils have been found on every continent. The largest numbers of sites are in the United States and Europe. At a fossil site, or dig, scientists use chisels to carefully free the fossils from the surrounding rock. Each fossil is cleaned and carefully packed in a plaster or foam jacket. Detailed notes are taken about where the bones were found.

The bones are then taken to a laboratory to be analyzed. Scientists try to determine how the bones may have fit together. This job is easier if the muscles have left marks, called muscle scars, where they were attached to the bones. A scientific artist sketches the bones and muscles, and adds skin. Drawing the skin is mostly guesswork. No one knows for sure whether dinosaurs had stripes or spots, or what color their skin was.

Interesting Dinosaurs

Dinosaurs began to appear in books during the mid-1800s. Today, some museums feature exhibits of dinosaurs. Dinosaur robots that move and make noises are made of steel and latex. They are shown throughout the world at theme parks and at museums.

THINK ABOUT IT

- Why do you think people in China thought dinosaur bones were from dragons?

The History of Dinosaur Discoveries

1677
First illustration of a dinosaur bone appears in a book.

1842
The group Dinosauria is named.

1853
First life-size models of dinosaurs are exhibited.

1600   1700   1800   1900   2000

1824/25
First dinosaurs are named: Megalosaurus and Iguanodon.

1987
Dinosaur skeleton is discovered in Antarctica, the only continent where dinosaurs had not been found before.

Atlantic Coast **Mid-Atlantic Ridge**

Charles Langmuir
PETROLOGIST, GEOCHEMIST

Charles Langmuir says that when he was a boy, his father played at science with him. They made musical instruments together and changed the tone of a flute by blowing carbon dioxide through it instead of air. They made a model of a diver in a bottle. They watched dry ice evaporate and grew crystals. All this play taught Langmuir that science was a combination of fun, amazement, and careful observation. Although his mother didn't play at science with him, Langmuir says she taught him other things. She taught him that exploration never stops, that limits don't matter, and that a sense of humor is important.

These lessons led Langmuir to the study of geology and petrology, the study of rocks. Langmuir began studying ocean rocks while in graduate school. Most of the rocks he studies are basalts, a type of igneous rock. Studying the ocean leads to greater knowledge about Earth's land. Learning about Earth's land gives more information about the ocean.

Langmuir thinks of the ocean floor as a wonderful frontier. He finds it exciting to be working with the two-thirds of Earth's surface that is underwater.

THINK ABOUT IT

1. What kinds of things would you expect to find on the ocean floor?

2. What school subjects do you "play at" outside school?

STREAK

What color streak do some minerals have?

Materials

- streak plate or piece of tile
- minerals common to your area, such as chalcopyrite, hematite, pyrite, talc, gypsum, sphalerite, muscovite, galena, fluorite, and calcite

Name of Mineral	Color of Mineral	Color of Streak

Procedure

❶ Make a chart like the one shown.

❷ Make a mark on the tile with the first mineral. Record the color of the mark it makes. The mark is called the streak.

❸ Repeat step 2 for each mineral. Record your results.

Draw Conclusions

Compare the color of the minerals with the color of the streaks. Are they the same? How could streaks help you identify minerals that may look alike?

MINERALS IN SAND

What minerals are found in sand?

Materials

- sand
- sheet of paper
- hand lens
- toothpick
- mineral descriptions

Procedure

❶ Spread the sand on a sheet of paper.

❷ Observe the colors and shapes of the sand grains with the hand lens. Each type of mineral grain has a different color and shape.

❸ Use the toothpick to move the grains of each mineral into a separate pile.

Draw Conclusions

Identify the minerals. Use the descriptions your teacher gives you. Which mineral is the most common?

Vocabulary Review

Use the terms below to complete the sentences 1 through 10. The page numbers in ( ) tell you where to look in the chapter if you need help.

mineral (C6)

rock (C8)

crust (C8)

mantle (C8)

core (C8)

igneous rock (C12)

sedimentary rock (C12)

metamorphic rock (C12)

rock cycle (C14)

fossil (C20)

1. A ____ is something that has lasted from a living thing that died long ago.

2. Rock that has been changed by heat and pressure in the Earth is ____.

3. The ____ is the iron layer at the center of the Earth.

4. A solid material made of minerals is a ____.

5. A ____ is a solid natural material found in the Earth.

6. Rock that forms from layers of sediment is ____.

7. The ____ is Earth's middle layer of soft rock.

8. One type of rock turns into another type as rocks move through the ____.

9. The ____ is Earth's outer layer.

10. Melted rock that has cooled is ____.

Connect Concepts

Write the terms where they belong in the concept map.

minerals   sedimentary

igneous   metamorphic

melted rock that cools and hardens

layers of sediment and plant and animal remains

rock that has been changed by heat and pressure inside the Earth

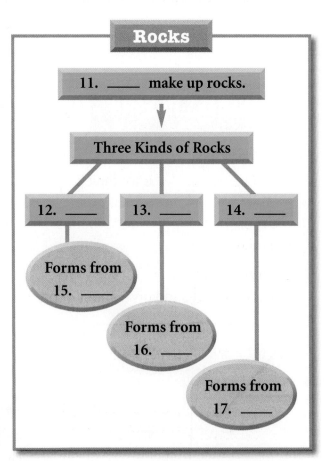

Rocks

11. ____ make up rocks.

Three Kinds of Rocks

12. ____   13. ____   14. ____

Forms from 15. ____

Forms from 16. ____

Forms from 17. ____

Check Understanding

Write the letter of the best choice.

18. A rock is made of —

  A only living things

  B one or more minerals

  C only two minerals

  D minerals that are hard

19. Heat helps form —

  F igneous and metamorphic rocks

  G sedimentary and metamorphic rocks

  H only igneous rocks

  J only metamorphic rocks

20. Fossils often last in sedimentary rocks because the rocks —

  A are very hot

  B are often near animals

  C have layers that save animal and plant shapes

  D don't ever change

21. A ___ mineral will scratch a ___ mineral.

  F rare, common   **H** hard, soft

  G soft, hard   **J** small, big

22. As you go deeper into Earth, —

  A the pressure increases and it gets hotter

  B the rocks get smaller

  C it gets cold

  D the pressure decreases and the rocks get smaller

Critical Thinking

23. Why are fossils not often found in igneous rocks?

24. You find a mineral sample. You think it may be calcite or quartz. How could you decide which mineral your sample is?

Process Skills Review

25. What tools are useful in putting minerals in **order** by hardness?

26. You want to **compare** three unknown rocks with three known rocks. What properties would you use?

27. How can you **make a model** of the way sedimentary rocks form?

Performance Assessment

Changing Rocks

Choose a type of rock. Tell how it could move through the rock cycle by changing into different types of rocks. Draw a picture showing the stages your rock could go through.

CHAPTER 2

Forces That Shape the Land

Vocabulary Preview

landform
mountain
valley
canyon
plain
plateau
barrier island
weathering
erosion
glacier
earthquake
volcano
flood

Over millions of years, a river wears away layer after layer of rock to form a canyon. Wind picks up sand and drops it in another place, forming a dune. Fast or slow, the land is always changing.

Fast Fact

There are many reasons why desert people move from place to place. One is that the sand surface they live on changes. As the wind blows the sand, dunes can move forward between 10 and 50 meters (33 to 164 ft) a year. Sand dunes have even been known to cover small villages.

Death Valley, California

Earthquakes can be destructive, but they can also make new landforms. In 1811 and 1822, three earthquakes centered in Missouri destroyed the town of New Madrid. But they also formed Lake Saint Francis in Arkansas.

The West Chop Lighthouse on Martha's Vineyard has had to be moved three times since 1817 to keep it from falling off the cliff! Every year the water wears away more of the rocky cliff it stands on.

Midwest Earthquakes

Damage to Homes	About How Often It Happens
Few repairs	Every year
Many repairs	Every 11 years
Heavy structural damage	Every 80 years
Most buildings heavily damaged	Every 377 years
Total destruction of buildings	Every 875 years

LESSON 1

What Are Landforms?

In this lesson, you can . . .

INVESTIGATE how mountains form.

LEARN ABOUT landforms.

LINK to math, writing, physical education, and technology.

Folds in Earth's Crust

Activity Purpose Scientists know that some mountains are formed by folds in Earth's surface. But how can the surface of Earth fold? In this investigation you will **use a model** to find out.

Materials

- 4 paper towels
- plastic cup
- water

Activity Procedure

1. Stack the four paper towels on a table. Fold the stack in half.

◄ This rock, called Devil's Tower, was once lava inside a volcano. Wind and rain have worn away the volcano that was around it.

2 Sprinkle water on the towels. They should be damp but not very wet.

3 Place your hands on the edges of the damp towels.

4 Push the edges slowly toward the center. (Picture A)

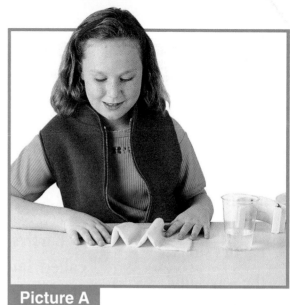
Picture A

Draw Conclusions

1. What happened as you pushed the edges of the towels together?

2. How did the height of the towels change as you pushed them?

3. **Scientists at Work** Scientists **use models** to understand how things happen. How did this model help you understand how mountains form?

Investigate Further Some mountains, such as the Rocky Mountains shown below, form when two separate pieces of Earth's crust push together. How would you **make a model** to show this process?

Process Skill Tip

You cannot see real mountains form. The process takes thousands of years. But you can **use a model** to find out about something that happens very slowly.

Earth's Surface

The Shape of the Surface

VOCABULARY

landform
mountain
valley
canyon
plain
plateau
barrier island

Earth's surface has many natural shapes, or features, called **landforms**. The landforms you've seen or know about are on land. But there are also interesting landforms under the oceans!

Look at the diagram below. You can see that the crust is thicker under the land than it is under the oceans. You can also see places where the crust rises above the water to form land.

✔ **What are landforms?**

Earth is made up of three layers. The crust is the thinnest layer. ▶

Mantle

Crust

Core

Types of Landforms

In the investigation you saw how Earth's crust can fold to form mountains. A **mountain** is a place on Earth's surface that is much higher than the land around it.

Some parts of Earth's surface are low areas. A **valley** is a lowland area between higher lands such as mountains. A **canyon** is a deep valley with very steep sides.

A **plain** is a flat area on Earth's surface. The middle of the United States is a large plain. A **plateau** (pla•TOH) is a flat area higher than the land around it. In some places plateaus have steep sides. They look like tables made of rock.

You might see another kind of landform at the seashore. A **barrier island** (BAIR•ee•er EYE•luhnd) is a thin island near a coast. Barrier islands have wide, sandy beaches.

✔ **List and describe three landforms.**

▲ A valley is a lowland between higher areas. Rivers can wear away rock to form valleys.

▲ A mountain is at least 600 meters (about 2,000 ft) higher than the land around it. Some mountains are tall and rocky. Others are rounded and covered with trees.

A plain is a flat area on Earth's surface. The soil of some plains is good for growing crops. ▼

▲ Barrier islands can form when sand in moving water is dropped near the shore.

NORTH CAROLINA

Elizabeth City

Nags Head

Greenville

New Bern

Ocracoke

Atlantic Beach

Wilmington

◄ The east coast of the United States has the longest chain of barrier islands in the world. They go from New York to Florida. In North Carolina, shown here, the islands (red) are called the Outer Banks.

A canyon can form where a river cuts a path through a plateau. The Grand Canyon is 1.6 kilometers (1 mi) deep. It took the Colorado River millions of years to cut the canyon in the Colorado Plateau. ►

Summary

Landforms are the shapes, or features, found on Earth's surface. Landforms include mountains, valleys, canyons, plains, plateaus, and barrier islands.

Review

1. What is a landform?
2. What is a mountain?
3. How are plateaus and plains different?
4. **Critical Thinking** Compare a valley with a canyon. How could a valley become a canyon?
5. **Test Prep** Which landform is higher than the land around it?
   A valley
   B plateau
   C plain
   D canyon

LINKS

MATH LINK

Compare and Order Numbers
Earth's core is 3,486 kilometers from its center to its edge. The mantle is 2,885 kilometers thick. The crust is 30 to 40 kilometers thick in some areas. List the layers in order from thinnest to thickest.

WRITING LINK

Informative Writing— Description What is the most unusual landform you've ever seen? What is special about it? Write a paragraph about the landform for your teacher. Explain what it looks like. Describe the land around it. Tell what you like best about it.

PHYSICAL EDUCATION LINK

Climbing Mountains Mountain climbing is a popular sport. It can be fun, but it can be dangerous. Find out what equipment people need to climb a mountain safely.

GO ONLINE TECHNOLOGY LINK

Learn more about landforms by visiting this Internet site.

www.scilinks.org/harcourt

SCi**LINKS**
THE WORLD'S A CLICK AWAY

C37

LESSON 2

What Are Slow Landform Changes?

In this lesson, you can . . .

INVESTIGATE how sand wears away rock.

LEARN ABOUT weathering and erosion.

LINK to math, writing, literature, and technology.

Sand at Work

Activity Purpose Wind picks up sand and blows it against rocks. This wears away the rock and changes its shape. In this investigation you will **interpret data** to learn how sand wears away rock.

Materials

- balance
- extra masses for the balance
- sandstone rocks
- sand
- glass jar with lid

Activity Procedure

1. Copy the table on page C39.

2. **Measure** the mass of all the rocks. **Record** your results in the table. (Picture A)

3. Fill the jar one-fourth full with sand. **Measure** the mass of the jar with the sand in it. **Record** your results. Add to get the total.

◄ Wind has worn away parts of this rock. Now it looks like an elephant. As more rock wears away, the elephant will lose its "trunk."

	Mass of Rocks	Mass of Jar and Sand	Total Mass of Rocks, Jar, and Sand
Before			
After			

4 Put the rocks into the jar. Put the lid on. Shake the jar for 30 minutes. Then put the jar aside. Shake the jar for 30 minutes every day for one week.

5 After one week, **measure** the mass of the jar and its contents. Then remove the rocks from the jar. **Measure** their mass. **Record** your results. Subtract to find the mass of the jar with the sand inside.

Picture A

Draw Conclusions

1. What did the sandstone look like before shaking? Did it look different after shaking? How?

2. **Compare** the masses before and after the shaking. How did the mass of the rocks change?

3. **Scientists at Work** Scientists **interpret data** to understand how things work. Use the data from this investigation to tell what happened to the sand and the rock.

Investigate Further **Design an experiment** to test this **hypothesis:** Larger pieces of rock weather faster.

Process Skill Tip

When you **interpret data,** you look for patterns in recorded information. Then you use the patterns to **draw conclusions** about what happened.

Slow Changes to the Land

FIND OUT

- why landforms are always changing
- how wind, water, and ice change Earth's surface

VOCABULARY

weathering
erosion
glacier

How Rocks Are Broken Down

In the investigation you saw how sand smashes against rock, wears it down, and breaks it apart. This process is called weathering. **Weathering** (WETH•er•ing) is the way rocks are broken down into smaller pieces. Weathering is always changing the surface of Earth.

You have learned that Earth's crust is rock. But most of the land around you is covered with soil, sand, or pebbles. That's because of weathering. Very slowly, weathering acts on rocks. Bit by bit the rocks are worn away. After thousands of years, the solid rocks are broken down into soil.

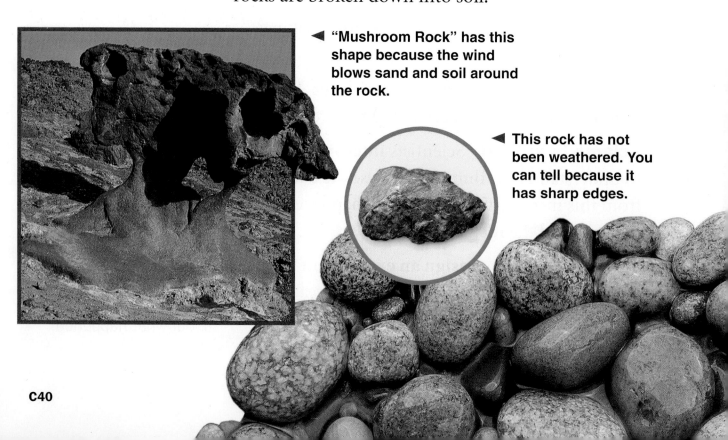

◀ "Mushroom Rock" has this shape because the wind blows sand and soil around the rock.

◀ This rock has not been weathered. You can tell because it has sharp edges.

Weathering is caused by more than the wind. Water also causes weathering. Even plants help break apart rocks on the surface of the Earth.

Water causes weathering when it freezes. Most things take up less space when they freeze. But frozen water takes up more space. Water flows into cracks and holes in rock. As the temperature drops, the water freezes. Since the ice takes up more space, it pushes against the rock around it. The force of the ice widens the cracks and breaks the rock into pieces.

Water also causes weathering when it is not frozen. The movement of water wears rock away. Also, rivers pick up rocks and bounce them around. This wears the rocks down.

Plants cause weathering, too. Roots grow into cracks in rock. As the roots get bigger, they split the rock.

✔ **What is weathering?**

▲ Tree roots grow into cracks in rocks to reach minerals and water. As the roots grow, they split the rocks.

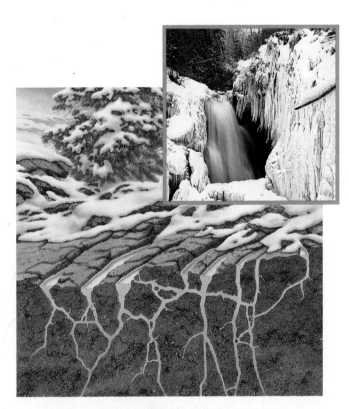

▲ Water breaks rock when it freezes in cracks. Water and ice are important causes of weathering.

◀ After weathering by water, a rock has rounded edges. These rocks tumbled in a river and smashed against other rocks. Their sharp edges were worn away.

How Rock Pieces Move

After weathering breaks up rocks, erosion moves the pieces around. **Erosion** (ee•ROH•zhuhn) is the movement of weathered rock and soil. Sometimes erosion happens very fast. The waves of a big storm can tear the sand away from a beach in just a few hours. A big dust storm can quickly blow away tons of soil. But most erosion happens very slowly.

Creep is a type of slow erosion. *Creep* is the movement of soil down steep hills. Creep happens so slowly that you don't notice it. But you can see what creep does. Sometimes a fence that was straight becomes crooked over a long time. The crooked fence shows that there was creep.

Erosion can be caused by water. Rain washes soil from hills and fields. The soil flows with the rainwater into rivers. The flowing water in rivers

▲ Creep moves trees and bends fences and walls. It can also push roads out of line.

Satellite view of the Mississippi Delta ▼

carries soil downstream. The soil is dropped whenever the rivers slow down. Sometimes the soil is dropped along the banks. But soil can also be dropped at the mouth of a river to form a delta. A delta is a piece of land that forms at the mouth of a river. Deltas are often shaped like triangles.

Just like water, wind carries loose pieces of rock and sand from one place to another. The faster the wind blows, the more rock and sand it can carry. When wind slows down, it drops some of the sand it carries.

✔ **What is erosion?**

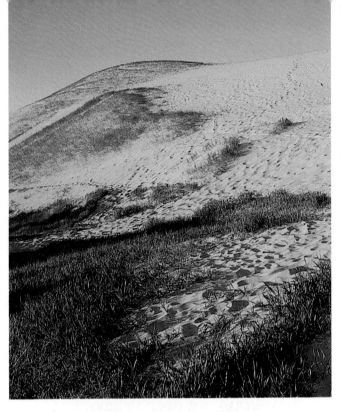

▲ Wind blows sand into large piles called dunes. Dunes form in deserts and along sandy coasts. The dunes in this picture are on the shore of Lake Michigan.

Erosion sometimes makes a delta by moving soil to the mouth of a river. The Mississippi River has one of the world's biggest deltas. It is larger than the states of New Jersey and Rhode Island combined. ▼

C43

How Glaciers Change the Land

Erosion can also be caused by moving ice. **Glaciers** (GLAY•sherz) are huge sheets of ice. They form in places where it's so cold all year that the snow doesn't melt. Glaciers move downhill, but they usually move very slowly. Most glaciers travel less than 30 centimeters (about 1 ft) each day.

Glaciers change the land as they slide over it. They scrape up rocks and soil and pile them up into hills. They scoop out rocks and soil to form huge holes. Sometimes these holes fill with water to become lakes.

Valley glaciers form near mountain peaks. They move slowly downhill like rivers of ice. As they move, they scoop out deep valleys.

Continental glaciers are sheets of ice that are much bigger than valley glaciers. They build up at the center of a continent.

✔ **What is a glacier?**

Glaciers (white) cover one-tenth of Earth's land surface. Most glaciers are found in valleys. Continental glaciers, which are bigger, cover most of Greenland and Antarctica. ▼

Longest Valley Glaciers

Glacier	Length (in mi)
Denman Glacier (Antarctica)	150 mi
Nimrod-Lennox-King Ice Passage (Antarctica)	179 mi
Arctic Institute Ice Passage (Antarctica)	225 mi
Novaya Zemlya (Russia)	260 mi
Lambert-Fisher Ice Passage (Antarctica)	320 mi

Length (in mi)

Summary

Weathering breaks the rock of Earth's crust into pieces. Erosion moves the broken rock and soil on Earth's surface. Wind, water, and glaciers shape the land by moving rock and soil.

Review

1. How can ice cause weathering?

2. How do plant roots break rock?

3. How do glaciers change Earth's surface?

4. **Critical Thinking** Why must weathering happen before erosion?

5. **Test Prep** Which causes erosion?

   A sand   **C** weathering

   B wind   **D** plant roots

LINKS

MATH LINK

Solve a Problem There is a straight fence on a steep hill. Creep moves the middle of the fence 5 centimeters per year. What will the fence look like in 1 year? In 10 years? How far will it have moved?

WRITING LINK

Narrative Writing—Personal Story Thousands of years ago, a huge glacier covered most of the northern United States. Ice and snow always covered the ground. Suppose that you lived at that time. Write a story for your family that describes a day in your life.

LITERATURE LINK

Find Out About Landslides Read about what causes erosion in *Landslides, Slumps, & Creep* by Peter H. Goodwin.

GO ONLINE TECHNOLOGY LINK

Visit the Harcourt Learning Site for related links, activities, and resources.

www.harcourtschool.com

WELCOME TO THE LEARNING SITE

What Are Rapid Landform Changes?

In this lesson, you can . . .

INVESTIGATE how volcanoes change the land around them.

LEARN ABOUT rapid changes in the land.

LINK to math, writing, social studies, and technology.

INVESTIGATE

A Model Volcano

Activity Purpose An erupting volcano sends out hot liquid rock and ash. An eruption quickly changes the look and shape of the land around the volcano. In this investigation you will **make a model** to see how a volcano can change the land around it.

Materials

- large tray
- wax paper
- tall, thin plastic jar
- safety goggles
- lab apron
- measuring spoons
- flour
- baking soda
- measuring cup
- red, green, and blue food coloring
- soil
- water
- white vinegar

Activity Procedure

1. Cover the tray with wax paper. Place the jar in the middle of the tray.

2. **CAUTION** **Put on safety goggles and a lab apron.** Mix $\frac{1}{2}$ teaspoon flour and 1 teaspoon baking soda in a measuring cup. Put this mixture into the jar. Add 10 drops of red food coloring.

◀ **Red-hot lava escapes from deep in the Earth through volcanoes.**

3. Moisten the soil slightly. Put the soil around the jar. Then mold the soil into the shape of a volcano. The top of the jar must be even with the top of the soil. (Picture A)

4. Slowly pour $\frac{1}{4}$ cup white vinegar into the jar. (Picture B)

5. **Observe** what happens. Remove the jar and throw away the contents. Replace the jar. Then wait 15 minutes for the "lava" to dry.

6. Repeat steps 2, 4, and 5 with the green food coloring and then with the blue food coloring.

Picture A

Picture B

Draw Conclusions

1. What happened when you poured the vinegar into the mixture in the jar?

2. What did the material that came out of your volcano stand for?

3. **Scientists at Work** Scientists **make a model** to understand how things happen in nature that are difficult to **observe** in person. How did your model help you understand the way an erupting volcano changes the land around it?

Investigate Further Different kinds of volcanoes have different kinds of eruptions. How could you find out what these eruptions are like? Choose one type of eruption, and **plan and conduct an investigation** to model it.

Process Skill Tip

An erupting volcano is dangerous. When you **make a model** of an eruption, you can **observe** the process without taking a risk.

Rapid Changes to the Land

FIND OUT

- how earthquakes and volcanoes change the land
- how floods change the land

VOCABULARY

earthquake
volcano
flood

Earthquakes

Earth's crust and mantle are made up of many pieces that fit together like pieces of a puzzle. These pieces move around in different ways. They push into each other. They pull away from each other. They slide past each other. Sometimes their movements cause earthquakes. An **earthquake** is the shaking of Earth's surface caused by movement of the crust where it meets the mantle.

Most earthquakes are too small to feel. But each year about 200 earthquakes cause great damage. Very big earthquakes can leave cracks and uneven areas in Earth's surface. They can destroy cities and move rivers. Earthquakes under the sea can cause huge waves that flood coastlines.

✔ What is an earthquake?

The San Andreas fault (left) is a crack in Earth's crust in California. A *fault* is a place where two pieces of Earth's crust are slowly sliding past each other. Sometimes the pieces of crust get stuck. Then they suddenly break free and move again. That's when the ground around the fault shakes. Earthquakes can destroy buildings and roads.

Volcanoes

A **volcano** is an opening in Earth's surface from which lava flows. Lava and ash build up around the opening to form a mountain.

You saw in the investigation that an erupting volcano can quickly change the land around it. The eruption can blow off mountaintops. It can cover the land with ash and liquid rock called *lava*. It can also send out hot clouds of ash, rock, and gases. The heat can burn nearby forests and buildings.

✔ **What is a volcano?**

▲ A volcano erupted on Montserrat, an island in the Carribean, in 1997. It destroyed Plymouth, the island's capital city. It set trees on fire and left ash on most of the island. Thousands of people had to leave their homes.

Floods

You have already read that water can cause slow changes on Earth's surface. Sometimes water can change Earth's surface quickly. Big storms dump heavy rain on the land. Then the rainwater runs into rivers. If the rivers can't hold all the water, they overflow their banks and cause a flood. A **flood** is a large amount of water that covers normally dry land.

Flood water flows into cities, towns, and farms near the rivers. Floods damage buildings, roads, and soil.

When flood water goes down, it leaves soil and sand behind. Buildings that have been flooded are left full of mud. But the flood also leaves rich soil on fields. This soil is good for growing crops.

✔ **What can cause a flood?**

▲ Mudslides begin when heavy rains fill soil with too much water. Soil turns to mud and slides downhill. The mud can take houses and trees with it as it moves.

THE INSIDE STORY

How Floods Affect the Land

Before the flood the river is at its normal level.

During the flood the river swells and covers low land.

After the flood the river returns to its banks. It leaves behind much of the soil it was carrying.

Summary

Several kinds of events can change Earth's surface quickly. Earthquakes shake Earth's surface and destroy buildings. Erupting volcanoes spread lava, ash, or rock in large areas around them. Floods wash away soil and buildings and can cause mudslides. But flood water leaves a new layer of soil on the land.

Review

1. What causes earthquakes?
2. What is lava?
3. What damage can be caused by a flood?
4. **Critical Thinking** Can people protect the land from floods? Explain your answer.
5. **Test Prep** Which can cause rapid changes to the land?

   A volcano   **C** wind

   B glacier   **D** weathering

LINKS

MATH LINK

Construct Graphs Look up earthquakes in an encyclopedia or almanac. Make a list of earthquakes that have happened during the past 40 years in the United States. Make a bar graph that shows the four strongest.

WRITING LINK

Informative Writing— Narration What would it be like to live in an area where there could be an earthquake? Write a story for your classmates that describes what you might see, hear, and feel.

SOCIAL STUDIES LINK

Report the News Research the eruption of a famous volcano. Write a news report about the event.

TECHNOLOGY LINK

To learn about how people can make buildings safer during an earthquake, watch the video *Earthquake Springs* on the **Harcourt Science Newsroom Video.**

CNN
Turner
Le@rning.

Yellowstone Geysers

What Is a Geyser?

A geyser is a hot underground spring that bubbles with steam and water. Geysers have long tubes, called pipes, that contain water and reach deep into the ground. The water in these pipes is warmed by heat within Earth's crust. Near the bottom of the pipes, the water is very hot and under great pressure. The heat causes the water nearer the surface to heat up and boil. When the water boils, it flows upward, which takes away pressure from the water below. This loss of pressure causes the water deep within the pipes to boil. That sudden, strong boiling action causes the rest of the water to *erupt*, or burst, from the geyser's opening and into the air.

The History of the Yellowstone Geysers

about 600,000 B.C.
A volcanic eruption occurs at what is now known as Yellowstone, leaving a large caldera.

1890
The United States army sets up a permanent post at Yellowstone in order to preserve and protect the land.

600,000 B.C. | 1800 | 1850 | 1900

Early 1800s
Explorers, missionaries, trappers, and miners travel the Yellowstone region.

1872
Congress names Yellowstone as the world's first national park.

YELLOWSTONE NATIONAL

Yellowstone National Park

More than 500,000 years ago, in the area now known as Yellowstone National Park in Wyoming, Montana, and Idaho, a volcano erupted and formed a giant crater called a *caldera*. Lava under the caldera forms a hot spot below Earth's surface.

In the early 1800s, when Yellowstone was first seen by American explorers, people often did not believe the stories of the steaming and erupting waters. In 1842 a man named Warren Ferris was the first to use the word *geyser* to describe these erupting waters. During the late 1800s, more and more people explored the Yellowstone region, and by 1872 President Ulysses S. Grant had established Yellowstone as a national park.

Geysers in Yellowstone

Today there are more than 500 geysers in Yellowstone National Park. Geysers can erupt as often as several times a day or as little as a few times every 10 years! Some geysers have fairly regular eruptions, while others do not.

One of the biggest and most famous geysers is Old Faithful. Old Faithful erupts about every 35 to 120 minutes. The eruptions last between 90 seconds and five minutes. When it erupts, Old Faithful can spray water 27 to 56 meters (89 to 184 feet) into the air.

Beehive Geyser is shaped like a hive at its base. Next to Beehive is a smaller geyser that begins to erupt about 20 minutes before a full eruption of Beehive.

Grand Geyser is one of the tallest geysers at Yellowstone. Its eruptions, which occur about every 8 to 12 hours, reach about 55 meters (180 feet) in height. Grand Geyser's eruptions usually last about 10 to 12 minutes, but they often stop after 9 minutes and then start again after one minute. The second eruption often brings the bigger burst.

THINK ABOUT IT

- What causes water to erupt from geysers?

1978
Yellowstone is declared a World Heritage site.

1950 2000

2000
On May 2, Steamboat Geyser erupts for the first time in nine years.

The Yellowstone caldera

Scott Rowland
VOLCANOLOGIST

Scott Rowland studies lava flows from volcanoes. He studied and now teaches at the University of Hawai'i. He also travels to such places as Mexico, Guatemala, and the Galápagos Islands to study volcanoes.

People who study volcanoes look at the nature and causes of eruptions. They set up observatories on the rims or slopes of volcanoes to learn more about the volcanoes. Their work can save many lives. When they know a volcano is about to erupt, they can warn people to leave the area.

Volcanoes are classified by the kind of material that comes out of the volcano and by the violence of the eruption. Most eruptions in Hawai'i are not very violent. The lava usually flows quietly out of vents in Earth's surface.

Volcanoes in Hawai'i have a built-in warning system. Many small earthquakes occur as magma collects and rises inside the volcano. As the magma collects, the outside of the volcano expands slightly. This expansion can be detected with sensitive scientific instruments.

THINK ABOUT IT

1. What would cause the outside of a volcano to expand before it erupts?

2. What is the advantage of an early warning that a volcano is about to erupt?

SHAKE THE EARTH

What are some effects of earthquakes?

Materials

- baking pan filled with gelatin
- plastic wrap
- large croutons

Procedure

① Cover the top of the gelatin with plastic wrap.

② Use croutons to make buildings on top of the gelatin.

③ Move the pan up and down. Then move the pan from side to side. Then tap one end of the pan as you move it. Observe the movement of the gelatin.

Draw Conclusions

Did the movement damage your buildings? **Record** your observations. How is this model like an earthquake?

WEATHERING

Can chemicals in water wear away rock?

Materials

- 6 small glass jars without labels
- wax pencil
- 3 types of rock chips (limestone, sandstone, quartzite)
- water
- white vinegar

Procedure

① Label two jars *limestone*. Write *sandstone* on two jars. Write *quartzite* on the last two jars.

② Put a few rock chips in each jar. Make sure the chips match the jar's label.

③ Fill one jar of each pair with water. Fill the other jar with vinegar.

④ Observe what happens. Wait 30 minutes, and observe again. Let the jars sit overnight. Then, observe them again.

Draw Conclusions

How did the vinegar and the water affect the rocks?

Vocabulary Review

Use the terms below to complete sentences 1 through 13. The page numbers in ( ) tell you where to look in the chapter if you need help.

landform (C34)   **weathering** (C40)

mountain (C35)   **erosion** (C42)

valley (C35)   **glacier** (C44)

canyon (C35)   **earthquake** (C48)

plain (C35)   **volcano** (C49)

plateau (C35)   **flood** (C50)

barrier island (C35)

1. A flat area on Earth's surface is a ___.

2. ___ breaks down rock into smaller pieces.

3. A lowland between higher lands such as mountains is a ___.

4. A ___ is a flat area higher than the land around it.

5. A place on Earth's surface that is much higher than the land around it is a ___ .

6. A ___ occurs when water covers an area of land that is normally dry.

7. The movement of weathered rock by wind, water, or ice is called ___.

8. A ___ is an opening in Earth's surface, from which lava may flow.

9. A ___ is any feature on Earth's surface.

10. An ___ is the shaking of Earth's surface, caused by movement in the crust and mantle.

11. A deep valley with steep sides is a ___.

12. A ___ is a large sheet of ice that moves slowly downhill.

13. A ___ is a thin, sandy island that forms near a coast.

Connect Concepts

Write the terms that complete the concept map.

C56

Check Understanding

Write the letter of the best choice.

23. Rivers can cut through land to form —

    A canyons   **C** mountains

    B plains   **D** crust

24. An example of erosion is —

    F plant roots growing

    G water freezing in cracks

    H water moving soil

    J ice that does not move

25. Creep causes —

    A dust storms   **C** mudslides

    B bent fences   **D** floods

26. Volcanoes can form —

    F mountains **H** barrier islands

    G plains   **J** canyons

27. Mountains can form —

    A when Earth's crust folds

    B when rivers cut through plateaus

    C when soil is smashed against rock

    D on barrier islands

Critical Thinking

28. Will Earth's landforms look the same 1,000 years from now? Explain your answer.

29. Would Earth's surface be different without weathering and erosion? Explain your answer.

30. How could it help people if we could predict earthquakes?

31. Why do some farmers plant crops next to rivers?

Process Skills Review

32. How could you **make a model** to show erosion caused by a glacier?

33. How could you **interpret data** to find how high the water got during a flood? What data would you need?

Performance Assessment

Changing Landforms

Draw a picture of a landform discussed in the chapter. Under your picture, write sentences about the landform. Tell how it formed and how it might change.

Soils

Soil covers almost all of Earth's land. We walk on it. We put buildings on it. We grow plants in it. We couldn't live without it!

Vocabulary Preview

soil
humus
topsoil
bedrock
clay
loam
resource
conservation
strip cropping
contour plowing

Fast Fact

Animals use soil too. Pigs need soil more than many animals. Because pigs can't sweat, they roll around in mud to keep cool.

You dig a hole. Worms crawl away. Tiny bugs scatter. What else lives in soil? If you could take a cross section of soil and remove 1000 grams of the living things, here's what you'd find:

Mass of Living Things in Soil

Plant Roots 660 g

Bacteria 171 g

Fungi 131 g

Other Stuff 28 g

Insects 3 g

Earthworms 7 g

Earth isn't the only planet with soil. Mars has soil also. The soil is red — that's why Mars looks red when we view it from Earth.

LESSON 1

How Do Soils Form?

In this lesson, you can . . .

INVESTIGATE how soils form.

LEARN ABOUT what is in soil.

LINK to math, writing, technology, and other areas.

Enrich the Soil

Activity Purpose There are many kinds of soils. Some are better for growing plants than others. In this investigation you will look at a way of changing soil. Then you will predict how this change will affect plant growth.

Materials

- 1-L wide-mouthed plastic jar
- measuring cup
- 2 cups of soil with humus mixed in
- teaspoon
- water
- apple peels
- banana slices
- $\frac{1}{4}$ cup dry unsweetened cereal
- plastic wrap
- rubber band
- pencil

Activity Procedure

1 Put one cup of soil into the jar. Sprinkle two teaspoons of water on top of the soil.

◄ Compost is a mixture of material from once-living things. People use food scraps and yard clippings to make compost. Then they add it to the soil to make plants grow better.

2 Spread the fruit and cereal on top of the soil. The apple peels and banana slices must touch the sides of the jar. (Picture A)

3 Put another cup of soil on top of the fruit and cereal. You should see pieces of fruit and cereal through the sides of the jar.

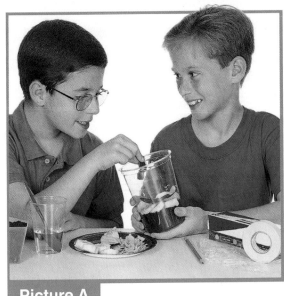

Picture A

4 Cover the jar with plastic wrap. Put a rubber band around the jar to hold the plastic wrap. Use a pencil point to make three small holes in the plastic wrap.

5 Leave the jar in a warm place, but do not put it in direct sunlight. Keep the jar there for four weeks.

6 Look at the jar once each week for four weeks. **Record** what you **observe.**

Draw Conclusions

1. What changes did you **observe** in the jar after one week? After four weeks?

2. **Form a hypothesis** about what would happen to the soil after eight weeks. To form your hypothesis, finish this sentence: After eight weeks, the soil will. . . .

3. **Scientists at Work** Scientists use their observations to form hypotheses. How did you use observations to form your hypothesis?

Investigate Further **Form a hypothesis** about the effects of compost on plant growth. **Plan an experiment** to test your hypothesis.

Process Skill Tip

When you **hypothesize,** you say what you think will happen. To form a hypothesis, you use your observations.

How Soils Form

FIND OUT

- where soil comes from
- why soil is important

VOCABULARY

soil
humus
topsoil
bedrock

What Soil Is

In the investigation you learned that decayed food scraps can become part of soil. Other things are part of soil, too. **Soil** is the loose material in which plants can grow in the upper layer of Earth.

Soil is a mixture of four different materials. Weathered rock is one part of soil. The bits of weathered rock contain minerals. These minerals make up most of soil. Soil also contains humus. **Humus** (HYOO•muhs) is the part of soil made up of decayed parts of once-living things. The compost and soil you worked with in the investigation could have become humus after more time. Humus is dark and soft. It contains much of what plants need for growth.

Between the bits of rock and humus are spaces. Air and water fill up the spaces. So soil also contains air and water.

Soil takes a long time to form. It takes 500 to 1,000 years to make 2.5 centimeters (1 in.) of soil. Deep soil takes thousands of years to form.

✔ **Name four things that soil contains.**

1 Soil forms in layers. **Topsoil** is the top layer. It is made up of the smallest grains. It also has the most humus, making it the richest layer of soil.

2 Subsoil is the layer under topsoil. It has larger grains and less humus than topsoil.

3 **Bedrock** is the solid rock under soil. Weathering breaks down bedrock into soil. Bedrock is made of different minerals in different places. So different soils contain different minerals.

C63

Life in Soil

Moles dig tunnels and make their homes underground. They may build small nests made of grass and twigs in the tunnels. Moles eat tiny worms and insects that live in the soil.

1 Pill bugs live in soil. They can roll into balls to protect themselves.

2 Ants build their homes underground. An anthill you see above the ground is the entrance to the ant nest below.

3 Earthworms need dark, wet places to live. As they make tunnels in the soil, worms use the soil for food.

Importance of Soil

You could not live without air or water. You also would have a hard time living without soil. That's because soil contains the minerals all living things need.

These minerals are found in Earth's crust. But plants and animals can't take minerals from solid rock. First, weathering has to break down Earth's crust into soil. Then, plants can grow in the soil. Through their roots, plants take the minerals from the soil. Plant-eating animals then get the minerals from the plants they eat. You get minerals from the plants and animals you eat, too.

✔ **Where do plants get the minerals they need?**

Summary

Soil is a mixture of weathered rock and humus that contains air and water. Soil is important to all living things. It contains minerals and other things that plants and animals need for growth. Soil takes a long time to form, so we must take care of it.

Review

1. What is humus?
2. What is topsoil?
3. How do people get the minerals they need?
4. **Critical Thinking** What would soil be like without weathering?
5. **Test Prep** Which of these is **NOT** part of soil?
   - **A** humus
   - **B** minerals
   - **C** water
   - **D** weathering

LINKS

MATH LINK

Find Elapsed Time How much time does it take to form 5 in. of new soil if it takes 500 years to form 1 in. of soil?

WRITING LINK

Persuasive Writing— Opinion Soil is an important material. Pretend you are selling soil. Write a radio or TV ad for adults that will get them to buy it.

SOCIAL STUDIES LINK

Crops What kinds of crops grow in the soil where you live? Which of the crops do you like to eat?

LITERATURE LINK

Explore Compost Take a close look at a compost pile. What lives there? Read *Compost Critters* by Bianca Lavies to find out.

GO ONLINE TECHNOLOGY LINK

Visit the Harcourt Learning Site for related links, activities, and resources.

www.harcourtschool.com

WELCOME TO THE LEARNING SITE

LESSON **2**

How Do Soils Differ?

In this lesson, you can . . .

INVESTIGATE different types of soil.

LEARN ABOUT how soils differ.

LINK to math, writing, physical education, and technology.

Types of Soil

Activity Purpose Soil has minerals, humus, air, and water in it. But different soils have different amounts of these things. In this investigation you will **observe** soils to see how they are different.

Materials

- 2 soil samples
- paper plates
- petri dish
- low-power microscope
- toothpick
- paper towel

Activity Procedure

1 Get two soil samples from your teacher.

2 Place a few grains of one sample in the petri dish. Put the dish under the microscope. (Picture A)

3 **Observe** the soil. Move the soil grains around with the toothpick. What do the grains look like? **Record** what you **observe.** Make a drawing of the grains.

◀ Many living things depend on soil. Without soil, there would be few plants. And without plants, most other living things could not survive.

Picture A

Picture B

4 Pick up some soil from the petri dish. Rub it between your fingers. How does it feel? **Record** what you **observe.** (Picture B)

5 Clean the petri dish with the paper towel. Repeat Steps 2 through 4 with the other soil sample.

Draw Conclusions

1. What senses did you use to **observe** the soil?

2. Describe your observations.

3. **Scientists at Work** Scientists **observe** to see how things are alike and how they are different. How were the soil samples alike? How were they different?

Investigate Further **Experiment** to find another way soils differ. How much water can different soils hold? Get two different types of soil from your teacher. Put each type into a separate jar. Now get two cups of water from your teacher. Pour one of the cups of water into each jar of soil. Which soil holds more water? How do you know?

Process Skill Tip

People use their senses to **observe** things. Many people think they can observe only with their eyes. But they can also observe by tasting, touching, smelling, and hearing.

Different Types of Soil

FIND OUT

- **how soils are different**
- **what kinds of soils are good for plants**

VOCABULARY

clay
loam

A Closer Look at Soil

In the investigation you observed two types of soil. But there are also many other types. They differ in color. They have different grain sizes. They contain different minerals. They hold different amounts of water.

Soil can be black, brown, gray, red, yellow, or white. The color of soil depends on what's in it. For instance, black soils have lots of humus. White soils often form from light rocks, such as limestone.

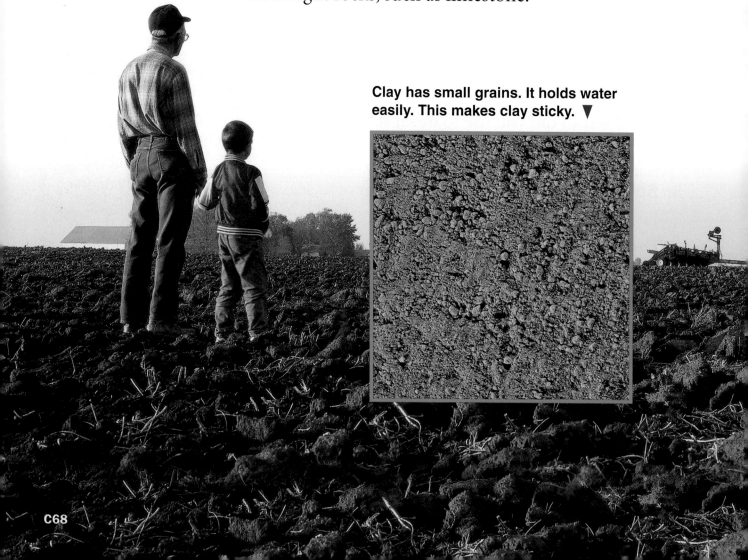

Clay has small grains. It holds water easily. This makes clay sticky. ▼

In the investigation you rubbed different types of soil between your fingers. You learned that not all soils feel the same. Some types, such as sand, have large grains. These types feel gritty. Other soils have small grains. **Clay** soil, for example, is made up of very small grains. When clay soil dries after a rain, it often forms hard clods. When the clods are broken up, they feel like powder.

Some soils hold water. Some soils do not. This difference is caused by the size of the spaces between the grains in the soil. Water drains out of sandy soils quickly. That's because sandy soils have large spaces between the grains. Clay soils have small spaces between the grains. Water becomes trapped there. This makes the clay soil wet and heavy and difficult for plant roots to grow through.

✔ What is clay?

Sand has large grains. It also has large spaces between the grains. This lets water leave it quickly. Sand has less humus than other soils. ▼

Loam has large and small grains. It also has lots of humus, which makes it dark and rich. Loam holds enough water for plants. But it also drains well. ▼

Soils Good for Growing Plants

Soil that is good for growing plants is called topsoil. Topsoil has more humus than other soil layers. Some topsoil has the things that plants need for growth.

Good topsoils have the right mixture of minerals and humus. **Loam** is one type of topsoil. It is a rich soil with lots of humus. It has a lot of water and air. Most farm soils are loam.

Other topsoils are not as good for plant growth as loam. Dry clays are too hard. Wet clays are too soggy. Sand is too dry and does not have enough nutrients.

Farmers can change the soil to make it better for plants. One way they can do this is to add fertilizers to poor soils. *Fertilizers* are materials that are rich in the things that plants need for growth.

✔ **What is topsoil?**

▲ Potting soil has a lot of humus. Once some sand is added to the soil, it is good for growing plants indoors.

The circle graph shows a soil that is good for plants. For every 100 grams of soil, 45 grams are minerals. Humus makes up 5 grams of this soil. There are 25 grams each of water and air. ▶

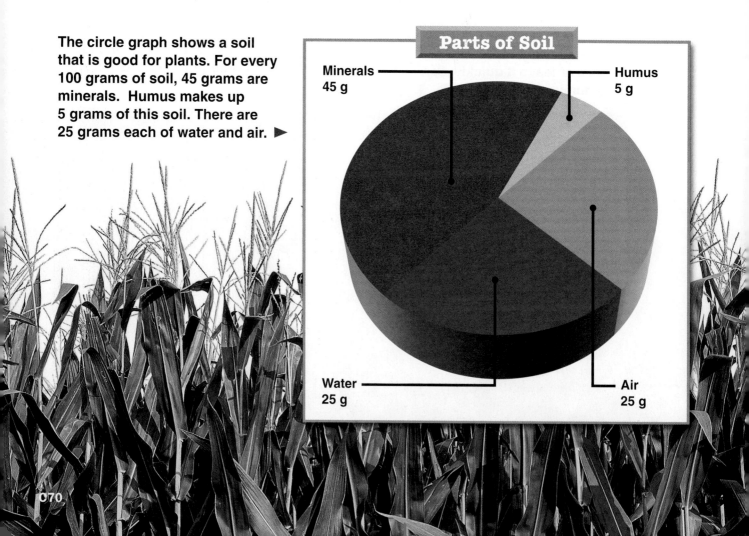

Parts of Soil

Minerals 45 g

Humus 5 g

Water 25 g

Air 25 g

Summary

There are many types of soil. Soils are made from different minerals. They have different colors and different-sized grains. Soils can hold different amounts of water. Soils that are best for plants have the right mixture of minerals and humus.

Review

1. Describe clay soil.
2. Describe loam soil.
3. Why do farmers add fertilizers to soil?
4. **Critical Thinking** Why is sand alone not good for plants?
5. **Test Prep** Which of these is a type of soil?
   A clay
   B limestone
   C fertilizer
   D bedrock

LINKS

MATH LINK

Construct Graphs Dig up a little soil. Observe the soil. Classify what you observe as plants, animals, or other. Use a computer graphing program such as *Graph Links* to make a bar graph that shows the numbers in each group.

WRITING LINK

Persuasive Writing— Business Letter Write to your state Department of Agriculture. Ask for information, maps, and pictures of the types of soil in your state. Use the information to write a paragraph for your teacher that describes the soils.

PHYSICAL EDUCATION LINK

Take a Hike Take a walk in your town with an adult family member. Collect soil from three places. Compare the soils.

 GO ONLINE **TECHNOLOGY LINK**

Learn more about soils by visiting the Smithsonian Institution Internet site.

www.si.edu/harcourt/science

 Smithsonian Institution®

LESSON

3

How Can People Conserve Soil?

In this lesson, you can . . .

INVESTIGATE how soils can be saved.

LEARN ABOUT how farmers conserve soil.

LINK to math, writing, music, and technology.

Saving Soil

Activity Purpose It takes a very long time for new soil to form. So it is important to save the soil we have. In this investigation you will **observe** soil with and without plants. Then you will **infer** how plants help save soil.

Materials

- 2 baking pans
- soil
- piece of sod
- 2 wooden blocks
- large Styrofoam cup with holes in the bottom
- pitcher
- water

Activity Procedure

1 Put soil in both baking pans. Put sod over the soil in one pan.

◀ Contour plowing stops soil from washing down hills.

2 Set one end of each pan on a wooden block. One end of each pan should be lower than the other.

3 **Predict** what will happen when water is dripped into each pan. **Record** your prediction.

4 **Make a model** of rain over the pan that has just soil. Have one person hold the cup over the upper end of the pan. Have another person pour water from the pitcher into the cup. (Picture A)

Picture A

5 **Observe** what happens in the pan. **Record** what you see.

6 Repeat Steps 4 and 5, using the pan that has sod.

Draw Conclusions

1. What did you **observe** in each pan? **Compare** your observations for the pans.

2. What caused the difference?

3. **Scientists at Work** Scientists use their **observations** to **infer** why things happen. Infer how you might keep soil from washing away in the rain.

Investigate Further **Plan and conduct an investigation** to show how soil can be conserved on the school grounds. For example, grass on the grounds reduces erosion.

Process Skill Tip

When you **observe** something, you use your senses to record what happens. When you **infer,** you use your observations to **draw a conclusion.**

How Soil Can Be Saved

FIND OUT

- what harms soil
- how soil can be saved

VOCABULARY

resource
conservation
strip cropping
contour plowing

How Soil Can Be Harmed

In the investigation you learned that plants help keep soil from eroding. Saving our soil is important because soil is an important resource. A **resource** (REE•sawrs) is a material found in nature that living things use.

Water, air, trees, and minerals are resources. Soil is a resource, too. Soil is used to grow food.

Many things can harm soil. Even farming can do this. It may harm the soil if the same type of crop is planted for many years on the same land. The plants use up the nutrients in the soil. Then the soil is too poor for growing more crops.

As you saw in the investigation, plants hold soil in place. Sometimes people cut down too many trees and other plants. Then water and wind carry away the soil.

✔ **What is a resource?**

◀ Wind blows away soil that is bare and dry. It takes thousands of years to replace the soil.

▲ Rain forests have many trees.

▲ Farmers cut them down to grow crops.

▲ But rain forests have thin, poor soil. Crops cannot grow in this soil for long. After the crops are harvested there are no plants to hold the soil in place. Heavy rain washes it away.

This is a pine forest in the western United States. ▼

People cut down pine trees to make paper and furniture. ▼

Then tree farmers plant more trees. A new forest can grow and will replace the trees that were cut down. ▼

Ways to Save the Soil

Farmers need good soil to grow crops. They practice conservation to save the soil. **Conservation** (kahn•ser•VAY•shuhn) is saving resources by using them carefully.

Some farmers use strip cropping to save soil. **Strip cropping** is planting strips of thick grass or clover between strips of crops. The thick mat of plants helps keep water in the soil. It also stops soil from washing away.

Some farmers use contour plowing. **Contour plowing** (KAHN•toor PLOW•ing) is planting rows of crops around the sides of hills instead of up and down. This keeps water from running off in straight lines, so the soil isn't washed away.

There are also other ways to save soil. In the fall after the harvest, many farmers turn over the soil in their fields. This is called *tilling*. Tilling leaves the soil loose until spring planting. This can add water and air to the soil. But it can also cause loss of soil. During the winter, wind and water can remove the loose soil. To save their soil, some farmers have stopped tilling.

✔ **What is conservation?**

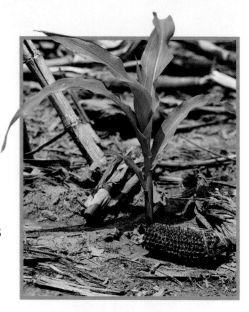

▲ The farmer has not tilled this field. New crops grow through plants left from the past year.

The farmer used strip cropping on this field. Strip cropping can save soil. ▼

Summary

Growing the same type of crop on the same land for many years removes minerals. When people remove plants and trees, soil may be washed away. Farmers conserve soil by strip cropping, contour plowing, and other methods.

Review

1. How does planting the same crop every year in the same soil harm the soil?

2. How does taking away plants harm soil?

3. How can tilling harm soil?

4. **Critical Thinking** In the United States many pine trees are cut down to make paper. A whole forest could be cut down at once and replanted. Or part of it could be cut down at a time. Which would be better? Explain your answer.

5. **Test Prep** Which of these is a method that farmers can use to save soil?

   A erosion

   B strip cropping

   C strip resourcing

   D clear-cutting

LINKS

 MATH LINK

Solve a Problem Suppose you are a farmer. You notice that there is less topsoil on your land every year. The first year you farmed there were 10 in. of topsoil. You are losing $\frac{1}{2}$ in. of topsoil every year. In how many years will no topsoil be left?

 WRITING LINK

Narrative Writing—Story Suppose that all the trees and other plants on Earth were cut down. Then all the soil on Earth was worn away. Write a story for your classmates about a day on Earth without soil.

 MUSIC LINK

On the Farm Do you know any songs about farms? Share them with the class. Bring a tape or CD, or sing the songs yourself.

 TECHNOLOGY LINK

To learn more about farming, watch *Agripost* on the **Harcourt Science Newsroom Video**.

FARMING with GPS

Farmers have used strip cropping and contour plowing to conserve soil for many years. Now farmers are using a new technology called GPS to help them protect and conserve soil.

What Is GPS?

GPS stands for Global Positioning System. GPS is a tracking system that uses satellites and radio transmitters and receivers to help guide ships, trains, and soldiers on the ground. Now farmers are using GPS and computers to get more crops from their land and plan for better use of their fields.

How Does GPS Help?

The combine, shown on page C78, is a machine used to harvest crops. This combine has a yield monitor and a radio receiver. As the combine moves through the corn and cuts it, the monitor keeps track of how much corn is collected. The receiver uses GPS to keep track of the exact location of the combine.

All this information is stored on a data card. At the end of the day, the farmer puts the card into a computer. The computer then makes color-coded maps that show the farmer the crop yield for each area. Then the farmer knows exactly how much corn each part of the field produced.

Farming with Computers

What the farmer learns from these maps is useful in many ways. This information can be used to calculate the right amounts of fertilizer, insecticide, herbicide, and water for each spot. Using the correct amounts will increase the amount of corn produced in the field. The amounts of fertilizer, insecticide, and herbicide that are used will probably decrease. Environmentalists hope that this new technology will reduce the waste water and chemicals that go into rivers and lakes.

By using both GPS and other information systems, farmers can learn immediately where their fields need help. In the past, farmers had to wait 10 to 15 years to see results. They used trial and error to make their fields produce more crops. Now farmers can learn about problems, fix them, and see the results in the next harvest.

THINK ABOUT IT

1. How can GPS and crop monitors help farmers increase crop yields?
2. How could knowledge gained by using GPS change the price of a field?

CAREERS
FARMER

What They Do Most farmers specialize in raising two or three crops that grow well in their region. The farmers of the United States produce 80 percent of all the food we use in this country.

Education and Training A farmer must have many skills. Many of today's farmers grew up on farms. Some of these farmers also get college degrees in agriculture. Farmers also need to know bookkeeping and the latest computer skills.

WEB LINK
For Science and Technology updates, visit the Harcourt Internet site.
www.harcourtschool.com

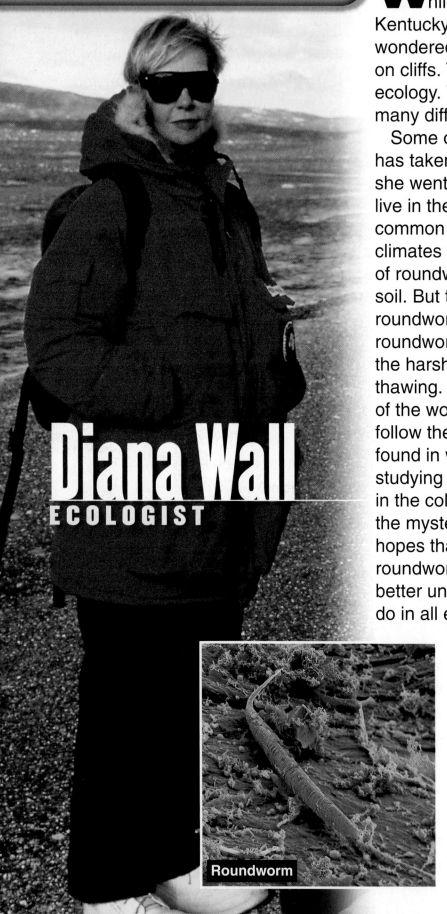

Diana Wall
ECOLOGIST

Roundworm

While growing up near the Kentucky River, Diana Wall wondered about the effect of water on cliffs. This led her to a career in ecology. Wall studies the soils of many different ecosystems.

Some of her most interesting work has taken place in Antarctica, where she went to study roundworms that live in the soil. Soil roundworms are common garden pests. In warm climates there may be 60 or 70 kinds of roundworms in just a handful of soil. But there are only 6 kinds of roundworms in all of Antarctica. The roundworms of Antarctica survive the harsh climate by freezing and thawing. No one knows how old any of the worms are, since they do not follow the life cycle of roundworms found in warmer climates. By studying the roundworms that live in the cold, Wall is helping solve the mysteries of their lives. She hopes that by understanding the roundworms of Antarctica, she can better understand what roundworms do in all ecosystems.

THINK ABOUT IT

- Why don't people know how old the roundworms in Antarctica are?

SOIL AND PLANTS

How does soil help plants grow?

Materials

- 4 plants of the same kind
- potting soil
- sand
- water
- measuring cup
- ruler

Procedure

1. Take the plants from their store pots. Dump out the soil. Rinse the roots.

2. Put each plant back into its empty pot. Put potting soil around two plants. Put sand around the other two plants. Water each plant with the same amount of water.

3. Put the plants in the same sunny place. Use the measuring cup to give the plants the same amount of water each day.

4. Observe the plants for 14 days. Measure their heights. Count the leaves.

Draw Conclusions

Which soil is best for growing the plants?

FOOD FROM SOIL

Where do the foods you eat come from?

Materials

- outline map of the United States
- an encyclopedia
- crayons or colored pencils

Procedure

1. Get a map of the United States from your teacher.

2. Make a list of some of the foods you like to eat. Find out where these foods are grown. Look up the information in an encyclopedia.

3. Use the map to share your findings. Draw a picture of each food on your list. Glue each picture onto the map to show where the food is grown.

Draw Conclusions

Where do the foods you eat come from?

Vocabulary Review

Use the terms below to complete the sentences 1 through 10. The page numbers in ( ) tell you where to look in the chapter if you need help.

soil (C62)   resource (C74)

humus (C62)   conservation (C76)

topsoil (C63)   strip

bedrock (C63)   cropping (C76)

clay (C69)   contour

loam (C70)   plowing (C76)

1. Rich soil with lots of humus is ___.

2. ___ is a type of soil with very small grains and small spaces between them.

3. Planting strips of different crops next to each other is ___.

4. A ___ is a material found in nature that living things use.

5. ___ is the layer of bits of rocks and humus found on Earth's crust.

6. ___ means saving resources by using them carefully.

7. The top layer of soil is ___.

8. ___ is planting rows of crops around hills instead of up and down their sides.

9. The decayed remains of dead plants and animals in soil is ___.

10. The layer of rock beneath the soil is ___.

Connect Concepts

Write the terms where they belong in the concept map.

minerals   humus   sand   not tilling the soil
bedrock   clay   air   strip cropping
topsoil   water   subsoil   contour plowing
loam

Soils			
Parts of Soil	**Layers of Soil**	**Three Types of Soil**	**Three Ways to Save Soil**
11._____	15._____	18._____	21._____
12._____	16._____	19._____	22._____
13._____	17._____	20._____	23._____
14._____			

Check Understanding

Write the letter of the best choice.

24. Plants get ___ from soil.

   A clay   **C** loam

   B minerals   **D** sand

25. ___ is a feature of loam.

   F Mostly large particles

   G White color

   H Lots of humus

   J A sticky feeling

26. ___ harms soil.

   A Strip cropping

   B Erosion

   C Contour plowing

   D Not tilling

27. The solid rock under soil is called —

   F bedrock   **H** subsoil

   G topsoil   **J** humus

Critical Thinking

28. Why is water an important part of soil?

29. Would loam or sand need fertilizer more?

Process Skills Review

30. Predict what might happen if plants and animals did not decay in soil.

31. Suppose someone gave you a soil sample and asked you to describe it. What features would you **observe**?

32. Suppose heavy rain falls. You **observe** soil washing down a bare hill. There are two other hills like the ones shown below. **Infer** which hill will lose more soil.

Performance Assessment

Identifying Soil

Work with a partner. Identify three soil samples by observing them. Make a chart to record your observations. Include features such as color, grain size, and water-holding ability.

C83

Earth's Resources

Every day you use Earth's resources. The paper you use is made from trees. Your soda can is made of metal that was dug out of the Earth. Plastic bottles are made from oil pumped out of the Earth. You can't live a single day without using hundreds of Earth's resources.

Vocabulary Preview

resource
renewable
   resource
reusable resource
nonrenewable
   resource
recycle

Fast Fact

The deepest lake on Earth is Lake Baikal in Russia. This giant lake, which is 1620 meters (5,300 ft) deep, holds one-fifth of Earth's liquid fresh water!

Air is one of Earth's resources. So are water and food. How much of these important resources do we use?

The Needs of an Average Adult

Resource	Daily Use
Air	30 pounds
Food	2 to 3 pounds
Water	4 to 5 pounds

Mining Resources

Activity Purpose

We use many materials from Earth's crust to make things. These materials are called *resources*. Some resources, such as oil, are pumped out of Earth's crust. Other resources, such as diamonds, must be dug out, or mined. In this investigation you will "mine" raisins from a cookie.

Materials

- oatmeal-raisin cookie
- paper plate
- dropper
- water
- toothpick

Activity Procedure

1 **Observe** your cookie. How many raisins do you see?

2 Fill the dropper with water. Put a few drops of water around each raisin. The cookie should be moist but not wet. (Picture A)

◀ This pump brings oil to Earth's surface. Gasoline and plastics are just two of the things made from oil.

LESSON **1**

What Are Resources?

In this lesson, you can . . .

INVESTIGATE how resources are mined.

LEARN ABOUT resources people use.

LINK to math, writing, literature, and technology.

Picture A

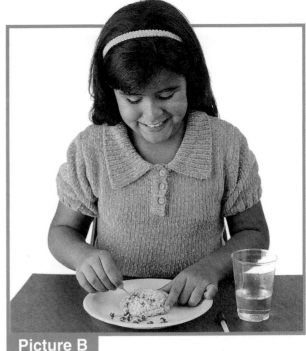

Picture B

3 Use the toothpick to "mine" all the raisins from the cookie. If the raisins are hard to get out, put a few more drops of water around them. Put the removed raisins on the plate. (Picture B)

4 **Observe** the cookie again. Were there any raisins you didn't see in the cookie the first time? Why didn't you see them?

Draw Conclusions

1. What did you "mine" from the cookie?

2. How did the water help you?

3. How is mining raisins from a cookie like mining materials from the Earth?

4. **Scientists at Work** Scientists **observe** things to see how they work. They use their observations to **infer** how similar things work. Use your observations to infer how mining could affect the land around the mine.

Process Skill Tip

When you **observe,** you use your senses to note what happens or how things work. When you **infer,** you use your observations to form an opinion.

Resources People Use

Where Resources Are Found

A **resource** is a material that is found in nature and that is used by living things. Think about the resources you use each day. You breathe air. You drink water. You ride in cars, trains, and buses. When you eat dinner, you use a metal fork. When you use a computer, you push plastic buttons that are made from oil. Air, water, gasoline, metals, coal, and oil are resources.

FIND OUT

- what resources are
- how we get resources

VOCABULARY

resource

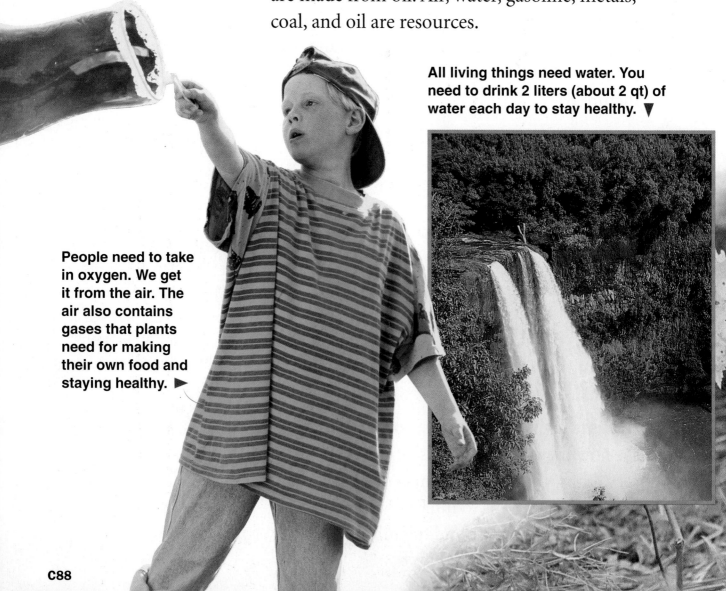

All living things need water. You need to drink 2 liters (about 2 qt) of water each day to stay healthy. ▼

People need to take in oxygen. We get it from the air. The air also contains gases that plants need for making their own food and staying healthy. ▶

C88

In the investigation you learned that some resources are found below Earth's surface. Some examples are oil, coal, and diamonds.

Some resources are on Earth's surface. Water and soil are important resources on Earth's surface. Water is so important that without it, there would be no life on Earth.

Air is a resource that is above Earth's surface. Air has many gases that living things need. One of these is oxygen, a gas you take in when you breathe.

✔ **Where do resources come from?**

Forests cover one-third of the land on Earth. People get wood, paper, food, and other resources from the plants and animals in these forests. ▼

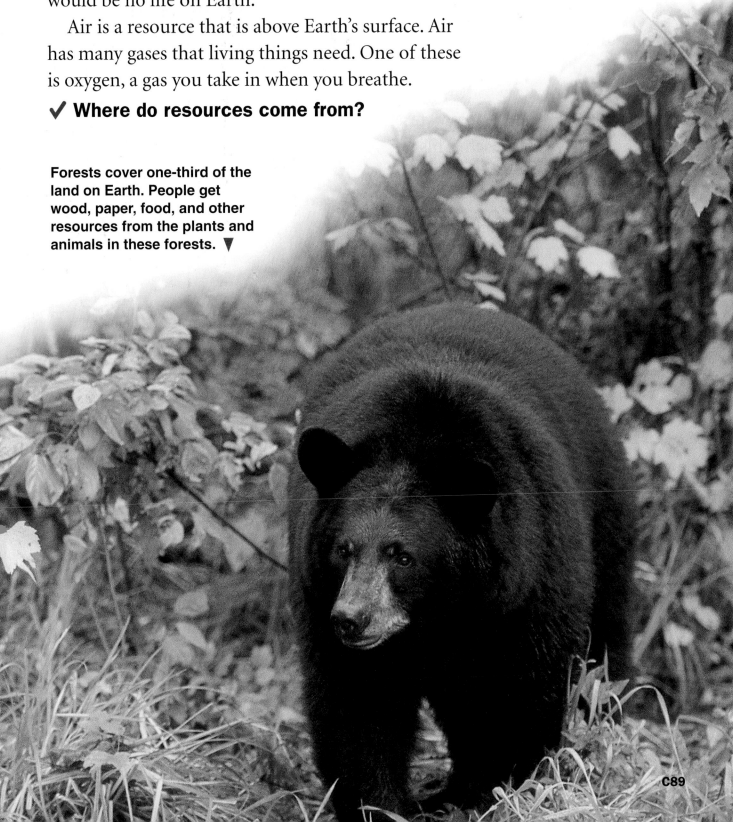

Resources Under Earth's Surface

Resources that are under Earth's surface are collected in different ways. Diamonds and emeralds are mined by people who dig tunnels deep under the ground. Some coal is mined in deep tunnels, too.

To mine other resources, big machines scrape away soil and rock. Then the machines take the materials from the holes that are left. This is known as strip mining. Some coal is strip-mined. The picture on page C91 shows copper being mined this way.

Still other resources, such as oil and water, are liquid and can be pumped from Earth's crust. People dig wells in the ground to reach these materials.

✓ **List three ways resources are taken from under Earth's surface.**

Oil is an important resource. Oil derricks hold equipment used to drill for oil. People use oil to make many things. ▶

▲ Gasoline is a fuel that comes from oil. Most cars use gasoline.

Some energy plants burn oil to produce electricity. ▼

◀ Plastic is made from some of the things that are found in oil.

▲ People mine copper from Earth's crust. This mine in Montana is one of the largest copper mines in the world.

Summary

A resource is a material that living things use. Resources include air, water, soil, trees, and minerals. We need resources such as air and water to live. We get many resources, such as minerals, from Earth's crust.

Review

1. List two products that come from trees.
2. Name two resources that people need to live.
3. List two ways people use oil.
4. **Critical Thinking** Is it harder to get resources from under Earth's surface or on it? Explain your answer.
5. **Test Prep** Which resource is found below Earth's surface?
   A trees   C air
   B oil   D soil

LINKS

MATH LINK

Collect and Display Data
Water is an important resource. How much of Earth's surface is covered by water? Visit the media center to find the answer to this question. Make a display that shows what you learn.

WRITING LINK

Narrative Writing—Story
Suppose you are a magazine writer. Write a story for young children about a resource that is in the news. Tell where it is found and how it is used.

LITERATURE LINK

Garbage Resources often become garbage after being used. But where does the garbage go? Find out in the book *Where Does Garbage Go?* by Isaac Asimov.

TECHNOLOGY LINK

Visit the Harcourt Learning Site for related links, activities, and resources.
www.harcourtschool.com

WELCOME TO THE LEARNING SITE

LESSON 2

What Are Different Kinds of Resources?

In this lesson, you can . . .

INVESTIGATE resources and the products made from them.

LEARN ABOUT how resources are classified.

LINK to math, writing, social studies, and technology.

Resource Use

Activity Purpose Every product around you is made from a resource. There are many kinds of resources. In this investigation you will **compare** pictures of resources with pictures of products. You will **classify** the products by the resources they are made from.

Materials
- resource picture cards
- product picture cards

◀ Many types of rocks are used as resources. These Chinese lions are made of marble.

Activity Procedure

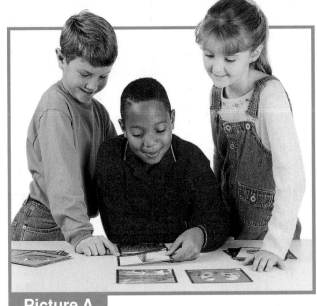

1. Look closely at all the cards. Sort the cards into two groups—resources and products.

2. **Classify** the products. To do this, match each product with the resource from which it comes. (Picture A)

3. Make a drawing to show how you sorted your cards.

Picture A

Draw Conclusions

1. How did you **classify** the products?

2. Does a product always look like the resource it was made from? Explain.

3. **Scientists at Work** Scientists **compare** objects to see how they are alike and how they are different. How did comparing the products to the resources help you **classify** the products?

Investigate Further Identify five or more products in your home. **Classify** the products by the resources they came from.

Process Skill Tip

When you **compare** things, you think about how they are alike and how they are different. When you **classify** things, you group things that are alike.

Kinds of Resources

FIND OUT

- which resources will never run out

- which resources could be used up one day

VOCABULARY

renewable
　resource
reusable
　resource
nonrenewable
　resource

Resources That Can Last Forever

Some resources can last forever. Some of these resources, called **renewable resources**, can be replaced in a human lifetime. Trees are renewable resources. When people cut down trees, they can plant new trees to replace the cut trees.

Other resources will never run out. **Reusable resources** are used over and over and can't be used up. Water and air are reusable resources. Even polluted water and air can be used again if they are cleaned. Earth's processes help clean water and air.

✔ **How are renewable and reusable resources different?**

Wood for houses, furniture, pencils, and paper comes from trees. Trees also provide places for animals to live. When trees are replanted, this resource is renewed for the future. ▼

▲ The air is always there for you to breathe. Sometimes, cars, trucks, and factories pollute the air. Wind and rain can clean the pollution out of the air. People can work to reduce pollution so the air will stay clean.

The sun never stops shining. It warms Earth's land and oceans. Plants use the sun's energy to make food. People use the sun's energy to heat water and to meet other needs. All living things on Earth use energy from this resource to live. ▼

◄ People need water every day for drinking, cooking, and bathing. Factories and farms use water to make products people use. Water is reusable, but dirty water must be cleaned before it can be used again.

Resources That Won't Last Forever

Some resources will not last forever. A **nonrenewable resource** is a resource that will be used up someday. It might surprise you just how many resources are nonrenewable. Coal, oil, iron, and copper are only a few of them.

Soil is a nonrenewable resource. You know that new soil can be formed, but it takes thousands of years for rocks to break down and become soil. That's why soil is called nonrenewable.

Trees are renewable resources. But some kinds of forests are nonrenewable. Old-growth forests have never been cut down. When people cut down an old-growth forest, they may plant new trees. But the new forest has fewer types of plants and animals than the old forest had.

✔ **What is a nonrenewable resource?**

▲ *Old-growth forests* have trees that are 200 years old or older. When people cut old-growth forests, the forests will never grow back exactly the way they were.

The United States mines a lot of coal. Coal is burned to produce electricity. When all the coal is burned, another fuel will have to be used. ▼

▲ Natural gas is an important fuel. Many people use it for heating their homes and cooking their food. When all the natural gas has been burned, there will be no more for people to use.

Summary

Renewable resources, such as trees, can be replaced. Reusable resources, such as air, water, and the sun, are used over and over again and do not run out. Nonrenewable resources can be used up. Oil, soil, minerals, and old-growth forests are nonrenewable resources.

Review

1. What are renewable resources?
2. Why is water a reusable resource?
3. Why is an old-growth forest nonrenewable?
4. **Critical Thinking** Why should nonrenewable resources be used wisely?
5. **Test Prep** Choose the resource that is nonrenewable.
   - A iron
   - C water
   - B air
   - D the sun

  LINKS

 MATH LINK

Solve a Problem Suppose your community has enough coal to produce energy for 20 years. Your community uses 5 tons of coal a year. But what if it used only 4 tons each year? How long would the coal last?

 WRITING LINK

Informative Writing— Explanation Make a list of the nonrenewable resources you used today. Choose one, and write a story for your teacher explaining how your life would be different without this resource.

 SOCIAL STUDIES LINK

Old Growth Where in the United States are old-growth forests found? Make a map that shows where they are. Are there any in your state?

GO **TECHNOLOGY LINK**
ONLINE

Learn more about resources by visiting this Internet Site.
www.scilinks.org/harcourt

 SCiLINKS
THE WORLD'S A CLICK AWAY

How Can We Conserve Earth's Resources?

In this lesson, you can . . .

INVESTIGATE items that can be recycled.

LEARN ABOUT how recycling conserves resources.

LINK to math, writing, music, and technology.

INVESTIGATE

Recycling

Activity Purpose Every day people use more and more of Earth's resources. Many of these resources end up as trash. Trash is taken away and put into landfills. In this investigation you will **record** one type of resource your family uses. Using data from all the members of your class, you will **use numbers** to find out how much landfill space your class could save by recycling aluminum cans.

Materials
- aluminum cans your family uses in one week
- large plastic trash bag
- bathroom scale

Activity Procedure

1 Get permission from a parent to participate in this activity. Save all of the aluminum cans your family uses for one week. Rinse them in the sink. Put the cans in the trash bag. (Picture A)

◀ **Recycling saves resources and reduces pollution.**

2 Weigh the cans. If your cans are too light to weigh, you can find their weight by multiplying the number of cans you have collected by 1.5 oz. **Record** the weight.

3 Bring your results to class. Use your data to draw a bar on the class graph. The graph will show the weight of each family's cans.

Picture A

4 Add up all the weights shown on the graph. The sum tells you how much aluminum all the families used in one week.

Draw Conclusions

1. Suppose that 1 lb of cans takes up 2 ft of space. How much landfill space would your class save by recycling all the cans you saved this week?

2. What other resources might be saved if your cans were recycled instead of thrown away?

3. **Scientists at Work** There are many ways you could tell someone how much aluminum was used in one week. In this investigation you **used numbers** to describe the weight of aluminum used. How does using numbers help you tell people what you found out?

Process Skill Tip

Using numbers helps you tell others exactly what data you have collected. Scientists use numbers to explain things such as how big or small things are, how hot or cold things are, and how fast things go.

Conserving Resources

FIND OUT

• what recycling is

• how recycling saves resources

VOCABULARY

recycle

Recycling

People use a lot of resources. They also throw a lot of resources away. Think about how much trash you have seen people throw away in one week. This trash is usually taken to landfills, where it is buried in the ground. Landfills take up space that could be used in other ways. They are also expensive to build and keep up. If people threw away less trash, less space would be needed for landfills. And the materials people save could be used again. When people **recycle**, they reuse a resource to make something new.

Recycling makes resources last longer. If aluminum is recycled, less aluminum ore, called *bauxite,* needs to be mined. If plastic is recycled, less oil is needed to make new plastic.

Many of the things people throw away can be recycled. Recycling saves resources. Every ton of recycled paper saves 17 trees. ▼

What People Throw Away

Percent of Total Trash

Paper, Plants, Metal, Glass, Food, Dairy, Furniture, Liquid

Materials

Recycling renewable resources is helpful, too. When paper is recycled, fewer trees must be cut down.

Recycling helps save energy. Recycling resources saves the energy needed to find, mine, or harvest more of the resource. It also saves the energy needed to move it from place to place.

Recycling helps reduce pollution. Making paper from trees pollutes both air and water. So does making new plastic from oil. Making products from recycled paper and plastic causes less pollution.

Many towns have recycling programs. Families save paper, aluminum, glass, and plastic. Trucks take the materials to recycling centers. These centers send the materials to factories. There the recycled materials are made into new products.

✔ **What does it mean to recycle?**

▲ **Plastic can be recycled. But fewer plastic containers are recycled than aluminum or glass containers.**

Each person in the United States throws away about 2 kilograms (about $4\frac{1}{2}$ lb) of trash every day. But we recycle more now than we did ten years ago. ▼

Most trash is buried in landfills. Recycling means using less space in landfills. ▼

Recycling Aluminum

Many things we use are made of aluminum. These include food cans and cooking pots. Aluminum is used to make foil and electrical equipment, too. Most aluminum objects are thrown away after being used once. But this is not true for aluminum cans. Out of every 100 aluminum cans used in the United States, almost 67 are recycled!

Billions of aluminum cans are made each year. Half the aluminum in most aluminum cans has been recycled. Recycling aluminum saves resources. Using one ton of recycled aluminum saves four tons of bauxite from being mined.

Recycling aluminum also saves electricity. It takes a lot of electricity to produce new aluminum from bauxite. Making products from recycled aluminum uses less electricity. Electric energy plants burn nonrenewable fuels such as coal and oil. So recycling aluminum saves fuel. It also reduces pollution.

✔ **How does recycling aluminum help save resources?**

THE INSIDE STORY

▲ Most bauxite is mined from open pits. This type of mining, also called strip mining, destroys soil and plants. Recycling aluminum means mining less bauxite.

1 Recycling starts with the cans you use. You finish your apple juice. Then you put the can into the recycling bin. Someone collects the bin of aluminum cans. A truck takes the aluminum to a recycling center.

2 People unload the cans at the recycling center. They put the cans on a moving belt. The belt takes the cans to a chopper. The chopper cuts the cans into many pieces.

3 The next job is removing paint from the pieces of can. The pieces go into a machine full of very hot air. The air has a temperature of 482° Celsius (900°F). The hot air melts the paint from the can pieces. But the hot air doesn't melt the aluminum. Clean pieces of aluminum come out of the machine.

4 The clean aluminum pieces then go to a furnace. The furnace is even hotter than the hot-air machine. It has a temperature of 660°Celsius (1,220°F). That's hot enough to melt aluminum. The furnace turns the aluminum into a hot silvery liquid.

5 The melted aluminum is poured out of the furnace. It flows into molds. The molds shape the hot metal into big blocks. The blocks cool. People use the blocks to make new cans and other products. Aluminum from the can you recycle today could be back in the store in eight weeks.

Conserving Resources

Some resources can't be recycled. People can't recycle the gasoline, oil, or coal that are used as fuels because they are burned up. But people can conserve them. When people *conserve,* they use less of a resource at one time. Conserving resources makes them last longer.

Coal and oil can be saved when people use less electricity. People can turn off lights when not using them. A house can be kept warmer in summer to use less air conditioning. It can be kept cooler in winter to use less heat.

Sometimes people must conserve water when there has been no rain. There may not be enough water for everyone in a community to use. If your community has a water shortage, here are some things you can do. Take short showers. Don't run the water while you brush your teeth. Make sure the dishwasher is full when you use it. Fix leaky faucets. Leaks waste lots of water.

Preventing pollution is a way to conserve resources. Earth's supply of air and water will never be used up. But air and water can become dirty. If they become too dirty, they are unhealthful to use. It's important for everyone to help keep Earth's air and water clean. You can help protect Earth's resources.

✔ **List three ways to save water during a water shortage.**

Summary

Recycling is using old or used materials. When we recycle, we need fewer new resources to make new products. This makes the resources last longer. People can conserve, or use less of a resource, when they can't recycle.

Review

1. What resources are saved when you recycle aluminum?
2. List the steps in recycling aluminum.
3. Name two ways to save water.
4. **Critical Thinking** Suppose the population of a city is growing. But the amount of water the city can use stays the same. Why is it important for people in the city to conserve water?
5. **Test Prep** Choose the resource that you can conserve by recycling paper.

   A aluminum   C gasoline

   B coal   D trees

LINKS

MATH LINK

Compare Data Make a table that lists the kinds of materials people recycle. Include paper, glass, aluminum, and plastic. Find out how much of each material is recycled in the United States. List the materials in order from the highest recycling rate to the lowest rate.

WRITING LINK

Informative Writing—How to Write a set of recycling directions for your class. What materials should students collect? When can the recyclables be picked up?

MUSIC LINK

Recycling Tune Write the words to a song that tells people why it's good to recycle. Use a tune you already know. Sing your song in class.

TECHNOLOGY LINK

To learn more about wise use of resources, watch *Graffiti Plastics* on the **Harcourt Science Newsroom Video**.

CNN
Turner
Le@rning®

Recycling Plastics to Make Clothing

▼ Flake

Putting a plastic bottle in a recycling bin is the first step in recycling. Next, the bottle must be made into something new that can be used again.

What Do They Do with Those Plastic Bottles?

Recycling plastic is not as easy as recycling glass, aluminum, or paper. There are seven kinds of plastic. Each kind needs to be treated in a different way. The easiest way to recycle plastic bottles and jars is to melt them all together. Then you can make big, solid objects from them, such as picnic tables and park benches.

Today machines are used to sort plastic bottles. Bottles that have a number 1 stamped on them can be used in a new, exciting way, so they are separated from the rest. Their labels and caps are removed. Then the

◀ **EcoSpun blankets**

bottles are crushed and chopped into tiny pieces called flake. The flake is melted and pulled into long, thin threads. The threads are then stretched and kinked. After that, they look like threads of cotton. In the last step, the threads are gathered up into big square bunches called bales.

What Happens to the Baled Threads?

The bales of thread are sent to factories. At the factories, the threads are pulled from the bales and twirled together to make yarn. The yarn is called EcoSpun™. EcoSpun can be knitted or woven to make almost anything that can be made from wool or cotton or other types of cloth. EcoSpun is used to make carpets, backpacks, blankets, T-shirts, soft suitcases, socks, and many other things.

How Does This Help the Environment?

When people know their recycled plastic is actually being used, they are more likely to recycle. And that's good for the environment. About two and one-half billion recycled plastic bottles are used every year to make EcoSpun. Instead of becoming trash, the bottles are becoming clothing. Instead of filling up the landfills, two and one-half billion bottles are being used again.

THINK ABOUT IT

- Can the products made from recycled plastic be used to help the environment even more? Explain.

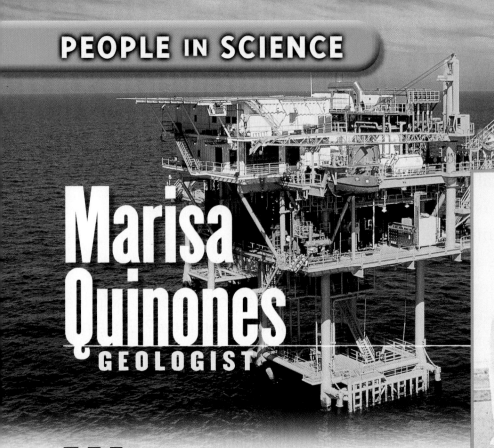

Marisa Quinones
GEOLOGIST

When you think of a geologist, you may think only of rocks. But geologists do many things. They study the history of Earth, find water in dry climates, and search for precious rocks and minerals, such as gold and diamonds. For Marisa Quinones, geology involves looking for oil underground. Oil companies look for oil by setting off an explosion in the ground or by firing an air gun into the ocean floor. The rocks underground respond to the sound waves that result. Their responses are recorded on a computer. Quinones studies the patterns of rock responses. By studying them, she can decide whether oil is likely to be found in a certain spot.

Once drilling begins, Quinones looks at the cuttings, or rock chips, from the hole. The cuttings help her predict whether there could be any danger as the drilling is being done. They also let her know when the area that holds the oil has been reached.

Quinones also supervises the lowering of scientific instruments into the hole that has been drilled. These instruments keep a record of what happens in the well. The record provides information about the underground rocks and areas that hold oil. These findings tell Quinones whether to continue drilling.

THINK ABOUT IT

1. What dangers might occur when drilling for oil?
2. Why do you think oil companies are searching for oil under the sea?

HOW MUCH WASTE?

How much waste does your class throw away each day?

Materials

- paper
- pencil

What We Threw Away Today	
Newspaper and Magazines	
Cardboard and Other Paper	
Glass Containers	
Plastic Containers	
Plastic Wrapping and Bags	
Other	

Procedure

❶ Copy one chart for the class. Put the chart and a pencil next to the trash can.

❷ All students in your class should record what they throw away. If a paper is thrown away, then a *1* is written in the Paper row. If 3 plastic bottles are thrown away, then *3 bottles* is written in the Plastic Containers row.

Draw Conclusions

After gathering data for one day, total all the things that were thrown away. How could your class recycle more?

REUSE IT!

How can some classroom materials be reused?

Materials

- large cardboard or plastic boxes
- black marking pen
- tape

Procedure

❶ Use the chart from "How Much Waste?" As a class, decide which materials could be reused instead of being thrown away. Work with your teacher to find a place in the room to store materials that can be reused.

❷ Find cardboard boxes or plastic bins for keeping the materials. Label each box with the material it will hold. Be sure that items that had food in them, such as plastic containers, are rinsed before being put in the boxes.

Draw Conclusions

After you have started your REUSE IT! center, check your trash again. How does the amount of trash compare with the amount of trash before the REUSE IT! center was started?

Vocabulary Review

Use the terms below to complete the sentences 1 through 5. The page numbers in ( ) tell you where to look in the chapter if you need help.

resource (C88)

renewable resource (C94)

reusable resource (C94)

nonrenewable resource (C96)

recycle (C100)

1. A resource that can be replaced after it is used is called a ____.

2. When you ____, you reuse a resource to make something new. Then the resource can be used again and again.

3. A ____ is a resource that will never run out.

4. A material found in nature that living things use is a ____.

5. A ____ is a resource that could be used up one day.

Connect Concepts

Write the terms where they belong in the concept map.

coal   renewable   water   reusable

oil   aluminum   air   old-growth forests

soil   natural gas

Kinds of Resources		
6. _____	Nonrenewable	13. _____
trees	7. _____	the sun
	8. _____	14. _____
	9. _____	15. _____
	10. _____	
	11. _____	
	12. _____	

Check Understanding

Write the letter of the best choice.

16. Most mineral resources are found ____ Earth's surface.
    - **A** above
    - **B** under
    - **C** alongside
    - **D** on

17. Oil is used to make —
    - **F** paper
    - **G** glass
    - **H** plastic
    - **J** aluminum

18. Trees are used to make —
    - **A** paper
    - **B** glass
    - **C** plastic
    - **D** aluminum

19. Which resource can get dirty but can never run out?
    - **F** trees
    - **G** water
    - **H** coal
    - **J** aluminum

20. Which resource can be renewed?
    - **A** soil
    - **B** water
    - **C** the sun
    - **D** trees

Critical Thinking

21. How would life be different without resources taken from under Earth's surface?

22. How can pollution stop people from using reusable resources?

Process Skills Review

23. List the resources that you can **observe** on your way to school. Be sure to include at least one of each type of resource.

24. Suppose people are mining a mineral from Earth's crust. What can you **infer** about the kind of resource it is? Explain your answer.

25. **Compare** renewable and reusable resources.

Performance Assessment

Classify Resources

Observe a group of objects. Classify each object as a renewable, a reusable, or a nonrenewable resource.

There are many places where you can learn more about Earth's land and resources. By visiting the places below, you can find out how some of these resources are used.

The Kentucky Coal Mining Museum

WHAT A museum displaying all aspects of a coal mine

WHERE Benham, Kentucky

WHAT CAN YOU DO THERE? Tour the exhibits, see the displays of equipment, and touch the coal from the mines.

John Day Fossil Beds National Monument

WHAT A land area long known for its rich fossil deposits

WHERE Kimberly, Oregon

WHAT CAN YOU DO THERE? Hike through the landscape, see geologic formations, and observe fossils.

GO ONLINE Plan Your Own Expeditions

If you can't visit the Kentucky Coal Mining Museum or the John Day Fossil Beds National Monument, visit a museum or national monument near you. Or log on to The Learning Site at **www.harcourtschool.com** to visit these science sites.

Cycles on Earth and in Space

UNIT D — EARTH SCIENCE

Cycles on Earth and in Space

UNIT EXPERIMENT

Air Pressure and Temperature

Air pushes on Earth. This pressure affects the weather. While you study this unit, you can conduct a long-term experiment to find out how temperature affects air pressure. Here is a question to think about. Does air press harder on Earth when it is warm outside or when it is colder? Plan and conduct an experiment to find answers to this question or others that you may have about temperature and air pressure. See pages x–xii for help in designing your experiment.

The Water Cycle

Vocabulary Preview

groundwater
estuary
evaporation
condensation
precipitation
water cycle

There's plenty of water on Earth. In fact, Earth is nearly covered with it. Most of the water on Earth is frozen or salty. And even though water seems to be everywhere, in some places on Earth there is almost no water at all.

Fast Fact

A leaky faucet wastes about 76 liters (20 gal) of water a day. If you wait a week to fix the leak, the faucet will drip 800,000 drops!

Where Is Water Found on Earth?

In this lesson, you can . . .

INVESTIGATE how much water covers Earth's surface.

LEARN ABOUT why water is important to living things.

LINK to math, writing, art, and technology.

INVESTIGATE

Land or Water

Activity Purpose Does Earth's surface have more land or more water? In this investigation you will play a game to **collect data** about Earth's surface. Then you will **use numbers** to estimate the amount of water on Earth's surface.

Materials
- plastic inflatable globe

Activity Procedure

1. Work in groups of five. Choose one person to be the recorder. The other four people will toss the ball.

2. Have the four ball tossers stand in a circle. The recorder hands the ball to the first person, who gently tosses the ball to another person in the circle. (Picture A)

◄ If you live in a cold place, you may see water in the form of snow.

Picture A

3 The catcher should catch the ball with open hands. Check to see if the tip of the catcher's right index finger is on land or water. The recorder should **record** this data.

4 Continue tossing and recording until the ball has been tossed 20 times.

5 Repeat Steps 3 and 4 two more times.

Draw Conclusions

1. Total your counts. How many times did the catcher's right index finger touch water? Touch land?

2. Where did the catchers' fingers land more often? Why do you think so?

3. **Scientists at Work** Scientists **use numbers** to **collect data.** Using your data, estimate how much of Earth's surface is covered by water.

Investigate Further You did this investigation 3 times. The more data you collect, the better your data becomes. How would doing the investigation 10 times change your data? Try it to find out.

Process Skill Tip

Collecting data by **using numbers** can help you answer questions. By doing the activity several times, you increase the amount of data you collect. Then you can **interpret the data** to find an answer to your question.

This view of Earth from space makes it easy to see why Earth is sometimes called the water planet. ▶

Water on Earth

FIND OUT

- why water is important
- where water is found on Earth

VOCABULARY

groundwater
estuary

The Importance of Water

From space, Earth looks like a blue marble. The water that covers most of the planet makes it look blue. Earth's lands are really small islands in the middle of huge oceans and seas.

Without water there could be no life on Earth. Plants and animals need water to live. So do people. Two-thirds of your body is water. People must drink at least 2 liters (about 2 qt) of water each day to stay healthy. Even the foods you eat are full of water. Chicken is three-fourths water. A potato is four-fifths water.

Water is important to Earth's environment. Without water there could be no rain or snow. Water helps make winds and storms. Water even changes the shape of Earth's surface.

All animals need water to stay alive. ▼

▲ Industry uses about half of our fresh water. Water is used to wash things, to cool things down, and to make products.

Look at a map of Earth. You can see that most water on Earth is found in the oceans. This water is salt water. Many plants and animals live in the ocean. But salt water isn't good for the plants and animals that live on land or in fresh water.

Living things on land need fresh water. Only a little of Earth's water is fresh water. But not all the fresh water can be used. Most fresh water is frozen as ice in glaciers or in icecaps near the poles. Only a small amount of Earth's fresh water can be used to meet the needs of living things.

✓ **What are the two types of water on Earth?**

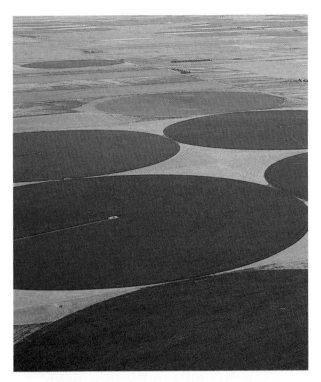

▲ Irrigation is the moving of water to dry places. Irrigation helps plants grow in dry areas. Almost two-fifths of Earth's liquid fresh water is used for irrigation.

Water on Earth

Fresh Water

Ice

If you could put all the water on Earth into 100 buckets, 97 buckets would hold the salt water of the oceans and seas, and 2 buckets would hold the frozen fresh water of glaciers and icecaps. Only 1 bucket would hold liquid fresh water.

Salt Water

Fresh Water

Nearly every person in the United States uses more than 380 liters (about 100 gal) of fresh water every day. You use fresh water when you take a drink. You take baths in fresh water. You water your plants with fresh water. You cook with fresh water. Farmers grow your food with fresh water. Factories use fresh water to make everything from bread to steel. People find the fresh water they need in many places. The rain or snow that falls to Earth is fresh water. This water flows over the ground and into rivers and streams. Ponds and most lakes also hold fresh water.

There is also fresh water under Earth's surface. This water is called **groundwater**. Groundwater begins as rain soaking into the soil. The water moves down through the soil and broken rocks under the soil until it reaches solid rock. Much of Earth's fresh water is stored underground as groundwater.

Fresh water is not found evenly on Earth's surface. Some places have a great deal of fresh water. Other places have very little. In those places there may not be enough water to meet the needs of the people who live there. In some places pollution makes the water dirty. Polluted water cannot be used by people.

◄ Most of Earth's fresh water is frozen. Glaciers and icecaps cover one-tenth of Earth's land surface. This iceberg has broken away from a glacier and is floating in the ocean.

To make sure there is enough clean, fresh water for everyone, it is important to conserve, or save, water when you can. Take short showers. Turn off the water when you brush your teeth. And don't pour paints, oils, or other harmful liquids down the drain. These liquids can get into the water people drink and make it unhealthful.

✔ **Where is fresh water found on Earth?**

THE INSIDE STORY

Water on Earth

Water that falls on the Earth collects in lakes, ponds, rivers, and streams.

Snow falls in cold areas.

The water from melted snow flows into streams and ponds.

Rain soaks into soil and rock. It becomes groundwater.

Some water from rain goes into rivers and streams.

Some water is stored in ponds and lakes.

Sometimes groundwater rises to the surface to form a lake.

Salt Water

Earth is a watery planet. Much of that water is salt water. The salt water of Earth's oceans covers more than two-thirds of our planet's surface. The Pacific Ocean is Earth's largest ocean. It is so big that all of Earth's land could fit inside it.

Most of the salt in salt water comes from the weathering of rocks. Rivers carry the salts from the rocks into ocean waters. Some inland seas and lakes also contain salt water.

▲ In some places fresh water is scarce. This water treatment plant removes the salt from ocean water to make fresh water.

The continents are really islands of land surrounded by Earth's large oceans. ▶

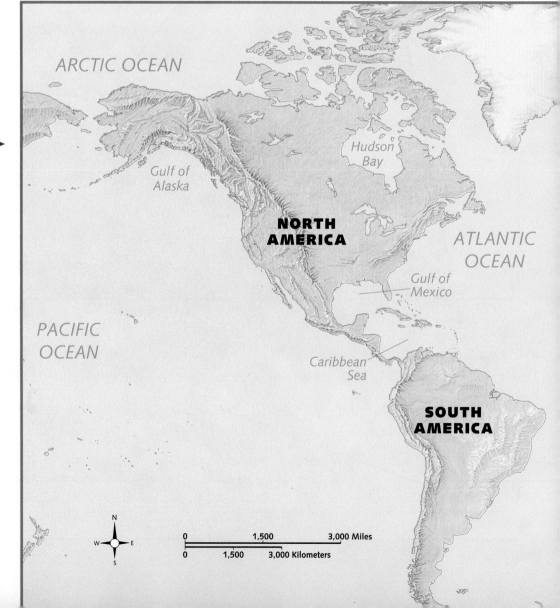

ARCTIC OCEAN

Hudson Bay

Gulf of Alaska

NORTH AMERICA

ATLANTIC OCEAN

Gulf of Mexico

PACIFIC OCEAN

Caribbean Sea

SOUTH AMERICA

N
W   E
S

0   1,500   3,000 Miles
0   1,500   3,000 Kilometers

The Great Salt Lake in Utah is one of the world's saltiest bodies of water.

You may think that ocean water isn't important because you don't drink it. But ocean water helps keep the planet from being very cold in some places and very hot in others. The sun warms ocean water near the equator. This warm water moves through the ocean, warming the cooler water around it as it moves.

The warm water helps keep the air above it warm, too.

The resources of the ocean are important. Fish and other ocean animals and plants are food for millions of people. Many useful products come from the ocean. For example, people pump oil from wells deep under the ocean. About one-fourth of our oil comes from wells under the sea.

✔ **Where is salt water found on Earth?**

Where Fresh Water and Salt Water Meet

Suppose you could walk along the whole coast of the United States. As you walked, you would find places where rivers bring fresh water to the ocean. These places are estuaries. An **estuary** (ES•tyoo•air•ee) is a place where fresh water from a river mixes with salt water from the ocean.

Estuaries are unusual ecosystems. The plants and animals there must be able to live in both fresh water and salt water.

Many kinds of animals live in or near estuaries. Birds build their nests in the plants on the edges of estuaries. Young fish, crabs, clams, shrimp, and oysters live and grow in the shallow waters of an estuary. Many people make their living by catching these animals, which are then sold as food.

Estuaries are important for other reasons, too. The roots of the many plants that live there slow down the water that enters the estuary. The roots also trap the soil that the slow water carries. This helps build up the land along the coast.

✔ **What is an estuary?**

▲ The Chesapeake Bay is the largest estuary in the United States. It is on the East Coast between Maryland and Virginia.

Tall grasses grow around the edges of estuaries. Many birds and other animals find food and shelter there. The roots trap soil and provide a home for small fish and other animals. ▼

▲ Mangrove trees grow in estuaries that are warm all year long. Because of the way their roots grow, mangroves provide a home for small fish and other animals.

Summary

More than two-thirds of Earth's surface is covered by water. Most of this water is the salt water of oceans and seas. Fresh water is found in lakes, ponds, rivers, and streams. Nothing could live on Earth without water.

Review

1. List three ways fresh water is used.
2. How does water get underground?
3. Where do the salts in Earth's oceans come from?
4. **Critical Thinking** Why don't estuaries hold only salt water?
5. **Test Prep** Which of the following is true of all ocean water?

   A It is warm.

   B It is salt water.

   C It is fresh water.

   D It is frozen.

LINKS

 MATH LINK

Construct Graphs Use a computer graphing program such as *Graph Links* to make a bar graph that shows the part of Earth's water that is salty and the part that is fresh.

 WRITING LINK

Persuasive Writing—Opinion Is it fun to visit the water? Write a paragraph describing a trip you have taken on a boat. Or describe a trip to a beach, lake, or river. What was it like? What did you do? What was the water like? Convince others that it would be a good place to visit.

 ART LINK

Mobile Find out about the kinds of animals that live in an estuary. Then make a mobile that shows some of these animals.

 TECHNOLOGY LINK

Learn more about the water on Earth by visiting the National Air and Space Museum Internet Site.
www.si.edu/harcourt/science

 Smithsonian Institution®

What Is the Water Cycle?

In this lesson, you can . . .

INVESTIGATE how fresh water and salt water evaporate.

LEARN ABOUT the movement of water on Earth and in the air.

LINK to math, writing, health, and technology.

◄ Water on these berries turned to ice in the cold night air. The sun's heat will melt the ice.

INVESTIGATE

Evaporation

Activity Purpose During a storm, rain forms puddles. After the rain stops, the puddles disappear. This process is called *evaporation*. In this investigation you will **control variables** to find out if some kinds of water evaporate faster than others.

Materials

- masking tape
- 4 identical jars
- measuring cup
- water
- salt
- spoon
- 2 jar lids
- ruler

Activity Procedure

1. Put a strip of masking tape down the side of each jar. (Picture A)

2. Using the measuring cup, pour $\frac{1}{2}$ cup water into each jar. Stir a spoonful of salt into 2 of the jars. Mark these jars with an *S*. Mark the other 2 jars with an *F*.

3 Make a mark on the tape on each jar to show how high the water is. Then put the lids on one *S* jar and one *F* jar. (Picture B)

4 **Predict** which jar the water will evaporate from first. **Record** your prediction.

5 Place the jars in a sunny place.

6 **Observe** the jars every day for a week. Each day, mark how high the water in each jar is.

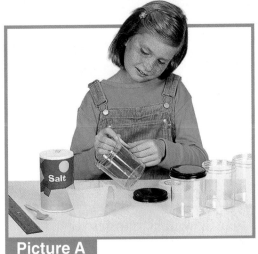
Picture A

Draw Conclusions

1. Did all the water evaporate from any of the jars? If so, which one?

2. **Compare** your prediction with your results. How did you make your prediction? Was your prediction correct?

Picture B

3. **Scientists at Work** To find the answers to some questions, scientists test things that will change. These things are called *variables*. Then they add something to the experiment that they know won't change. This is called a *control*. What were the controls in this investigation?

Investigate Further **Infer** what would happen if you repeated the activity but used different amounts of salt. How would the results change? Try the activity to see if your inference was correct. Don't forget to use controls.

Process Skill Tip

A control shows what would happen if no variable were being tested. **Controlling variables** is one way scientists make sure that their experiments are fair tests.

The Water Cycle

FIND OUT

• how water changes form

• how water moves from place to place

VOCABULARY

evaporation
condensation
precipitation
water cycle

How Water Changes

Water is the only material on Earth that has three forms in nature. You can find liquid water in lakes and rivers. You can find ice on a freezing winter day. Water is in the air around you in the form of a gas you can't see. It is called water vapor.

The form that water takes depends on the amount of heat, or *thermal energy,* in it. Adding heat or taking away heat changes the form of water.

Water changes form as temperatures change. The warm rays of the sun melt ice. Cold temperatures turn liquid water back into ice again. The sun warms a rain puddle, and the water becomes invisible water vapor.

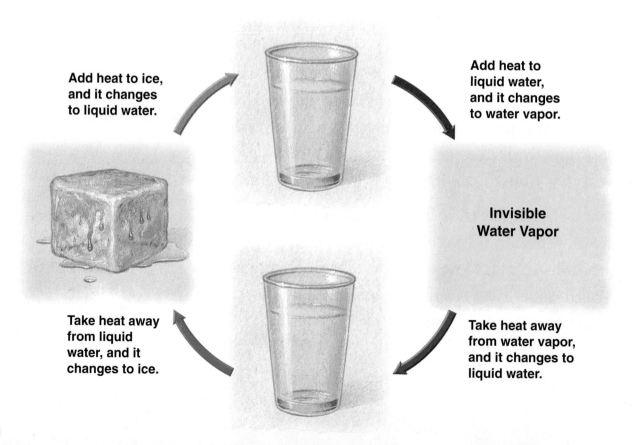

Add heat to ice, and it changes to liquid water.

Add heat to liquid water, and it changes to water vapor.

Invisible Water Vapor

Take heat away from liquid water, and it changes to ice.

Take heat away from water vapor, and it changes to liquid water.

Clouds form as water vapor cools and forms tiny water drops.

Small drops bump into each other to form larger drops.

When the drops are too big and heavy, they fall as rain.

In the investigation you used the sun to heat water. The heat changed the liquid water in the open jars into a gas that spread out in the air. **Evaporation** is the changing of a liquid into a gas. Heat must be added to a liquid to make it evaporate. Evaporation changes liquid water into invisible gas—water vapor.

When you see rain falling, you are seeing what happens because of cooling. **Condensation** is the changing of a gas into a liquid. Taking heat away from a gas, or cooling it, changes the gas into a liquid. When water vapor cools, the water changes form. It becomes liquid water.

✔ **What three forms can water take?**

Water vapor in the air can condense to form dew. On cool mornings you can see dew on spider webs and on leaves. ▼

Water vapor in the air can also freeze as it condenses, to form frost. Air must be cold for frost to form. ▼

Water Changes and Moves

Water evaporates all the time from Earth's surface. So why hasn't all the water on Earth turned into water vapor? After water becomes vapor, it cools to form water again. The water returns to Earth as precipitation. **Precipitation** is water that falls to Earth as rain, snow, sleet, or hail.

Earth uses the same water over and over again. The water you use to brush your teeth is billions of years old. This recycling of water over and over again is called the water cycle. The **water cycle** is the movement of water from Earth's surface into the air and back to the surface again. This cycle is powered by heat from the sun. The picture below shows how the water cycle works.

✔ **What is the water cycle?**

The Water Cycle The sun's rays warm the land and water on Earth's surface. This causes water to evaporate and form water vapor. Warm air carries water vapor upward.

Cooler temperatures high in the air make water vapor condense. Little water droplets form clouds.

Water droplets join to make bigger drops. Rain or snow falls from clouds.

Rivers take some of the rain to oceans.

Rain flows across the ground. It goes into rivers and lakes.

Some of the rain soaks into the soil. It becomes groundwater.

The sun warms the water. Water evaporates from oceans, rivers, and lakes to start the cycle again.

Summary

Evaporation changes water from a liquid into a gas. Condensation changes water from a gas back into a liquid. The water cycle is the movement of water from Earth's surface into the air and back to the surface again. The water moves by evaporation and condensation.

Review

1. What is evaporation?
2. What is condensation?
3. What is the water cycle?
4. **Critical Thinking** What would happen if water could evaporate but could not condense?
5. **Test Prep** How does water on land return to Earth's oceans in the water cycle?

   A by evaporating
   B by turning to ice
   C by the flow of rivers
   D by entering plants

LINKS

MATH LINK

Solve a Problem Suppose that 100 liters of water evaporate from a lake; 50 liters fall back on the lake as rain; 10 liters turn to ice on a mountain. The rest of the water flows back to the lake from a river. How much of the 100 liters does the river carry?

WRITING LINK

Informative Writing—Description Find pictures in magazines that show the parts of the water cycle. For each picture, write a sentence that tells what is happening. Share your work with a family member.

HEALTH LINK

Keeping Cool Evaporation helps keep your body cool on a hot day. Look up *perspiration* in a health book to find out how.

TECHNOLOGY LINK

Learn more about how people use technology to control water by watching *Inflatable Dams* on the **Harcourt Science Newsroom Video.**

A Filter for CLEAN WATER

Scientists developed a filter to clean water in the space shuttle. Now they are using what they learned to clean water on Earth.

Why Clean Water?

In the United States, most people use water that has been cleaned at a water treatment plant or pumped from the ground. You get water from the faucet, knowing it is safe to drink. Some places in the world, however, don't have clean water. The people in those places often drink unsafe water. The World Health Organization estimates that one billion people are not able to get clean, safe drinking water every day.

Water in Space

Astronauts taking long space flights need lots of water. But water is heavy and takes up a lot of room. The space shuttle can't carry all the clean water that astronauts need. So scientists at NASA and at the Umpqua Research Company developed a filter to clean the used water on the space shuttle. Astronauts take only a little water on each mission, and they use the filter to clean the water after they use it.

The Umpqua Filter

After its success in space, scientists decided to use the filter on Earth. Communities suffering from natural disasters like floods and hurricanes need to clean their water. So do communities that don't already have water treatment systems.

The Umpqua filter doesn't remove dirt and chemicals from the water. It only kills bacteria. So water is first passed through another filter that removes dirt and chemicals. Then it goes through the Umpqua filter.

Several companies are now making small water-cleaning systems that use the Umpqua filter to kill bacteria in water. These filters last a long time. And it costs less than one cent per gallon to clean water by using these systems.

THINK ABOUT IT

1. Why is cleaning water at a disaster site better than shipping in bottled water?
2. Why is it important for people to have clean water to drink?

Lisa Rossbacher
GEOLOGIST

When you think of the National Aeronautics and Space Administration (NASA), you may not think of rocks and minerals. But some people who work at NASA study rocks and minerals. Learning about rocks and landforms on Earth helps us understand more about other planets.

Lisa Rossbacher has helped NASA study erosion on the planet Mars. She uses maps and images made by space probes. She compares the patterns of erosion she sees on Mars with those she has studied on Earth. From her observations she makes inferences about how the landforms on Mars may have been shaped. She has inferred that water once moved over the surface of Mars, just as it does on Earth. Other geologists agree with her.

Rossbacher applies what she learns from her studies to help people. Geologists such as Rossbacher can help people by telling them where floods, landslides, earthquakes, or sinkholes are likely to occur. Once a community knows about the danger, it can make plans to use the land wisely. For example, people who live in areas that may flood might build dams to control the flow of water. In areas where earthquakes are likely, builders try to make buildings safer in case of an earthquake.

THINK ABOUT IT

1. What kinds of science skills does Rossbacher use in her work?
2. How might you use photographs of Mars to study erosion there?

CLOUD IN A JAR

How do raindrops form?

Materials

- metal pie pan
- freezer
- glass jar without lid
- hot water
- ice cubes

Procedure

❶ Put the pan in the freezer for an hour.

❷ Just before you take the pan out, have your teacher fill the jar halfway with hot water.

❸ Remove the pan from the freezer, and fill it with ice cubes. Place the pan on top of the jar. Leave it there for a few minutes.

Draw Conclusions

Observe what happens inside the jar. How is this like part of the water cycle?

MAKING RAINDROPS

Why do raindrops fall?

Materials

- dropper
- water
- clear plastic coffee-can lid
- pencil

Procedure

❶ Fill the dropper with water.

❷ Turn the lid so the top of the lid rests flat on the table. Drop small drops of water onto the lid. Put as many drops as you can on the lid without having the drops touch.

❸ Quickly turn the lid over.

❹ Holding the lid upside down, move drops together with the pencil point. What happens?

Draw Conclusions

How is this similar to what happens in clouds?

Vocabulary Review

Use the terms below to complete the sentences 1 through 6. The page numbers in ( ) tell you where to look in the chapter if you need help.

groundwater (D8)

estuary (D12)

evaporation (D17)

condensation (D17)

precipitation (D18)

water cycle (D18)

1. Water that falls to Earth as rain, snow, sleet, or hail is ____.

2. The process that changes a liquid into a gas is ____.

3. An ____ is a place where fresh water from a river mixes with salt water from the ocean.

4. The process that changes a gas into a liquid is ____.

5. The ____ is the movement of water from Earth's surface into the air and back to the surface again.

6. Fresh water found under Earth's surface is ____.

Connect Concepts

Write the terms where they belong in the concept map. Use the terms in the Word Bank. One term will be used twice.

water vapor   **liquid water**   **ice**

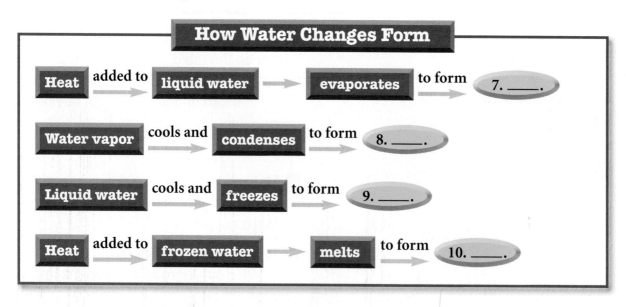

How Water Changes Form

Heat *added to* **liquid water** → **evaporates** *to form* 7. ____.

Water vapor *cools and* **condenses** *to form* 8. ____.

Liquid water *cools and* **freezes** *to form* 9. ____.

Heat *added to* **frozen water** → **melts** *to form* 10. ____.

Check Understanding

Write the letter of the best choice.

11. Which is mostly water?
    A rocks   C shells
    B plants   D soil

12. The oceans help control —
    F types of soil
    G temperature
    H groundwater
    J sunlight

13. Where does the energy for the water cycle come from?
    A the sun   C the soil
    B the wind   D the ocean

14. Fresh water is **NOT** found —
    F under Earth's surface
    G in lakes
    H in oceans
    J in rivers

15. Rain and snow are forms of —
    A precipitation
    B transpiration
    C condensation
    D evaporation

Critical Thinking

16. Some people think Earth's glaciers are important resources. Why might they think so?

17. Why is it important to not pour paint, oil, and other harmful liquids down a drain?

18. Why is an estuary an important environment?

19. Explain why the sun is important to the water cycle.

Process Skills Review

20. Suppose you are asked to keep track of the water used by your class. Tell how **using numbers** could make it easier to organize this data.

21. You see drops of rain falling. How could you **make a model** to find out what happens to the rain? Tell how you could **control variables** to find out.

Performance Assessment

Diagram the Water Cycle

Work with a partner. Together, draw a simple picture of the water cycle. Label the changes in the water. Tell whether water has been warmed or cooled to make each change.

Observing Weather

Vocabulary Preview

atmosphere
weather
temperature
front
wind
anemometer
weather map

No matter where you go, it seems someone is talking about the weather. That's because the weather affects what people do every day. Should you wear a coat? Will it rain during your picnic? Many of life's decisions depend on the weather.

Fast Fact

Called the "snow eater," the Chinook is a hot wind that roars down the Rocky Mountains in winter. Within seconds, a Chinook can go from a gentle breeze to over 160 kilometers (100 mi) per hour, melting several feet of snow in just a few hours!

The biggest storms on Earth are hurricanes. If the energy in one average hurricane could be captured, it would supply the United States with electricity for six months!

Record Hurricanes

Record Type	Where	When	Name
Deadliest 6,000 killed	Galveston, Texas	1900	unnamed
Strongest Winds 322 kph (about 200 mph)	Florida Keys	1935	"Labor Day"
Costliest $25 billion	Louisiana and South Florida	1992	Andrew

What Is Weather?

In this lesson, you can . . .

 INVESTIGATE the properties of air.

 LEARN ABOUT what weather is.

 LINK to math, writing, social studies, and technology.

 INVESTIGATE

Properties of Air

Activity Purpose Air is all around you. You can't see it, but you can **observe** its properties. In this investigation you will make observations. Then you will use them to **infer** some of the properties of air.

Materials

- plastic container
- water
- paper towel
- plastic cup
- index card

Activity Procedure

Part A

1 Half-fill the plastic container with water.

2 Crumple the paper towel. Push it to the bottom of the plastic cup.

◀ Water in the air can form clouds. These tall storm clouds are called thunderheads.

3 Turn the cup upside down. Push the cup to the bottom of the plastic container. Do not tilt the cup as you are pushing it downward. Then pull the cup straight up and out of the water. **Observe** the paper towel. **Record** your observations. (Picture A)

Part B

4 Remove the paper towel from the cup. Half-fill the cup with water. Put the index card over the cup opening.

5 Hold the cup over the plastic container. Use your right hand to hold the cup and your left hand to hold the index card in place. Quickly turn the cup over. Take your left hand off the index card. **Record** your observations. (Picture B)

Picture A

Picture B

Draw Conclusions

1. What did you **observe** in Part A?

2. What did you **observe** in Part B?

3. **Scientists at Work** Scientists **observe** things that happen all around them. They use their observations to **infer** why those things happen. Use your observations to infer one property of air for each part of this investigation.

Investigate Further Suppose you repeat Part B with a cup that is almost filled with water. **Predict** what will happen. Then try it.

Process Skill Tip

When you **observe**, you use your senses to examine things. Then you can **record** what you observe. When you **infer**, you use your observations to explain why something happens.

Where Weather Happens

FIND OUT

- about the layers of the atmosphere
- what weather is

VOCABULARY

atmosphere
weather

The Air Around You

It's easy to observe the air around you. But how do you study the air high above the planet? Long before the airplane was invented, scientists had wanted to study air high above the Earth. Some scientists put weather instruments on kites that they sent into the atmosphere. The **atmosphere** (AT•muhs•feer) is the air that surrounds Earth. The atmosphere contains water vapor as well as small pieces of dust and pollution.

Today we know a lot about the atmosphere. We know that it has layers. We also know that the air in the atmosphere has certain properties. Air takes up space. That's why the paper towel in the cup stayed dry. Air also has weight and presses on things. In the investigation air pushed up on the index card, holding it in place. This pressing by the air is called *air pressure.*

The atmosphere acts like a blanket for Earth. The sun shines on Earth's surface and warms it. The surface gives off heat. Earth's atmosphere holds in the heat. Without the atmosphere, most of the energy that keeps Earth warm would escape into space.

✔ **What is the atmosphere?**

◄ A person flew in a hot-air balloon for the first time in 1783. After that, scientists flew in balloons to study the atmosphere.

The Atmosphere

The atmosphere has layers. You can't see where the layers begin and end. But the air in each layer is different.

1 thermosphere

2 mesosphere

3 stratosphere

4 troposphere

1 Temperatures in the *thermosphere* (THER·muhs·feer) can be higher than 2,000°C (3,632°F). Air particles can be miles apart in this part of the atmosphere. Some parts of this layer glow as the sun's rays hit them. Those parts form the northern and southern lights.

2 Temperatures are lower in the *mesosphere* (MES·uhs·feer) and can go below ¯120°C (¯184°F).

3 The *stratosphere* (STRAT·uhs·feer) contains the atmosphere's ozone. Ozone is a type of oxygen. It absorbs harmful rays from the sun. Because ozone absorbs some of the sun's energy, temperatures increase as you go higher in the stratosphere. Even so, the temperatures are usually below freezing. Long-distance jets sometimes fly low in the stratosphere.

4 The *troposphere* (TROH·puhs·feer) is the layer of the atmosphere where you live. Air particles in this layer are close enough for you to breathe easily. All our weather takes place in the troposphere. Near the surface, temperatures are warm. But the higher you go in the troposphere, the cooler the air temperature gets. At the top of the troposphere, the temperature drops to ¯80°C (¯112°F).

Weather

Earth's atmosphere is more than 160 kilometers (100 mi) thick. But weather takes place only in the 10 kilometers (6 mi) of air directly above Earth's surface.

Everybody talks about the weather, but what is it? **Weather** is what is happening in the atmosphere at a certain place. Temperature, wind, and precipitation are all parts of weather.

There would be no weather without the sun. The sun's heat causes clouds, winds, and precipitation to form.

Meteorologists are scientists who study weather and the atmosphere. They measure and record changes in air. These changes help them know if the weather will be sunny or stormy.

✔ **What is weather?**

▲ Blizzards are large snowstorms. They have low temperatures and strong winds of 50 kilometers per hour (about 31 mph) or more. These winds blow the snow so that it is almost impossible to see.

▲ Hurricanes are strong, dangerous storms that form over warm ocean waters. Hurricanes have winds of 120 kilometers per hour (about 75 mph) or more.

Rain can come as gentle showers or pouring storms. ▼

▲ Tornadoes are violent windstorms. The winds are so strong that they can destroy homes and lift trains from their tracks. More tornadoes occur in the United States than anywhere else on Earth.

Summary

The atmosphere has layers. Weather takes place in the lowest layer of the atmosphere. Weather is what is happening in the atmosphere at a certain place. Temperature, wind, and precipitation are all parts of weather.

Review

1. List three properties of air.
2. What does ozone do?
3. List three things that are parts of the weather.
4. **Critical Thinking** What might Earth be like without the atmosphere?
5. **Test Prep** Where does weather happen?
   A in the layer of the atmosphere next to Earth's surface
   B in the coldest layer of the atmosphere
   C where air particles are far apart
   D in the ozone layer

LINKS

 MATH LINK

Organize Data How windy has it been lately? Look on the weather page in a newspaper to find out. Record the wind speed for seven days. Write the speeds in order from most windy to least windy.

 WRITING LINK

Expressive Writing—Poem
Pick a type of weather, and write the letters of the name down the side of a page. For each letter, think of words that describe the weather. Use your words to make a poem for a younger child.

 SOCIAL STUDIES LINK

Bad Weather Report on the worst weather disaster that has happened where you live. Interview someone who was there. Record the interview on tape, and share it with others.

 GO ONLINE TECHNOLOGY LINK

Learn more about weather by visiting the National Air and Space Museum Internet Site.
www.si.edu/harcourt/science

 Smithsonian Institution®

How Are Weather Conditions Measured?

In this lesson, you can . . .

INVESTIGATE
how a thermometer works.

LEARN ABOUT
how weather is measured.

LINK to math, writing, physical education, and technology.

INVESTIGATE

Measuring Temperature

Activity Purpose Temperatures change from place to place. In this investigation you will **use numbers** and a simple thermometer to **compare** temperatures.

Materials

- water
- 1-L plastic bottle
- red food coloring
- clear drinking straw
- clay
- clear plastic cup
- dropper
- metric ruler

Activity Procedure

1 Put water in the bottle until it is almost full. Add ten drops of food coloring.

2 Put the straw in the bottle. Three-fourths of the straw should stick out of the bottle. Seal the opening around the straw with clay. (Picture A)

◀ **Wind vanes show wind direction. The head of the lobster points toward the direction the wind is blowing.**

3 Half-fill the cup with water. Add three drops of food coloring.

4 Use the dropper to put water from the cup into the straw. Add water until you can see the water in the straw above the clay stopper.

5 Make a mark at the water level in the straw. You have made a thermometer. The higher the level of liquid in the straw, the higher the temperature.

Picture A Picture B

6 Take the thermometer to five different places at school. Leave it at each place for 15 minutes. Use a ruler to **measure** the water level in the straw from the mark to the top of the water level. Do not squeeze the bottle while you measure. **Record** the measurement and the location. (Picture B)

Draw Conclusions

1. What happened to the water levels in the straw in the different locations?

2. What information could you learn by using your thermometer? What information is impossible to learn by using your thermometer?

3. **Scientists at Work** Scientists sometimes **use numbers** to put things in order. Look at the numbers you recorded. Use the numbers to order the locations from warmest to coolest.

Process Skill Tip

You can **use numbers** to do many things. You can count, put things in order, and **compare** one set of things to another.

How Weather Is Measured

Measuring Temperature

The highest temperature ever measured on Earth was 58°C (136°F) in northern Africa. The lowest temperature was ⁻89°C (⁻128°F) in Antarctica. **Temperature** is a measure of how hot or cold something is. Temperatures on Earth can feel burning hot or freezing cold. Thermometers are used to measure temperatures.

Air temperature is always changing. You've probably noticed changes in temperature from day to night. Air is warmer in the sun. It is cooler after the sun sets. During the day the sun warms the ground more in some places than in others. It warms land faster than water.

Usually, air over land is warm and dry. Air over water is cool and damp. A large body of air with the same temperature and moisture is called an *air mass.* An air mass can be hundreds of kilometers wide. It can cover many states or a whole ocean. A moving air mass causes many weather changes.

✓ **What is temperature?**

Temperature	
40°C/104°F	Heat wave
30°C/86°F	Good day for a swim
20°C/68°F	Perfect day!
10°C/50°F	A bit chilly—wear a light jacket!
0°C/32°F	Time for a coat (water freezes)
⁻10°C/14°F	Bundle up! It's cold outside!
⁻20°C/⁻4°F	There's ice on the windows!
⁻40°C/⁻40°F	Brrrrrr! Stay inside!

°C   °F
50 — 120
40 — 100
30 — 80
20 — 60
10 — 40
0 — 20
10 — 0
20 — 20
30 — 40
40 —

MADE IN U.S.A.

Air masses are always moving. A front is a place where two air masses of different temperatures meet. Most weather changes happen at fronts.

At a cold front, cold air bumps into warmer air. The cold air is heavier. It pushes the warm air up quickly. This forms tall clouds and thunderstorms. Wind and heavy rain often occur. Cold fronts move fast, so the rain doesn't last long. Cold air replaces the warm air at the surface. This makes the temperature drop after the rain.

At a warm front, warm air bumps into colder air. The warm air is pushed up gently by the cold air. It forms a long line of clouds. Warm fronts bring long periods of gentle rain, gray skies, and light winds. Warm air replaces the cold air at the surface. This makes the temperature rise after the rain.

Measuring Precipitation

Many people live near rivers. Rivers are usually good neighbors, helping people move goods, supplying sources of power, and providing places to fish and swim. But when there are heavy rains, rivers can rise and spill over their banks. Flood waters can cover fields and towns, causing much damage.

People need to know when a flood might occur. That's one reason it's important to measure precipitation. Precipitation is any kind of water that falls from the sky. It might be rain, snow, sleet, or hail.

Meteorologists measure rain by using rain gauges. A rain gauge looks like a cup or a glass. It collects precipitation as it falls.

Meteorologists measure snow by using snow boards. Snow boards are like long rulers. People stick them into snow to see how high it is. During storms, people measure snow levels every six hours. It takes 10 inches of snow to equal the amount of water in 1 inch of rain.

✔ How is precipitation measured?

Rain gauges, like this one, are used to measure precipitation. ▶

The ways clouds look often give us clues about the coming weather. Stratus clouds are low gray clouds. They usually show that rain is on the way. ▼

Cumulus clouds are puffy and white. Small cumulus clouds appear in clear, sunny weather. If the clouds gather and grow tall, a storm is coming. ▼

Inside a Thunderhead

Thunderheads are giant clouds that form along cold fronts.

Strong upward movement of air causes tall clouds to form.

Quickly rising air

Sinking air

As the clouds grow taller, the air inside them cools and begins to sink.

Lightning

Strong winds

Heavy rainfall

Heavy rains, lightning, and sometimes hail and tornadoes form as air moves up and down within the cloud.

Eventually, the air cools so much that it is no longer pushed upward. Then the rain stops, and the cloud breaks up.

Measuring Wind

Winds can be helpful. They cool us on a hot day. They clear pollution from the air. But winds also can do damage. They can blow down buildings or tear up trees.

Wind is the movement of air. Wind happens because air pressure is different in different places. Air, in the form of wind, moves from areas of high pressure to areas of low pressure—like water flowing downhill.

The direction the wind comes from can be recorded, and its speed can be measured. A weather vane shows wind direction. An **anemometer** (an•uh•MAHM•uht•er) measures wind speed.

Beaufort Wind Scale

One way to estimate the speed of the wind is to look at the movements of objects around you. The pictures show one way to estimate the speed of the wind. This wind scale is called the Beaufort (BO•furt) Wind Scale.

0 Air is still; smoke rises straight up.

1 Smoke drifts; flags hang still.

2 Smoke drifts with wind.

3 Flags and leaves move gently.

4 Loose paper blows.

5 Small waves on water.

6 Umbrellas blow inside out.

7 Hard to walk into wind.

8 Branches ripped off trees.

9 Roofs and chimneys damaged.

10 Trees snapped in half.

11 Cars turned over.

12 Buildings destroyed.

The strongest winds occur in storms. Hurricanes are the biggest storms on Earth. They can be 650 kilometers (400 mi) across. The slowest hurricane winds are 120 kilometers per hour (75 mph).

Tornadoes are shaped like spinning funnels. They are much smaller than hurricanes, but they have stronger winds. The wind at the center of a tornado can be more than 480 kilometers per hour (300 mph).

✔ **What is wind?**

Summary

Many weather changes happen at fronts. People use tools to measure changes in weather. Thermometers measure temperature. Rain gauges measure rainfall. Anemometers measure wind speed.

Review

1. What is an air mass?
2. What is a front?
3. What makes the wind blow?
4. **Critical Thinking** What changes happen when a front passes through an area?
5. **Test Prep** An anemometer measures wind —

   A direction   **C** sounds
   B destruction   **D** speed

LINKS

MATH LINK

Collect and Display Data
Make a table showing each day's high and low temperature for one week. Which day had the greatest difference in temperature? What was the difference?

WRITING LINK

Informative Writing— Description Write a paragraph to describe today's weather. How does the weather make you feel? Read your description in class. Compare your description with those of your classmates.

PHYSICAL EDUCATION LINK

Fly a Kite Find directions for making a kite. Look in books with projects on wind, weather, air, and Earth science. Fly your kite on different days when the wind is blowing at different speeds. When does your kite fly best?

TECHNOLOGY LINK

To learn more about measuring weather, watch *Phoenix Monsoon* on the **Harcourt Science Newsroom Video.**

CNN Turner Le@rning®

What Is a Weather Map?

In this lesson, you can . . .

INVESTIGATE how to read a weather map.

LEARN ABOUT the way people predict weather.

LINK to math, writing, social studies, and technology.

Reading Weather Maps

Activity Purpose Maps show a lot of data. Often the data is shown as symbols. In this investigation you will **interpret data** on a weather map. Then you will answer questions about the weather.

Materials

- weather map

Activity Procedure

1 Study the weather map and the key to the symbols that it uses.

2 Use the map to answer the questions.

◀ These red and black flags tell people that a hurricane is coming.

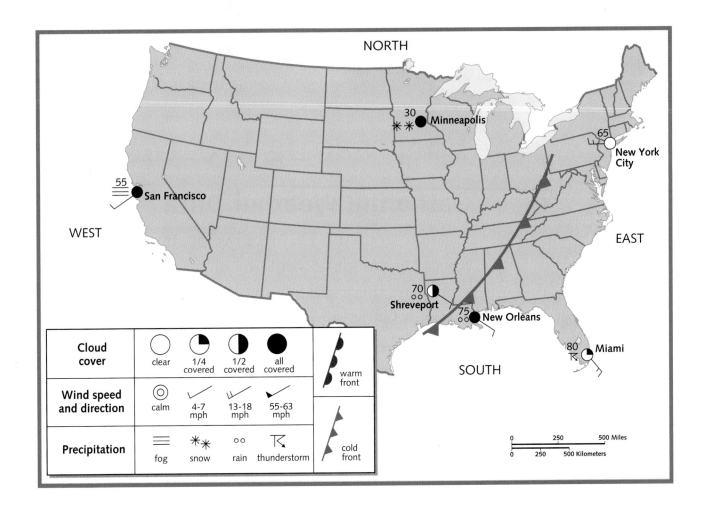

Cloud cover	○ clear	◔ 1/4 covered	◐ 1/2 covered	● all covered	warm front
Wind speed and direction	◎ calm	╱ 4-7 mph	╱ 13-18 mph	╲ 55-63 mph	
Precipitation	≡ fog	✳✳ snow	∘∘ rain	�📐 thunderstorm	cold front

Draw Conclusions

1. Where is there a thunderstorm?

2. Find the cold front. What can you tell about the weather along the cold front?

3. **Scientists at Work** Scientists **interpret data** on weather maps to learn about the weather in different places. Interpret data on this map to describe the weather in Minneapolis, Minnesota.

Investigate Further The weather in the United States generally moves from west to east. Imagine that you are in New York City. Use the data on the map to **predict** what your weather may be like about one week from now.

Process Skill Tip

When you **interpret data**, you must first **observe** it and try to understand it. Then you use the data to answer questions, to make predictions, or to make inferences.

Forecasting Weather

FIND OUT

- **how people forecast the weather**

- **how to read a weather map**

VOCABULARY

weather map

Gathering Weather Data

You turn on the TV. Joyce Bishop, the weather forecaster, stands in front of a big map. She points to it and says there will be rain tomorrow. So you know you should take an umbrella to school.

You depend on the TV weather forecaster. But she doesn't predict the weather by herself. She has help.

Information about the weather comes from thousands of weather stations all over the world. At each station, data about temperature, precipitation, air pressure, wind, and clouds are recorded.

◄ Thousands of stations collect weather data each day. The government runs some of the stations like this one. Some people have instruments at their homes to collect data.

▲ Weather satellites circle Earth many times each day. Satellite data can show cloud patterns over large areas.

◀ Doppler radar helps forecasters see the movement of thunderstorms. This radar also shows where tornadoes are likely to form.

LIGHT, HEAVY, SEVERE

▲ TV weather forecasters get data and forecasts from the National Weather Service. Sometimes they use the data to make their own forecasts for a local area.

Weather planes gather data about storms. Meteorologists on these planes try to find out how strong the winds are and what direction a storm is likely to move.

Data also comes from weather balloons. Meteorologists send up weather balloons every 12 hours. Instruments carried by the balloons take readings of temperature, precipitation, and wind. They record data on weather high in the atmosphere.

Satellites in space send weather data back to Earth. Satellites also take pictures that show clouds and storms as they move across the country.

Each day the National Weather Service collects all these pieces of data. The data goes into computers that organize the information into maps. Computers also help meteorologists make predictions. They send all this information to the weather forecasters you see on TV.

✔ **Name three sources of weather data.**

Weather Maps

Meteorologists use the data from the National Weather Service to make forecasts. They also use the data to make weather maps. A **weather map** is a map that shows weather data for a large area. The maps show temperatures and precipitation. They show warm fronts and cold fronts. They show areas of high air pressure and low air pressure.

Some weather maps use station-model symbols. You saw some of these symbols in the investigation. A station model is shown on the next page. Meteorologists often use these symbols instead of the symbols used in many newspapers. These symbols give more exact data about the weather in a certain place.

✔ **What is a weather map?**

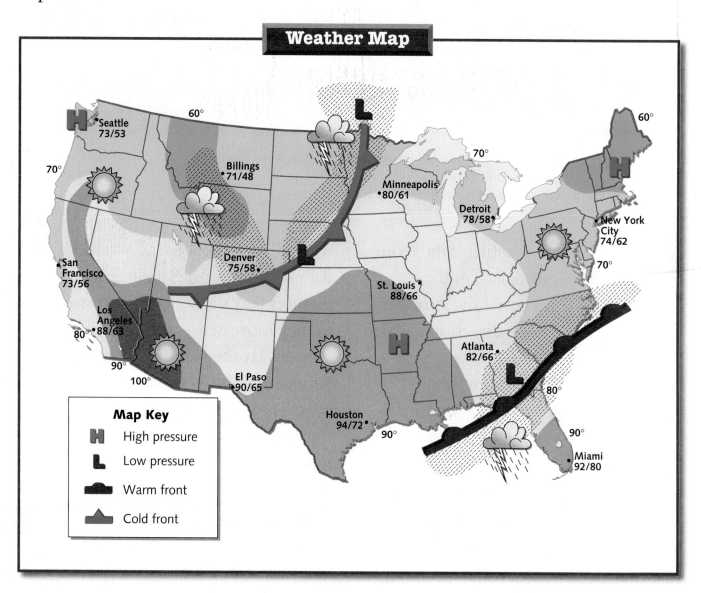

Weather Map

Seattle 73/53
Billings 71/48
Minneapolis 80/61
Detroit 78/58
New York City 74/62
San Francisco 73/56
Denver 75/58
St. Louis 88/66
Los Angeles 88/63
El Paso 90/65
Atlanta 82/66
Houston 94/72
Miami 92/80

Map Key
H High pressure
L Low pressure
🌡 Warm front
🔺 Cold front

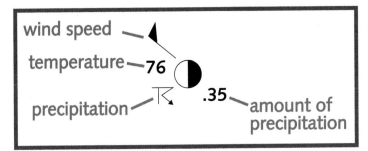

wind speed

temperature — 76

precipitation — .35 — amount of precipitation

▲ A station model shows the weather at one place. The weather at this station is cloudy with winds out of the northwest at about 55–63 miles per hour. The temperature is 76°F, and there are thunderstorms.

Summary

Meteorologists use data from surface stations, airplanes, weather balloons, and satellites. Weather maps use symbols to show weather conditions over large areas.

Review

1. What kinds of weather data do we get from airplanes?
2. How do satellites help meteorologists predict the weather?
3. What is a station model?
4. **Critical Thinking** Why do meteorologists collect data many times each day?
5. **Test Prep** A weather map does **NOT** show —

    A temperature
    B precipitation
    C seasons
    D wind speed

LINKS

MATH LINK

Write Fractions Keep track of the TV weather forecast for five days. Each day check to see if the forecast was right or wrong. Write a fraction to compare how many forecasts were right (top number) with the total number of forecasts (bottom number).

WRITING LINK

Informative Writing— Explanation Suppose a meteorologist comes to your class. Write one question about weather. With your classmates, find the answers to the questions. Publish your findings.

SOCIAL STUDIES LINK

Types of Maps A weather map is only one kind of map. Find another kind of map in a book or a magazine. Explain to the class what the map shows.

TECHNOLOGY LINK

Learn more about weather maps by visiting this Internet Site.

www.scilinks.org/harcourt

Spotting and Chasing TORNADOES

Tornadoes are powerful, dangerous windstorms. Their high winds have been known to lift objects such as cars and cattle, and even to blow a blade of straw through a tree! While many people head to safe places when they hear a tornado warning, some people, known as storm chasers, do just the opposite. They track and follow tornadoes. The work can be very dangerous, but many of these people gather important scientific information about storms.

Can a Tornado Be Predicted?

The violent winds of a tornado rotate from 64 to 606 kilometers (40 to 379 miles) per hour. A tornado can travel at speeds of 48 to 112 kilometers (30 to 70 miles) per hour, and its path can change suddenly. Tornadoes form within large thunderstorm systems. Although there is no way to predict a tornado exactly, weather forecasters study thunderstorm patterns to predict where and when a tornado *might* strike. These forecasters use their experience, knowledge, and special equipment to try to predict a tornado's path.

Storm Spotters

A storm spotter is someone who watches for severe weather, such as tornadoes. Although special radar equipment is used, it cannot find every dangerous storm. Spotters warn people in the community about tornadoes and other unsafe weather. Usually, local groups of storm spotters and radio broadcasters help get warnings to people quickly. Groups such as the National Weather Service and local emergency centers provide training for storm spotting.

Storm Chasers

Some meteorologists who want to learn more about tornadoes become storm chasers. These storm chasers study thunderstorms by closely following their paths. They use computers and other equipment to track and collect data. Before a chase, storm chasers begin gathering information from computer models, news reports, and other weather centers to find out if conditions are right for a tornado to form. Once the chase begins, storm chasers may travel hundreds of miles to follow a storm. Cars, trucks, and vans are used to carry chasers and their equipment. While on a chase, storm chasers need to watch out for high winds, lightning, hail, and flash floods. During months when there is little or no storm activity, chasers spend time analyzing data and studying books about weather.

THINK ABOUT IT

- What is the difference between a storm chaser and a storm spotter?

June Bacon-Bercey

METEOROLOGIST

June Bacon-Bercey was discouraged from becoming a meteorologist. That's why she decided to set up a scholarship fund for women who want to be meteorologists. Meteorologists are people who study weather. They observe weather and map weather conditions. They use information from computers to predict the weather.

Bacon-Bercey has been interested in the weather since she was a young girl. She has worked on television as a meteorologist. She has also worked for the National Weather Service. In 1979 she became chief administrator of television activities for the National Oceanic and Atmospheric Administration. She coordinates the agency's services to schools, the government, and the general public.

Bacon-Bercey has seen a lot of changes in the ways weather data is gathered and shared with people. Years ago people who gave TV weather reports just read information a weather service gave them. Now many TV stations hire their own meteorologists.

THINK ABOUT IT

1. What might a person who studies the weather talk about if he or she came to your school?

2. If you were going to set up a scholarship fund, what groups of people would you most like to help?

MEASURE PRECIPITATION

How can you find out how much rain falls?

Materials

- masking tape
- ruler
- clear plastic 1-L bottle with top cut off

Procedure

❶ Tape the ruler to the outside of the bottle. The 1-in. mark should be at the bottom of the bottle.

❷ Put your rain gauge outside before it rains. Do not place it under a tree or under an object that might block the rain.

❸ Check the amount of water in the bottle after the rain stops.

Draw Conclusions

Look on the weather page of the newspaper. How much rain fell the day you used your gauge? Was your measurement correct? How close was your measurement?

MEASURE THE WIND

How fast does the wind blow?

Materials

- 2 cardboard strips
- scissors
- stapler
- wire
- cap of a ballpoint pen
- 4 small paper cups (3 white, 1 red)
- watch with second hand

Procedure

❶ Make an X with the cardboard strips. Staple the strips together.

❷ Use the scissors to make a hole in the middle of the X. Push the pen cap into the hole as shown.

❸ Cut a slit in the opposite sides of each cup. Attach the cups as shown.

❹ Push the piece of wire deep into the ground outside. Balance the pen cap on the wire.

❺ Count the times the red cup spins by in 1 minute. Divide this number by 10. The answer tells how many miles per hour the wind is blowing.

Draw Conclusions

Measure the speed of the wind over the next several days. How does the speed change?

Vocabulary Review

Use the terms below to complete the sentences 1 through 8. The page numbers in ( ) tell you where to look in the chapter if you need help.

atmosphere (D30)

weather (D32)

temperature (D36)

front (D37)

wind (D40)

anemometer (D40)

weather map (D46)

1. What is happening in the atmosphere at a certain place is ___.

2. A tool that measures wind speed is an ___.

3. A ___ shows the weather over a large area.

4. The air that surrounds Earth is the ___.

5. The ___ is the measure of how hot or cold something is.

6. The movement of air is ___.

7. A ___ is a place where two air masses meet.

8. Weather occurs in the lowest layer of the ___.

Connect Concepts

Write the terms where they belong in the concept map.

anemometer   **temperature**

precipitation   **wind vane**

rain gauge

Weather Measuring Tools	
Weather Condition	**Tools That Measure It**
9. _____	thermometer
wind	11. _____
	12. _____
10. _____	13. _____
	snow board

Check Understanding

Write the letter of the best choice.

14. The atmosphere is important to our weather because —
    A it is clear
    B it holds in Earth's heat
    C winds are light
    D it has ten layers

15. At a cold front, —
    F warm air replaces cold air
    G there is gentle rain
    H winds are light
    J there can be thunderstorms

16. A ___ collects weather data on the ground.
    A satellite   C weather station
    B airplane   D weather balloon

Critical Thinking

Use the diagram below to answer the questions.

17. What type of front is shown?

18. What will the weather be like along the front?

19. How will the weather change as the front moves on?

Process Skills Review

20. **Observe** the table below, which shows the high temperature in one place for five days in a row. **Interpret the data**. What can you **infer** about the weather during the week?

Day	High Temperature (°F)
Monday	20°
Tuesday	19°
Wednesday	21°
Thursday	45°
Friday	47°

21. How would you **use numbers** to find out how much rain is equal to 10 in. of snow?

Performance Assessment

Reading Weather Maps

Use the weather map to tell what the weather is like in Atlanta, Georgia. Next, use the data from the map to forecast how Atlanta's weather will change. Then, draw a new station model for Atlanta showing what the weather will be like after the change.

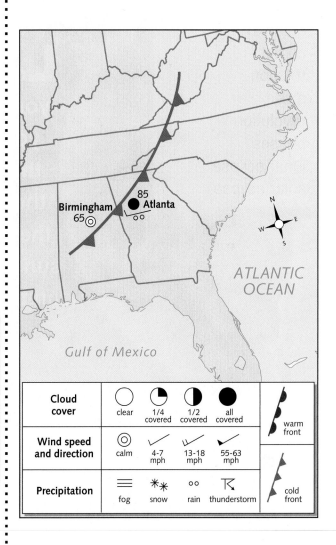

Earth and Its Place in the Solar System

Vocabulary Preview

solar system
orbit
planet
asteroid
comet
rotation
axis
revolution
phases
lunar eclipse
solar eclipse

Looking up at a clear night sky, you will see tiny points of light. If you could leave Earth and travel through space to get closer to those lights, you would see that they are other worlds and other suns, but not like the Earth and the sun that we know.

Fast Fact

If you want to find the coldest place in the solar system, go to Triton, Neptune's largest moon. Temperatures there average −235 degrees C. It's so cold on Triton that volcanoes erupt with ice instead of lava!

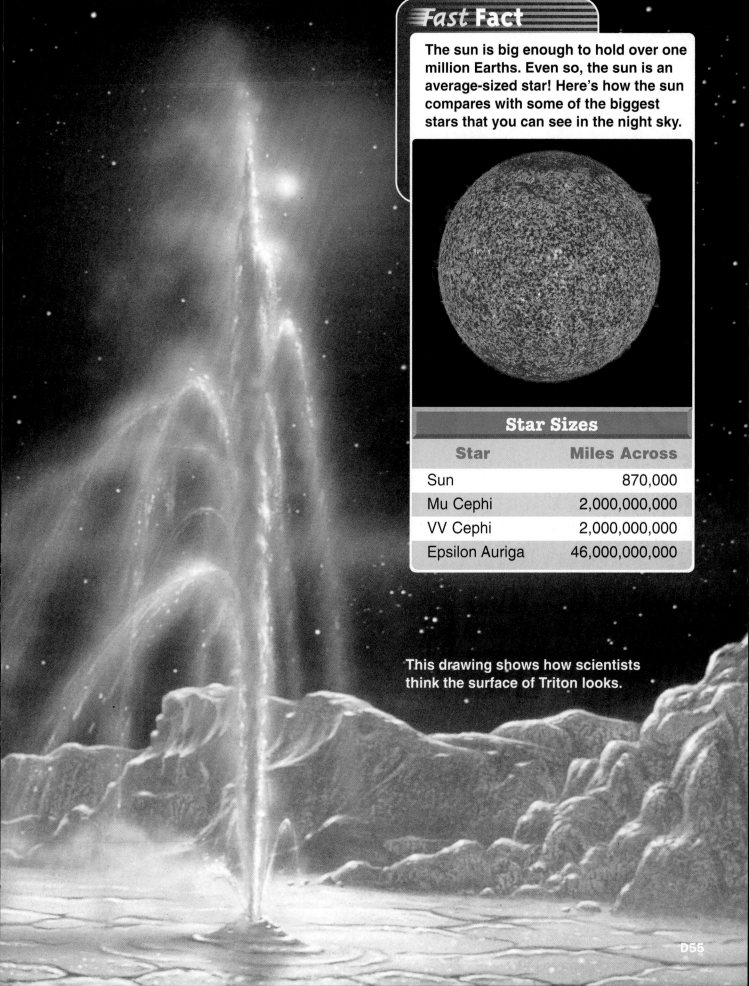

The sun is big enough to hold over one million Earths. Even so, the sun is an average-sized star! Here's how the sun compares with some of the biggest stars that you can see in the night sky.

Star Sizes	
Star	**Miles Across**
Sun	870,000
Mu Cephi	2,000,000,000
VV Cephi	2,000,000,000
Epsilon Auriga	46,000,000,000

This drawing shows how scientists think the surface of Triton looks.

What Is the Solar System?

In this lesson, you can . . .

INVESTIGATE the planets.

LEARN ABOUT objects in the solar system.

LINK to math, writing, health, and technology.

◄ Telescopes help us see things that are far away.

INVESTIGATE

The Planets

Activity Purpose Nine planets circle the sun. They are not all alike. In this investigation you will use some of the planets' properties to **order** them. Then you will **classify** the planets by using the data you have organized.

Materials

- pencil
- paper
- planet picture cards (optional)

Activity Procedure

1 Copy the Ordering Planet Data chart.

2 **Use numbers** from the data table to find each planet's distance from the sun. **Record** in your table the names of the planets, beginning with the one closest to the sun.

3 **Use numbers** from the data table to find the distance across each planet. The planet with the shortest distance across is the smallest planet. Use numbers to **order** the planets by size. **Record** the names of the planets in order, beginning with the smallest planet.

Ordering Planet Data

Closest to the Sun to Farthest from the Sun	Smallest to Largest	Shortest Year to Longest Year

Planet Data			
Planet	Distance from Sun (in millions of kilometers)	Distance Across (in kilometers)	Length of Year (y=Earth year d=Earth day)
Earth	150	12,750	365 d
Jupiter	778	143,000	12 y
Mars	228	6,800	2 y
Mercury	58	4,900	88 d
Neptune	4,505	49,000	165 y
Pluto	5,890	2,300	248 y
Saturn	1,427	120,000	29 y
Uranus	2,869	51,000	84 y
Venus	108	12,000	225 d

Draw Conclusions

1. Which planet is closest to the sun? Farthest from the sun?

2. Which is the largest planet? The smallest?

3. **Scientists at Work** Scientists sometimes **use numbers** to put things in **order**. Scientists have studied the same data you used in this investigation.

Investigate Further **Plan and conduct an experiment** that **makes a model** to show one set of your planet data. You may wish to use the planet picture cards in your model.

Process Skill Tip

You can **use numbers** to put objects in **order.**

The Solar System

The Structure of the Solar System

The **solar system** is the sun and the objects that orbit around it. An **orbit** is the path an object takes as it moves around another object in space. All the planets you studied in the investigation, including Earth, are in orbit around the sun.

You learned about some parts of the solar system in the investigation. The solar system has nine planets, including Earth. A **planet** is a large body of rock or gas that orbits the sun. The solar system also has many moons. Moons are large, rocky objects that orbit planets. Earth has one moon. Other planets have no moons or many moons.

✔ **What is the solar system?**

THE INSIDE STORY

The Solar System

All of the planets are much smaller than the sun. The distances tell how far from the sun each planet really is.

Jupiter
(778 million km)

Mercury
(58 million km)

Earth
(150 million km)

Venus
(108 million km)

Mars
(228 million km)

Sun

The Sun

The sun is the center of the solar system. It is a *star*—a hot ball of glowing gases. It looks different to us from other stars because it is closer to us than other stars are.

The sun is very hot and bright. The sun is also big. All of the planets and moons of the solar system could fit inside it.

Gravity on the sun is very strong. That's because of its great size. *Gravity* is the force of one object's pull on another. The sun's gravity helps hold the objects in the solar system in orbit.

✔ **What is the sun?**

The sun is 1.35 million kilometers (about 838,900 mi) across. The Earth is tiny compared with the sun. The sun could hold more than one million Earths inside it. ▶

Earth

Saturn
(1,427 million km)

Pluto
(5,890 million km)

Uranus
(2,869 million km)

Neptune
(4,505 million km)

The Inner Planets

In the investigation you found a way to put the planets in order by their distances from the sun. Scientists use this same order to put the planets into two groups. The four planets closest to the sun are in one group. They are called the *inner planets*. The five other planets are the *outer planets*.

The inner planets are Mercury, Venus, Earth, and Mars. They are alike in many ways. They all have rocky surfaces. Because they are

Mercury

Mercury

Sun

Fun Fact: In the daytime Mercury's surface is hot enough to melt lead.

Length of Day: 59 Earth days
Length of Year: 88 Earth days
Moons: none
Surface: rocky, with many craters
Distance Across: 4,900 kilometers (about 3,100 mi)

Venus

Venus

Sun

Fun Fact: Venus rotates backward compared with most of the other planets.

Length of Day: 243 Earth days
Length of Year: 225 Earth days
Moons: none
Surface: rocky, with constant cover of thick clouds
Distance Across: 12,000 kilometers (about 7,500 mi)

closer to the sun, they are warmer than the outer planets. The inner planets are also smaller than most of the outer planets. None of them has more than two moons.

Earth is different from the other inner planets. It has a watery surface. It is the only planet with a lot of oxygen in its atmosphere. Earth also has plant life and animal life.

✔ **List the inner planets in order from the sun.**

Earth

Earth

Sun

Fun Fact: Earth is the only planet known to support life.

Length of Day: 24 hours (1 Earth day)
Length of Year: $365\frac{1}{4}$ days (1 Earth year)
Moons: 1
Surface: mostly water
Distance Across: 12,750 kilometers (about 7,920 mi)

Mars

Mars

Sun

Fun Fact: Mars has the largest volcano in the solar system, Olympus Mons.

Length of Day: almost 25 Earth hours
Length of Year: almost 2 Earth years
Moons: 2
Surface: rocky, with volcanoes, canyons, and red dust
Distance Across: 6,800 kilometers (about 4,200 mi)

The Outer Planets

The five planets farthest from the sun are called the outer planets. The outer planets are Jupiter, Saturn, Uranus, Neptune, and Pluto.

The outer planets are alike in many ways. They are made mostly of frozen gases. They are very far from the sun, so their surfaces are much colder than the inner planets. All but Pluto are much larger than the inner planets. Jupiter is the solar system's largest planet. It is more than 1,000 times larger than Earth. Most of the outer planets have many moons. Many also have rings of dust and ice around them.

Pluto is different from the other outer planets. It is the smallest planet in the solar system. It is smaller than Earth's moon.

✔ **List the outer planets in order from the sun.**

Jupiter

Sun — Jupiter

Fun Fact: Two Earth-sized circles could fit inside Jupiter's Great Red Spot, a huge hurricane-like storm on Jupiter's surface.

Length of Day: 10 Earth hours
Length of Year: about 12 Earth years
Moons: 16 known
Surface: no solid surface
Distance Across: 143,000 kilometers (about 88,900 mi)

Saturn

Sun — Saturn

Fun Fact: Saturn has a large system of rings that reaches 416,000 kilometers (260,000 mi) from its surface.

Length of Day: about 10 Earth hours
Length of Year: 29 Earth years
Moons: 18 known
Surface: frozen gases
Distance Across: 120,000 kilometers (about 75,000 mi)

Uranus

Uranus

Sun

Fun Fact: Uranus rolls on its side as it orbits the sun.

Length of Day: 17 Earth hours
Length of Year: 84 Earth years
Moons: 18 known
Surface: made of frozen gases
Distance Across: 51,000 kilometers (about 32,000 mi)

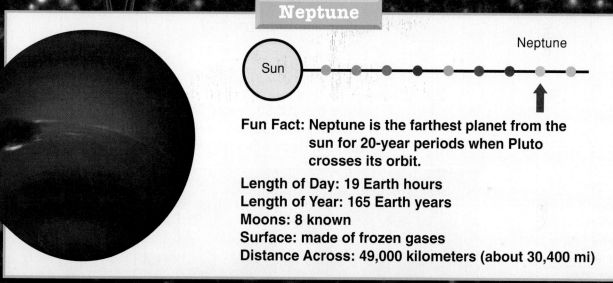

Neptune

Neptune

Sun

Fun Fact: Neptune is the farthest planet from the sun for 20-year periods when Pluto crosses its orbit.

Length of Day: 19 Earth hours
Length of Year: 165 Earth years
Moons: 8 known
Surface: made of frozen gases
Distance Across: 49,000 kilometers (about 30,400 mi)

Pluto

Pluto

Sun

Fun Fact: Pluto is made of ice. It has a moon almost as large as it is.

Length of Day: 6 Earth days
Length of Year: 248 Earth years
Moons: 1
Surface: made of frozen gases
Distance Across: 2300 kilometers (about 1,500 mi)

Other Bodies in the Solar System

The sun, the planets, and their moons are the largest objects in the solar system. But asteroids and comets, while smaller, are parts of the solar system, too.

An **asteroid** is a chunk of rock or metal that orbits the sun. There are thousands of asteroids in the asteroid belt between Mars and Jupiter.

A **comet** is a large ball of ice and dust that orbits the sun. The orbit of a comet is shaped like a large, flat oval. One part of a comet's orbit might come very close to the sun. But the other part can reach far past Pluto.

A comet can be seen only when it gets close to the sun. The heat from the sun melts a comet's ice to form glowing gases. The gases stream out in a long tail that looks like a bright streak in the sky. The tail can be millions of kilometers long.

✔ **What are asteroids and comets?**

Meteors are chunks of rock from space. Many come from the asteroid belt. Each day, hundreds of meteors enter Earth's atmosphere. Those that don't burn up hit the surface and are called meteorites. ▼

More than 20,000 asteroids are in the asteroid belt. Some are small. Others are hundreds of kilometers wide. ▼

Comets orbit the sun, too. Halley's comet can be seen from Earth every 76 years.

Summary

The solar system has nine planets that orbit the sun. Earth is one of those planets. Asteroids and comets are also parts of the solar system.

Review

1. What is a planet?
2. List three ways the inner planets are alike.
3. List three ways the outer planets are alike.
4. **Critical Thinking** How are asteroids and meteorites alike? How are they different?
5. **Test Prep** A comet is visible in the sky only when it is close to —

   A the sun

   B Earth

   C Mars

   D Pluto

LINKS

MATH LINK

Construct a Graph Make a bar graph showing the number of moons each planet has. How does the number of Earth's moons compare with the number of moons of other planets?

WRITING LINK

Narrative Writing—Story Pick a planet. Write a story for your teacher that tells what life would be like on that planet. Describe what it might be like to visit there. Share your story with your classmates.

HEALTH LINK

Sun Safety The sun's rays can harm the skin. That's why people use sunscreen. Sunscreens have an SPF number. Find out what *SPF* means. What SPF number sunscreen should you wear every day to protect you from the sun?

TECHNOLOGY LINK

Learn more about Mars by viewing *Mars Pathfinder Discovery* on the **Harcourt Science Newsroom Video**.

CNN
Turner
Le@rning

What Causes Earth's Seasons?

In this lesson, you can . . .

INVESTIGATE how Earth's tilt causes seasons.

LEARN ABOUT the seasons.

LINK to math, writing, art, and technology.

INVESTIGATE

How the Sun Strikes Earth

Activity Purpose Many places on Earth are hot in summer and cold in winter. In this investigation you will find out why. You will **compare** the way light rays strike a surface. Then you will **infer** how this affects Earth's temperatures.

Materials

- clear tape
- graph paper
- large book
- flashlight
- meterstick
- black marker
- wooden block
- red marker

Activity Procedure

1 Tape the graph paper to the book.

2 Hold the flashlight about 50 cm above the book. Shine the light straight down. The beam will make a circle on the paper. If the circle is bigger than the paper, bring the light closer.

◄ **The leaves of some trees turn red, orange, or gold in the fall.**

3 Have a partner use the black marker to draw around the light beam on the paper. (Picture A)

4 **Observe** the brightness of the light on the squares. **Record** your observations.

5 Keep the flashlight in the same position. Have a partner put the block under one end of the book and use the red marker to draw around the light on the paper. (Picture B)

6 **Observe** the brightness on the squares again. **Record** your observations.

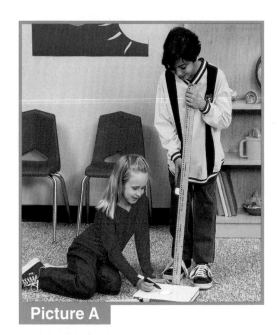
Picture A

Draw Conclusions

1. How many squares are inside the black line? How many squares are inside the red line?

2. Inside which line was the light brighter?

3. **Scientists at Work** Scientists **compare** things to find out how they are the same and how they are different. Compare the results of Steps 3 and 5 of the investigation. Do straight light rays or tilted light rays give stronger light? Suppose the paper is Earth's surface. The light is the sun. Which area would have warmer weather? Explain.

Picture B

Investigate Further **Form a hypothesis** about what will happen if the book is tilted even more. **Plan and conduct an experiment** to test your hypothesis.

Process Skill Tip

When you **compare**, you **observe** the properties of two or more things to see how they are alike and how they are different.

The Seasons

FIND OUT

- why there are seasons
- what causes day and night

VOCABULARY

rotation
axis
revolution

How Earth Moves in Space

You are sitting reading this book. It seems like you are still. But you're not. Earth is traveling through space at almost 107,800 kilometers (67,000 mi) per hour. You are moving with Earth. You are also flying around the solar system as Earth orbits the sun.

Earth moves in two ways. First, Earth spins like a top. This is called rotation. **Rotation** (roh•TAY•shuhn) is the spinning of an object on its axis. Earth's **axis** (AK•sis) is an imaginary line that goes through the North Pole and the South Pole. Earth rotates on its axis once every 24 hours. One rotation takes one day.

Earth also circles the sun. This is called revolution. A **revolution** (rev•uh•LOO•shuhn) is the movement of one object around another object. Earth makes one revolution around the sun every $365\frac{1}{4}$ days. One revolution takes one year.

Earth rotates on its axis as it revolves around the sun. ▶

Sun

Earth

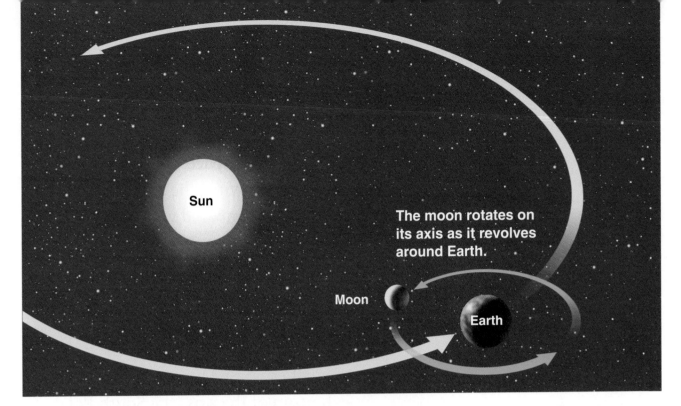

▲ Both Earth and the moon rotate. The Earth rotates
once a day. The moon rotates about once a month.

The moon also rotates and revolves. It rotates on its axis. It revolves around Earth. A day on the moon, or one rotation, is about 29 Earth days long. The moon takes this same amount of time to revolve around Earth.

Objects on Earth cast shadows. Shadows can help us observe Earth's rotation. As Earth rotates, the sun's position seems to change in the sky. But it is really the Earth that is moving.

In the morning the sun seems low in the sky. Objects cast long shadows. As the Earth rotates, the sun seems to move higher in the sky. Shadows get shorter. At noon, the sun is overhead. Objects cast short shadows—or no shadows at all. As Earth continues to rotate, the sun looks lower in the sky again. Shadows get longer until the sun sets.

✔ **What is rotation?**

Shadows are short at noon. They're longer at
2:00 P.M. because the sun is lower in the sky. ▼

What Causes Seasons

In most places on Earth, summer and winter are different. Summer is hot. There are many hours of daylight. Sunlight is strong. Winter is cold. The hours of daylight are shorter. Sunlight is weaker. Summer and winter are two seasons.

Earth has seasons because its axis is tilted. This means Earth is tipped to one side, like the book in the investigation was tilted. The tilt changes the way sunlight hits Earth at different times of the year. Sometimes the sun's rays are almost straight when they hit Earth's surface. At other times the sun's rays are slanted. This changes the amount of light and heat the surface gets.

Earth's axis is always pointing the same way in space. But because Earth is moving, the axis changes position compared with the position of the sun.

For part of the year the top of the axis (the North Pole) points in the direction of the sun. When Earth is in this position, it is summer in the northern half. During that time the bottom of the axis (the South Pole) points away from the sun. When Earth is in this position, it is winter in the southern half.

Earth has a curved surface. Some sunlight hits the surface straight on. Some sunlight hits the surface on a slant. ▼

Seasons on Earth's Northern Half

Spring

Winter

Summer

Fall

Whichever end of Earth's axis points in the direction of the sun, the sun shines more directly on that part of Earth. This direct sunlight heats the ground and the air. It is summer.

Earth is always moving around the sun. Three months after summer starts, the top of the axis is not pointing in the direction of the sun anymore. Neither is the bottom of the axis. Days and nights are of equal length. Both the top half and the bottom half of the Earth get the same amount of light. Temperatures are cooler than in summer and warmer than in winter. It is fall in the northern half.

Three months later the northern half of the Earth points away from the sun. The sun shines less directly on its surface. Rays are slanted. Slanted rays cover a larger area, so the ground and the air are heated less. This makes the northern half of the Earth colder. It is winter.

Another three months pass. Again neither axis points in the direction of the sun. Days and nights are almost equal in length. Now it is spring. A full year has passed. Then the cycle starts again with summer.

Seasons in the northern and southern halves of Earth are reversed. When the northern half of Earth has spring, the southern half has fall. When the northern half has winter, the southern half has summer. Australia is on the southern half of Earth. So in Australia December is in the middle of summer. July is in the middle of winter.

✔ **Why are there seasons?**

What Causes Day and Night

It's 4:00 P.M. Your family decides to call a friend in Asia. When your dad makes the call, he wakes up your Asian friend. He was sleeping. It's the middle of the night there.

As you move from place to place on Earth, time changes. When you are eating dinner, people on the other side of the world might be having breakfast.

▲ When it is day in Chicago, Illinois, . . .

. . . it is night in Hong Kong, China. Hong Kong is on the other side of Earth from Chicago. ▼

Sunlight always shines on half of Earth. The other half is in darkness. ▼

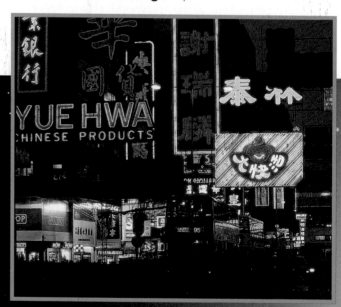

Sun

D72

Earth's rotation causes this difference in time. At any one time, half of Earth is in sunlight. The other half is in darkness. The half in sunlight has day. The half in darkness has night.

✔ **How much of Earth's surface is in sunlight at one time?**

Summary

Earth rotates on its axis and revolves around the sun. Earth has seasons because its axis is tilted. The sun heats Earth's surface differently at different times of the year. Night and day happen as Earth rotates. Places on Earth's surface move from sunlight into darkness and back.

Review

1. What is a revolution?
2. When it is winter in the northern half of Earth, what season is it in the southern half?
3. Why are many places warmer in summer than in winter?
4. **Critical Thinking** How would day and night be different if Earth did not rotate?
5. **Test Prep** The tilt of Earth's axis causes —

   A rotation

   B day and night

   C seasons

   D sunlight

How Do the Moon and Earth Interact?

In this lesson, you can . . .

 INVESTIGATE the phases of the moon.

 LEARN ABOUT why the moon seems to change.

 LINK to math, writing, literature, and technology.

INVESTIGATE

The Moon's Phases

Activity Purpose If you look at the moon each night, you will see that its shape seems to change. These shapes are called *phases*. In this investigation you will **observe** how a light shining on a ball looks different as you move around the ball.

Materials

- lamp with no shade
- softball

Activity Procedure

1 Work with a partner. Turn on the lamp. Your teacher will darken the room.

2 Have Person 1 hold the ball and stand with his or her back to the lighted bulb. Hold the ball as shown. Continue holding the ball this way until the end of the procedure. (Picture A)

◀ You see the moon rise from Earth. But if you were on the moon, you would see Earth rise!

3 Have Person 2 stand in position 1 in Picture A. **Observe** the ball. Make a drawing of the ball's lighted side.

4 Person 2 now moves to position 2. Turn toward the ball. Make a drawing of the lighted part of the ball.

5 Have Person 2 move to position 3. Make a drawing of the lighted part of the ball.

Picture A

6 Person 2 again moves. This time to position 4. Turn toward the ball. Make a drawing of the lighted part of the ball.

7 Switch roles and repeat the procedure so Person 1 can observe the patterns of light on the ball.

Draw Conclusions

1. What part of the ball was lighted at each position?

2. The ball represents the moon. What does the light bulb represent? What represents a person viewing the moon from Earth?

3. **Scientists at Work** Scientists **use models** to make **inferences** to explain how things work. If the ball represents the moon, what can you infer that the different parts of the lighted ball represent?

Process Skill Tip

When you **observe** something, you use your senses to get information about it. When you **infer**, you use your observations to form an opinion.

How the Moon and Earth Interact

FIND OUT

• what the moon's phases are

• what causes eclipses

VOCABULARY

phase
lunar eclipse
solar eclipse

The Phases of the Moon

If you watch the moon for a month, its shape seems to change. Sometimes it looks like a big round ball. At other times you see a thin sliver. Why do these changes happen?

The half of the moon that faces the sun is always lighted. As the moon moves around Earth, different amounts of its lighted and dark sides face Earth. The moon's phase depends on the part of the lighted half you can see. **Phases** are the different shapes the moon seems to have in the sky.

It takes about one month for the moon to revolve around Earth. It takes the same amount of time for the moon to rotate. This causes the same side of the moon to always face Earth. ▶

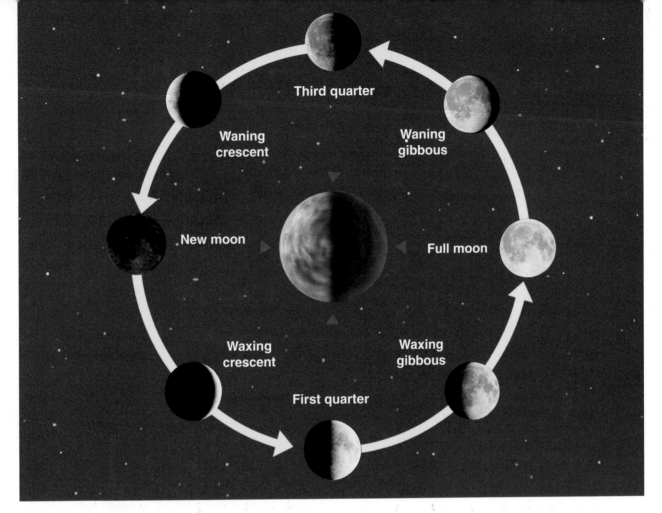

Third quarter

Waning crescent

Waning gibbous

New moon

Full moon

Waxing crescent

Waxing gibbous

First quarter

▲ The photographs show what the moon looks like from Earth.

The moon goes through all of its phases every $29\frac{1}{2}$ days. During the phase called the new moon, the lighted half faces away from Earth. You can't see the moon at all. After the new moon, the moon seems to get bigger.

As the moon continues in its orbit around Earth, one lighted edge comes into view. This is a crescent moon. About one week after the new moon, half of the moon's lighted face can be seen. This is the first quarter. The next phase is the gibbous moon.

It shows a little less than $\frac{3}{4}$ of the moon's lighted side.

About two weeks after the new moon, you see the full moon. At full moon you can see the whole face of the moon. The moon has completed half of its orbit around Earth.

After the full moon, the phases reverse. The lighted part you see gets smaller. First you see the gibbous moon again. Then you see the third quarter. The last phase is another crescent moon.

✔ **What are the moon's phases?**

Eclipses of the Moon

Everything the sun shines on casts a shadow. Earth and the moon cast shadows, too. Most of the time these shadows fall on empty space. But sometimes these shadows can be seen from Earth's surface.

You know the moon revolves around Earth. At times the Earth is between the sun and moon. If the sun, Earth, and moon are in a straight line, Earth blocks some of the sun's light from falling on the moon. Although you should see a full moon, the moon gets dark for a time. This is called a lunar eclipse. A **lunar eclipse** happens when Earth's shadow falls on the moon.

✔ **What causes a lunar eclipse?**

When the sun shines on you, you cast a shadow. ▶

Sun

A total lunar eclipse causes all of the moon's face to look dark red. Total lunar eclipses do not happen as often as partial eclipses. This is because the sun, the Earth, and the moon need to be in a straight line for Earth's shadow to completely cover the moon.

A partial lunar eclipse blocks only part of the sun's light. Watching partial eclipses helped early scientists figure out that Earth is round. Why would eclipses help them see that Earth is round? ▼

The sun shines on objects in space. They cast shadows, too. Sometimes Earth's shadow falls on the moon. This causes a lunar eclipse. ▼

Earth

Moon

Eclipses of the Sun

A shadow slowly covers the sun. The whole sky turns dark in the middle of the day. Ancient peoples thought this was the end of the world. Today we know it's a solar eclipse. A **solar eclipse** happens when the moon's shadow falls on Earth. This happens when the moon moves between the Earth and the sun.

During a total solar eclipse, the moon blocks out the sun. Only a halo of sunlight remains around the moon. The areas where a total eclipse can be seen is small. Outside this area only part of the sun is covered.

✔ **What causes a solar eclipse?**

A total solar eclipse happens when the moon moves between Earth and the sun. These photos show what the sun looks like as a total solar eclipse takes place. Total solar eclipses are rare. ▶

People in the small shadow area see the total eclipse. Those outside the shadow see a partial eclipse. ▼

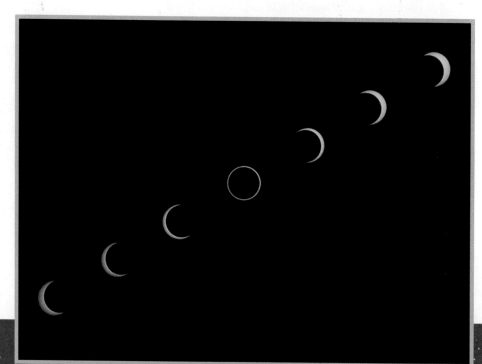

Sun

Summary

Phases are the different shapes the moon seems to have in the sky. The moon goes through its phases every $29\frac{1}{2}$ days. Eclipses happen when one object in space moves into the shadow of another. There are lunar eclipses and solar eclipses.

Review

1. Describe a new moon.
2. Compare and contrast a lunar and a solar eclipse.
3. What do you see from Earth during a total solar eclipse?
4. **Critical Thinking** Tell what phase the moon is in during a lunar eclipse. Explain your answer.
5. **Test Prep** Which of these is **NOT** a phase of the moon?

   A new   C crescent
   B full   D eclipse

Moon   Earth

 # LINKS

 MATH LINK

Estimate Elapsed Time
Sketch the shape of the moon each night for one month. Start with the new moon. How much time does it take for all eight phases to take place? Predict the date of the next new moon.

 WRITING LINK

Narrative Writing—Personal Story When the sun got dark in ancient times, people thought the sun was gone. Suppose that you lived then. You are seeing a solar eclipse. Write a story for a younger child to explain what you think is happening.

 LITERATURE LINK

Find Out More Find out more about the sun, the moon, or eclipses by reading *The Sun and the Moon* by Patrick Moore.

 TECHNOLOGY LINK

Learn more about interactions in space by investigating *Blast Off into Orbit* on **Harcourt Science Explorations CD-ROM.**

Earth from Space

Today, people know Earth is round. But thousands of years ago, many people thought Earth was flat. Many believed that ships that sailed over the horizon had "fallen off" Earth. In time, scientists hypothesized that Earth is shaped like a big, round ball, or sphere. These ideas were shown to be correct when explorers returned home after trips around the world. Still, it wasn't until the late 1950s that space exploration made possible pictures of Earth from space.

Ideas About Earth

4000 B.C.
Egyptians believe that Earth is a disk, a flat layer of ground with water below it and sky above it.

| 4000 B.C. | 600 B.C. | B.C./A.D. | 1522 |

6th century B.C.
Pythagoras, a Greek mathematician and philosopher, believes that Earth is a sphere.

September 1522
Juan Sebastián de Elcano returns a ship to Spain, completing the first successful trip around Earth.

Views of Earth

Technology has allowed scientists to see Earth from space. By studying Earth as a whole, scientists have learned much about its shape, size, and atmosphere. They've also learned about its position in the solar system compared to the moon, the sun, and other planets.

One of the first space photos of Earth was taken by a camera on a weather satellite in 1960. Six years later a much clearer photograph of Earth was taken from the spacecraft *Lunar Orbiter 1*. Like the weather satellite before it, *Lunar Orbiter 1* did not have astronauts on board. Once astronauts began traveling into space, they could see Earth's shape with their own eyes.

What Is Earthrise?

Earthrise is similar to a moonrise, except that it is seen from the moon. In an Earthrise, Earth appears to rise above the moon's horizon. Earthrise can be seen from spacecraft orbiting the moon. Many spacecraft, such as the one used in the *Apollo 10* mission in 1969, have taken photographs of Earthrise.

EarthKAM

Scientists use many instruments to view Earth from space. Images of Earth are taken from space probes and weather satellites. The National Aeronautics and Space Administration (NASA) uses a project called EarthKAM, in which photos are taken from the space shuttles. These photographs show many different Earth features, such as volcanoes, fires, hurricanes, mountain ranges, and even cities.

THINK ABOUT IT

- Even though people already knew that Earth is round, why do you think they would want to view it from space?

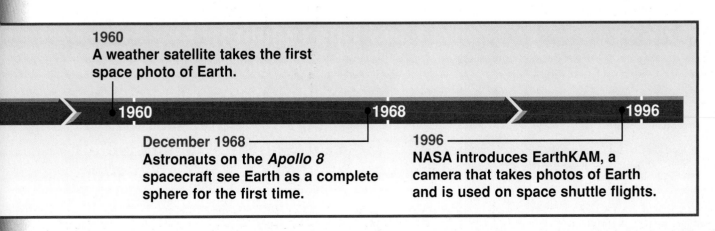

1960
A weather satellite takes the first space photo of Earth.

1960   1968   1996

December 1968 —
Astronauts on the *Apollo 8* spacecraft see Earth as a complete sphere for the first time.

1996 —
NASA introduces EarthKAM, a camera that takes photos of Earth and is used on space shuttle flights.

Mae Jemison
ASTRONAUT, PHYSICIAN, BIOMEDICAL ENGINEER

Mae Jemison was the first African-American woman in space. She was a mission specialist on the 1992 *Endeavour* space shuttle flight. Before the flight, she helped check the shuttle, its computer software, and the tiles that protect the ship from burning up when returning to Earth.

For Jemison, becoming an astronaut was a childhood dream come true. She began her career by going to medical school. While a student, she traveled to Thailand, Cuba, and Kenya to offer medical help. She joined the Peace Corps after graduating from medical school. She spent two years in West Africa.

Jemison returned to the United States and became a doctor in Los Angeles. She applied to the National Aeronautics and Space Administration (NASA) to be an astronaut. She was not accepted the first time she applied. She applied again and was accepted. After five years of training and working at NASA, she was selected for the *Endeavour* mission. All her hard work had paid off!

THINK ABOUT IT

1. How could living in a foreign country help a person get ready for a trip in outer space?

2. How can studying in school help a person make his or her dreams come true?

EARTH MODEL

Why do we have seasons?

Materials

- Styrofoam ball
- flashlight
- two pencils

Procedure

❶ Stick a pencil through the middle of the ball. This represents Earth's axis.

❷ With the other pencil, draw a line around the middle of the ball. This is

the equator. Put the Earth on a table. The axis should lean to the right.

❸ Shine the flashlight on the left side of the Earth. The light represents the sun. Place the light about 13 cm away. Observe where the light rays hit the ball.

❹ Shine the light on the right side of the Earth. Where do the light rays hit the ball? Compare how the light hits the ball each time.

Draw Conclusions

How does this explain seasons in the northern half of the Earth?

A LOOK AT ROTATION

How does day become night?

Materials

- a small self-stick note
- spinning Earth globe
- flashlight

Procedure

❶ Write where you live on the self-stick note. Place the note on your state on the globe.

❷ Shine the flashlight on the globe. Your teacher will then turn off the lights.

❸ Slowly spin the globe counterclockwise.

Draw Conclusions

What happens to the place where you put your note? What does this represent?

D85

Vocabulary Review

Use the terms below to complete the sentences 1 through 11. The page numbers in ( ) tell you where to look in the chapter if you need help.

solar system (D58)   **axis** (D68)
orbit (D58)   **revolution** (D68)
planet (D58)   **phases** (D76)
asteroid (D64)   **lunar eclipse** (D78)
comet (D64)   **solar eclipse** (D80)
rotation (D68)

1. A large body of rock or gas that orbits the sun is a ____.

2. An ____ is a chunk of rock or metal that orbits the sun.

3. When the moon's shadow falls on Earth we see a ____.

4. The spinning of an object on its axis is called ____.

5. A ____ is a large ball of ice and dust that orbits the sun.

6. The moon has ____ that make it seem to change shape.

7. Earth has an imaginary line, or ____, that runs through the North Pole and the South Pole.

8. The movement of one object around another object is called ____.

9. The ____ is made up of the sun and all the objects that orbit around it.

10. An ____ is the path of an object as it moves around another object in space.

11. When Earth's shadow falls on the moon, we see a ____.

Connect Concepts

The motions of the Earth and the moon cause certain things to happen. Choose a term below to fill in the chart and complete each sentence.

day and night   **seasons**
lunar eclipses   **solar eclipses**
phases   **years**

Motions of the Earth and the Moon	
Earth's tilt	causes 12. ____.
Earth's rotation	causes 13. ____.
Earth's revolution	causes 14. ____.
Earth's shadow	causes 15. ____.
The moon's shadow	causes 16. ____.
The moon's movement	causes 17. ____.

Check Understanding

Write the letter of the best choice.

18. The outer planets are —
    A like Earth
    B Mars and Jupiter
    C mostly larger than Earth
    D made of rock

19. Two revolutions of Earth take —
    F two days   H two months
    G two weeks   J two years

20. When the moon looks like a lighted circle in the sky, it is in the ___ phase.
    A full moon
    B new moon
    C crescent moon
    D gibbous moon

Critical Thinking

21. In what ways is Pluto like an inner planet?

22. How would Earth be different if its axis were not tilted?

Process Skills Review

23. You can use distance from the sun to classify planets. Some are inner planets. Some are outer planets. **Classify** the inner planets as those *with moons* and those *without moons.*

24. **Compare** the revolutions of the moon and Earth. How are they alike? How are they different?

25. It is always cold at the North Pole. What can you **infer** about the way the sun's rays hit the North Pole?

Performance Assessment

Ordering Planets

Use the table to put the planets in order from largest to smallest based on their mass. Record your results. Then sort the planets into two groups, those with rings and those without rings. Compare your lists. What conclusions can you draw by organizing this data?

Planet	Mass of Planet (The mass of Mercury = 1.)	Planet Has Rings?
Earth	17	no
Jupiter	5300	yes
Mars	2	no
Mercury	1	no
Neptune	288	yes
Pluto	$\frac{1}{5}$	no
Saturn	1587	yes
Uranus	243	yes
Venus	14	no

UNIT D EXPEDITIONS

There are many places where you can observe cycles on the Earth and in space. You can learn how weather and our solar system are a part of these cycles by visiting the places below.

WHNT TV, Weather

WHAT A television broadcast station weather room

WHERE Huntsville, Alabama

WHAT CAN YOU DO THERE? Tour the building, find out about weather, and learn about Dan's Wild Wild Weather Page.

Rose Center for Earth and Space

WHAT A museum and planetarium at the American Museum of Natural History

WHERE New York, New York

WHAT CAN YOU DO THERE? Explore the many exhibits and visit the new Hayden Planetarium.

GO ONLINE Plan Your Own Expeditions

If you can't visit WHNT TV, Weather or the Rose Center for Earth and Space, visit a weather station or space museum near you. Or log on to The Learning Site at **www.harcourtschool.com** to visit these science sites.

Investigating Matter

UNIT E — PHYSICAL SCIENCE

Investigating Matter

UNIT EXPERIMENT

Freezing Point of Water

Pure water freezes at 0°C (32°F). While you study this unit, you can conduct a long-term experiment to find out how other substances affect the freezing point of water. Here are some questions to think about. Can the freezing point of water be lowered by adding something to water? Can the freezing point of water be raised by adding some other substance to water? Plan and conduct an experiment to find answers to these or other questions you may have about the freezing point of water. See pages x–xii for help in designing your experiment.

Properties of Matter

Every day we look at, listen to, feel, smell, and taste different kinds of matter. We even breathe it! Because matter comes in so many shapes and sizes, people have come up with many ways to measure it.

Vocabulary Preview

matter
physical property
solid
liquid
gas
atom
evaporation
volume
mass

Fast Fact

People use lasers and satellites to measure really big objects. Mt. Everest in the Himalayas is the tallest mountain in the world. At 8848 meters (29,028 ft), it is as tall as a building with 2,950 stories!

Our senses help us observe and describe matter. Dogs are famous for their sense of smell. Bloodhounds can use their sense of smell to follow a trail more than 100 miles long and 100 hours old.

Type of Animal	Best Smeller
Insects	Silkworm moths
Fish	Sharks
Mammals	Elephants
Amphibians	Newts
Birds	Petrels and albatrosses
Reptiles	Snakes and lizards

LESSON 1

What Are Physical Properties of Matter?

In this lesson, you can . . .

INVESTIGATE kinds of matter.

LEARN ABOUT the properties of different objects.

LINK to math, writing, art, and technology.

Physical Properties

Activity Purpose Can you pour paper? Can you fold milk? Why not? Different objects have different properties. In this investigation you will **observe** different properties of matter.

Materials

- penny
- nickel
- marble
- key
- cotton balls
- piece of peppermint candy
- index card
- book
- uncooked macaroni
- twist tie
- peppercorns

Activity Procedure

1 Copy the charts shown.

2 Look at the objects you have been given. Notice whether they look shiny or dull. Notice how many colors each one has. **Record** your **observations.**

◄ **This picnic basket is made of straw. The basket can hold many other things that are made of matter.**

How It Looks				How It Feels			
Object	Color	Dull	Shiny	Hard	Soft	Rough	Smooth

How It Smells				How It Sounds			
Object	Sweet	Sharp	No Smell	Loud	Soft	Makes a Ping	No Sound

3. Touch the objects. Feel whether the objects are hard or soft. Feel whether they are rough or smooth. **Record** your **observations.** (Picture A)

4. Next, tap each object lightly with your fingernail. What kind of sound does it make? **Record** your **observations.**

5. Smell each object. **Record** your **observations.**

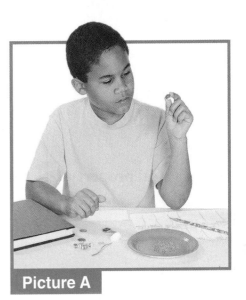
Picture A

Draw Conclusions

1. Which objects are hard and rough? Which are hard and smooth? Which are soft and rough? Which are soft and smooth?

2. **Compare** your chart with the chart of another group. Are any objects in different columns? Why?

3. **Scientists at Work** Scientists learn about the world by **observing** with their five senses. Which of the five senses did you *not* use in the investigation?

Investigate Further **Form a hypothesis** about how physical properties change with the size of the sample. **Plan and conduct an experiment** to test your hypothesis.

Process Skill Tip

Scientists study the world closely and **record** what they sense. This is called **observing.** Observing is one way scientists answer questions about matter.

Physical Properties of Matter

FIND OUT

• how to observe matter

• about three states of matter

VOCABULARY

matter
physical property
solid
liquid
gas

Matter

Look around your classroom. You may see desks, books, other students, and the teacher. What else do you see? Everything you see takes up space. Your classroom must have enough space to hold you and all the other things that are in it. Everything in the classroom is matter. **Matter** is anything that takes up space.

Look at your desk. Can you pick it up with one arm? It is probably too heavy. Can you bend it? It is probably too stiff. You can use many different words to describe your desk. Each word you use to describe an object names a physical property of the object. A **physical property** (FIZ•ih•kuhl PRAHP•er•tee) is anything you can observe about an object by using your senses.

✔ **What is matter?**

◀ The girl, the raincoat, and the rain are matter. Even the air is matter. Everything in this picture is matter.

What Matter Looks Like

You can observe some physical properties of matter with your sense of sight. In the investigation you observed some things that are dull and some things that are shiny. You also looked at the colors of the objects.

There are some things, such as most glass windows, that you can see through. Some of these things don't have any color. Then you can see the colors of the things on the other side. But some things you can see through, such as tinted windows, do have color. Then you can't tell the colors of things on the other side.

Another physical property you can see is size. Have you ever seen a group of basketball players? They don't seem tall by themselves. But when a player is standing next to you, you can see that the player is tall. Size is easiest to see when you can compare one object to another.

A property you cannot see is temperature. But you can see the effects of temperature. You can

▲ The glass has no color, so when you look through it, you can see that the liquid in it is pink. You can tell the drink is cold because it has ice in it. The steam rising from the cup of tea lets you infer that it is hot.

infer that something is hot if you see steam coming from it. You can guess that something is cold if you see it with ice or snow.

✔ **What properties of matter can you learn about with your sense of sight?**

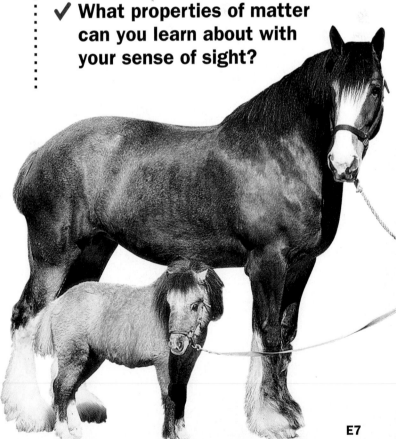

One of these horses is much larger than the other one. Size is a physical property of matter. ▶

What Matter Feels Like

Many people wear shirts under wool sweaters because wool sweaters feel scratchy. You can learn about some physical properties of matter by using your sense of touch.

Sandpaper feels rough, but sand feels smooth. The bark on a tree and gravel both feel rough. *Smooth* can describe objects as different as a mirror and a desk top.

You can feel some things that you can't see. You can feel the push of the wind. You can also feel whether something is hot or cold.

Different parts of the same object may feel different. A wool jacket feels rough, but the buttons may feel smooth. A cat's fur is soft, but its claws are sharp.

✔ **What are some words you can use to describe how matter feels?**

◄ **You can't see air, but you can see how the air moves this windsock.**

◄ **Snow feels cold and wet. Temperature and wetness are both physical properties of matter.**

Different parts of these slippers feel different. The fur is soft, but the soles feel hard and smooth. ▼

What Matter Tastes and Smells Like

People have to be careful about tasting things. Some things can make you ill, even if you taste just a small piece of them. But if you are careful, you can learn by tasting things. Your tongue can taste things that are sweet, sour, salty, and bitter.

You enjoy your favorite foods partly because of their smell. You may begin to feel hungry when good smells come from the kitchen.

Not all smells are pleasant. But people can get used to smells so they don't notice them anymore. Barnyards have strong smells. A visitor from the city might notice them right away. A farmer who works every day in a barn may not notice the strong smells at all. But smell comes from matter, and it is a physical property of matter.

✔ **What can we learn from our senses of taste and smell?**

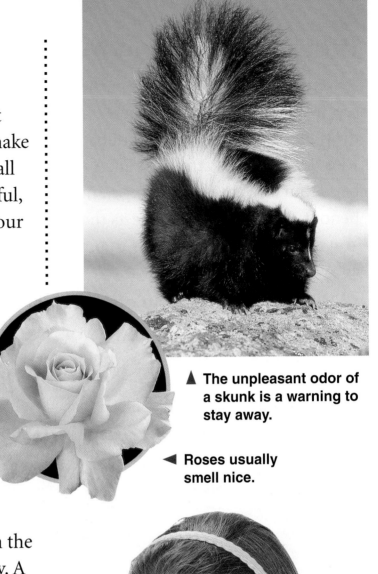

▲ **The unpleasant odor of a skunk is a warning to stay away.**

◀ **Roses usually smell nice.**

Humans can taste many foods but don't always like what they taste. ▶

E9

Other Properties of Matter

Matter has many other properties that you can see, hear, and feel. Many objects break if you drop them. Others bounce. Rubber bands stretch. Kite string doesn't stretch at all. A paper clip can bend, but a twig will snap in two if you try to bend it. Magnets attract objects that contain iron. You can feel the force it takes to pull the object away from the magnet.

✔ **What are some of the other properties of matter?**

▲ Magnets attract objects that contain iron.

Putty, clay, and this gel are things that can bend. ▼

▲ Many objects break easily if you drop them.

Three States of Matter

Matter has different forms, called states. The three states of matter we can observe are solids, liquids, and gases.

Solids A **solid** takes up a specific amount of space and has a definite shape. A solid does not lose its shape. For example, a book keeps its shape when it is on a shelf or in your hands. A solid also has a volume that stays the same. That means a solid object takes up the same amount of space all the time.

▲ This sculpture of a fish is made of ice. Ice is a solid. As long as the sculpture stays frozen, it will keep its shape. If the ice warms up, it will melt and become a liquid. Then the sculpture will lose its shape.

▲ Solid

Liquid

▲ Gas

Liquids A **liquid** has a volume that stays the same, but it can change its shape. A liquid takes the shape of any container it is put into. But one cup of water always takes up one cup of space, in any container.

One cup of water might not look like very much in a short, wide glass. But in a tall, skinny glass, one cup of water can look like a lot. No matter what it looks like, it is the same volume of water in both glasses.

Gases You may know that a gas takes the shape of the container it is in. A **gas** does not have a definite shape or a definite volume. It takes up all the space in its container. The air in your classroom is a gas. It takes the shape of your classroom. It also takes up all the space inside the classroom. If you put the same amount of air into a larger classroom, the air would spread out to take up all the space in that room.

✔ **What are the three states of matter we can observe?**

▲ The shape of the water changes as it falls. When it hits the stream, the banks help it hold a shape.

We breathe the mixture of gases in the atmosphere. We call it air. ▼

Summary

Matter is anything that takes up space. Matter has many physical properties that you can observe using your five senses. You can feel matter, taste matter, see matter, hear matter, and smell matter. Matter has different states. The three states we can observe are solids, liquids, and gases.

Review

1. What is matter?
2. What is a physical property?
3. How can we learn about matter?
4. **Critical Thinking** Think of last night's dinner. What properties of matter did you observe?
5. **Test Prep** Which set of words all name physical properties of matter?
   A solids, liquids, diamonds
   B ice, water, steam
   C hard, soft, sticky
   D rocks, rubies, emeralds

LINKS

MATH LINK

Compare Capacity How many cups of matter does it take to fill a liter container? A gallon container?

WRITING LINK

Narrative Writing—Story Helium is a gas that is lighter than air. When you fill a balloon with helium, the balloon rises. Write a story for your classmates about the travels of a helium balloon that floats away.

ART LINK

Statues in Stone Sculptors choose their stone carefully. Different kinds of stone have different physical properties that can make it easier or harder to work with. Investigate the stone statues in your city or state. Find out what kind of stone they are made from.

TECHNOLOGY LINK

To learn more about properties of matter, watch *Fun With Matter* on the **Harcourt Science Newsroom Video.**

CNN
Turner
Le@rning

What Are Solids, Liquids, and Gases?

In this lesson, you can . . .

 INVESTIGATE three states of matter.

 LEARN ABOUT the differences between the three states of matter.

 LINK to math, writing, language arts, and technology.

INVESTIGATE

One Way Matter Can Change

Activity Purpose Matter can change from one state to another. Think about what happens when you make ice cubes. You put water in a freezer, and it turns into ice. What might happen to an ice cube that is left out in a warm room? Investigate to see if your idea is correct.

Materials

- clear plastic cup
- paper towel
- 2 ice cubes
- marker

Activity Procedure

1 Place the plastic cup on the paper towel. Put the ice cubes in the cup. (Picture A)

◄ Three states of matter surround us everywhere. Liquid water is in the ocean and in fog. The lighthouse is a solid. We breathe air, which is a gas.

2 **Form a hypothesis** about what will happen to the ice cubes after 45 minutes.

3 **Observe** what's in the cup after 45 minutes. **Record** what you see. Was your hypothesis correct?

4 Mark the outside of the cup to show how high the water is. **Form another hypothesis** about what will happen to the water if you leave it out all night. Then leave the cup sitting out.

Picture A

5 **Observe** the cup the next morning. **Record** what you see.

Draw Conclusions

1. What do you think caused the ice to change?

2. What do you think happened to the water when you left it out all night?

3. **Scientists at Work** Scientists **form hypotheses** based on things they have **observed** before. What had you observed before that helped you make your predictions?

Investigate Further **Plan and conduct an experiment** to test this **hypothesis:** Water freezes faster than orange juice.

Process Skill Tip

When you **hypothesize,** you explain observations you have made in the past. A hypothesis can be used to make predictions that you can test.

Solids, Liquids, and Gases

FIND OUT

- what matter is made of
- how matter changes

VOCABULARY

atom
evaporation

Atoms

A puzzle has many pieces that fit together to form a picture. If you look closely, you can see each piece. If you look even more closely, you can see the tiny dots of color on each piece. All matter is like the puzzle. The more closely you look, the smaller the pieces you can see.

Some pieces of matter are so small that you can see them only by using special tools. Some pieces are so small that you cannot see them at all. But scientists can observe the effects of what these pieces of matter do. These pieces are called atoms. **Atoms** are the basic building blocks of matter.

✔ **What are atoms?**

◀ From far away, you can see the carved figure of a woman sitting down.

◀ When you move closer, you can see the colors and roughness of the stone.

◀ If you use a microscope, you can see some of the tiny pieces that make up the stone.

How Particles Are Connected

The particles in matter are arranged differently in each state of matter. But in all the ways they are arranged, the particles move.

▲ In a gas, such as this iodine gas, the particles are not connected to each other and are not close to each other. Each particle moves in a straight line until something stops it. Then it bounces. It moves off in another straight line until something else stops it.

▲ In a liquid the particles are more loosely arranged than in a solid. This allows the particles to slide past each other.

▲ A solid is hard because its particles do not move very much.

How Matter Changes States

Adding heat or taking heat away causes matter to change states. This is because adding heat makes the particles in matter move faster. Taking away heat, or cooling, makes the particles slow down.

In the investigation the warm air in the classroom added enough heat to the ice to change it to liquid water. The heat caused the particles in the ice to move faster. As the particles moved faster, the connections between them became looser. In time, the connections got so loose that the particles could slide past each other. At that point, the solid ice became liquid water.

With still more heat, the particles broke apart from each other completely. The liquid became a gas. The process by which a liquid becomes a gas is called **evaporation** (ee•vap•uh•RAY•shuhn).

If you take heat away from liquid water, the opposite happens. The particles slow down and solid ice forms.

✔ **What causes matter to change state?**

Hot lava, or liquid rock, comes from this volcano. When the lava hits water, the heat in the lava causes some of the water to turn to steam. Then the lava cools and changes into solid rock. ▼

Summary

Atoms are small particles that make up matter. In solids atoms fit tightly together and do not move very much. In liquids, they slide past each other. The atoms in gases are far apart and are not connected. They keep moving until something stops them. Adding or taking away heat can cause matter to change states.

Review

1. What are the building blocks of matter?
2. In which state of matter are the particles most tightly connected?
3. Why does gas **NOT** have a definite shape?
4. **Critical Thinking** When you boil water, what makes the liquid water turn into a gas?
5. **Test Prep** Which set of words names three states of matter?
   A solid, gas, water
   B solid, liquid, gas
   C hard, soft, smooth
   D salty, sweet, sour

LINKS

MATH LINK

Measure Temperature
People often need to know the temperature of what they cook. Find out the names of two kinds of kitchen thermometers and what each kind is used for.

WRITING LINK

Informative Writing— Description Write a description of a lake or pond for a younger child. Tell what it is like in each season. Be sure to describe what happens to the water in each season.

LANGUAGE ARTS LINK

Parts of Speech Find out what parts of speech the words *solid, liquid,* and *gas* are. Use each word in a sentence.

TECHNOLOGY LINK

Learn more about how matter changes state by investigating *Solids, Liquids, and Gases* on **Harcourt Science Explorations CD-ROM.**

LESSON 3

How Can Matter Be Measured?

In this lesson, you can . . .

INVESTIGATE the mass and volume of objects.

LEARN ABOUT ways to measure mass and volume.

LINK to math, writing, language arts, and technology.

Measuring Mass and Volume

Activity Purpose
If you pick up a C-cell battery and a D-cell battery, which feels heavier? In this investigation you will find out the difference in mass between the two batteries. You will also **measure** the amount of space a liquid takes up.

Materials

- balance
- 3 C-cell batteries
- 3 D-cell batteries
- clear plastic cup
- marker
- water
- masking tape
- 3 clear containers of different sizes

Activity Procedure

Part A

1. Put a C-cell in the pan on the left side of the balance. Put a D-cell in the pan on the right side. **Record** which battery is heavier. (Picture A)

◄ Tools have been invented for measuring all sorts of things. Here an elephant is being weighed.

E20

2 Add C-cells to the left side and D-cells to the right side until the pans are balanced. You may need to use some of the small masses from the balance to make the cells balance perfectly. **Record** the number of C-cells and D-cells you use.

Part B

3 Fill the cup half-full with water. Use a piece of tape to mark how high the water is in the cup. **Predict** how high the water will be in each container if you pour the water into it. Mark each prediction with a piece of tape. Write *P* (for *Prediction*) on the tape.

4 Pour the water into the next container. (Picture B) Mark the height of the water with a piece of tape. Write *A* (for *Actual*) on the tape.

5 Repeat Step 4 for each of the other containers.

Picture A

Picture B

Draw Conclusions

1. **Compare** the numbers of C-cells and D-cells it took to balance the pans. **Draw a conclusion** from these numbers about the masses of the batteries.

2. Describe the height of the water in each container. Why did the same amount of water look different in the different containers?

3. **Scientists at Work** Scientists **measure** matter by using tools that are marked with standard amounts. What was the standard amount you used in this activity to measure the water?

Process Skill Tip

Using tools to **measure** allows scientists to study and **compare** different pieces of matter.

Measuring Matter

FIND OUT

- how to measure matter
- how to use tools to measure matter

VOCABULARY

volume

mass

Measuring Volume

Suppose you fill a glass all the way to the top with orange juice. Then you try to put ice cubes into it. The orange juice will spill out over the top of the glass. The orange juice takes up space, and the ice cubes take up space. If you want to add ice cubes to the drink, you have to leave enough space for them.

All matter takes up space. The amount of space matter takes up is called its **volume** (VAHL•yoom). Scientists measure volume by using tools. The volume of a liquid can be measured by using a measuring cup.

✔ **What is volume?**

The same volume of liquid looks different in different containers. A measuring cup will show the volume in a standard unit you can understand.

Like liquids, solids have volume. Since a solid holds its shape, you cannot measure its volume easily in a measuring cup. A rock egg, a rock, or a marble will not take the shape of the cup. ▶

◀ You can measure the volume of the blue rock egg. Pour some water into a measuring device. Record the level of the water. Gently place the egg in the water. Record the new water level. The difference in the water levels equals the volume of the egg.

Measuring Mass

All matter has mass. **Mass** is the amount of matter in an object. You can't tell how much mass an object has if you just look at it. A golf ball and a Ping Pong ball are about the same size. But a golf ball has much more mass than a Ping Pong ball. You have to measure to find out how much mass an object has.

In the investigation you used a pan balance to measure mass. You may have used another kind of balance in the grocery store to measure the

The balloon filled with air has more mass than the empty balloon. This shows that air has mass. ▶

An empty pan balance has the same amount of mass on both sides. ▼

masses of fruits and vegetables. You may use a scale at home to measure your own mass.

You can't see air. In fact, you can't see most gases. But like all matter, gases have mass. Look at the balloons on the previous page. You can see that when you put air into a balloon you add to its mass. If you put too much air into a balloon, the balloon will pop. Then you can feel the mass of air rushing out of the balloon.

✔ **What is mass?**

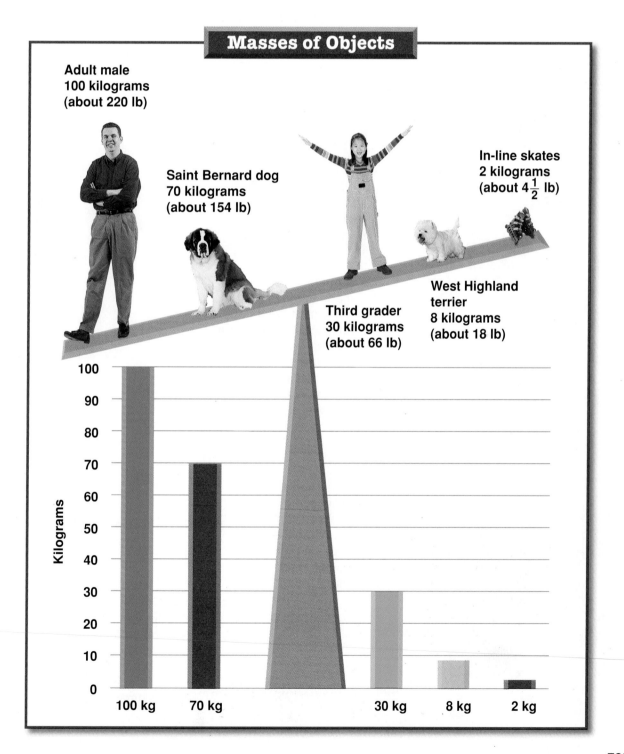

Masses of Objects

Adult male
100 kilograms
(about 220 lb)

Saint Bernard dog
70 kilograms
(about 154 lb)

In-line skates
2 kilograms
(about $4\frac{1}{2}$ lb)

West Highland terrier
8 kilograms
(about 18 lb)

Third grader
30 kilograms
(about 66 lb)

Kilograms

| 100 | 90 | 80 | 70 | 60 | 50 | 40 | 30 | 20 | 10 | 0 |

100 kg   70 kg   30 kg   8 kg   2 kg

Tools for Measuring Mass and Volume

Suppose you need 1 teaspoon of salt. You would use a measuring spoon, not a scale. Measuring tools are made for certain tasks. Using the right tool makes measuring easy.

This scale makes measuring the masses of fruits and vegetables easy. The large pan can hold big items like bags of apples or bunches of bananas. ▶

▲ When you need medicine, it is important to take the right amount. This spoon measures the correct volume of medicine.

▲ A postage scale is made to measure the masses of letters and packages. A letter has a small mass. To measure its mass, you need a scale that can measure small masses.

◀ To find a person's mass, you need a scale a person can stand on. When the boy stands on this scale, he can read his mass.

▲ Restaurants make food in large volumes. This measuring tool can hold large amounts of liquid.

◀ Scientists often measure liquids. This container, called a *graduate,* is marked along the side. By using it, a scientist can see exactly what the volume of a liquid is.

E26

Adding Masses

Suppose you draw a picture on a large sheet of paper. Then you cut the paper into pieces to make it into a puzzle. When you put the puzzle back together, it's the same size as the whole sheet of paper. And it still has the same mass.

Suppose you measure the mass of an apple. Then you cut the apple in half and measure the mass of each piece. If you add the masses of the two pieces, you will find that the total is the same as the mass of the whole apple.

When you cut the apple in half, you still have the same amount of apple to eat. In any way matter is arranged, its mass stays the same.

✔ **What happens to the mass of an object when you cut the object into pieces?**

The balance is holding two identical boxes of crayons. Taking the crayons out of the box does not change their mass. The mass is the same when the crayons are in the box and when they are out of the box. ▼

Comparing Mass and Volume

Different kinds of matter can take up the same amount of space but have different masses. A Ping Pong ball takes up about the same amount of space as a golf ball. But the Ping Pong ball has much less mass. A lime has about the same volume as an egg. But the lime has more mass.

✔ **Which do you think has more mass, a cup of water or a cup of air?**

Mass and Volume

All the jars are filled. They all have the same volume of matter in them. But look closely at the matter in each jar. Each kind of matter has a different mass. The jelly beans have more mass than the pasta. The sand has more mass than the marbles.

Summary

Volume is the amount of space an object takes up. Mass is how much matter is in an object. The mass of an object stays the same in any way its matter is arranged. Different objects can have the same volume but different masses.

Review

1. Name one kind of tool for measuring the volume of a liquid.
2. Do objects that are the same size always have the same mass? Explain.
3. Name some tools you could use to measure mass.
4. **Critical Thinking** Name two kinds of fruit. Which do you think has more mass? Explain.
5. **Test Prep** Choose the best definition of *volume*.
   - **A** the amount of air an object holds
   - **B** how much something weighs
   - **C** the amount of matter in an object
   - **D** the amount of space something takes up

LINKS

MATH LINK

Measure Volume Fill a film canister to the top with water, and put the lid on it. Measure the height of the canister. Then freeze it. In two hours, measure the height of the canister again. What happened to the water?

WRITING LINK

Informative Writing— Explanation Think about going shopping for milk. Tell what it would be like if there were no standard volumes of milk sold. Write a story for your teacher that explains what you would have to do.

LANGUAGE ARTS LINK

Many Word Meanings Look up the words volume and mass in a dictionary. Write two sentences for each word. But use meanings that are not from science.

GO ONLINE TECHNOLOGY LINK

Learn more about measuring matter by visiting this Internet Site.

www.scilinks.org/harcourt

SCiLINKS
THE WORLD'S A CLICK AWAY

GOLD

The history of gold dates back thousands of years. In fact, some scientists think gold may have been the first metal used by humans. For centuries gold has been valued by people around the world. Gold is not only one of the heaviest and strongest metals but also one of the softest and most bendable. Gold's strength, along with its high melting point of 1063°C (1,945°F), is a major reason why it is used in building computers, spacecraft, and other equipment. Gold also is a good conductor of heat and electricity.

The History of Gold

4000 B.C.
Gold is discovered and used in Egypt and Mesopotamia.

100 A.D.
Gold is mined in Spain.

Mid-1700s
Large amounts of gold are discovered in Brazil and Russia.

| 4000 B.C. | 2300 B.C. | A.D. 100 | 1700 |

2300 B.C.
Gold particles are first mined from river sands by separating the heavier gold particles from sand grains.

Gold History

Throughout history, people have found gold in riverbeds, rocks, and even ocean water. Archeologists, or scientists who study historical remains, say that gold was first discovered thousands of years ago in ancient Egypt and Mesopotamia. Gold will stay shiny for thousands of years, as archeologists discovered when they found perfectly preserved gold objects from ancient Egypt. Archeologists could tell from these objects that gold was used in Egypt to make or decorate jewelry, weapons, statues, drinking cups, and many other things. Because of its beauty and value, gold often was used to decorate religious objects.

By the 1400s, much of the world's gold was being mined in South America. Over time, the search for gold prompted many explorations of the Western Hemisphere. In the 1850s gold was discovered in California. This led to a "gold rush," in which people from across the world came to California to try to get rich by finding gold. From the 1870s to the early 1900s, gold was used to make most of the world's money.

The Many Uses of Gold

Because it is soft, gold can be shaped and stretched. In fact, a tiny piece of gold can be hammered into a sheet only 0.025 mm (0.001 in.) thick. These sheets are called gold leaf. Gold leaf is used to decorate metal, wood, glass, plaster, and other materials by covering them with a thin layer of gold.

In jewelry and coins, gold is often alloyed, or mixed with other metals, such as silver, copper, zinc, and nickel. This makes the metal harder so that the jewelry, coins, and other gold products can keep their shape.

THINK ABOUT IT

- What happens to the particles in gold when gold is heated to 1063°C (1,945°F)?

1848
Gold is discovered in California, beginning the California gold rush.

Late 1900s
The electronics, computer, and space industries use gold in their products.

| 1800 | 1900 | 2000 |

1936
A bomb-proof building is built in Fort Knox, Kentucky, to hold most of the gold owned by the United States government.

Insulin

Dorothy Crowfoot Hodgkin
CHEMIST

Dorothy Crowfoot Hodgkin won the Nobel Prize in chemistry in 1964. She was only the third woman ever to win it. By the time she won the award, she had spent more than 30 years studying insulin. Insulin is a chemical made in the body that allows us to use sugar for energy. The results of her studies helped fight diseases and save lives.

Hodgkin did most of her research at Oxford University in England. While there, she attended meetings of the research club. At these meetings she was able to communicate her ideas and research findings with other students and scientists.

Hodgkin loved studying how things were put together. She became interested in crystals. She used X rays to find the shapes of the crystals. She did much of her work before computers had been invented, so her research took a very long time. She used the first IBM computers to help her make calculations. Later, she sent her data to a professor in Los Angeles who had a faster computer. They used mail and telegrams to send information back and forth.

Hodgkin traveled around the world to meet and talk with other chemists. She continued to do research, teach, and travel throughout her life.

THINK ABOUT IT

1. How did not having a computer slow down Hodgkin's research?

2. How can communicating with others help solve a problem?

PROPERTIES OF METALS

Which metals have magnetic properties?

Materials

- magnet
- penny
- piece of aluminum foil
- straight pin
- scissors
- dime
- paper clip

	Objects
Magnetic	
Non-Magnetic	Objects

Procedure

❶ Copy the chart onto a sheet of paper.

❷ Place the magnet close to the penny. Is the penny attracted to the magnet? Write down the results on your chart.

❸ Repeat Step 2 for each of the other objects. Write down the results for each one on the chart.

Draw Conclusions

Study your completed chart. Are all metals attracted by a magnet? Which kinds are?

MASS OF LIQUIDS

Which of three liquids has the greatest mass?

Materials

- clear measuring cup
- water
- oil
- red vinegar

Procedure

❶ Will water float on oil? Or will oil float on water? Predict which liquid will float on the other.

❷ Pour $\frac{1}{3}$ cup water into the measuring cup.

❸ Add $\frac{1}{3}$ cup oil. Observe what happens to the oil. Write down your observations. Was your prediction correct?

❹ Will the vinegar float on the water? Make a prediction.

❺ Pour $\frac{1}{3}$ cup red vinegar into the measuring cup. Let it stand still for five minutes. Write down your observations.

Draw Conclusions

The lightest liquid floats on the others. List the liquids from lightest to heaviest.

Vocabulary Review

Use the terms below to complete the sentences 1 through 9. The page numbers in ( ) tell you where to look in the chapter if you need help.

matter (E6)

physical property (E6)

solid (E11)

liquid (E12)

gas (E12)

atoms (E16)

evaporation (E18)

volume (E22)

mass (E24)

1. A ____ is matter that has a definite shape.

2. All matter is made of ____.

3. Stickiness is a ____ of matter.

4. ____ is the amount of matter in an object.

5. Everything that takes up space is ____.

6. The amount of space that matter takes up is its ____.

7. A ____ has no definite shape but a definite volume.

8. A ____ has no definite shape and no definite volume.

9. When a liquid changes into a gas, the process is called ____.

Connect Concepts

Write the terms needed to complete the concept map.

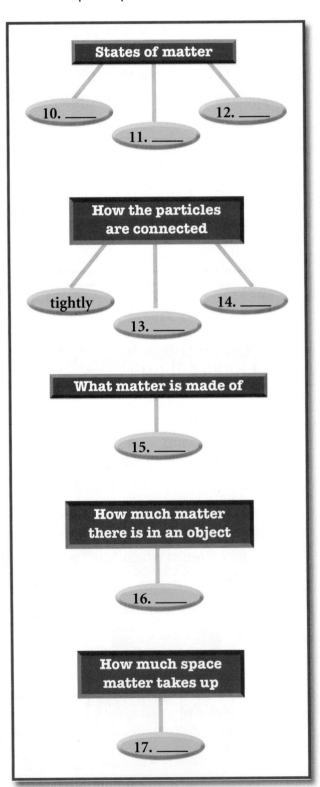

States of matter

10. ____

11. ____

12. ____

How the particles are connected

tightly

13. ____

14. ____

What matter is made of

15. ____

How much matter there is in an object

16. ____

How much space matter takes up

17. ____

Check Understanding

Write the letter of the best choice.

18. There are two jars that are the same size. One is filled with peanut butter, and the other is filled with jelly. They have the same volume, but they may not have the same —

  A heat   **C** evaporation

  B mass   **D** gas

19. One physical property that a football and a soccer ball share is that both —

  F bounce   **H** fold

  G stretch   **J** crackle

20. Syrup pours because its atoms are —

  A tightly connected

  B not connected

  C loosely connected

  D split

21. A shallow pond can dry up because of —

  F ice

  G cold weather

  H heat and evaporation

  J snow falling during the winter

Critical Thinking

22. Explain what happens to a liquid when heat is added to it.

23. A solid has a definite shape. Sand can take the shape of its container. Then why is sand a solid?

Process Skills Review

Write *True* or *False*. If a statement is false, change the underlined words to make it true.

24. **Predicting** means explaining what underlined happened in the past.

25. **Measuring** is using tools to find the volume or mass of something.

26. **Observing** means watching something for a second.

Performance Assessment

Make Models

Make clay models of the particles in a solid, a liquid, and a gas. Make the models small, but be sure each one looks different. Use an index card to make a label for each model. Place the labels in front of the models.

Changes in Matter

When you put the silverware away, it's easy to separate the spoons from the forks. But if you tried to unscramble an egg, you'd have a pretty hard time. What changes mixtures so you can't separate them? In this chapter, you'll find out.

Fast Fact

When you cut yourself, blood looks like a thick red liquid. But blood is really a mixture of liquids and cells of different sizes. Here are some other things that you might not think of as mixtures.

Different Kinds of Mixtures

Kinds of Matter Mixed	Result
Carbon and iron	Steel
Water and gelatin	Jelly
Air and rock	Pumice
Fat and water	Milk
Ash and air	Smoke
Water and air	Fog

This photograph shows how a drop of blood looks through a powerful microscope.

Fast Fact

Sometimes new products are found by accident. In the 1940s, James Wright mixed all sorts of things together trying to find a substitute for rubber. When he mixed boric acid and silicone oil, he got something more fun than rubber—a new product!

What Are Physical Changes?

In this lesson, you can . . .

INVESTIGATE how to separate mixtures.

LEARN ABOUT physical changes in matter.

LINK to math, writing, social studies, and technology.

INVESTIGATE

Separate a Mixture

Activity Purpose In a mixture of sand, shells, twigs, and seaweed, you might want to separate the shells. You could do it easily with your hands. To separate other mixtures, you might need to use different methods or tools. **Plan and conduct an investigation** to discover methods for separating mixtures.

Materials

- 4 clear plastic cups
- 6 marbles
- water
- steel paper clips
- rice
- magnet
- measuring cup
- paper towels
- funnel

Activity Procedure

1 In one cup, make a mixture of marbles and water. Plan a way to separate the marbles from the water. Try it. **Record** your method and your results.

◄ Heat causes a physical change in the ice pop. It melts.

2 In another cup, make a mixture of marbles, paper clips, and rice. Plan a way to separate the mixture. Try it. **Record** your method and your results.

3 If your method doesn't work, plan a different way to separate the mixture. Try different methods until you find one that works. Try using the magnet. **Record** each method you try.

4 In another cup, mix $\frac{1}{4}$ cup of rice with 1 cup of water. How could you separate the rice from the water? **Record** your ideas.

5 Make a filter with the paper towels and the funnel. **Predict** how this tool could be used to separate the mixture. Then use the filter to separate the mixture. (Picture A)

Picture A

Draw Conclusions

1. When would it be easy to use only your hands to separate a mixture?

2. When might you need a tool to separate a mixture?

3. **Scientists at Work** Scientists often use charts to **record** the results of an investigation. How would setting up charts help you **plan and conduct an investigation**?

Investigate Further Make a mixture of sand and water. **Plan and conduct an experiment** to separate the mixture. Would a tool be useful? Which tool would you use?

Physical Changes in Matter

FIND OUT

- how matter can change and still be the same

- about two kinds of mixtures

VOCABULARY

physical change
mixture
solution

Kinds of Physical Changes

When you wash your clothes, they get wet, soapy, and wrinkled. Even with all these changes, they are still your clothes. No new kinds of matter are formed. Changes to matter in which no new kinds of matter are formed are called **physical changes**.

Some physical changes make objects look very different. Paper can be cut, painted on, written on, torn, folded, and glued. Each time, the paper looks different, but it is still paper.

Changing the temperature can make matter change. Cooling makes liquid water change to ice. The ice has the same particles in it that the liquid water had. No new kinds of matter are formed.

✔ **What are some ways that matter can change and still be the same matter?**

People make paper so they can use it. ▼

One way people change paper is by giving it a different shape. ▶

◀ Another way people change paper is by cutting it into smaller pieces.

Mixtures

A **mixture** is a substance that contains two or more different types of matter. The types of matter in a mixture can be separated. After a mixture is separated, the matter is the same as it was before it was mixed.

In the investigation you made a mixture of rice, paper clips, and marbles. Then you separated the pieces back into separate piles of rice, paper clips, and marbles. Making a mixture is a physical change.

Separating the parts of a mixture is another physical change.

Some mixtures can be separated by hand. You separated the rice from the marbles with your hands. Some mixtures can be separated by evaporation or by condensation. In *evaporation* a liquid part of a mixture turns into a gas. This leaves the other parts behind. In *condensation* a gas in a mixture turns into a liquid. The liquid can be separated from the rest of the mixture.

✔ **What is a mixture?**

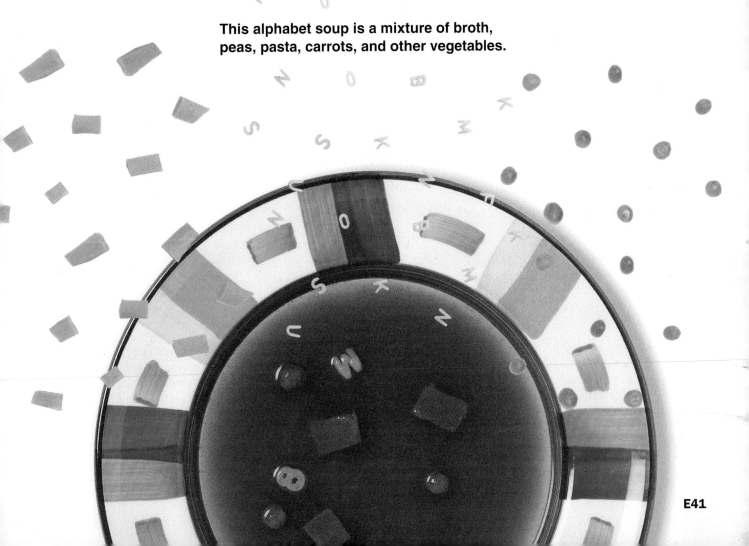

This alphabet soup is a mixture of broth, peas, pasta, carrots, and other vegetables.

Solutions

Have you ever put sugar in iced tea? After you stir the tea, you can't see the sugar anymore. You know the sugar is still there because you can taste it. This mixture of sugar and tea is called a solution. In a **solution** the particles of the different kinds of matter mix together evenly.

The different kinds of matter in a solution can't be separated by hand. But evaporation can separate some solutions. If you heat the iced tea or leave the glass out for a while, the water in the tea will evaporate. Then the sugar will be left.

✔ **What is a solution?**

THE INSIDE STORY

Solutions

This bright-blue substance is called copper sulfate. Watch what happens when it is mixed with water.

Copper sulfate mixes with water to form a solution. Like the copper sulfate, the solution is a bright-blue color.

To separate the copper sulfate from the water quickly, you can heat the solution. The heat makes the water evaporate.

After the water is gone, only the copper sulfate is left.

Summary

Matter can change size, shape, and state. Matter can be mixed. Changes to matter that don't form any new kinds of matter are called physical changes. A mixture contains two or more types of matter. A solution is a kind of mixture. In a solution the particles of the different kinds of matter are mixed evenly.

Review

1. What is a physical change?
2. Name three ways to cause a physical change in matter.
3. What is the difference between a mixture and a solution?
4. **Critical Thinking** Suppose you have a mixture of water and salt. You use evaporation to separate the water from the salt. Where does the water go?
5. **Test Prep** Which one is a solution?

   A marbles mixed in water

   B sugar mixed in water

   C clay, rocks, and twigs

   D rice mixed in water

◄ Mixture

LINKS

MATH LINK

Add Fractions Make a food mixture. Use a $\frac{1}{4}$-cup measuring cup and a 2-cup measuring cup. Measure $\frac{1}{4}$ cup each of raisins, dried banana chips, sunflower seeds, and pretzel circles. Put all these into the 2-cup measuring cup. How much trail mix do you have altogether?

WRITING LINK

Expressive Writing—Song Lyrics Almost all soups are mixtures. Choose a familiar tune and write song lyrics for a younger child about your favorite soup.

SOCIAL STUDIES LINK

Gold Rush Look up the California gold rush. Find out how people separated mixtures of water, sand, and rock to find gold.

GO ONLINE **TECHNOLOGY LINK**

Visit the Harcourt Learning Site for related links, activities, and resources.

www.harcourtschool.com

WELCOME TO THE LEARNING SITE

What Are Chemical Changes?

In this lesson, you can . . .

INVESTIGATE a change in matter.

LEARN ABOUT how new matter is formed.

LINK to math, writing, language arts, and technology.

INVESTIGATE

Chemical Changes

Activity Purpose You mix flour, eggs, milk, and oil. Then you pour some of the mixture into a hot pan. Pancakes! The pancakes are a different kind of matter than the flour and eggs. Many changes happen to cause the new kind of matter to form. You can **observe** a new kind of matter being formed in this investigation.

Materials

- safety goggles
- cookie sheet
- large glass bowl
- measuring cup
- baking soda
- vinegar

Activity Procedure

1 **CAUTION** Put on your safety goggles.

◀ The yellow liquid mixes with the clear liquid. Together they form a new kind of matter that is a pink solid.

2 Place the cookie sheet on the table. Place the bowl on the cookie sheet.

3 **Measure** $\frac{1}{4}$ cup of baking soda. Pour it into the bowl.

4 **Measure** $\frac{1}{4}$ cup of vinegar. Hold the cup with the vinegar in one hand. Use your other hand to fan some of the air from the cup toward your nose. Do not put your nose directly over the cup. (Picture A)

Picture A

5 Pour the vinegar into the bowl.

6 **Observe** the matter in the bowl. **Record** what it looks like. Use the procedure from Step 4 to smell the matter in the bowl. Record what it smells like.

Draw Conclusions

1. How is the material in the bowl like the baking soda and vinegar you started with? How is it different?

2. What can you **infer** about where the bubbles came from?

3. **Scientists at Work** Scientists **observe** changes. Then they **record** their observations. Describe the changes you observed in the bowl.

Investigate Further Mix warm water and a fresh packet of dry yeast. **Observe** the mixture. **Record** what you see. What can you **infer** about the changes you see?

Process Skill Tip

Scientists **observe** matter carefully. Sometimes they see things they don't understand right away. Sometimes they can use their experience to **infer** what those things mean. When you infer, you use your observations to form an opinion.

Chemical Changes in Matter

FIND OUT

- how new kinds of matter are formed
- some ways we use chemical changes every day

VOCABULARY

chemical change

Forming Different Kinds of Matter

Matter is always changing. Some changes are physical changes. In physical changes the kind of matter stays the same.

Some changes form new kinds of matter. Changes that form different kinds of matter are called **chemical changes**. In chemical changes the particles in the matter change. Cooking food makes new kinds of matter. Flour, eggs, milk, and oil turn into pancakes. The particles in the flour, eggs, milk, and oil change. The pancakes will never be just flour, eggs, milk, and oil again.

✔ **What is a chemical change?**

▲ **This liquid looks like water. It is actually a solution with lead in it.**

This is a solution with iodine in it. It also looks like water. ▶

When the two liquids are mixed, they form a yellow solid. This is an example of a chemical change. ▶

Some Chemical Changes

Burning People burn things every day. Many people burn oil or gas to heat their homes. When things burn, different kinds of matter form. So burning is a chemical change. When wood burns, it combines with the oxygen in the air. The matter that forms includes smoke and ash. Another kind of matter forms that you can't see. It is a gas that mixes with the air.

Rusting Have you ever noticed orange-brown spots on the metal of a bike or a car? This orange-brown matter is rust. Rust forms when air and water mix with the iron in metal. The rust is a different kind of matter. It is flaky and soft. It is not strong like iron. When a metal gets rusty, it loses some of its strength. Often you can break the rusty part off. Rusting is a chemical change.

✔ **What are two common chemical changes?**

A chemical change is happening in this fire. The wood is combining with oxygen in the air to form new kinds of matter. ▼

The new bolt is shiny. The other bolts are old. The iron in the old bolts has rusted. It has combined with air and water to form a new kind of matter. ▼

▲ When wood burns, one of the new kinds of matter that forms is ash. The ash doesn't look like the wood.

Using Chemical Changes

Chemical changes go on all around us. We burn fuel to heat our homes. The engines of cars and buses burn fuel to make them move. Chemical changes happen when we cook food. Many of the materials in our clothes are made by chemical changes. Plants use chemical changes to make their food. The film in a camera goes through chemical changes to make photographs.

✔ **Name three chemical changes.**

1 First you take a picture.

2 The film inside a camera has chemicals on it. These chemicals change when light hits them. The changes are the beginning of your photograph.

3 Film is made into negatives. On a negative, the colors are backward. The negative is used to make a print.

4 A machine shines light through the negative and onto a sheet of paper. This sheet of paper is coated with chemicals. The paper is put through a chemical bath. It is washed off, and your picture is finished!

Summary

Chemical changes cause new kinds of matter to form. Chemical changes can be very useful. We use chemical changes to cook. We use chemical changes to take pictures. Some chemical changes are harmful. Rust on metal makes the metal weak.

Review

1. What happens to particles of matter in a chemical change?
2. Name two common chemical changes.
3. Describe some ways we use chemical changes to help us.
4. **Critical Thinking** What is the difference between a chemical change and a physical change?
5. **Test Prep** Which of the following is a chemical change?
   - **A** tearing
   - **B** soaking
   - **C** rusting
   - **D** folding

LINKS

MATH LINK

Solve a Problem A log had a mass of 5 kilograms before it burned. After the fire was out, the ashes had a mass of 1 kilogram. What was the mass of the smoke and gas that were formed?

WRITING LINK

Narrative Writing—Story Write the story of a forest fire for your teacher. Tell how the fire begins. Describe what is left of the forest when the fire is over.

LANGUAGE ARTS LINK

Many Uses of Fire Look up the word *fire* in a dictionary. Write two sentences that use the word. But use the word in ways that are different from the way *fire* is used in science. Explain what *fire* means in each sentence.

TECHNOLOGY LINK

To learn more about how matter that has undergone a chemical change can be used, watch *Recycled Roads* on the **Harcourt Science Newsroom Video.**

CNN
Turner Le@rning®

E49

PLASTIC BRIDGES

Physical changes can be useful. When you fold a sheet of paper, you want it to change shape. And you want a plastic bag to change its shape to hold the groceries you buy at the store. But if a bridge you were driving on changed shape as much as the paper or the plastic bag, you'd be in trouble.

Choosing Materials

When engineers design and make something, they choose their materials carefully. They use materials that change in ways that are useful and don't change in ways that cause problems. When they want to build a bridge, they use materials that are strong. They look for materials that won't bend or break when cars and trucks drive over them. They might use steel, or concrete—or plastic.

Why Build Plastic Bridges?

People don't usually think of plastic when they think of bridges. Plastic bags get holes in them. Plastic milk bottles bend and break. Even the hard plastic used in toys and computers breaks. But scientists have developed a new kind of plastic that is strong enough to hold the weight of cars and trucks. It is a kind of composite, or a material made of several different things put together.

Composite plastic is as strong as steel, but it is much lighter. Bridges built with plastic can be put together

► Plastic building material

Plastic is also being used to fix old bridges. Plastic can be wrapped around parts of these bridges to add support. The plastic coating also keeps the bridges from being damaged by heat, cold, wind, water, and salt.

THINK ABOUT IT

1. Why do we still need to use concrete and steel to make bridges?

2. Why might you want to wrap plastic around the supporting parts of a building?

and ready to use in about a day. Bridges made with steel and concrete take much longer to build.

Weathering wears out bridges made of steel and concrete. Heat, cold, rain, ice, and wind slowly break them apart. Water can erode cement and make steel rust. But water and salt don't affect composite plastic. The plastic doesn't break down or rust.

Using Plastic in Bridges

Today plastic bridges are being tested in different places around the country. These bridges aren't made completely of plastic. They still have steel rails on the sides and concrete on the road surface. They look just like the bridges you're used to. But scientists hope they will last longer.

Enrico Fermi
PHYSICIST

◄ The first atomic bomb

Enrico Fermi was a man who lived on a schedule. It was noon and he was hungry. So work on his great experiment could wait awhile. That afternoon, December 2, 1942, his experiment succeeded and made it possible to develop the atomic bomb. The work of many scientists over several years had been completed.

Fermi became interested in atoms after reading about the research done by other scientists. In 1938 he was awarded the Nobel Prize in physics.

After Fermi, his wife, and their two children went to Sweden to accept the prize, they did not return to Italy. Fermi's wife, Laura, was Jewish. She was in danger because of the prejudice against Jews in Italy. So the Fermi family came to the United States. Fermi taught at Columbia University. A few years later, he went to the University of Chicago, where many of his experiments took place.

In 1943 Fermi went to Los Alamos, New Mexico, to help develop the first atomic bomb. All of the major countries involved in World War II were racing to make this bomb. After the war ended, Fermi returned to the University of Chicago.

THINK ABOUT IT

1. Why did all the major countries in the war want to make an atomic bomb?

2. Why is it important for scientists to write about their discoveries?

CHANGES IN COOKING

What happens to muffins as they bake?

Materials

- 1 box of muffin mix
- other needed ingredients
- mixing bowl
- spoon
- muffin pan

Procedure

❶ Read and follow the directions on the box of muffin mix.

❷ Halfway through the cooking time, open the oven or turn on the oven light and observe the muffins. Record your observations.

Draw Conclusions

What is happening to the muffins?

MAKING A SOLUTION

Which works better, hot water or cold water?

Materials

- 2 small, heat-proof glass containers
- cold water
- spoon
- sugar
- clock with second hand
- warm water (from the tap)

Procedure

❶ Fill one container with cold water.

❷ Mix a spoonful of the sugar into the water. Stir until the sugar dissolves.

❸ Watch the clock to see how long it takes. Record the number of seconds it takes.

❹ Repeat Steps 1–3 using warm water.

Draw Conclusions

How were the results different? Why do you think they were different?

Vocabulary Review

Choose a term below to match each definition. The page numbers in ( ) tell you where to look in the chapter if you need help.

physical change (E40)

mixture (E41)

solution (E42)

chemical change (E46)

1. Matter that contains two or more different things that can be separated

2. A change in which no new kinds of matter are formed

3. A change that makes new kinds of matter

4. A mixture in which the particles of the different kinds of matter mix together evenly

Connect Concepts

Complete the diagram below by listing three examples of physical change and two examples of chemical change.

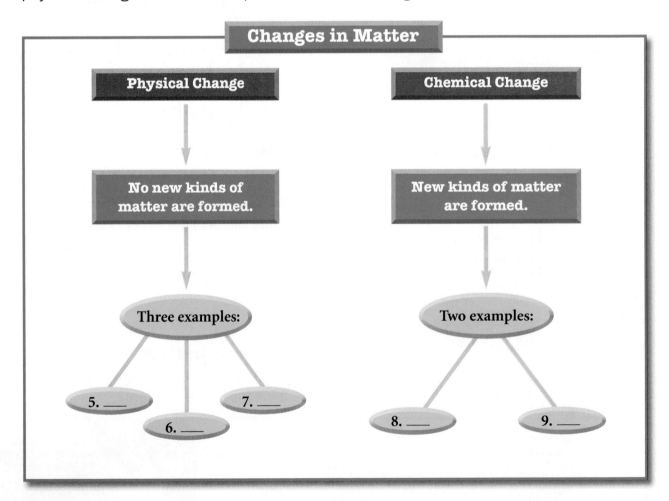

Changes in Matter

Physical Change → No new kinds of matter are formed. → Three examples: 5. ___ 6. ___ 7. ___

Chemical Change → New kinds of matter are formed. → Two examples: 8. ___ 9. ___

Check Understanding

Write the letter of the best choice.

10. Which of the following involves a chemical change?
    A dissolving soap in water
    B cutting paper with scissors
    C burning paper
    D filling a balloon with air

11. Which of the following is a physical change?
    F mixing blueberries, strawberries, and raspberries
    G rusting of iron on a car
    H burning a log
    J cooking pancakes

12. When you add heat to ice to turn it into liquid water, you make a —
    A solution   C chemical change
    B mixture   D physical change

13. Which of the following is a solution?
    F twigs, leaves, and bugs
    G sugar and water
    H newspapers and magazines
    J milk and cereal

14. What new kind of matter forms when iron is mixed with air and water?
    A wood   C ice
    B rust   D ash

Critical Thinking

15. Think of the investigation you did with vinegar and baking soda. What happened that showed a gas was forming?

16. Suppose you leave a shovel out in the rain. Two weeks later there are orange-brown spots on it. Explain what has happened.

Process Skills Review

Write *True* or *False*. If the statement is false, change the underlined part to make it true.

17. A scientist who <u>wants to find an answer to a question</u> **plans and conducts an investigation.**

18. When you **observe** something, you <u>watch it carefully</u>.

19. When you **infer**, you <u>make a wild guess</u>.

Performance Assessment

Mixtures and Solutions

Work together with three or four other students. Your teacher will give you the following things: a pitcher of water, two cups, paper clips, safety pins, salt, a spoon, and unpopped popcorn. Make one mixture and one solution and correctly label each.

There are many places where you can learn about matter. By visiting the places below, you can find out more about the properties of matter and the ways it changes.

Oregon Museum of Science and Industry

WHAT A museum where open-ended science exploration is encouraged

WHERE Portland, Oregon

WHAT CAN YOU DO THERE? Tour the many exhibits in the building and learn about matter in the Chemistry Lab.

Corning Museum of Glass

WHAT A museum that displays glassware and provides educational tours

WHERE Corning, New York

WHAT CAN YOU DO THERE? Visit the museum, tour the exhibits, and see how glass is made.

GO ONLINE Plan Your Own Expeditions

If you can't visit the Oregon Museum of Science and Industry or the Corning Museum of Glass, visit a museum near you. Or log on to The Learning Site at **www.harcourtschool.com** to visit these science sites where you can learn about matter.

Exploring Energy and Forces

Exploring Energy and Forces

UNIT EXPERIMENT

Evaporation

Evaporation occurs when a liquid becomes a gas.
While you study this unit, you can conduct a long-term experiment to find out how evaporation is related to heat. Here are some questions to think about. When water evaporates from a dish, does it gain heat or lose heat? Do liquids other than water act the same way? Plan and conduct an experiment to find answers to these or other questions you may have about evaporation and heat. See pages x–xii for help in designing your experiment.

Energy

Energy is all around you. It is in sunlight, moving water, gasoline, and batteries. It can move and change from one form to another. Without energy, plants could not grow, animals could not move, and machines could not operate.

Vocabulary Preview

energy
potential energy
kinetic energy
electricity
fossil fuel
vibrate
circuit

Fast Fact

The Earth is struck by lightning 100 times every second. Most lightning strikes do not cause any damage, but sometimes they start fires. About 75,000 forest fires are started every year by lightning.

Fast Fact

It takes a ray of sunlight 8 minutes to travel from the sun to Earth. It would take a car going 60 miles per hour about 170 years to travel the same distance.

Fast Fact

Animals get their energy from the food they eat. Racehorses can run as fast as 43 miles per hour. But ostriches can run even faster—up to 45 miles per hour.

Running Speeds	
Human	22 mph
African elephant	25 mph
Cat	30 mph
Alligator	35 mph
Pronghorn antelope	55 mph
Cheetah	62 mph

LESSON 1

How Is Energy Stored?

In this lesson, you can . . .

INVESTIGATE
how energy can be stored.

LEARN ABOUT
the different ways stored energy can be used.

LINK to
math, writing, health, and technology.

► This hurricane lamp burns oil to produce light energy.

Twisting Up Energy

Activity Purpose You use energy to do lots of things every day. It takes energy to brush your teeth, walk to the bus stop, play kickball, or jump rope.

In this investigation, you will **hypothesize** what happens to the energy you use to twist two clothespins held together by a rubber band.

Materials
- safety goggles
- 1 rubber band
- 2 clothespins

Activity Procedure

1 **CAUTION** Put on safety goggles to protect your eyes in case a clothespin pops loose.

2 Attach the rubber band to each clothespin. Work with a partner to twist the rubber band between the clothespins. (Picture A)

3 When you have finished, the rubber band should be twisted and curled up. (Picture B)

4 Holding the clothespins tightly, lay them on the table and **hypothesize** what will happen to them when you let them go. **Communicate** your hypothesis to your partner.

5 **Observe** what happens to the clothespins when you let them go. Then do the investigation again, this time twisting the pins more tightly than you did before. **Compare** what the clothespins did the first time with what they did the second time.

Picture A

Picture B

Draw Conclusions

1. Describe what happened each time you put the clothespins on the table and let go of them. How did your hypothesis compare to the actual results?

2. Where did the energy to move the clothespins come from?

3. **Scientists at Work** Scientists **conduct simple experiments** to learn more about how things work. What did you learn about energy and twisted rubber bands from your investigation?

Investigate Further **Observe** what happens to a third clothespin that you twist around the other two with a second rubber band.

Process Skill Tip

When you **hypothesize** before **conducting an experiment**, you are explaining what you think will happen. Then you can plan other experiments to explore your results further.

What Energy Is

Energy to Live and Move

VOCABULARY

energy
potential energy
kinetic energy
electricity
fossil fuel

Think about what happens when you are riding your bike. How are you able to pump the pedals or stop? These actions use energy. **Energy** is the ability to cause change. Energy allows movement in the world.

Energy comes from many places, including the sun, food that you eat, gas that allows cars to run, and oil to heat your home. But all objects can have energy. The energy an object has because of where it is or its shape is called **potential** (poh•TEN•shul) **energy**. For example, a rock on top of a hill has potential energy. If the rock is pushed, that energy is released as the rock rolls down the hill.

Potential energy can change into kinetic energy. **Kinetic** (kih•NET•ik) **energy** is the energy of motion. Any moving object has kinetic energy. The rock rolling down the hill has kinetic energy. A bigger rock would have greater kinetic energy. The heavier a moving object is, the more kinetic energy it has.

✔ **What is energy?**

The bouncing of this ball is possible because of kinetic energy.

Sources of Energy

Almost all energy on Earth comes from the sun. The food we eat, the gas we put in our cars, even the electricity that lights our homes can all be traced back to the sun's energy.

Light and heat are forms of energy that come directly from the sun. Plants need energy from sunlight to make food. Heat from the sun warms everything on Earth.

What kinds of energy come indirectly from the sun? The food we eat is one example. Food contains the energy we use to power our bodies. Another example is fuels. Fuels, such as coal and oil, contain huge amounts of energy.

Fuels can release energy that can be changed into electricity. **Electricity** is a form of energy that people make by using other kinds of energy found in nature, such as wind, moving water, oil, or coal.

Energy that comes into our homes as electricity can be used to light lamps, run computers, or cook popcorn.

Wind and moving water can also be used in other ways. Wind can be used to keep a hang glider or a kite up in the air. Moving water can be used to carry logs downstream to a sawmill.

People can use other kinds of energy to open cans, print newspapers, or lift steel beams to build a skyscraper. Energy is needed for almost all the activities that make up our lives.

✔ **Where does almost all the energy on Earth come from?**

These children skate by using the energy from the food they have eaten. ▼

Stored Energy

At all times, the sun's rays are striking about half of Earth's surface. Plants use the energy in sunlight to make food, which they then use to grow and reproduce. Animals eat the plants to get the energy stored in the plant tissues. Then the animals use this energy to run, climb, hunt, and stay warm. So, organisms use a lot of the energy just by the things they do every day to stay alive. The energy that they don't use is stored in their bodies as potential energy.

People can use the potential energy of plants and animals. You use potential energy when you eat a hamburger or ride the school bus. Fuel and food are both forms of potential energy that people use.

Fuel Have you ever seen a fire burning? What was used to make the fire? Chances are, it was wood. Wood comes from trees. Like other plants, trees store energy from the sun. When wood burns, this stored energy is released as heat. The heat warms you as you sit near the fire.

All living organisms store energy. When they die, their bodies are slowly buried by soil and rocks. Over millions of years, some of this material may be pressed together until it turns into fuel, like oil or coal. This kind of fuel is called **fossil fuel**. Gasoline and heating oil are made from fossil fuels.

To release the energy stored in fossil fuels, the fuels must be burned. Burning releases heat that can be changed into other types of energy.

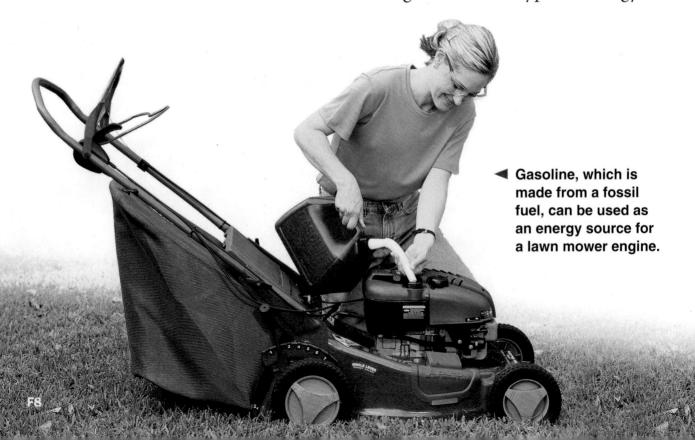

◄ Gasoline, which is made from a fossil fuel, can be used as an energy source for a lawn mower engine.

Food Just before winter, when it begins to get colder outside, do you notice anything different about the squirrels in your neighborhood? Watch them closely. You will soon see that they are collecting nuts, berries, and other bits of food. They hide some of the food and eat it later in the winter when food is hard to find.

Food is one way energy from the sun can be stored. Leaves, stems, roots, and fruits are structures in which plants store energy.

When an animal eats a plant, it gets the energy stored inside the plant and uses it to keep warm and move around. Squirrels get the energy they need to keep warm during the long, cold winter months by eating the food they collected in the fall.

Squirrels will eat a lot of nuts over the winter. Any energy from the nuts that their bodies don't use will be stored as fat. Suppose that another animal, such as a fox, eats a squirrel.

The fox gets the energy stored in the squirrel's body. So while acorns are food for squirrels, squirrels are food for foxes.

✔ **Where does the energy in food and fuels come from?**

▲ Energy from the sun is stored in many of the fruits and vegetables we eat, including apples, broccoli, bananas, and lettuce.

This mountain goat is eating grass. The goat's body will break down the grass to release the energy stored inside. ▶

Batteries

In nature, energy is stored in the form of food and fuel. But people can store energy too. You can store energy in a battery.

Batteries come in many shapes and sizes. Some are so small that they have to be handled with tweezers. Others are bigger than a suitcase—and a whole lot heavier. You probably use batteries that look like cylinders, or tubes.

Companies that make batteries charge them. To do this, the batteries are filled with chemicals that contain energy. Batteries change the energy in the chemicals into the electricity needed to make many things work.

THE INSIDE STORY

How a Battery Works

A paste in the battery holds a lot of energy. It makes electricity that flows out of the battery.

A rod runs through the center of the battery.

Things that get energy from the battery must be hooked up to the top and the bottom of the battery. This way, electricity can leave one end of the battery and then come back in the other end.

After the battery has been used for a while, the energy in the paste gets weaker and can't make as much electricity. Eventually, the battery wears out.

▲ Flashlights use the energy from batteries to make light.

▲ You can tell that the battery in your calculator is out of energy when you can't see numbers on the screen anymore.

▲ Batteries in this stereo supply the energy needed to play the radio or the cassette inside.

The stereo that you use to play music probably takes many big batteries. These batteries supply the stereo with the electricity it needs to play the music. Do you wear a wristwatch? Chances are, there is a small, flat battery inside. That battery provides the electricity needed for the hands to turn or the digital numbers to change on the face of the watch.

As batteries are used, the energy inside is used up. Some batteries can be recharged, or refilled with energy. Others cannot be recharged and must be recycled or thrown away.

✔ **How are batteries charged?**

The remote-control device for this toy gets its energy from batteries inside the control box. ▶

F11

How Stored Energy Can Be Used

You have just learned that energy can be stored as food or fuel. You also saw that energy can be stored in batteries. People store energy so they can use it when they need it. During the day, you might feel warm and be able to see objects clearly. But on a dark, cold night, you need energy to supply heat and light to your home.

Think about what you and your family did last night after supper. Maybe you had the radio on as you all played a game. The energy to play the music came from energy that was produced so that you could use it when you needed it.

Look at the picture of the women rowing in the boat below. Their muscles need energy to be able to pull the oars and move the boat forward. To get this energy, they eat foods such as sandwiches, spaghetti, and fruit. All this food originally got its energy from sunlight.

Fuel is a form of stored energy that people depend on a great deal. We either burn it to release the energy inside or use it to make electricity, which is another form of energy that can be used to make all sorts of things work. Fuel gives us energy to heat our homes, to cook our food, and to drive our cars.

✔ **Why is stored energy useful?**

These athletes are using energy from food they have eaten to pull the oars on this boat, called a racing shell. ▼

Summary

Energy is the ability to cause change. All living things need energy to survive. Tools and machines need energy to operate. Energy comes mainly from the sun and can be found in many different forms. It can be stored and used later when it is needed. Food and fuel are both forms of stored energy. Electricity is a form of energy that is made by using other forms of energy.

Review

1. What is the main source of energy on Earth?
2. What are fossil fuels?
3. Why are batteries useful?
4. **Critical Thinking** What would the world be like if the sun did not shine?
5. **Test Prep** Which of the following is not a source of energy?
   A wind   C engine
   B moving water   D coal

LINKS

MATH LINK

Multiply Whole Numbers
Scientists estimate that the sun produces about 4 million metric tons of energy every second. About how many metric tons does it produce each minute?

WRITING LINK

Persuasive Writing— Business Letter Fossil fuels are still commonly used in the United States. Scientists are trying to develop other kinds of fuels. Write a letter to the Department of Energy to find out more about other fuels being explored.

HEALTH LINK

Recycling Batteries People throw away millions of used batteries. Find out what recycling centers do with old batteries.

TECHNOLOGY LINK

To learn more about energy from the sun, watch Solar Float on the **Harcourt Science Newsroom Video** in your classroom video library.

How Does Energy Move?

In this lesson, you can . . .

INVESTIGATE
how energy moves as waves.

LEARN ABOUT
how warm objects can become cold and how cold objects can become warm.

LINK to math,
writing, social studies, and technology.

INVESTIGATE

Waves of Energy

Activity Purpose Energy can move through the air, through water, through wires—even through our bodies! One way energy moves is as waves.

In this investigation, you will **use models** to show two of the ways energy can move.

Materials

- rope about 6 feet long
- coiled spring toy

Activity Procedure

1 Do this investigation with a partner. Hold one end of the rope while your partner holds the other. Stand so that the rope hangs loosely between you.

2 While your partner holds his or her end of the rope still, move your end of the rope gently up and down. Now move the rope faster. **Compare** what the rope looked like before with what it looks like now. (Picture A)

◄ This coiled spring toy can be used to show one way energy can move.

3 Now take the coiled spring toy and place it on a table or on the floor. Hold one end, and have your partner hold the other. (Picture B)

4 Ask your partner to hold the end still as you quickly push your end of the toy in about 4 inches. Now push and pull the end backward and forward. **Observe** what happens to the coils.

5 Draw and label a diagram explaining what happened to the rope when you moved one end. Make another diagram showing what happened to the coiled spring toy when you pushed one end in.

Picture A

Picture B

Draw Conclusions

1. What happened to the rope when you moved one end up and down? How did it move? What happened when you moved it faster?

2. What happened when you pushed your end of the coiled spring toy toward your partner? What happened when you moved it back and forth?

3. **Scientists at Work** When things in nature can't be seen, scientists **use models** to see how they work. They then **communicate** what they learn. How did your diagram help you to communicate what you learned about how energy moves as waves?

Process Skill Tip

Using models is a good way to learn more about things that you can't see. Carefully drawn and labeled diagrams can then be used to **communicate** what you learned.

Energy Can Move as Waves

FIND OUT

- how energy can move as waves
- how energy can move as electricity

VOCABULARY

vibrate

circuit

Kinds of Waves

Have you ever seen a painting of the ocean? How did the artist draw the waves? Most of the waves we see every day look like curvy lines. If you were to draw a wave, it would probably start low, go up high, and then come back down low again. It would keep going like this over and over again.

Wind moving over water makes waves on the surface. Sometimes the waves are small, but at other times they are big enough to toss a boat about. You may even have made your own waves in the bathtub as you moved around. Waves in water are the easiest waves to see.

Look at the diagram below of a wave. If you wanted to measure the wave, what would you do? You might look at how high and how low each curve went. Or you might measure the distance from the top of one curve to the top of the next curve.

One kind of wave, like the one you made with the rope, moves up and down. ▼

▲ The kind of wave you make with a coiled spring toy moves back and forth.

But what about the other kind of wave you made in the investigation? You don't see this kind of wave every day. It moves back and forth instead of up and down.

Look at the diagram above. It shows the kind of wave you made by using a coiled spring toy. If you look closely, you'll notice that some parts of the spring are very close together and others are spread out.

If you wanted to measure this wave, what would you do? You could look at the distance between one bunched-up part and the next.

Energy often moves. Light is one kind of energy that moves from the sun to Earth. Sound is another kind of energy that moves. It travels from our mouths to the ears of people when we speak.

Some forms of energy, including light and sound, move through the air as waves. Light moves as up-and-down waves, like the rope wave. Sound moves as back-and-forth waves, like the coiled spring toy waves.

✔ **How is a rope wave different from a coiled spring toy wave?**

This sailboat is being tossed about by ocean waves. ▼

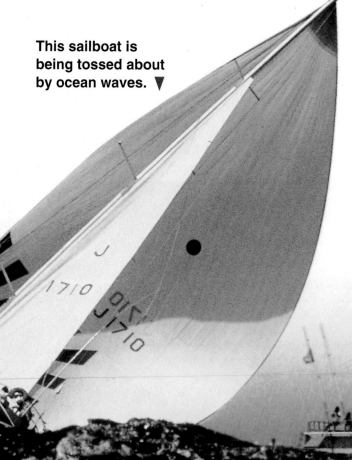

Light Waves

Light is a form of energy we use every day. We need it to see the things around us. Light comes from many different sources. The sun is the most important. Other light sources, such as lamps and candles, provide light when the sun doesn't give us light.

Light has something in common with water waves. When you throw a pebble into a pond, ripples move away from the spot where the pebble hit. In the same way, light waves move away from a light source. Light, like water, moves in up-and-down waves. Light waves travel until they come to an object. When the waves strike the object, some bounce off it so that we can see the object.

You cannot see light waves. Light waves move too fast for you to see them. They move about 300,000 kilometers (186,000 mi) each second.

Light travels through air and through space. It also travels through clear materials such as glass and water. You know this because you can see fish in an aquarium. Light doesn't travel through most objects, though. A shadow is made whenever an object, like your body, stops the path of light waves. When you stand outside on a sunny day, light waves from the sun hit your body, but they can't move through you to the ground behind you. Your body blocks the light, and a shadow forms.

✔ **How does light travel?**

Lights placed all along this runway give off light waves, allowing pilots to see the runway and to land the plane safely—even at night. ▼

Sound Waves

Sound is another kind of energy that travels in waves. Sound travels as back-and-forth waves, like the coiled spring toy in the investigation.

Think of different sounds you hear every day—the voice of a friend, the jingle of a bell, the slamming of a door, the buzz of an insect, a song on the radio. Even though these sounds seem different, they all travel the same way.

Think about the sound from a bell. When you ring a bell, the clapper inside hits the sides of the bell. The sides then start to **vibrate**, or move back and forth very quickly. This makes the air around the bell vibrate too. Waves of vibrating air move away from the bell in all directions. When these waves reach your ears, your brain hears the bell ring.

◄ When this old-fashioned fire alarm rings, sound waves are sent out in all directions, warning people of the danger.

Have you ever been in a storm with lightning and thunder? As the storm was coming toward you, you probably saw the lightning before you heard the thunder. But the lightning and the thunder began at the same time. You saw the lightning first because light waves travel much faster than sound waves.

✔ **How does sound travel?**

Instruments made with wood, strings, and metal can be used to make beautiful sounds that we hear as music. ►

Energy Can Move as Electricity

Light and sound are both forms of energy, and both travel in waves. Another way energy can travel is as electricity.

In the last lesson you learned that batteries can store energy so that it can be used later. The kind of energy that batteries produce is called electricity. Electricity is also produced by energy companies and sent to your home. You can use this electricity by plugging something into a wall socket.

Electricity can be used to do many things. This is because electricity can easily be changed to other forms of energy. It can be used to start a car engine, to light a lamp, to turn the blades of a fan, or to make your favorite toy move.

▲ Energy, in the form of electricity, moves out of batteries and turns the blades of this fan.

Have you ever made a bulb light by using a battery and some wires? The bulb lights because energy moves as electricity from the battery, through the wires, to the bulb, and back to the battery. When the bulb lights, electric energy is changed to light energy. The path the electricity follows from the battery, through the bulb, and back again is called a **circuit**.

◄ In a circuit, energy moves from the battery, through the wires, to the bulb, and then back to the battery.

Electricity can change form to make things move or turn. The battery in a hand-held fan supplies electricity to a little motor in the fan that turns the blades of the fan.

✔ **What is a circuit?**

Summary

Energy can move in many ways. Light energy moves as up-and-down waves. Sound energy moves as back-and-forth waves. Electricity is a form of energy that can move from a battery to other objects.

Review

1. What are two kinds of waves?
2. What do all sounds have in common?
3. How does electricity move to light the light bulbs in a room?
4. **Critical Thinking** What types of energy can be produced by a battery? Why is this energy important?
5. **Test Prep** What sort of energy moves by waves?
   A electricity
   B sound
   C batteries
   D lightning

LINKS

MATH LINK

Solve a Problem About 30 parts of every 100 parts of the energy coming to Earth from the sun reflect back into space when it hits the Earth's atmosphere. What part reaches the Earth's surface?

WRITING LINK

Narrative Writing—Description On the oceans there are different kinds of waves. Some you can see. Others you can't. Write a description for your teacher about an ocean and all the waves you might see or feel.

SOCIAL STUDIES LINK

Ringing the Bell Research the role of the bell tower in ancient times. Why was the bell located in the middle of town? Who was in charge of ringing it? How was it used to send out information?

TECHNOLOGY LINK

Learn more about sound waves and music by investigating *Waves of Music* on **Harcourt Science Explorations CD-ROM**.

LESSON 3

How Can Energy Be Changed?

In this lesson, you can . . .

INVESTIGATE how energy flows from a battery to light a bulb.

LEARN ABOUT how some forms of energy can be changed into other forms.

LINK to math, writing, and technology.

Lighting a Bulb

Activity Purpose Have you ever put batteries in a flashlight the wrong way? What happened? In order for the bulb to light up, the batteries need to be connected to the bulb in a certain way.

In this investigation you will **experiment** with a battery, a bulb, and wires.

Materials

- masking tape
- D-cell battery
- 2 pieces of insulated electrical wire
- miniature light bulb

Activity Procedure

1 Use a piece of masking tape to tape the battery to your desk. This way, it won't roll around. (Picture A)

2 As your partner holds the light bulb a few inches away from the battery, use the wires to connect the ends of the battery with the base of the bulb. (Picture B)

◄ the sun

3 Now switch the wires. Do you **observe** any changes?

4 Try to make the bulb light by touching the wires to the glass part of the bulb. Can you make it light?

5 Can you make the bulb light by touching the wires to the sides of the battery?

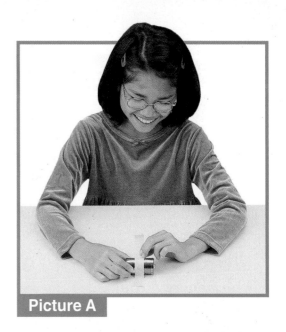
Picture A

Draw Conclusions

1. What happened when you connected the ends of the battery to the base of the light bulb by using the wires?

2. What happened when you switched the wires?

3. Could you make the bulb light by touching the wires to the glass part of the bulb? Did the bulb light when you touched the wires to the sides of the battery?

Picture B

4. **Scientists at Work** Scientists know that the results of experiments don't often turn out exactly the same every time. This can be caused by differences in materials or differences in procedure. How could you change the materials in this investigation to see if the results would change?

Investigate Further **Plan and conduct a simple investigation** to find out if you can make the bulb light by using something other than wires to connect the battery and the bulb. **Control variables** by using the same battery and bulb for each trial.

Process Skill Tip

When you **experiment** with materials to see how they interact, you can figure out how to make them do something, like light a bulb. By experimenting, you can see the evidence that helps you **draw conclusions** about how things work.

F23

Energy Can Change Forms

FIND OUT

- how energy from sunlight can be changed into other forms
- how food, fuel, and electricity can produce motion and heat

From Sunlight to Electricity

Sunlight brings us light and heat every day. We need light to see and heat to keep us warm. But sunlight cannot run our washing machines or play our radios. To do those things, we need electricity.

Electricity is a form of energy we use every day. You have probably already used electricity several times today. Electricity comes from many different sources, but almost all of them can be traced back to energy from the sun.

You may remember that plants can make their own food by using the energy from sunlight. When animals eat the plants, they convert, or change, the energy into energy they can use. When wood burns, the energy stored in the wood changes into thermal energy. These are just some of the ways that energy can be changed from one form to another.

✔ **Where did the energy in oil come from?**

Electricity is carried through wires to places where it is needed, like our homes. There, we change it into heat, light, motion, or other forms of energy. ▼

F24

The Formation of Fossil Fuels

Millions of years ago, plantlike organisms lived in the water. There were also many plants on land, near the water, at that time.

When the plantlike organisms that lived in the water died, they were slowly covered with layers of soil and rock. Dead plants were buried in the same way.

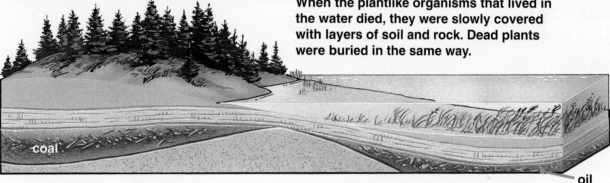

Over millions of years, the energy in the plantlike organisms was pressed into a liquid fuel, called oil. Land plants that were buried and crushed became solid fuel, called coal.

Today, people pump up oil and mine coal from beneath the ground. Then the oil and coal are converted to electricity.

Energy Into Motion and Heat

Recall that squirrels collect nuts for the winter. The nuts are like little packages of energy. When the squirrel does eat the nuts, its body will convert the food energy to the energy of motion and heat.

All animals convert food energy into the energy of motion and heat. When you eat a turkey sandwich, the energy contained in the meat and bread gives you the energy you need to walk to class, play kickball, and run across the schoolyard. Your body also uses the food energy to produce thermal energy to keep you warm.

Have you played outside on a cold day? Were you cold when you started and then warm once you had been playing for a while? This is because the energy of motion also produces heat. So it is better to move around on cold days than to stand still.

Machines also use energy to produce motion and heat. Fuel is the energy source. A car or boat engine uses fuel to produce motion. Furnaces use fuel to warm air or water.

Sometimes machines produce heat for no special purpose. Have you ever touched the hood of a car after a long trip? If you did, you would have noticed that the hood felt hot. As the engine worked to convert fuel energy into the energy of motion, heat was produced. This heat is called *waste heat* because it was not used for any purpose.

✔ **How are the energy of motion and heat energy related?**

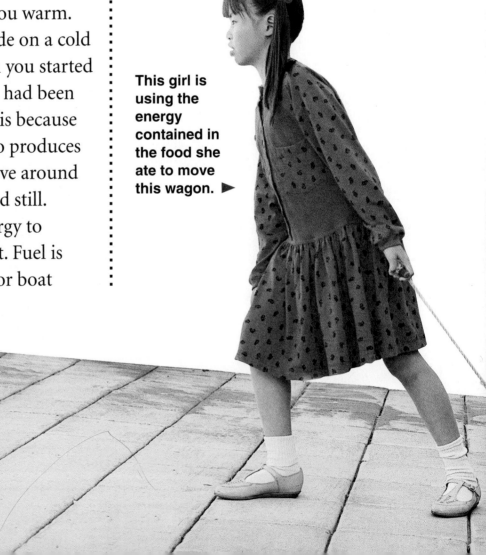

This girl is using the energy contained in the food she ate to move this wagon. ▶

Summary

Energy can change forms. Sunlight can be changed into food, fuel, or electricity. Electricity can be changed into other kinds of energy, like light energy. Food and fuel can be changed into motion and heat by animals and by machines. The energy of motion often produces waste heat.

Lesson Review

1. How can sunlight be changed into electricity?
2. Where do you get the energy to climb stairs?
3. **Critical Thinking** If all fossil fuels disappeared tomorrow, could you still watch TV? Explain your answer.
4. **Test Prep** A car engine feels hot after a long ride because —

   A it contains a lot of electrical energy

   B the sun heats the engine

   C the energy of motion produces waste heat

   D the battery keeps it warm

LINKS

MATH LINK

Solve a Problem Scientists measure the energy we get from the food we eat in units called Calories. A gram of fat provides about 9 Calories. Bread, pasta, and meat provide about 4 Calories per gram. If you ate 112 grams (about 4 oz) of meat on 84 grams (about 3 oz) of bread with 56 grams (about 2 oz) of butter, about how many Calories would you consume?

WRITING LINK

Narrative Writing— Description Write a paragraph for a classmate describing how to make a bulb light up by using a battery, a bulb, and two pieces of wire. Then exchange paragraphs with a partner. Mark any places in the paragraph that you didn't understand. Rewrite your paragraph to make it clearer.

GO ONLINE TECHNOLOGY LINK

Learn more about changing electricity to light by visiting the Smithsonian Institution Internet site.
www.si.edu/harcourt/science

Smithsonian Institution®

SOLAR POWER
An Airplane That Soars on Sunlight

Most airplanes use fuel to run their engines. *Pathfinder* is not most airplanes; it is a solar-powered airplane. It runs on sunshine. *Pathfinder* is very lightweight and can fly higher than any other propeller-driven plane. The scientists who built *Pathfinder* think that solar-powered planes can do many of the same jobs that satellites do.

A Flimsy Flying Wing

Pathfinder is made of thin plastic film stretched over a skeleton of plastic and Styrofoam. It weighs only about 455 kilograms (1,000 lb)—about as much as five big men. *Pathfinder* doesn't look like an ordinary plane. It has one wing that's 40 meters (about 130 ft) long. The top surface of this long wing is covered with solar cells that turn sunlight into electricity. The electricity runs motors that turn *Pathfinder's* eight propellers.

Pathfinder doesn't go very fast— only about 28 kilometers per hour (17 mph). Most kids can pedal a bike that fast! But it can go almost 42 kilometers (25 mi) high.

Pathfinder can't carry passengers. It doesn't even have a pilot. The plane is controlled by radio signals sent from the ground. So what good is a big, slow plastic airplane high in the sky? It can do some of the same jobs that satellites

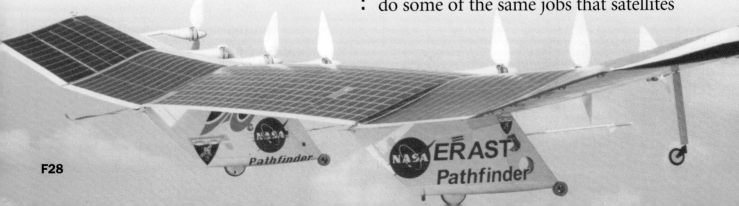

do. *Pathfinder* can take pictures while it is flying. The pictures can be used to keep track of hurricanes and to help predict the weather, just like satellites do. It can carry instruments that help scientists learn about pollution, and it can relay signals for radios and cellular telephones.

What Happens When the Sun Goes Down?

Pathfinder can fly only when the sun is shining. It has to land at night. But engineers at AeroVironment are working on a new solar-powered plane with batteries that can store energy during the day. Energy from the batteries will keep the propellers spinning during the night. The new plane is called *Helios*, from the Greek word that means "sun." *Helios* could stay in the air for a long time. By using sunlight during the day and batteries at night, *Helios* could fly for six months without landing.

Where Else Could It Fly?

Pathfinder flies where the atmosphere is very thin. The atmosphere on other planets is thin, too. Scientists at NASA—the National Aeronautics and Space Administration—think a plane like *Pathfinder* could be used to explore other worlds. NASA hopes to have a small, lightweight solar-powered plane flying on Mars in 2003.

THINK ABOUT IT

1. Satellites use solar power in outer space. Have you seen any machines that use solar power on Earth?
2. What are some advantages and disadvantages of using sunlight for energy?

CAREERS
ENERGY MANAGER

What They Do
Energy managers help people decide on the best way to use energy in homes, offices, and factories. They make suggestions about what kinds of lights to use, when to turn air conditioning or heating on and off, and what kind of machines are the most efficient.

Education and Training An energy manager needs a college degree. He or she must know about different kinds of lighting, heating systems, and other machines that use energy. Energy managers also need to know about electricity and accounting.

WEB LINK
For Science and Technology updates, visit the Harcourt Internet site.
www.harcourtschool.com

Steven Chu
PHYSICIST

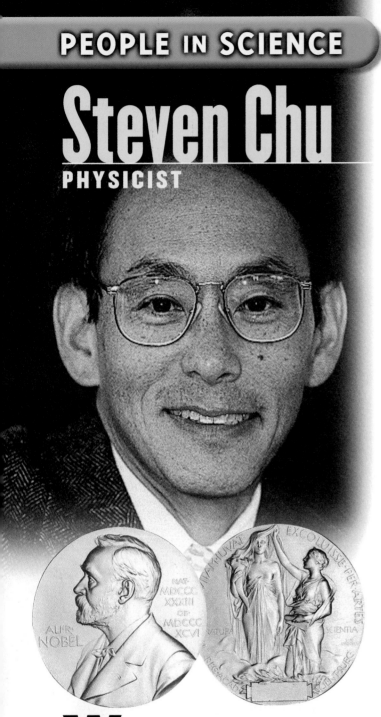

When Steven Chu was growing up in Garden City, New York, he wasn't crazy about school. "Learning seemed like work. I wanted it to be an adventure," he says. So he began asking questions that made learning fun—questions like "Why does that happen?"

Steven Chu was on his way to becoming a particle physicist—a scientist who studies atoms and the forces that hold them together or make them come apart.

In high school, Chu met a science teacher who encouraged him to keep learning about things by asking simple questions and then creating experiments that would give answers. Soon he was experimenting with chemistry sets and homemade rockets.

Chu's curiosity has led to some important questions and answers. In 1997 he received one of the most important awards in science—the Nobel Prize in physics. He won the award for thinking of a way to slow down tiny particles so other scientists can study them more carefully.

Steven Chu wants other people to know how much adventure there is in asking questions. He is a teacher at Stanford University in California. He loves working with students there. "They figure out that textbooks and professors don't know everything, and then they start to think on their own," he says. "Then I begin learning from them."

THINK ABOUT IT

1. What are you curious about? Pick a question, and try to think of some experiments that could help you find the answer.

2. Look for a story about science in a newspaper or magazine. What questions were the scientists asking?

HOT ICE

What environments make ice cubes melt fastest?

Materials

- 3 ice cubes of equal size
- 3 foam cups

Procedure

❶ Place one ice cube in each cup.

❷ Choose three different places to leave the cups. Predict which ice cube will melt most during a half-hour.

❸ Place the cups in their locations. Thirty minutes later, get the cups and observe the ice cubes.

❹ Which ice cube melted the most? Did your results support your hypothesis?

Draw Conclusions

How did heat affect your ice cubes?

SUNNY WINDOW   BOOKCASE   CLOSET

BIG EARS

How do big ears help animals hear?

Materials

- sheet of plain paper

Procedure

❶ Work with a partner for this activity. Standing about 3 meters from your partner, have him or her whisper something to you. Can you hear what he or she said?

❷ Now roll your sheet of paper into a cone, and hold the small end to your ear. Have your partner whisper at the same level as before. Were you able to hear your partner better this time?

Draw Conclusions

Explain how you think the cone helped you hear the whispering better. Use the term *sound waves* in your explanation.

Vocabulary Review

Use the terms below to complete the sentences 1 through 7. The page numbers in ( ) tell you where to look in the chapter if you need help.

energy (F6)

potential energy (F6)

kinetic energy (F6)

electricity (F7)

fossil fuel (F8)

vibrate (F19)

circuit (F20)

1. The energy an object has because of where it is or its shape is ____.

2. A ____ is made up of a battery, a bulb, and wires.

3. When objects ____, they make sounds.

4. The energy of motion is ____.

5. A source of stored energy called ____ was made over millions of years as the bodies of dead plants and animals were pressed together.

6. The ability to cause change is ____.

7. Other forms of energy can be used to make ____, which is the most common form of energy that we use.

Connect Concepts

Use the terms in the Word Bank to complete the concept map.

motion **food** **sunlight** **batteries**

animals **fuel** **electricity**

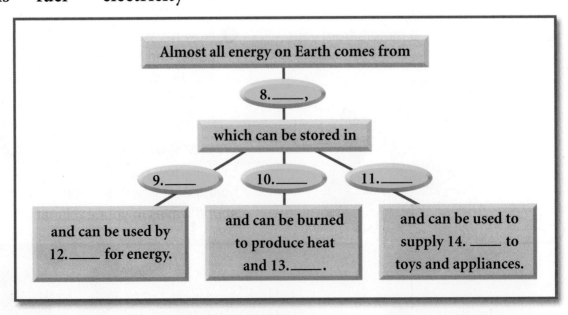

Almost all energy on Earth comes from

8.____,

which can be stored in

9.____ 10.____ 11.____

and can be used by 12.____ for energy.

and can be burned to produce heat and 13.____.

and can be used to supply 14.____ to toys and appliances.

Check Understanding

15. Almost all energy on Earth comes from —

A batteries   C the sun

B electricity   D fuel

16. Sound waves move ____ light waves.

F slower than

G faster than

H at the same speed as

J in front of

17. If two rocks are rolling down the same hill, which rock has more kinetic energy?

A the smaller rock

B the larger rock

C They have the same kinetic energy.

D They have no kinetic energy.

18. Which object has potential energy?

F a glass on a table

G a stretched rubber band

H a cat in a tree

J All of the above.

19. Light waves can move through —

A water   C walls

B shadows   D the ground

Critical Thinking

20. What forms of energy can be found in your home? How does your family use each form?

21. Why do we need to store energy?

22. Draw a diagram that shows how a fossil fuel is formed.

Process Skills Review

23. **Compare** food to fuel. How is each formed? What are they used for? Who are they used by? Present your ideas in a table.

24. Based on your **observations** of the rubber bands and clothespins, what can you **infer** about what happened to the energy you used to twist up the rubber bands?

Performance Assessment

Diagram Energy

Working with a partner, draw a diagram showing everything you know about the energy in sunlight— who uses it directly, how it moves, how it can be stored, and into what other forms of energy it can be converted.

Heat

Have you ever been to a crowded basketball game? The more the people move around, the hotter it gets. Matter acts in much the same way. Matter is made of little particles that move. The more the particles move, the hotter the matter gets.

Vocabulary Preview

thermal energy
heat
friction
conduction
conductor
insulator
convection
radiation
thermometer

Fast Fact

Have you ever wanted to know the temperature when you didn't have a thermometer? Next time this happens, just count the number of times a cricket chirps in one minute and use this table.

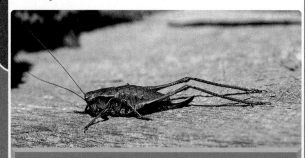

Cricket Chirp Thermometer

Number of Chirps per Minute	Temperature
10	40°F
40	47°F
80	57°F
120	67°F
160	77°F
200	87°F
240	97°F

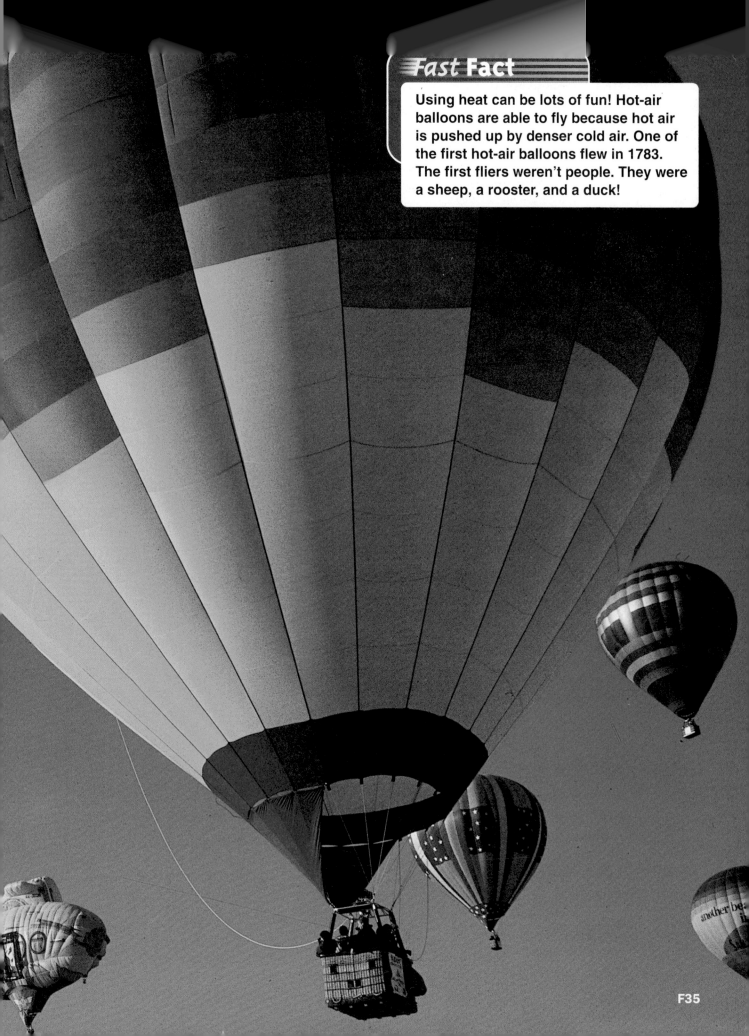

Using heat can be lots of fun! Hot-air balloons are able to fly because hot air is pushed up by denser cold air. One of the first hot-air balloons flew in 1783. The first fliers weren't people. They were a sheep, a rooster, and a duck!

1

What Is Heat?

In this lesson, you can . . .

INVESTIGATE a way to get thermal energy.

LEARN ABOUT thermal energy and heat.

LINK to math, writing, health, and technology.

INVESTIGATE

Rubbing Objects Together

Activity Purpose
Scientists use what they know to make statements about how the world works. Then they do tests to see if their statements are correct. The statements they test are called **hypotheses**. In this investigation you will make hypotheses about heat.

Materials
- metal button
- small piece of wool
- penny
- sheet of paper

Activity Procedure

1 Hold your bare hands together, palms touching. Do your hands feel cold, hot, sticky, or damp? **Record** what you **observe**.

◀ Standing close to a grill, you can feel the heat. It begins in the coals. Then the sides of the grill get hot. When the fire is ready for cooking, almost any part of the grill feels hot.

2 Make a **hypothesis**. What would you feel if you rubbed your hands together? **Record** your hypothesis.

3 Now rub your palms together very fast for about ten seconds. **Record** what you **observe**. (Picture A)

4 What might you feel if you rubbed the button with the wool? The penny with the paper? Form a **hypothesis** for each test. **Record** each one.

5 Rub the button with the wool for about ten seconds. Touch the button. Touch the wool. **Record** what you **observe**. (Picture B)

6 Then rub the penny with the paper for about ten seconds. Touch the penny. Touch the paper. **Record** what you **observe**.

Picture A

Picture B

Draw Conclusions

1. What changes did you **observe**? What actions did you perform that caused the changes you observed?

2. Were your **hypotheses** correct? If not, how could you change them based on what you learned?

3. **Scientists at Work** Scientists use their knowledge and experiences to help them **hypothesize**. What knowledge and experiences did you use in this investigation to help you hypothesize?

Process Skill Tip

A **hypothesis** is tested by **controlling variables** while conducting an **experiment**. This is called a fair test.

Thermal Energy

Energy

FIND OUT

- what thermal energy is
- what heat is
- what thermal energy can do

VOCABULARY

thermal energy
heat
friction

It's hot outside. My soup's cold. Don't touch the stove—it's hot. It's cold out—put on your coat. You've heard these things many times. You know what hot and cold feel like. But do you know what causes them? It's heat.

The story of heat begins with energy. Recall that energy is the ability to cause change. There are many ways matter can change. A sheet of paper can be cut into pieces. Baking soda and vinegar can be mixed together to make a new kind of matter. But these changes don't happen by themselves. The paper doesn't cut itself. The baking soda and vinegar don't mix themselves. Energy has to be added to make the changes happen. Your energy cuts the paper. Your energy also mixes the baking soda and the vinegar. Energy in the baking soda and the vinegar makes the new kind of matter. There are many different kinds of energy. All kinds of energy cause changes in matter.

✔ **What is energy?**

You use energy to fold paper. Your energy changes the paper into a different shape. ▼

◄ The energy in the flame melts the candle wax. This energy makes the matter in the candle change states.

F38

Thermal Energy

Even though you can't see them, the particles in all matter are always moving. The particles in solids move back and forth in place. The particles in liquids slide past each other. The particles in gases fly off in all directions. If you have ever moved a heavy chair across the living room, you know it takes a lot of energy. Moving anything from one place to another takes energy. Even moving the tiny particles in matter takes energy. The energy that moves the particles in matter is called **thermal energy**.

We feel thermal energy as heat. Something that is hot has more thermal energy than something that is cold. The particles in a hot stove are moving very fast. They have a lot of thermal energy. The particles in a bowl of cold soup are moving more slowly. They have less thermal energy.

✔ **What is thermal energy?**

A horseshoe is a solid. Its particles are packed tightly together, but they still move a little bit. ▶

A blacksmith puts the horseshoe into the fire. The thermal energy from the fire moves into the horseshoe. When the particles in the fire bump into the particles in the horseshoe, they make them start to move faster too. ▼

Heat

Thermal energy can move from one thing to another. Suppose you warm some cocoa on the stove. Then you pour the cocoa into a cup. When you touch the cup, it feels hot. Thermal energy moves from the hot cocoa to the cool cup. Then thermal energy moves from the warmed cup to your hand. The movement of thermal energy from one place to another is called **heat**.

When you touch a hot cup of cocoa, thermal energy moves from the cup to your hand. If you touch a cold glass of milk, thermal energy moves from your hand to the cold glass. Thermal energy always moves from a hot place to a cold place. It never moves from a cold place to a hot place.

✔ **What is heat?**

These children are blowing warm air onto their hands. Doing this keeps their hands warm on a chilly day. ▼

▲ Fire produces thermal energy. The thermal energy from the stove is used to cook food.

Ways to Make Things Hot

Every time two objects rub together, they produce thermal energy. In the investigation you rubbed your hands together. The particles in your left hand rubbed against the particles in your right hand because of friction. **Friction** is the force between two moving objects that tries to keep the objects from moving freely. Friction made the particles in both hands move faster. So you felt heat.

Burning also produces thermal energy. When a gas stove is lighted, the potential energy in the gas particles changes into thermal energy. The thermal energy cooks your food.

Some materials produce thermal energy when they are mixed together. When iron oxide and aluminum are mixed together, they make a hot fire. The fire is so hot that it can even melt metals.

Some gardeners like to use natural materials to make the soil richer. They pile up leaves, soil, food scraps, and grass clippings. Tiny living things in the soil, called *bacteria,* "eat" the leaves and other matter. The bacteria change the mixture into a rich, dark soil-like material called *compost.* During this change, thermal energy is produced.

✔ **Name three ways to produce thermal energy.**

▲ Aluminum mixes with iron oxide to produce a lot of thermal energy.

▲ A gardener turns the compost pile. Turning mixes the bacteria. The more the bacteria "eat," the more thermal energy is produced.

Ways to Use Thermal Energy

You may not think about it, but you use thermal energy every day. It cooks your food. It keeps you warm. You probably use hot air to dry your clothes and hair. You wash your face with warm water. Factories use thermal energy to form metal parts for cars and refrigerators. On the Fourth of July, thermal energy helps give us fireworks. People could not live without thermal energy.

✔ **How do we use thermal energy?**

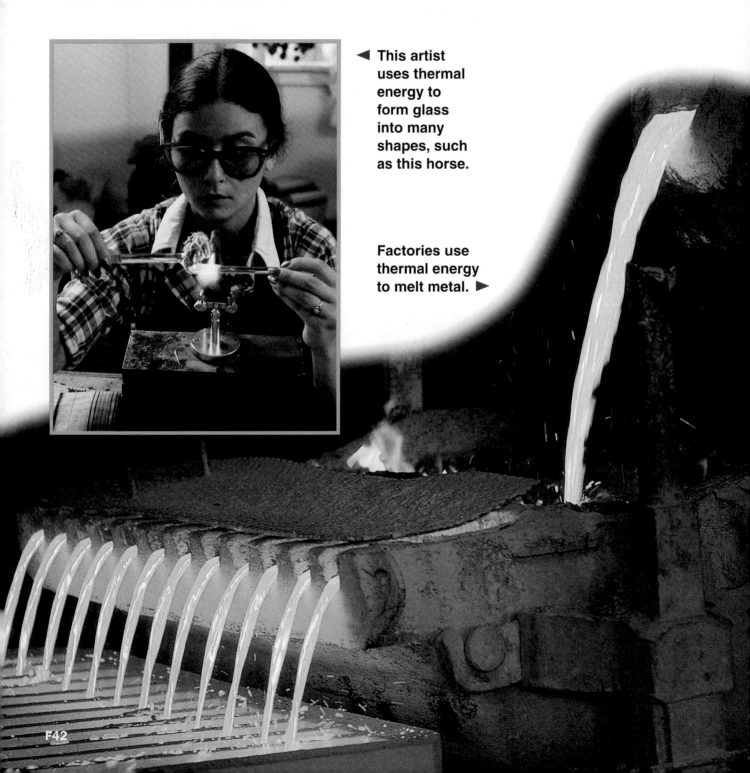

◀ **This artist uses thermal energy to form glass into many shapes, such as this horse.**

Factories use thermal energy to melt metal. ▶

▲ A warm home lets you enjoy the snow.

Summary

Energy is the ability to cause matter to change. Thermal energy is the energy that moves the particles inside matter. Thermal energy that moves from one thing to another is called heat.

Review

1. How can you use energy?
2. What does thermal energy do to matter?
3. Name two ways thermal energy can be made.
4. **Critical Thinking** Why do we need thermal energy?
5. **Test Prep** Which is a good definition of heat?

   A ice melting

   B thermal energy that moves

   C fire

   D the energy that moves the particles in matter

 LINKS

 MATH LINK

Find Elapsed Time A pie has to bake at 425°F for 15 minutes. Then it has to bake at 350°F for 45 minutes. What is the difference between the two temperatures?

 WRITING LINK

Narrative Writing—Story Write a story about a day without thermal energy. Read your story to a younger child.

 HEALTH LINK

Keeping Warm People have used wool for centuries to keep warm. Find out four kinds of animals that we get wool from.

 TECHNOLOGY LINK

Learn more about ways thermal energy can be used by watching *Solar Float* on the **Harcourt Science Newsroom Video**.

How Does Thermal Energy Move?

In this lesson, you can . . .

INVESTIGATE what kinds of objects get hot.

LEARN ABOUT three ways thermal energy moves.

LINK to math, writing, health, and technology.

◄ Two colored liquids are inside this lamp. They move because one liquid gets hotter than the other.

INVESTIGATE

What Gets Hot

Activity Purpose When you were little, you learned not to touch the stove. You had to learn this lesson to keep safe. Now that you are older, you can learn what kinds of things may get hot and what things almost never get hot. **Experiment** to find out.

Materials

- wooden spoon
- plastic spoon
- metal spoon
- 3 foam cups
- water
- ceramic mug
- plastic cup with handle
- metal cup with handle

CAUTION

Activity Procedure

1. Make charts like the ones shown to **record** your **observations**.

2. Touch the three spoons. Are they hot or cold? **Record** what you **observe**.

3. **CAUTION** **Be careful with hot water. It can burn you.** Fill three foam cups with hot tap water. Set them on the table in front of you. Put one spoon in each cup. Wait one minute.

Spoons		
Wooden	Plastic	Metal

Picture A

Cups		
Ceramic	Plastic	Metal

4 Gently touch each spoon. Which one is hottest? **Record** how hot each spoon is. Use words like *cool, warm,* or *hot.* (Picture A)

5 Next, fill each cup with hot tap water. Wait one minute. Then gently touch the handle of each cup. Which one is hottest? (Picture B)

6 Use the words you wrote in Step 4 to **record** how hot each cup handle is.

Picture B

Draw Conclusions

1. Study your Spoons chart. Did all the spoons get hot? Which spoon got the hottest?

2. Look at both charts. Which material got hot in both experiments? How did the plastic items change in the hot water?

3. **Scientists at Work** As they test their ideas, scientists may change their **experiments** in small ways. Suppose you want to see if wood always stays cool when it is placed near heat. What kinds of wooden objects could you use in your experiment?

Process Skill Tip

Scientists wonder how things work. They **form hypotheses** to explain how things work. To test their hypotheses, they do experiments. An **experiment** is a kind of test done very carefully to find out new information.

The Movement of Thermal Energy

Bumping Particles

FIND OUT

• three ways thermal energy moves

• how to keep thermal energy from moving easily

VOCABULARY

conduction
conductor
insulator
convection
radiation

In the investigation you put a metal spoon into hot water. At first the spoon was cool. But after it had been in the water, it got hot. Thermal energy moved from the hot water to the cool spoon.

There are three ways thermal energy can move from one place to another. The first way happens when things are touching each other.

When objects touch each other, their particles bump into each other. The particles in a hot object move faster than the particles in a cold object. The faster, hotter particles give some of their energy to the slower, cooler particles. Then the slower particles speed up and get hotter. This movement of thermal energy is called **conduction**.

✔ **How does thermal energy move between objects that touch each other?**

The particles in the hot pancakes bump against the cold butter particles. They hit so hard that they shake the butter particles loose, and the butter melts. ▶

Conductors

Thermal energy moves very quickly in some materials. Metals are an example. Most cooking pots and pans are made of metal because these materials let thermal energy move easily. The energy has to move from the hot stove to the pan to the food. Then the thermal energy will cook the food. Materials in which thermal energy moves easily are called **conductors**.

✔ **What is a conductor?**

▲ The iron in the Dutch oven makes this a good cooking pot. The iron heats easily so the food can cook.

Insulators

Sometimes you don't want thermal energy to move from one object to another. Suppose you are using a metal cookie sheet to use the thermal energy in the oven to bake some cookies. But then you need to take the cookie sheet out of the oven. Now you need something to keep the thermal energy away from your hands! You need an insulator. An **insulator** is a material in which thermal energy can't move easily. Its particles don't move much when particles from a hot object bump into them. Oven mitts are good insulators.

✔ **What is an insulator?**

▲ This pizza holder does not take in thermal energy easily. The thermal energy from the pizza moves very slowly to the holder. The holder is an insulator.

Moving Liquids and Gases

The second way thermal energy moves from one place to another is in moving liquids and gases. This type of movement is called **convection**. The particles in liquids and gases can move from one place to another. Particles in hot liquids and gases often move to new places before they transfer thermal energy. In some homes, furnaces use fire to heat air. Then fans blow the hot air into the cold rooms in the house. The hot air from the furnace gives its thermal energy to the whole house.

Even when they're not pushed by fans, hot liquids and gases move. When a liquid or gas is heated, its particles spread out. This makes the hot liquid or hot gas lighter. Hot air is lighter than cold air. Cold air sinks to the floor, pushing the hot air up.

✓ **Why does hot air move up?**

Heat from the Sun

The third way thermal energy moves from one place to another happens when things aren't touching each other. When you feel warm standing in the sun, you are not touching the sun. So how do you get warm without touching something that is warm? Thermal energy that moves without touching anything is called **radiation**.

✓ **How can thermal energy move without touching anything?**

▲ In the desert the hot ground warms the air. The hot air is pushed up by cooler air. As the hot air moves, it makes things around it look wavy.

◄ Energy from the sun warms the air and the Earth. We cannot touch the sun, but we can feel its heat.

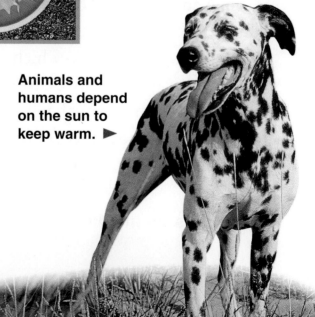

Animals and humans depend on the sun to keep warm. ▶

Summary

When things touch each other, their particles bump and thermal energy moves between them by conduction. Conductors let thermal energy travel easily. Insulators are materials in which thermal energy doesn't move easily. Heated liquids and gases transfer thermal energy through convection. We get thermal energy from the sun by radiation.

Review

1. Describe the three ways thermal energy can move.
2. Is a potholder a conductor or an insulator? Explain.
3. Is the metal in a pot a conductor or an insulator? Explain.
4. **Critical Thinking** Animals that have wool keep warm because of their wool. A sweater or coat made of wool keeps you warm too. Why?
5. **Test Prep** Which is the best way to describe what happens to air when it gets warm?

   A Warm air sinks.

   B The particles in warm air get close to each other.

   C Warm air is pushed up by cooler air.

   D Warm air is very still.

LINKS

MATH LINK

Find Elapsed Time Suppose the burner under a pot of water is turned on at 2:15 P.M. It begins to boil at 2:35 P.M. How long did it take the water to come to a boil?

WRITING LINK

Informative Writing— Explanation Some sports are often done in the warm sunshine. Write a paragraph for your teacher explaining why people who swim outdoors usually do so only when it's warm.

HEALTH LINK

Safety Rules People need thermal energy, but using it can be dangerous. Write two rules for staying safe in the kitchen when food is cooking on the stove.

GO ONLINE TECHNOLOGY LINK

Visit the Harcourt Learning Site for related links, activities, and resources.

www.harcourtschool.com

How Is Temperature Measured?

In this lesson, you can . . .

 INVESTIGATE tools for measuring temperature.

 LEARN ABOUT ways to control thermal energy.

 LINK to math, writing, social studies, and technology.

INVESTIGATE

Measuring Temperature

Activity Purpose Many people don't leave home in the morning without finding out what the temperature outside is. Knowing the temperature is especially handy when you're getting dressed! In this investigation you will find out how to **measure** temperature.

Materials
- 2 cups
- water
- thermometer

Activity Procedure

1 Make a chart like the one shown.

2 **CAUTION** **Be careful with hot water. It can burn you.** Fill one of the cups with cold tap water. Fill the other with hot tap water.

◀ **Thermometers come in many shapes and sizes. This one is used to measure body temperature.**

3 Put the thermometer into the cup of cold water. **Observe** what happens to the liquid in the thermometer. On your chart, **record** the temperature. (Picture A)

Water	Temperature
Cold water, Step 3	
Hot water, Step 4	
Cold water, Step 5	
Hot water, Step 6	

4 Put the thermometer into the cup of hot water. **Observe** what happens to the liquid in the thermometer. On your chart, **record** the temperature.

5 Put the thermometer back into the cup of cold water. **Observe** what happens to the liquid in the thermometer. On your chart, **record** the temperature.

Picture A

6 Wait one minute. Put the thermometer back into the cup of hot water. **Observe** what happens to the liquid in the thermometer. On your chart, **record** the temperature.

Draw Conclusions

1. What happened to the liquid inside the thermometer each time you put the thermometer in the hot water? What happened when you put it in the cold water?

2. Was the temperature of the hot water the same both times you **measured** it? What do you think caused you to get the measurements you got?

3. **Scientists at Work** Scientists **measure** carefully. Write directions for how to measure temperature by using a thermometer.

Process Skill Tip

Scientists look for answers to questions, but they do not ever make up the answers. To try to answer their questions, they **measure** with care. Then anyone who wants to check the answers can take the same measurements.

Measuring Temperature

FIND OUT

- **how to measure temperature**
- **ways to control thermal energy**

VOCABULARY

thermometer

Thermometers

In the investigation you used a thermometer. A **thermometer** is a tool used to measure how hot or cold something is. The liquid in your thermometer expanded when it got hot. It needed more space, so it moved up the tube. Many thermometers work this way. When the liquid cools, its particles don't move as fast. They get closer together. Then the liquid sinks down the tube.

Thermometers have numbers printed on them much like rulers do. Instead of inches or centimeters, they use scales called Fahrenheit and Celsius. By learning to read these scales, you can read the temperature from a thermometer.

✔ **How does a liquid thermometer work?**

Scientists have measured the temperatures of many kinds of things. Some examples are shown here.

▲ One kind of thermometer has the scale printed in a circle. It is a dial thermometer. It uses a metal coil instead of a liquid.

-200°C (-328°F)
Air becomes liquid

-89°C (-128°F)
Earth's lowest temperature

0°C (32°F)
Freezing point of water

58°C (136°F)
Earth's highest temperature

◄ This thermometer was invented about 300 years ago. The temperature of the air outside the glass causes the liquid inside the tube to move up or down.

14 million°C (25 million°F)
Center of the sun

30,000°C (54,000°F)
Average bolt of lightning

5530°C (10,000°F)
Surface of the sun

3027°C (5,480°F)
Metals can be welded

1535°C (2,795°F)
Melting point of iron

660°C (1,220°F)
Natural gas flame

327°C (620°F)
Melting point of lead

250°C (482°F)
Wood burns

184°C (363°F)
Paper burns

100°C (212°F)
Boiling point of water

Most thermometers hold liquid in a straight tube. You can see two scales printed on this thermometer. The numbers on the right are for the Celsius scale. The numbers on the left are for the Fahrenheit scale. ►

°F   °C
120   50
100   40
80   30
60   20
40   10
FREEZE⇨   0
20   10
0   20
20   30
40   40
60   50
          60

Controlling Thermal Energy

Humans can die from being too cold or too hot. People's bodies need to stay at a certain temperature. We can live in cold weather and in hot weather because we have learned how to control heat.

One way we control heat is by wearing clothes. In hot weather we dress lightly. In cold weather we dress warmly. Animals adjust to different temperatures also. In the winter a dog's coat gets thicker. By summer its fur is thinner.

One way to control heat inside a building is to use a thermostat. Almost every building has one. It looks like a little box or circle on the wall. Thermostats have temperature scales, just like thermometers. In fact, they have thermometers inside them.

✔ **Name two ways people control heat.**

Thermostats

A thermostat turns the furnace and the air conditioner off and on. Most large buildings, like schools, have several furnaces. Each furnace or air conditioner has its own thermostat.

Inside this thermostat is a coiled piece of metal made of two different kinds of metals glued together. Each kind of metal gets bigger when it gets warm. But the metal on the bottom gets bigger faster than the metal on the top. So when the room gets warmer, the coil gets bigger. It turns on the switch for the air conditioner. Then the air conditioner can cool the room.

◄ This thermostat is round. You can set it to the temperature you want in the room.

Summary

Thermometers are used to measure temperature. In a liquid thermometer, thermal energy makes the liquid inside the tube move up. We can read the temperature on a scale next to the tube. A thermostat helps control the temperature inside a building.

Review

1. What does a thermometer do?
2. Why does a liquid thermometer work as it does?
3. What kinds of scales are used on thermometers?
4. **Critical Thinking** Why would you need to know what the temperature outside is?
5. **Test Prep** Two different kinds of metals make up thermostat coils because —
   A it's cheaper to make them using two metals
   B they look better that way
   C there is not enough of one kind of metal
   D one metal gets bigger faster than the other

LINKS

MATH LINK

Skip-Count Look at the scale on a thermometer. Do you need to skip-count by 5s or by 10s to read it?

WRITING LINK

Informative Writing— Description Write a weather forecast for your class. Pretend you are on the TV news. Describe what the weather will be like for the next five days.

SOCIAL STUDIES LINK

Geography Use a world map or a globe to find two countries that have extremely cold winters. Find two tropical countries that are warm all year. Explain how you chose your countries.

GO ONLINE ### TECHNOLOGY LINK

Learn more about measuring temperature by visiting this Internet Site.

www.scilinks.org/harcourt

SC*i*LINKS™
THE WORLD'S A CLICK AWAY

Technology Delivers HOT PIZZA

You know that thermal energy always moves from hot objects to cold objects. This means thermal energy moves from a hot pizza to the cooler air around it. In the process, the hot pizza gets cold. And who wants cold pizza?

We Want It Hot

A recent survey found that more than half of all take-out food was delivered to homes rather than picked up. Keeping pizza hot while the delivery person finds the right house is sometimes a problem. Customers want their food delivered fast, and they want it to arrive piping hot. Companies that deliver cold pizzas are soon out of business. So it's good news that science is helping pizza companies deliver your pizza hot to your door.

Foam

pizza

Our Pizza Is the Greatest...
Fresh & Oven Hot
MADE WITH THE FINEST INGREDIENTS

Thank You For Your Patronage, Please Call Again

Thermal Retention

A new product is being used to keep take-out food hot. It is called the hot bag, and it keeps the heat of the food inside the container.

The hot bag is made with three layers of material. The inside liner, made of nylon and vinyl, reduces condensation. It also has a shiny silver color to reflect the heat of the food back inside the container.

The middle layer is a dense foam. This layer is the insulator for the bag. Thermal energy doesn't move easily through the foam. That means the heat is trapped inside the bag. The foam also prevents air from moving into or out of the bag. Even though the inside of the bag is hot, the outside of the bag remains cool and easy to handle.

The outside of the bag is made of heavy vinyl. This makes the bag waterproof. The hot-bag makers use strips of Velcro to seal the bag, keeping even more thermal energy in. The hot bag also has two small openings that allow steam to escape. They keep the pizza crust from becoming soggy on its trip to your home.

Hot Delivery

The makers of the hot bag promise that food in this bag will remain at 80°C (176°F) for at least 15 minutes. After 30 minutes the temperature inside the bag may drop 5° to 8°C (about 10° to 15°F). But thanks to the new materials, the pizza remains 17°C (31°F) hotter than it would using the old way. The crust stays crisp, and the cheese stays gooey. Hot-bag manufacturers are always watching for new technology that can help them deliver your pizza just the way you like it—hot from the oven.

THINK ABOUT IT

1. What other types of fast-food companies could use the hot bag to help them in their deliveries?
2. Would these bags be helpful for delivering ice cream? Explain.

CAREERS
PIZZA CHEF

What They Do Pizza chefs work with fresh ingredients and pizza dough to make pizza. Pizza chefs often work until late at night to make pizzas for parties and other events.

Education and Training A person who is hired to be a pizza chef will spend some time learning on the job from an experienced chef. After training, the new chef is able to work on his or her own.

WEB LINK
For Science and Technology updates, visit the Harcourt Internet site.
www.harcourtschool.com

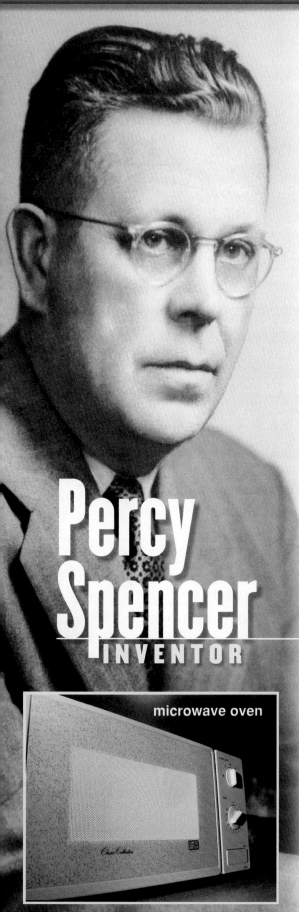

Percy Spencer
INVENTOR

microwave oven

Have you ever made popcorn in a microwave oven? That's how microwave ovens were invented in 1945. Percy Spencer was touring one of the laboratories at the Raytheon Company, where he worked. He was standing close to the power tube that drives a radar set. Suddenly he realized that the chocolate bar in his pocket was beginning to melt. He asked for some unpopped popcorn to test his theory that the machine could cook food.

Percy Spencer was awarded 120 patents during his lifetime. His patent for the microwave oven was given in 1952. The first microwave oven was more than 5 feet tall and weighed 750 pounds! It was designed for cooking large amounts of food in restaurants, on ocean liners, and on railroad cars.

Today microwaves are used to do many things besides heat food. Microwaves are used in radar. Some researchers are working to use microwaves to sterilize food. Some industries have begun using microwaves as well. Microwaves are used to bake the tiles that protect a space shuttle from heat when it returns to the Earth's atmosphere.

One of the most exciting possibilities is that microwaves might be used to treat some kinds of cancer. Cancer tissue begins to die at 109°F. Researchers hope they can use microwaves to kill the cancer and not harm the healthy tissue.

THINK ABOUT IT

1. How do you know that Percy Spencer was creative?
2. Have you ever had an unexpected discovery? What was it?

TESTING INSULATORS

Is wool or sand a better insulator?

Materials

- 1 small coffee can with plastic lid
- 2 wool socks
- scissors
- 1 long lab thermometer
- clock with a second hand
- hair dryer
- 3 cups of sand

Procedure

1 Stuff the can with the socks. Put the lid on. Cut a small hole in the middle of the lid for the thermometer. Make sure the thermometer is surrounded by wool. After five minutes, read and record the temperature.

2 Start the hair dryer. Warm the outside of the can. Watch the thermometer and the clock. See how long it takes the temperature to go up 10°C.

3 Repeat using sand in the coffee can.

Draw Conclusions

Compare results. Which is the better insulator? How do you know?

COOLING WATER

How long does it take for warm water to cool?

Materials

- 2 foam cups
- measuring cup
- 2 thermometers
- clock with a second hand
- warm water

Procedure

1 Fill one cup with 1 cup of warm water. Fill the other cup with $\frac{1}{2}$ cup of warm water.

2 In which cup will the water cool faster? Make a hypothesis to answer the question. Write down your hypothesis.

3 Make a chart to record temperatures. Record the starting temperature in each cup. Then record the temperature of each cup every minute until one cup of water reaches room temperature.

Draw Conclusions

Was your hypothesis correct? Explain.

Vocabulary Review

Choose a term below to match each definition. The page numbers in ( ) tell you where to look in the chapter if you need help.

thermal energy (F39)   **conductor** (F47)

heat (F40)   **insulator** (F47)

friction (F41)   **convection** (F48)

conduction (F46)   **radiation** (F48)

     thermometer (F52)

1. The movement of thermal energy in two solids that are touching

2. Matter in which thermal energy doesn't move easily

3. The movement of thermal energy from one place to another

4. The force between two objects that keeps the objects from moving freely

5. Matter in which thermal energy moves easily

6. The movement of thermal energy when objects are not touching

7. A tool that measures temperature

8. The energy of the moving particles inside matter

9. The movement of thermal energy in liquids and gases

Connect Concepts

Write the terms to complete the concept map.

hot   the sun   liquids   gases   particles   thermal energy   cold

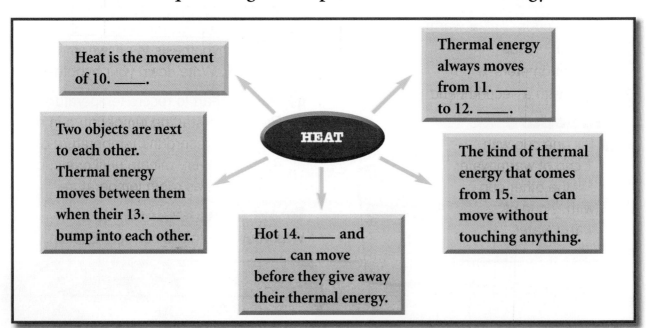

Heat is the movement of 10. ____.

Thermal energy always moves from 11. ____ to 12. ____.

HEAT

Two objects are next to each other. Thermal energy moves between them when their 13. ____ bump into each other.

Hot 14. ____ and ____ can move before they give away their thermal energy.

The kind of thermal energy that comes from 15. ____ can move without touching anything.

Check Understanding

Write the letter of the best choice.

16. Which is an insulator?

    A silver spoon

    B aluminum foil

    C stainless steel spoon

    D wooden spoon

17. Which is a conductor?

    F wooden spoon

    G oven mitt

    H aluminum foil

    J wool sweater

18. Heat from the sun gets to Earth by —

    A conduction

    B convection

    C radiation

    D bumping into Earth's particles

19. Moving anything from one place to another takes —

    F heat   H a thermometer

    G energy   J a thermostat

Critical Thinking

20. You take a dish out of a hot oven. Before you set the dish on the table, you put down a thick straw pad. Why?

21. You are holding an ice cube. Is thermal energy moving from your hand to the ice or from the ice to your hand? Explain.

Process Skills Review

22. Two people **measure** the temperature of the same cup of hot water. They use two different thermometers. One person says the temperature of the water is 40°C. The other says it is 50°C. What can cause the different answers?

23. What **experiment** could you do to find out why the temperatures in Question 22 were different?

24. It is July. The sun is shining. What **hypothesis** can you state about the temperature? How could you check your hypothesis?

Performance Assessment

Diagram a Thermometer

Water boils at 100°C and freezes at 0°C. Draw a picture of a liquid thermometer in a pot of boiling water. Draw a picture of the same thermometer in a pot of freezing water. Explain what happens to the thermometer when it moves from the boiling water to the freezing water.

Forces and Motion

Vocabulary Preview

force
motion
speed
gravity
weight
work
simple machine
lever
inclined plane

Do you ever wonder if you could throw a ball so fast that it wouldn't fall back to Earth? It takes a lot of energy to overcome gravity. Gravity is the force that pulls things back to Earth's surface. Rockets are the only human-made things that have been able to overcome Earth's gravity and make it into space.

Fast Fact

You may never travel fast enough to escape Earth's gravity. But how fast can you go? A race car goes about 354 kilometers (220 mi) per hour. To go the 4715 kilometers (2,930 mi) between New York and San Francisco, it would take a race car $13\frac{1}{2}$ hours!

Time to Travel from New York to San Francisco		
Object	Speed	Time
8-year-old runner	19 kph	248 hours
Propeller plane	483 kph	$9\frac{3}{4}$ hours
Supersonic jet	2,173 kph	2 hours
Space shuttle	40,233 kph	7 minutes
Fast meteoroid	241,395 kph	1 minute
Light	299,330 km per second	$\frac{16}{1,000}$ second

To throw a ball that doesn't come back down, you'd have to throw it at a speed of at least 40,000 kilometers per hour (24,856 mph)! A good fastball pitcher can throw a baseball at about 161 kilometers per hour (100 mph).

How Do Forces Cause Motion?

In this lesson, you can . . .

INVESTIGATE how forces are measured.

LEARN ABOUT how forces act.

LINK to math, writing, social studies, and technology.

INVESTIGATE

Measuring Pushes and Pulls

Activity Purpose Suppose you pull an empty wagon down the street. Then a friend gets in the wagon, and you pull again. The second time, you have to pull a lot harder. Scientists use a tool called a spring scale to **measure** pulls. In this investigation you will use a spring scale to measure pulls.

Materials

- spring scale
- 2 pieces of string
- 2 wooden blocks

Activity Procedure

1 Work with a partner. One of you should hold one end of the spring scale while the other gently pulls on the hook. Read the number on the scale. The number is in newtons. Newtons measure pushes and pulls. **Record** the number. (Picture A)

◀ Pushes and pulls can make things move. A yo-yo moves up and down on a string as you drop it down and pull it back.

2 Tie one piece of string around one of the wooden blocks. Tie the other end of the string to the hook on the scale.

3 Begin to pull on the spring scale. Pull as hard as you can without making the block move. **Record** the number on the scale.

Picture A

4 Now pull hard enough to make the block move. **Record** the number on the scale. Carefully pull the block across the room. Watch the scale. Make sure the number doesn't change as you pull. (Picture B)

5 Repeat Step 4. This time, pull so that the number on the scale changes. **Record** your observations.

6 Tie the second wooden block to the first one. Repeat Steps 3 through 5. **Record** your observations.

Picture B

Draw Conclusions

1. How many newtons did it take to pull on the block without moving it? How many newtons did you use to move the block in Step 4?

2. How did you pull differently in Steps 4 and 5?

3. How did your results change when you added the second block?

4. **Scientists at Work** Scientists make charts to help them **interpret data**. Make a chart to organize the data you collected in this investigation.

Process Skill Tip

Every measurement you make is a piece of data. Scientists **gather and interpret data** for every experiment. Often, scientists make different kinds of charts to help them organize and interpret their data.

Forces and Motion

FIND OUT

- **how motion begins**
- **how to find speed**
- **what gravity is**

VOCABULARY

force
motion
speed
gravity
weight

Forces

A **force** is a push or a pull. You push on a door. You pull on a wagon. Each push or pull is a force. There are many different forces. The force of the wind pushes sailboats and windmills. Forces in car engines can pull cars down the street.

In the investigation you pulled a wooden block. You used a spring scale to measure how hard you pulled. The spring scale measured the amount of force you used. The amount of force you have to use to move an object depends on its mass. The more mass something has, the more force you have to use to make it move. In the investigation you added a second block. How did that change the amount of force it took to move the blocks?

✔ **What is a force?**

◀ **This boy is pushing the snowball. The push of the boy is a force.**

This boy and his dog are pulling on the rope. Each pull is a force. ▶

Motion

Birds fly across the sky. Insects crawl across the ground. Leaves move back and forth in the breeze. The wheels on a bicycle go around in a circle. All these things are in motion. **Motion** is a change in position.

Every time you see something in motion, you know a force somewhere got it going. Every motion is started by a force. And every motion is stopped by a force. Once something is in motion, it will move until some force stops it.

✔ **What is motion?**

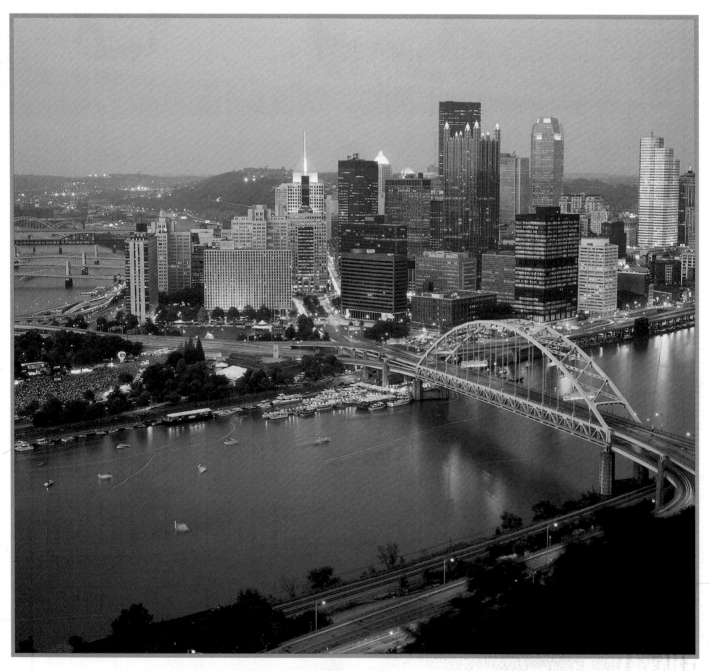

▲ Look at the picture of the river and the city. Each streak of light shows that an object is moving. What other motion can you identify?

Person biking
60 kmh
(37 mph)

Person walking
5 kmh
(3 mph)

Race horse
70 kmh
(43 mph)

Snail
$\frac{5}{100}$ kilometers per hour (kmh)
$\frac{3}{100}$ miles per hour (mph)

Motion

Suppose you want to move a soccer ball down the field. To start the ball moving, you have to apply a force. You give the ball a push with your foot. The ball starts moving. Now suppose you want to stop the ball. Again you have to apply a force. You have to put your foot up and push on the ball to stop it. If you don't stop the ball, it will keep rolling until some other force stops it.

Not all forces stop or start motion. Suppose you and a friend push on a box. You push one way. Your friend pushes the opposite way. The forces on the box are balanced, so the box doesn't move. But if another person starts pushing on your side, the forces aren't balanced anymore. Now the box moves.

✔ **Why does a rolling ball stop rolling?**

When this clown rides her unicycle, the forces pushing on the left side are the same as the forces pushing on the right side. This keeps her from falling sideways. ▼

Space shuttle
30,000 kmh
(18,600 mph)

Jumbo jet
1000 kmh
(621 mph)

Race car
380 kmh
(236 mph)

Speed

Glaciers are large sheets of ice that move very slowly. Most glaciers move less than 30 centimeters (about 1 ft) a day. A train can move much faster. A train can move more than 2000 kilometers (about 1,200 mi) in a day. The measure of how fast something moves over a certain distance is its **speed**. Something that moves a greater distance in the same amount of time has greater speed.

To find speed, you divide the distance you go by the time it takes you to get there. It's about 440 miles from Washington, D.C., to Boston. If you drive it by car in 8 hours, your speed is 440 miles divided by 8 hours, which is 55 miles per hour. An airplane can make the same trip in about 2 hours. The speed of the airplane is 880 miles divided by 2 hours, which is 440 miles per hour. Which has the greater speed, the car or the airplane?

✔ **What is speed?**

Most glaciers move slowly. ▼

Gravity

There is a force that pulls us and everything around us down. That's why when you drop something, it falls down. The force is called gravity. **Gravity** (GRAV•ih•tee) is the force that pulls objects toward each other. All objects are acted on by gravity.

The more mass two things have, the more gravity pulls them toward each other. Earth has a very large mass, so the pull between objects and Earth is large. The moon has less mass than Earth. The pull between the moon and objects is about one-sixth of what it is on Earth.

Weight (WAYT) is a measure of the pull of gravity on an object. On Earth you have one weight. But if you were to go somewhere with a different amount of gravity, you would have a different weight. On the moon, for example, you would weigh one-sixth what you weigh on Earth.

✔ **What is weight?**

Gravity is the force that pulls objects toward Earth. On Earth, all things fall toward the ground. ▼

This astronaut is on the moon. His weight is $\frac{1}{6}$ what it is on Earth. If he weighs 180 lb on Earth, he weighs 30 lb on the moon. ▶

Summary

A force is a push or a pull. Motion is a change in position. All motion is caused by forces. Gravity is the force that pulls objects toward each other. Earth's gravity is so strong that it causes all things near Earth to fall toward Earth. Weight is a measure of gravity's pull on an object.

Review

1. What is force?
2. What happens if you start something moving and no force stops it?
3. What two things do you need to know to tell how fast something is moving?
4. **Critical Thinking** What would happen to a rock in a garden if no forces were ever applied to it?
5. **Test Prep** Which sentence is the best definition of *weight*?

   A Weight measures how big something is.

   B Weight measures how fast something can travel.

   C Weight measures the pull of gravity on an object.

   D Weight measures the height of an object.

LINKS

MATH LINK

Subtract A cheetah can run as fast as 70 mph. A zebra can run 40 mph. How much faster can a cheetah run?

WRITING LINK

Expressive Writing—Poem
Write a short poem for your classmates, describing how the force of the wind moves the leaves on a plant.

SOCIAL STUDIES LINK

History of the Metric System
Find out where the metric system came from. Who invented it? What is the metric unit that measures force?

TECHNOLOGY LINK

To learn more about forces and motion, watch *Big Machine Summer* on the **Harcourt Science Newsroom Video**.

What Is Work?

In this lesson, you can . . .

INVESTIGATE the scientific definition of *work*.

LEARN ABOUT what work is.

LINK to math, writing, language arts, and technology.

INVESTIGATE

Measuring Work

Activity Purpose Scientists say that whenever you move an object, you do work. When you make your bed, put books onto shelves, or take out the trash, you do work. In this investigation you will gather information about work. Then you will **infer** how work is related to force.

Materials

- mug
- spring scale
- meterstick
- shoe with laces
- hat
- stapler
- string

Activity Procedure

1 Make a table like the one shown.

2 Hook the mug onto the spring scale. Work with a partner. One of you should hold the meterstick on the table, with the 1-cm mark toward the bottom. The other person should rest the mug on the table next to the meterstick. (Picture A)

◀ A forklift can lift heavy loads. It is made to do work.

Distance x Force = Work			
Object	Distance (centimeters)	Force (newtons)	Work (newton-centimeters)

3 Gently lift the scale, and pull the mug off the table. Keep the scale and the mug next to the meterstick. **Record** the height you lifted the mug. (Picture B)

4 Read the number of newtons on the spring scale. **Record** the number.

5 Multiply the number of newtons you used times the distance you moved the mug. This is the amount of work that was done. **Record** this number in your table under the heading *Work*.

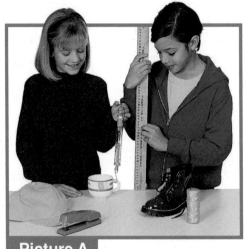

Picture A

6 Repeat Steps 2 through 5, using each of the other objects. You may need to use the string to attach the objects to the spring scale. Lift each object the same distance you lifted the mug.

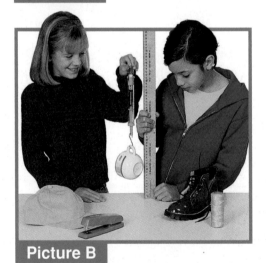

Picture B

Draw Conclusions

1. Which object took the most force to lift? Which object took the least force to lift?

2. Describe the math you did in the chart.

3. In this investigation one of the measurements was kept the same. Which one was it?

4. **Scientists at Work** Scientists **infer** from data. Look at the data you collected. Infer how work is related to force.

Process Skill Tip

Scientists **infer** from data they collect when they **experiment**. After making inferences, they continue experimenting to see if they are right.

Work

FIND OUT

- what work is
- what force has to do with work

VOCABULARY

work

Doing Work

For scientists the word *work* has a specific meaning. **Work** is the measure of force it takes to move an object a certain distance. In the investigation you did work when you lifted a mug off the table. Scientifically, you do work when you plant flowers, ride your bike, or help put away groceries. In each of these activities, you use a force to make something move. You don't do work when you push on a door and can't get it open. If you and a friend push against a box as hard as you can but the box doesn't move, you aren't doing any work.

This boy is pushing as hard as he can against a wall. He's not doing any work, though, because the wall doesn't move. ▼

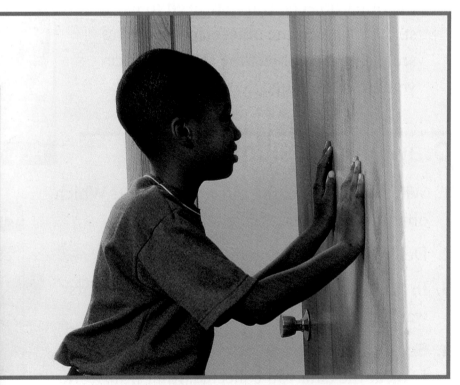

▲ This time he pushes on a door. The door moves. Now he's doing work.

To figure out how much work is done, scientists multiply the force needed to move the object times the distance the object moves. If you use 3 newtons of force to pull a wagon 10 meters, you do 30 newton-meters of work.

✔ **What is work?**

Summary

In science, work is done when a force moves an object. If the object doesn't move, no work is done. To figure out the amount of work done, scientists multiply the force that is used times the distance the object moves.

Review

1. At the beginning of this lesson there is a picture of a forklift. Is it doing work? How do you know?

2. To a scientist, what is work?

3. How do scientists find the amount of work done?

4. **Critical Thinking** Describe a scene in which someone is using force but is not doing work.

5. **Test Prep** For which activity would you be doing work?
   A watching TV
   B pushing on a box that doesn't move
   C reading a page in a book
   D raking leaves

LINKS

MATH LINK

Solve a Problem Marie used 3 newtons to move a chair 2 meters. Latifa used 2 newtons to lift her kitten 1 meter. Who did more work?

WRITING LINK

Informative Writing—How-To Write step-by-step instructions for your brother in first grade. Tell him how to do some kind of work. It might be how to hit a ball or how to make a bed. Be creative or funny.

LANGUAGE ARTS LINK

Many Meanings Write four sentences using the word *work*. Make two sentences with the scientific meaning and two sentences with the everyday meaning.

TECHNOLOGY LINK

Visit the Harcourt Learning Site for related links, activities, and resources.
www.harcourtschool.com

WELCOME TO THE LEARNING SITE

What Are Simple Machines?

In this lesson, you can . . .

INVESTIGATE
how simple machines help us do work.

LEARN ABOUT
kinds of simple machines.

LINK to math, writing, social studies, and technology.

INVESTIGATE

Moving Up

Activity Purpose People often get help when they do work. Sometimes they ask friends to help. Sometimes they use machines to help. In this investigation you will **compare** two ways of doing work.

Materials

- string
- spring scale
- toy car
- chair
- meterstick
- wooden board (about 1 m long)
- masking tape

Activity Procedure

1. Using the string, attach the spring scale to the toy car. With the spring scale, slowly lift until the bottom of the car is at the same level as the seat of the chair. Read the spring scale, and **record** the number. (Picture A)

2. Use the meterstick to **measure** how high you lifted the car. **Record** this number, too.

◀ Nutcrackers use simple machines called levers. They make the job—in this case cracking nuts—easier to do.

3. Prop up one end of the board on the seat of the chair. Tape the board to the floor so the board does not move. (Picture B)

4. Now place the toy car at the bottom of the board. Slowly pull the car to the top of the board at a steady rate. As you pull, read the force on the spring scale. **Record** it.

5. **Measure** the distance you pulled the car up the board. **Record** it.

Picture A

Draw Conclusions

1. Multiply the force you **measured** by the distance you moved the toy car. How much work did you do without the board? How much work did you do with the board?

2. **Compare** the force used without the board to the force used with the board. Which method used less force?

3. **Compare** the distance the car moved each time. Which method used less distance?

Picture B

4. **Scientists at Work** Scientists often **compare** their data. Compare your answers to Question 1 to the answers of your classmates. What did you find out?

Investigate Further Repeat the activity using boards of several different lengths. **Record** the results. Did you use less force with longer boards or with shorter ones?

Process Skill Tip

Scientists look at the data they collect. They want to see what it means. Sometimes they have to **compare** two pieces of data. This means they look at the pieces of data to see how they are alike and how they are different.

Machines

FIND OUT

- what a simple machine is
- names of simple machines

VOCABULARY

simple machine
lever
inclined plane

Simple Machines

A **simple machine** is a tool that helps people do work. It doesn't change the amount of work. It just makes a job easier to do. Some simple machines reduce the amount of force you have to use. Other simple machines change the direction of the force you use. Some simple machines do both.

There are six simple machines. These machines are the lever, the pulley, the wheel and axle, the inclined plane, the wedge, and the screw. The board you used in the investigation was an inclined plane. When you pull something up an inclined plane, you use less force than you use to pick it straight up. But you have to move it a longer distance with the inclined plane. A pulley changes the direction of the force. As you pull down on one end of the rope, you lift up whatever is attached to the other end. Because of gravity, pulling down is easier than pulling up.

✔ **What is a simple machine?**

A **lever** (LEV·er) is a bar that moves on or around a fixed point. For a seesaw, the board you sit on is the bar. The fixed point, called the *fulcrum,* is the stand. You can go up and down on the seesaw as it moves on the fulcrum. ▶

A pulley is used on a flagpole to raise and lower the flag. A pulley is a rope over a wheel. It changes the direction of the force you use. When you pull down on one end of the rope, the object attached to the other end moves up. ▶

◀ A wedge, such as this doorstop, is two inclined planes stuck back to back.

An inclined plane (IN·klynd PLAYN) is a flat surface set at an angle to another surface. It has many uses. Here it is used as a ramp for wheelchairs. ▼

▲ Look closely at a screw. It has an inclined plane winding around it. A screw is like an inclined plane wrapped around a pencil.

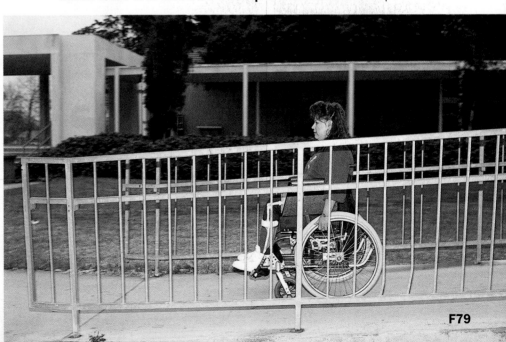

Scissors

Several simple machines put together make a compound machine. A pair of scissors is made up of two wedges and two levers. Look closely. Each blade is a wedge. The very narrow edges of the wedges meet and can cut through paper or fabric.

To make the blades meet every time, you need another machine. Each wedge moves around a bolt in the center. This bolt turns the wedges into levers.

wedge

lever

In a wheel and axle, the wheel is larger than the axle. It takes less force to move the wheel than it does to move the axle. But when the wheel makes a circle, it goes a longer distance than the axle. ▶

Summary

Simple machines do not change the amount of work, but they make a job easier to do. They reduce the amount of force you use or change the direction of the force. They can be used by themselves, or they can be parts of more complicated machines.

Review

1. Name two ways simple machines can make work seem easier.
2. What kind of simple machine is a ramp?
3. When you turn a wheel and axle, which moves farther, the wheel or the axle?
4. **Critical Thinking** A hand-cranked can opener contains a wheel and axle, a wedge, and two levers. Tell what part of a can opener each of these is.
5. **Test Prep** Which simple machine is a kind of inclined plane?
   - **A** wheel and axle
   - **B** pulley
   - **C** screw
   - **D** lever

LINKS

MATH LINK

Solve a Problem Evan used 2 newtons of force to roll a rock 6 meters up a ramp. Janet attached the same rock to a pulley and used 6 newtons of force to raise it 2 meters. Who did more work?

WRITING LINK

Informative Writing— Description Write a paragraph describing a machine you have designed to make it easier to carry your books to school.

SOCIAL STUDIES LINK

Log Cabins How were log cabins built? In a group, talk about how the logs had to be cut and lifted into place. Decide which simple machines the pioneers may have used.

TECHNOLOGY LINK

Learn more about simple machines and how they work by investigating *Simple Machines* on **Harcourt Science Explorations CD-ROM.**

Skyscrapers

How high is the world's tallest building? Fifty meters? One hundred meters? A set of buildings, called the Petronas Towers, in the country of Malaysia, is 452 meters (1,483 ft) high. The Sears Tower, in Chicago, is 443 meters (1,453 ft)—110 stories high. At one time people used the term skyscrapers to describe buildings that were 10 to 20 stories high. But as people continued making taller and taller buildings, the word skyscraper came to mean a building with more than 40 stories.

Petronas Towers

Buildings Over Time

12,000 B.C.
People built homes they could move with them from animal skins and wood.

1350-1570
During the Renaissance, the main types of tall buildings were domes, towers, and churches.

| 12,000 B.C. | 10,000 B.C. | 3000 B.C. | 1300 | 1800 |

10,000 B.C.
During the Agricultural Revolution, clay and stone were used to make homes that lasted longer.

2465 B.C.
Egyptians made large tombs called pyramids, using ramps and levers to move stones.

1857
The first passenger elevator was used in a department store in New York City. This allowed people to travel easily to different floors.

Buildings Change Over Time

Long ago, many people lived in simple huts or tents made from wood and animal skins. Most people moved from place to place, following the animals they hunted. As they moved, they took their homes with them. Around 10,000 B.C., clay was first used to weatherproof wooden buildings. Thousands of years later, in Egypt, triangle-shaped stone buildings called pyramids were built. Some pyramids stood as high as 147 meters (about 482 ft). As time passed, building styles changed even more. In the 1300s, for example, the tallest buildings were large towers, domes, and churches made from stone and glass.

Industrial Age

By the late 1800s, cities were springing up throughout the world. Because of growth, more and more tall buildings were being built. Many of these buildings were made of materials such as iron, steel, stone, brick, and concrete. Over time, builders used steel frames, which were stronger and lighter than iron rods, to produce even taller buildings. Machines, such as cranes, were used to carry heavy materials to these "high-rise" buildings.

What Keeps Buildings from Falling?

As you know, a force is a push or a pull. Tall buildings experience many different kinds of forces. When a force acts on a building, it is called a load. When wind blows on a structure, for example, it is called the wind load. Wind is a major concern of building designers. They must make buildings sturdy enough to withstand strong winds and other types of dangerous weather.

The dead load is the weight of a building. The live load is a building's weight plus everything in it, such as people, cars, and furniture. If forces such as these loads were powerful enough, buildings could crumble and fall. Builders, however, use materials such as concrete beams and steel bars to make strong buildings.

THINK ABOUT IT

1. What materials did people use to build taller and taller skyscrapers?

2. What is the difference between a live load and a dead load?

1973
The Sears Tower in Chicago was built. At 110 stories and 443 meters high (about 1,453 ft), it was now the tallest building in the world.

1900   **2000**

1931
The Empire State Building was built. At that time, it was the tallest building in the world, at 381 meters (1,250 feet) high.

Christine Darden
ENGINEER

One of Christine Darden's childhood loves was fixing things. If her bicycle was broken, she tried to fix it herself. Another of her loves was math. She wanted to make her living with it.

After teaching math for several years, Darden went back to school. She became a mathematician at the National Aeronautics and Space Administration (NASA). There she became fascinated by the work she saw the engineers doing.

Darden wanted to become an engineer, but NASA didn't approve of the idea at first. It is not easy to switch fields of study. Finally NASA decided to allow it, and she returned to school, where she earned a degree in engineering.

Darden is now working with others to make a plane that flies faster than the speed of sound but does not cause a sonic boom. Planes that make these loud noises are banned in the United States.

In 1992 Darden won the Women in Science and Engineering (WISE) Award. Every year, WISE honors three women for their important work in science and engineering.

THINK ABOUT IT

1. Which do you think is more important—finding a job easily or doing work you love to do?
2. How did Christine Darden show her determination?

MOVEMENT FROM AIR

How can you move a Ping Pong ball with your breath?

Materials

- Ping Pong ball
- 3 straws
- colorful tape

Procedure

❶ Work in groups of three. Each person needs a straw. Clear a space on the floor. With tape, mark a course on the floor. Make sure the course has some twists and turns in it.

❷ Put the Ping Pong ball at the beginning of the course. With your partners, blow on the ball to make it follow the path.

Draw Conclusions

From which angle did you blow to make the ball move farthest? Which made the ball move farther, blowing softly or blowing hard? Which made the ball move farther, blowing steadily or blowing in short puffs?

MEASURING WEIGHT

How can you make your own spring scale?

Materials

- paper cup
- a large, heavy rubber band
- 2 rulers
- string
- tape
- objects

Procedure

❶ With your pencil, punch two small holes on each side of the paper cup. Place the rubber band as shown. Thread a piece of string through each pair of holes in the cup and tie the cup to the rubber band.

❷ Hold the ruler straight, and have your partner use another ruler to measure the length of the rubber band from the top of the cup to the ruler.

❸ Compare the weights of different objects by putting them in the cup and measuring the length of the rubber band.

Draw Conclusions

How is the length of the rubber band related to the weight of the objects put in the cup?

Vocabulary Review

Choose a term below to match each definition. The page numbers in ( ) tell you where to look in the chapter if you need help.

force (F66)   **simple machine**
motion (F67)   (F78)
speed (F69)   **lever** (F78)
gravity (F70)   **inclined**
weight (F70)   **plane** (F79)
work (F74)

1. How fast an object moves from one position to another

2. A flat surface set at an angle to another surface

3. A change in position

4. A force that pulls all objects toward each other

5. A tool that helps people do work

6. A bar that moves on or around a fixed point

7. A push or a pull

8. A measure of the pull of gravity on an object

9. Measure of a force moving an object

Connect Concepts

Study the diagram. Then use terms from the chapter to complete the sentences.

10. Your push on the truck is a ____.

11. The length of the ramp is the ____ the truck must move.

12. The distance the truck moves divided by the time it takes is the truck's ____.

13. The simple machine the truck is moving up is an ____.

14. The force to push the truck times the distance the truck moves is the ____ done to push the truck up the ramp.

Check Understanding

Write the letter of the best choice.

15. A rock sat on the edge of a cliff. One day the rock fell off. The force that caused this motion was probably —

   A energy   C work
   B a pulley   D gravity

16. Workers at an airport put suitcases on an airplane. They use a moving ramp. What kind of simple machine is it?

F an inclined plane   H a wedge

G a screw   J a pulley

17. A jet flies at 550 mph. This is a measure of —

A height   C fuel

B speed   D weight

18. Alice uses 2 newtons of force to push her little sister's stroller 5 meters. How much work does she do?

F 2 newton-meters

G 5 newton-meters

H 7 newton-meters

J 10 newton-meters

Critical Thinking

19. Suppose you use a screwdriver to pry the top off a can. Explain which kinds of simple machines you use and how they work for this job.

20. Anthony moved dirt all day with a wheelbarrow. He moved it 20 meters from the vegetable garden to the flower garden. Max sat in his room and studied science. Who would scientists say did more work? Why?

Process Skills Review

21. A red car and a blue car both travel to a town 60 miles away. The red car gets there first. What can you **infer** about the speeds of the two cars?

22. You tried four different ways to lift a bag of sand 1 meter. With the pulley, you used 5 newtons of force. You used 3 newtons when you dragged the bag up the inclined plane. When you pushed the bag up with the lever, you used 2 newtons of force. And when you picked it up by yourself, you used 5 newtons of force. Make a table to help you **interpret the data. Compare** the methods. Tell which used the most force and which used the least force.

Performance Assessment

Simple Machines

Work with a partner to design and construct a device that can be used to move a textbook from one side of a desk to the other. Be sure your device contains at least one simple machine.

UNIT F EXPEDITIONS

There are many places where you can study energy and forces. By visiting the places below, you can learn how energy is used and see how simple machines use forces.

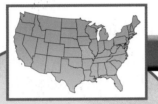

Thomas Hill Energy Center

WHAT A coal-based electrical generating plant

WHERE Clifton Hill, Missouri

WHAT CAN YOU DO THERE? Tour the power plant, see its equipment, and discover how electricity is generated.

Shenandoah Valley Discovery Museum

WHAT A museum with a variety of interactive hands-on exhibits and science programs

WHERE Winchester, Virginia

WHAT CAN YOU DO THERE? See the exhibits, try some of the activities, and discover how simple machines work.

SIMPLE MACHINES

GO ONLINE Plan Your Own Expeditions

If you can't visit the Thomas Hill Energy Center or the Shenandoah Valley Discovery Museum, visit a power plant or museum near you. Or log on to The Learning Site at **www.harcourtschool.com** to visit these science sites.

References

Using Science Tools

Using a Hand Lens

1. Hold the hand lens about 12 centimeters (5 in.) from your eye.

2. Bring the object toward you until it comes into focus.

Using a Thermometer

1. Place the thermometer in the liquid. Never stir the liquid with the thermometer. Don't touch the thermometer any more than you need to. If you are measuring the temperature of the air, make sure that the thermometer is not in line with a direct light source.

2. Move so that your eyes are even with the liquid in the thermometer.

3. If you are measuring a material that is not being heated or cooled, wait about two minutes for the reading to become stable, or stay the same. Find the scale line that meets the top of the liquid in the thermometer, and read the temperature.

4. If the material you are measuring is being heated or cooled, you will not be able to wait before taking your measurements. Measure as quickly as you can.

Caring for and Using a Microscope

Caring for a Microscope

- Carry a microscope with two hands.
- Never touch any of the lenses of a microscope with your fingers.

Using a Microscope

1. Raise the eyepiece as far as you can using the coarse-adjustment knob. Place your slide on the stage.

2. Start by using the lowest power. The lowest-power lens is usually the shortest. Place the lens in the lowest position it can go to without touching the slide.

3. Look through the eyepiece, and begin adjusting it upward with the coarse-adjustment knob. When the slide is close to being in focus, use the fine-adjustment knob.

4. When you want to use a higher-power lens, first focus the slide under low power. Then, watching carefully to make sure that the lens will not hit the slide, turn the higher-power lens into place. Use only the fine-adjustment knob when looking through the higher-power lens.

You may use a Brock microscope. This sturdy microscope has only one lens.

1. Place the object to be viewed on the stage.

2. Look through the eyepiece, and raise the tube until the object comes into focus.

A Light Microscope

A Brock Microscope

Pans

Middle mark

Standard masses

Using a Balance

1. Look at the pointer on the base to make sure the empty pans are balanced. Place the object you wish to measure in the left-hand pan.

2. Add the standard masses to the other pan. As you add masses, you should see the pointer move. When the pointer is at the middle mark, the pans are balanced.

3. Add the numbers on the masses you used. The total is the mass in grams of the object you measured.

Using a Spring Scale

Measuring an Object at Rest

1. Hook the spring scale to the object.

2. Lift the scale and object with a smooth motion. Do not jerk them upward.

3. Wait until any motion of the spring comes to a stop. Then read the number of newtons from the scale.

Measuring an Object in Motion

1. With the object resting on a table, hook the spring scale to it.

2. Pull the object smoothly across the table. Do not jerk the object.

3. As you pull, read the number of newtons you are using to pull the object.

Measuring Liquids

1. Pour the liquid you want to measure into a measuring container. Put your measuring container on a flat surface, with the measuring scale facing you.

2. Look at the liquid through the container. Move so that your eyes are even with the surface of the liquid in the container.

3. To read the volume of the liquid, find the scale line that is even with the surface of the liquid.

4. If the surface of the liquid is not exactly even with a line, estimate the volume of the liquid. Decide which line the liquid is closer to, and use that number.

Beaker   Graduate

Using a Ruler or Meterstick

1. Place the zero mark or end of the ruler or meterstick next to one end of the distance or object you want to measure.

2. On the ruler or meterstick, find the place next to the other end of the distance or object.

3. Look at the scale on the ruler or meterstick. This will show the distance or the length of the object.

Using a Timing Device

1. Reset the stopwatch to zero.

2. When you are ready to begin timing, press *Start.*

3. As soon as you are ready to stop timing, press *Stop.*

4. The numbers on the dial or display show how many minutes, seconds, and parts of seconds have passed.

Table of Measurements

SI Measures (Metric)

Temperature
Ice melts at 0 degrees Celsius (°C)
Water freezes at 0°C
Water boils at 100°C

Length and Distance
1000 meters (m) = 1 kilometer (km)
100 centimeters (cm) = 1 m
10 millimeters (mm) = 1 cm

Force
1 newton (N) = 1 kilogram $\times$
   meter/second/second (kg-m/s^2)

Volume
1 cubic meter (m^3) = 1m $\times$ 1m $\times$ 1m
1 cubic centimeter (cm^3) =
   1 cm $\times$ 1 cm $\times$ 1 cm
1 liter (L) = 1000 milliliters (mL)
1 cm^3 = 1 mL

Area
1 square kilometer (km^2) =
   1 km $\times$ 1 km
1 hectare = 10 000 m^2

Mass
1000 grams (g) = 1 kilogram (kg)
1000 milligrams (mg) = 1 g

Rates (Metric and Customary)
kmh = kilometers per hour
m/s = meters per second
mph = miles per hour

Customary Measures

Volume of Fluids
8 fluid ounces (fl oz) = 1 cup (c)
2 c = 1 pint (pt)
2 pt = 1 quart (qt)
4 qt = 1 gallon (gal)

Temperature
Ice melts at 32 degrees
   Fahrenheit (°F)
Water freezes at 32°F
Water boils at 212°F

Length and Distance
12 inches (in) = 1 foot (ft)
3 ft = 1 yard (yd)
5,280 ft = 1 mile (mi)

Weight
16 ounces (oz) = 1 pound (lb)
2,000 pounds = 1 ton (T)

Health Handbook

Bicycle Safety

A Safe Bike

You probably know how to ride a bike, but do you know how to make your bike as safe as possible? A safe bike is the right size for you. When you sit on your bike with the pedal in the lowest position, you should be able to rest your heel on the pedal. Your body should be 2 inches (about 5 cm) above the support bar that goes from the handlebar stem to the seat support when you are standing astride your bike with both feet flat on the ground. After checking for the right size, check your bike for the safety equipment shown below. How safe is *your* bike?

headlight

horn

white front reflector

red rear reflector

clear reflector

pedal reflectors

clear reflector

Your Bike Helmet

About 400,000 children are involved in bike-related crashes every year. That's why it's important to *always* wear your bike helmet. Wear your helmet flat on your head. Be sure it is strapped snugly so that the helmet will stay in place if you fall. If you do fall and strike your helmet on the ground, replace it, even if it doesn't look damaged. The padding inside the helmet may be crushed, which reduces the ability of the helmet to protect your head in the event of another fall. Look for the features shown here when purchasing a helmet.

approval sticker

quick-release strap

padding

hard shell

air vent

Safety on the Road

Here are some tips for safe bicycle riding.

- Check your bike every time you ride it. Is it in safe working condition?

- Ride in single file in the same direction as traffic. Never weave in and out of parked cars.

- Before you enter a street, **STOP. Look** left, then right, then left again. **Listen** for any traffic. **Think** before you go.

- Walk your bike across an intersection. **Look** left, then right, then left again. Wait for traffic to pass.

- Obey all traffic signs and signals.

- Do not ride your bike at night without an adult. Be sure to wear light-colored clothing and use reflectors and front and rear lights for night riding.

Safety in Emergencies

Fire Safety

Fires cause more deaths than any other type of disaster. But a fire doesn't have to be deadly if you prepare your home and follow some basic safety rules.

- Install smoke detectors outside sleeping areas and on every other floor of your home. Test the detectors once a month and change the batteries twice a year.

- Keep a fire extinguisher on each floor of your home. Check them monthly to make sure they are properly charged.

- Make a fire escape plan. Ideally, there should be two routes out of each room. Sleeping areas are most important, as most fires happen at night. Plan to use stairs only, as elevators can be dangerous in a fire.

- Pick a place outside for everyone to meet. Choose one person to go to a neighbor's home to call 911 or the fire department.

- Practice crawling low to avoid smoke.

- If your clothes catch fire, follow the three steps shown here.

1. STOP

2. DROP

3. ROLL

Earthquake Safety

An earthquake is a strong shaking or sliding of the ground. The tips below can help you and your family stay safe in an earthquake.

Before an Earthquake	During an Earthquake	After an Earthquake
• Attach tall, heavy furniture, such as bookcases, to the wall. Store the heaviest items on the lowest shelves.	• If you are outdoors, stay outdoors and move away from buildings and utility wires.	• Keep watching for falling objects as aftershocks shake the area.
• Check for fire risks. Bolt down gas appliances, and use flexible hosing and connections for both gas and water lines.	• If you are indoors, take cover under a heavy desk or table, or in a doorway. Stay away from glass doors and windows and from heavy objects that might fall.	• Check for hidden structural problems.
• Strengthen and anchor overhead light fixtures to help keep them from falling.	• If you are in a car, drive to an open area away from buildings and overpasses.	• Check for broken gas, electric, and water lines. If you smell gas, shut off the gas main. Leave the area. Report the leak.

Storm Safety

- **In a Tornado** Take cover in a sheltered area away from doors and windows. An interior hallway or basement is best. Stay in the shelter until the danger has passed.
- **In a Hurricane** Prepare for high winds by securing objects outside or bringing them indoors. Cover windows and glass with plywood. Listen to weather bulletins for instructions. If asked to evacuate, proceed to emergency shelters.
- **In a Winter Storm or Blizzard** Stock up on food that does not have to be cooked. Dress in thin layers that help trap the body's heat. Pay special attention to the head and neck. If you are caught in a vehicle, turn on the dome light to make the vehicle visible to search crews.

First Aid

For Choking . . .

The tips on the next few pages can help you provide simple first aid to others and yourself. Always tell an adult about any injuries that occur.

If someone else is choking . . .

1. Recognize the Universal Choking Sign—grasping the throat with both hands. This sign means a person is choking and needs help.

2. Put your arms around his or her waist. Make a fist and put it above the person's navel. Grab your fist with your other hand.

3. Pull your hands toward yourself and give five quick, hard, upward thrusts on the choker's belly.

If you are choking when alone . . .

1. Make a fist and place it above your navel. Grab your fist with your other hand. Pull your hands up with a quick, hard thrust.

2. Or, keep your hands on your belly, lean your body over the back of a chair or over a counter, and shove your fist in and up.

For Bleeding . . .

If someone else is bleeding . . .

Wash your hands with soap, if possible.

Put on protective gloves, if available.

Wash small wounds with soap and water. Do *not* wash serious wounds.

Place a clean gauze pad or cloth over the wound. Press firmly for ten minutes. Don't lift the gauze during this time.

If you don't have gloves, have the injured person hold the cloth in place with his or her own hand.

If after ten minutes the bleeding has stopped, bandage the wound. If the bleeding has not stopped, continue pressing on the wound and get help.

If you are bleeding . . .

- Follow the steps shown above. You don't need gloves to touch your own blood.

- Be sure to tell an adult about your injury.

For Nosebleeds . . .

- Sit down, and tilt your head forward. Pinch your nostrils together for at least ten minutes.
- You can also put an ice pack on the bridge of your nose.
- If your nose continues to bleed, get help from an adult.

For Burns . . .

Minor burns are called first degree burns and involve only the top layer of skin. The skin is red and dry and the burn is painful. More serious burns are called second or third degree burns. These burns involve the top and lower layers of skin. Second degree burns cause blisters, redness, swelling, and pain. Third degree burns are the most serious. The skin is gray or white and looks burned. All burns need immediate first aid.

Minor Burns

- Run cool water over the burn or soak it in cool water for at least five minutes.
- Cover the burn with a clean, dry bandage.
- Do *not* put lotion or ointment on the burn.

More Serious Burns

- Cover the burn with a cool, wet bandage or cloth. Do *not* break any blisters.
- Do *not* put lotion or ointment on the burn.
- Get help from an adult right away.

For Insect Bites and Stings . . .

- Always tell an adult about bites and stings.
- Scrape out the stinger with your fingernail.
- Wash the area with soap and water.
- Ice cubes will usually take away the pain from insect bites. A paste made from baking soda and water also helps.

▲ deer tick

- If the bite or sting is more serious and is on the arm or leg, keep the leg or arm dangling down. Apply a cold, wet cloth. Get help immediately!
- If you find a tick on your skin, remove it. Crush it between two rocks. Wash your hands right away.
- If a tick has already bitten you, do not pull it off. Cover it with oil and wait for it to let go, then remove it with tweezers. Wash the area and your hands.

For Skin Rashes from Plants . . .

Many poisonous plants have three leaves. Remember, "Leaves of three, let them be." If you touch a poisonous plant, wash the area. Put on clean clothes and throw the dirty ones in the washer. If a rash develops, follow these tips.

- Apply calamine lotion or a baking soda and water paste. Try not to scratch. Tell an adult.

▲ poison ivy

- If you get blisters, do *not* pop them. If they burst, keep the area clean and dry. Cover with a bandage.
- If your rash does not go away in two weeks or if the rash is on your face or in your eyes, see your doctor.

Being Safe at Home

When Home Alone

Everyone stays home alone sometimes. When you stay home alone, it's important to know how to take care of yourself. Here are some easy rules to follow that will help keep you safe when you are at home by yourself.

Do These Things

- Lock all the doors and windows. Be sure you know how to lock and unlock all the locks.

- If someone calls who is nasty or mean, hang up. Your parents may not want you to answer the phone at all.

- If you have an emergency, call 911 or 0 (zero) for the operator. Describe the problem and give your full name, address, and telephone number. Follow all instructions given to you.

  - If you see anyone hanging around outside, tell an adult or call the police.

  - If you see or smell smoke, go outside right away. If you live in an apartment, do not take the elevator. Go to a neighbor's home and call 911 or the fire department immediately.

- Entertain yourself. Time will pass more quickly if you are not bored. Try not to spend your time watching television. Instead, work on a hobby, read a book or magazine, do your homework, or clean your room. Before you know it, an adult will be home.

Do NOT Do These Things

- Do NOT use the stove, microwave, or oven unless an adult family member has given you permission and you are sure about how to use these appliances.

- Do NOT open the door for anyone you don't know or for anyone who is not supposed to be in your home.

  - If someone rings the bell and asks to use the telephone, tell the person to go to a phone booth.

  - If someone tries to deliver a package, do NOT open the door. The delivery person will leave the package or come back later.

  - If someone is selling something, do NOT open the door. Just say, "We're not interested," and nothing more.

- Do NOT talk to strangers on the telephone. Do not tell anyone that you are home alone. If the call is for an adult family member, say that they can't come to the phone right now and take a message. Ask for the caller's name and phone number and deliver the message when an adult family member comes home.

- Do NOT have friends over unless you have gotten permission from your parents or other adult family members.

Being Physically Active

Planning Your Weekly Activities

Being active every day is important for your overall health. Physical activity helps you manage stress, maintain a healthful weight, and strengthen your body systems. The Activity Pyramid, like the Food Guide Pyramid, can help you choose a variety of activities in the right amounts to keep your body strong and healthy.

The Activity Pyramid

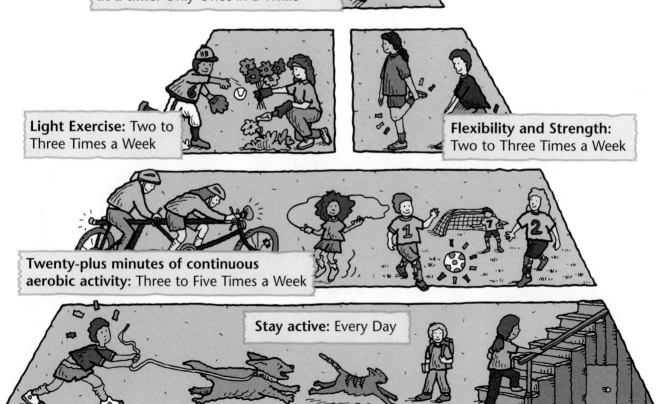

Sitting for more than thirty minutes at a time: Only Once in a While

Light Exercise: Two to Three Times a Week

Flexibility and Strength: Two to Three Times a Week

Twenty-plus minutes of continuous aerobic activity: Three to Five Times a Week

Stay active: Every Day

Guidelines for a Good Workout

There are three things you should do every time you are going to exercise—warm up, work out, and cool down.

Warm-Up When you warm up, your heart rate, breathing rate, and body temperature increase and more blood flows to your muscles. As your body warms up, you can move more easily. People who warm up are less stiff after exercising, and are less likely to have exercise-related injuries. Your warm-up should include five minutes of stretching, and five minutes of low-level exercise.

Workout The main part of your exercise routine should be an aerobic exercise that lasts 20 to 30 minutes. Aerobic exercises make your heart, lungs, and circulatory system stronger.

Some common aerobic exercises are shown on pages R22–R23. You may want to mix up the types of activities you do. This helps you work different muscles, and provides a better workout over time.

Cool-Down When you finish your aerobic exercise, you need to give your body time to cool down. Start your cool-down with three to five minutes of low-level activity. End with stretching exercises to prevent soreness and stiffness.

Being Physically Active

Warm-Up and Cool-Down Stretches

Before you exercise, you should warm up your muscles. The warm-up exercises shown here should be held for at least fifteen to twenty seconds and repeated at least three times.

At the end of your workout, spend about two minutes repeating some of these stretches.

▲ **Shoulder and Chest Stretch** HINT—Pulling your hands slowly toward the floor gives a better stretch. Keep your elbows straight, but not locked!

▶ **Hurdler's Stretch** HINT—Keep the toes of your extended leg pointed up.

◀ **Sit-and-Reach Stretch** HINT—Remember to bend at the waist. Keep your eyes on your toes!

▲ **Upper Back and Shoulder Stretch**
HINT—Try to stretch your hand down
so that it rests flat against your back.

▼ **Thigh Stretch** HINT—
Keep both hands flat on
the ground. Lean as far
forward as you can.

▲ **Calf Stretch** HINT—Keep
both feet on the floor during
this stretch. Try changing the
distance between your feet.
Is the stretch better for you
when your legs are closer
together or farther apart?

Tips for Stretching

- Never bounce when stretching.
- Hold each stretch for fifteen to twenty seconds.
- Breathe normally. This helps your body get the oxygen it needs.
- Do NOT stretch until it hurts. Stretch only until you feel a slight pull.

Being Physically Active

Building a Strong Heart and Lungs

Aerobic activities cause deep breathing and a fast heart rate for at least twenty minutes. These activities help both your heart and your lungs. Because your heart is a muscle, it gets stronger with exercise. A strong heart doesn't have to work as hard to pump blood to the rest of your body. Exercise also allows your lungs to hold more air. With a strong heart and lungs, your cells get oxygen faster and your body works more efficiently.

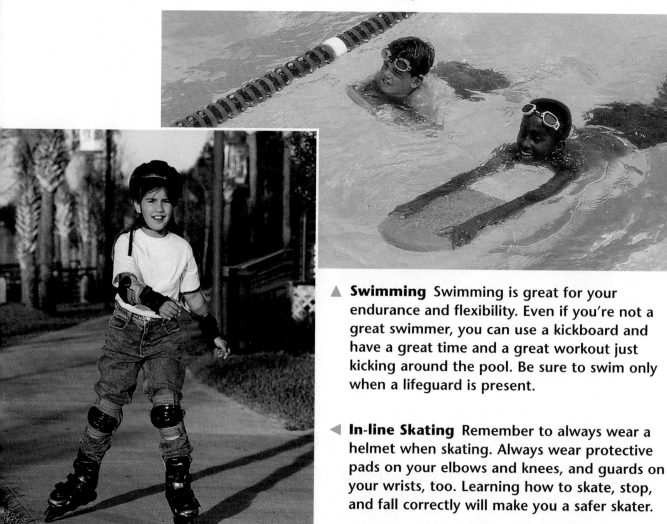

▲ **Swimming** Swimming is great for your endurance and flexibility. Even if you're not a great swimmer, you can use a kickboard and have a great time and a great workout just kicking around the pool. Be sure to swim only when a lifeguard is present.

◄ **In-line Skating** Remember to always wear a helmet when skating. Always wear protective pads on your elbows and knees, and guards on your wrists, too. Learning how to skate, stop, and fall correctly will make you a safer skater.

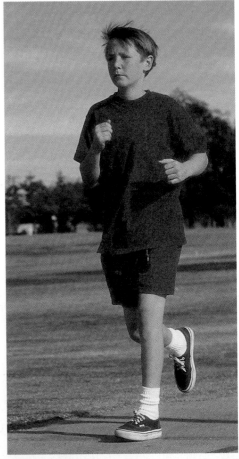

▼ **Walking** A fast-paced walk is a terrific way to build your endurance. The only equipment you need is supportive shoes. Walking with a friend can make this exercise a lot of fun.

▲ **Jumping Rope** Jumping rope is one of the best ways to increase your endurance. Remember to always jump on an even surface and always wear supportive shoes.

▼ **Bicycling** Bicycling provides good aerobic activity *and* a great way to see the outdoors. Be sure to learn and follow bicycle safety rules. And *always* remember to wear your helmet!

Good Nutrition

The Food Guide Pyramid

No one food or food group supplies everything your body needs for good health. That's why it's important to eat foods from all the food groups. The Food Guide Pyramid can help you choose healthful foods in the right amounts. By choosing more foods from the groups at the bottom of the pyramid and fewer foods from the group at the top, you will eat the foods that provide your body with energy to grow and develop.

Fats, oils, and sweets
Eat sparingly.

Meat, poultry, fish, dry beans, eggs, and nuts 2–3 servings

Milk, yogurt, and cheese
2–3 servings

Fruits
2–4 servings

Vegetables
3–5 servings

Breads, cereals, rice, and pasta 6–11 servings

Estimating Serving Sizes

Choosing a variety of foods is only half the story. You also need to choose the right amounts. The table below can help you estimate the number of servings you are eating of your favorite foods.

Food Group	Amount of Food in One Serving	Some Easy Ways to Estimate Serving Size
Bread, Cereal, Rice, Pasta Group	1 ounce ready-to-eat (dry) cereal	large handful of plain cereal or a small handful of cereal with raisins and nuts
	1 slice bread, $\frac{1}{2}$ bagel	
	$\frac{1}{2}$ cup cooked pasta, rice, or cereal	ice cream scoop
Vegetable Group	1 cup of raw, leafy vegetables	about the size of a fist
	$\frac{1}{2}$ cup other vegetables, cooked or raw, chopped	
	$\frac{3}{4}$ cup vegetable juice	
	$\frac{1}{2}$ cup tomato sauce	ice cream scoop
Fruit Group	medium apple, pear, or orange	a baseball
	$\frac{1}{2}$ large banana or one medium banana	
	$\frac{1}{2}$ cup chopped or cooked fruit	
	$\frac{3}{4}$ cup of fruit juice	
Milk, Yogurt, and Cheese Group	$1\frac{1}{2}$ ounces of natural cheese	two dominoes
	2 ounces of processed cheese	$1\frac{1}{2}$ slices of packaged cheese
	1 cup of milk or yogurt	
Meat, Poultry, Fish, Dry Beans, Eggs, and Nuts Group	3 ounces of lean meat, chicken, or fish	about the size of your palm
	2 tablespoons peanut butter	
	$\frac{1}{2}$ cup of cooked dry beans	
Fats, Oils, and Sweets Group	1 teaspoon of margarine or butter	about the size of the tip of your thumb

Preparing Foods Safely

Fight Bacteria

You probably already know to throw away food that smells bad or looks moldy. But food doesn't have to look or smell bad to make you ill. To keep your food safe and yourself from becoming ill, follow the steps outlined in the picture below. And remember—when in doubt, throw it out!

FIGHT BAC!

Keep Food Safe From Bacteria

CLEAN
Wash hands and surfaces often.

SEPARATE
Don't cross-contaminate.

CHILL
Refrigerate promptly.

COOK
Cook to proper temperatures.

BAC

TM

Food Safety Tips

Tips for Preparing Food

- Wash hands in warm, soapy water before preparing food. It's also a good idea to wash hands after preparing each dish.
- Defrost meat in the microwave or the refrigerator.
- Keep raw meat, poultry, fish, and their juices away from other food.
- Wash cutting boards, knives, and countertops immediately after cutting up meat, poultry, or fish.

Tips for Cooking Food

- Cook all food completely, especially meat. Complete cooking kills the bacteria that can make you ill.
- Red meats should be cooked to a temperature of 160°F. Poultry should be cooked to 180°F. When done, fish flakes easily with a fork.
- Never eat food that contains raw eggs or raw egg yolks, including cookie dough.

Tips for Cleaning Up the Kitchen

- Wash all dishes, utensils, and countertops with hot, soapy water. Use a soap that kills bacteria, if possible.
- Store leftovers in small containers that will cool quickly in the refrigerator. Don't leave leftovers on the counter to cool.

Sense Organs

Eye

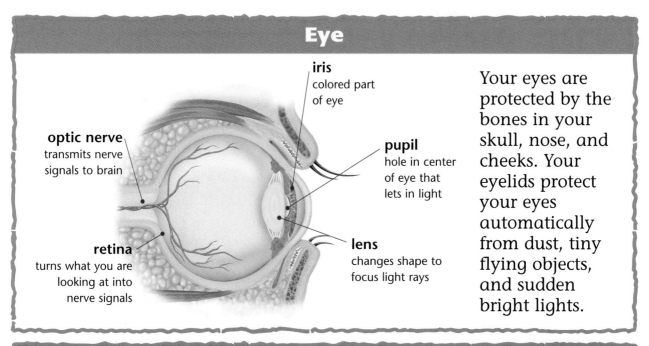

iris
colored part of eye

optic nerve
transmits nerve signals to brain

pupil
hole in center of eye that lets in light

retina
turns what you are looking at into nerve signals

lens
changes shape to focus light rays

Your eyes are protected by the bones in your skull, nose, and cheeks. Your eyelids protect your eyes automatically from dust, tiny flying objects, and sudden bright lights.

Ear

Earwax is made inside your ears to help keep them clean. Dust, dirt, and germs stick to the earwax instead of going farther into your ear. When you move your mouth by chewing and talking, old wax works its way to your outer ear.

Outer ear   Middle ear   Inner ear

eardrum
moves back and forth when hit by sound waves

ear canal
connects outer ear to middle ear

Caring for Your Eyes and Ears

- Have your eyesight (vision) checked every year.

- Wear safety glasses when participating in activities that can be dangerous to the eyes, such as sports and mowing grass.

- Wash in, around, and behind your outer ear. Do not try to clean your ear canal with cotton-tip sticks or other objects.

Nose

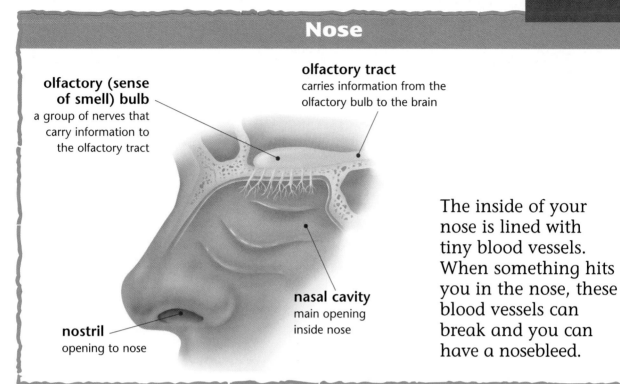

olfactory (sense of smell) bulb
a group of nerves that carry information to the olfactory tract

olfactory tract
carries information from the olfactory bulb to the brain

nasal cavity
main opening inside nose

nostril
opening to nose

The inside of your nose is lined with tiny blood vessels. When something hits you in the nose, these blood vessels can break and you can have a nosebleed.

Caring for Your Nose, Tongue, and Skin

- If you get a nosebleed, sit, lean forward slightly, and pinch just below the bridge of your nose for ten minutes. Breathe through your mouth.

- When you brush your teeth, brush your tongue too.

- Always wear sunscreen when you are in the sun.

Tongue

Germs live on your tongue and in other parts of your mouth. Germs can harm your teeth and give you bad breath.

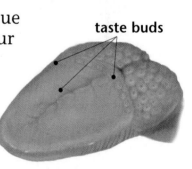

taste buds

Skin

protective outer layer

strong, springy middle layer

fatty lower layer

Your skin protects your insides from the outside world. It keeps fluids you need inside your body and fluids you don't need, such as swimming pool water, outside your body.

Skeletal System

Each of your bones has a particular shape and size that allow it to do a certain job. You have bones that are tiny, long, wide, flat, and even curved. The job of some bones is to protect your body parts.

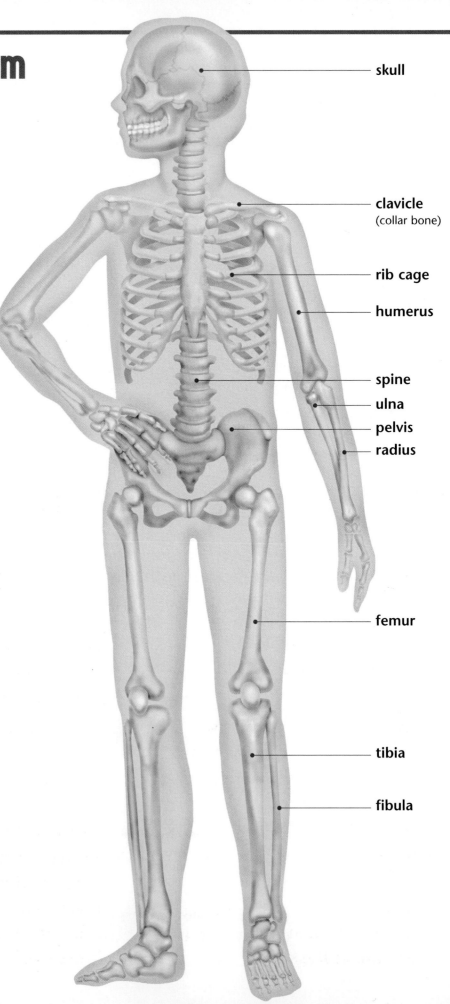

skull

clavicle
(collar bone)

rib cage

humerus

spine

ulna

pelvis

radius

femur

tibia

fibula

Bones That Protect

Rib Cage Your rib bones form a cage that protects your heart and lungs from all sides. Your ribs are springy. When something strikes you in the chest, your ribs push the object away instead of letting it hit your heart and lungs.

Your ribs are connected to your breastbone (sternum) by springy material called cartilage. The springy connection lets your ribs move up and down. This happens when your rib cage gets bigger and smaller as you breathe in and out.

Skull The bones in your head are called your skull. Some of the bones in your skull protect your brain. The bones in your face are part of your skull too.

cartilage

rib

sternum

jaw

Caring for Your Skeletal System

- Calcium helps bones grow and makes them strong. Dairy products like milk, cheese, and yogurt contain calcium. Have 2–3 servings of dairy products every day.

- Exercise also makes your bones strong. When bones aren't used, they can become brittle and may break.

Activities

1. Look at the picture of the skeleton. Name a long bone. Name a short bone. Name a curved bone.

2. Put a tomato inside a wire cage. Gently throw a wad of paper at the cage. What happens? The cage protects the tomato in the same way your ribs protect your heart.

3. Measure around your rib cage with a string. How big is it when you breathe in? How big is it when you breathe out? Which measurement is greater?

Muscular System

Like your bones, each muscle in your body does a certain job. Muscles in your thumb help you hold things. Muscles in your neck help you turn your head. Muscles in your arms help you pull or lift objects.

deltoid

biceps

triceps

flexors

abdominal muscles

quadriceps

flexors

How Muscles Move Your Body

Muscle Pairs Your arm can reach forward and pull back. Your hand can open and close. Muscles can only pull. Moving part of your body in more than one direction takes more than one muscle. It takes a pair of muscles for your arm to bend and straighten.

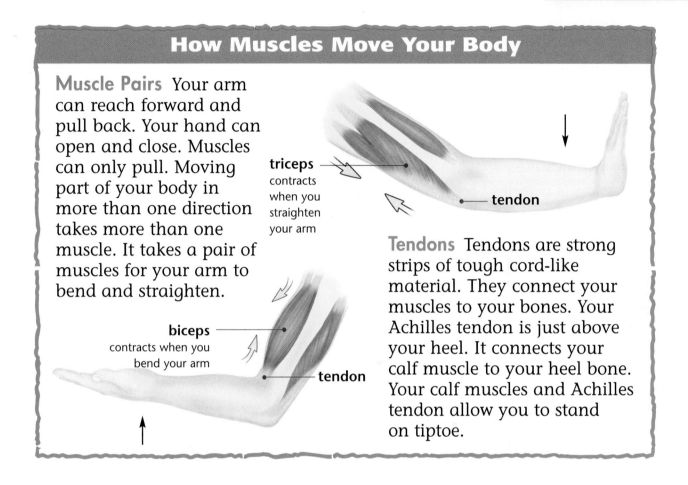

triceps
contracts when you straighten your arm

tendon

biceps
contracts when you bend your arm

tendon

Tendons Tendons are strong strips of tough cord-like material. They connect your muscles to your bones. Your Achilles tendon is just above your heel. It connects your calf muscle to your heel bone. Your calf muscles and Achilles tendon allow you to stand on tiptoe.

Caring for Your Muscular System

- Exercise makes your muscles stronger.
- Stretching before you exercise makes muscles and tendons more flexible and less likely to get hurt.

Activities

1. Tie your shoe without using your thumb. What happens?

2. Pull up on a desk with one hand. With your other hand, feel which arm muscle is working. Now push on the desk. Which arm muscle is working?

3. Ask a friend to push down on your arms for one minute while you push up as hard as you can. When your friend lets go, what happens?

Digestive System

Food is broken down and pushed through your body by your digestive system. Your digestive system is a series of connected parts that starts with your mouth and ends with your large intestine.

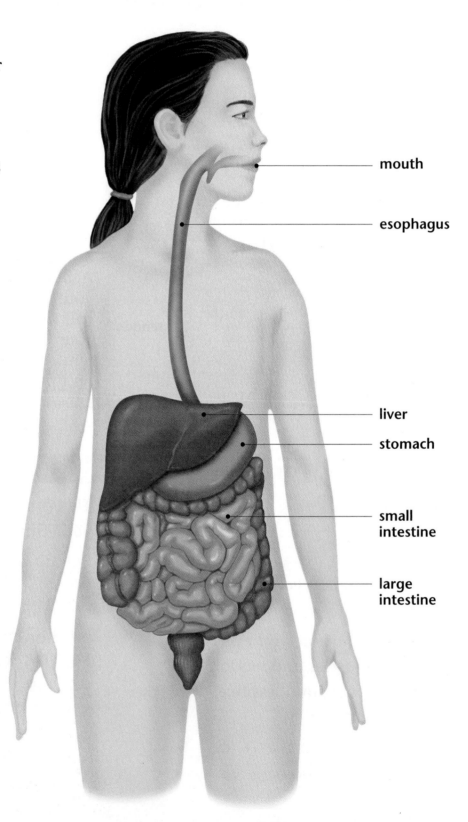

mouth

esophagus

liver

stomach

small intestine

large intestine

From Mouth to Stomach

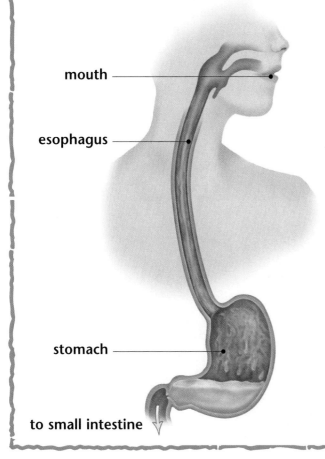

mouth

esophagus

stomach

to small intestine

Esophagus Your esophagus, or food tube, is a tube that connects your mouth to your stomach. After you swallow a bite of food, muscles in your esophagus push the food into your stomach.

Stomach Your stomach is filled with acid that helps dissolve food. The stomach walls are strong muscles that mix food with the acid. The stomach walls are protected from the acid by a thick layer of mucus. From your stomach, food moves to the small intestine and then to the large intestine.

Caring for Your Digestive System

- Chew everything you eat carefully. Well-chewed food is easier to digest.
- Do not overeat. Overeating can cause a stomachache.

Activities

1. Measure 25 feet (about 8 m) on the floor. This is how long your digestive system is.

2. Cut a narrow balloon so that it is open on both ends. Put a wad of paper in one end. Squeeze the outside of the balloon to push the paper through and out the other end. This is similar to how your esophagus pushes food to your stomach.

Circulatory System

Food and oxygen travel through your circulatory system to every cell in your body. Blood moves nutrients throughout your body, fights infection, and helps control your body temperature. Your blood is made up mostly of a watery liquid called plasma.

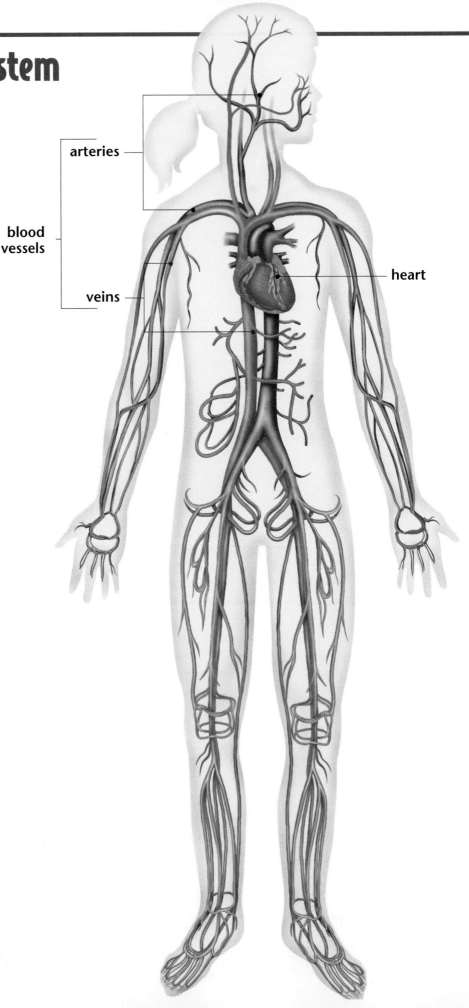

arteries

blood vessels

veins

heart

Blood Vessels

Arteries Arteries carry blood away from the heart. Blood in arteries is brighter red because it has come from the lungs and has lots of oxygen. Arteries bring oxygen and nutrients to all parts of the body.

Veins Veins carry blood to the heart. Veins have one-way valves that allow blood to move only toward the heart.

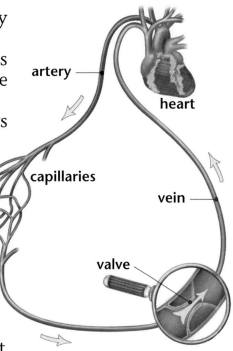

artery

heart

capillaries

vein

valve

Capillaries Capillaries are very small pathways for blood. When blood flows through capillaries, it gives oxygen and nutrients to the cells in your body. Blood also picks up carbon dioxide and other waste.

Caring for Your Circulatory System

- Never touch another person's blood.

- Eat a healthy, balanced diet throughout your life to keep excess fat from blocking the blood flowing through your arteries.

- Get regular exercise to keep your heart strong.

Activities

1. Take the bottom out of a paper cup. Bend the top together like a clamshell. Hold the cup and drop a marble through from the bottom. Now try to drop one into the top. The clamshell-shaped cup is like the one-way valve in a vein.

2. Find the blue lines under the skin on your wrist. These are veins. Press gently and stroke along the lines toward your elbow. Now stroke toward your hand. What do you see?

Respiratory System

Your body uses its respiratory system to get oxygen from the air and get rid of excess carbon dioxide. Your respiratory system is made up of your nose and mouth, your trachea (windpipe), your two lungs, and your diaphragm—a dome-shaped muscle under your lungs.

nose

mouth

trachea
(windpipe)

lungs

diaphragm

Breathing

When you inhale, or breathe in, air enters your mouth and nose and goes into your trachea. Your trachea connects your nose and mouth to your lungs. Your trachea divides into two smaller tubes that go to your lungs. Your lungs fill with air. When you exhale, or breathe out, your diaphragm pushes upward. Air is forced up your trachea and out your mouth and nose.

INHALING

air goes into mouth and nose

lungs fill with air

diaphragm moves down

EXHALING

air comes out of mouth and nose

air leaves lungs

diaphragm moves up

Caring for Your Respiratory System

- Exercise. When you exercise your body, you exercise your respiratory system too. Your muscles use more oxygen, so you breathe faster and deeper.

- Get enough sleep to help your resistance to colds.

Activities

1. Sit in a chair and count how many breaths you take in 30 seconds. Then exercise for two minutes. When you stop, count how many breaths you take in 30 seconds. When do you breathe more?

2. Put your hand on your bellybutton and take a deep breath in and out. How does your hand move?

Nervous System

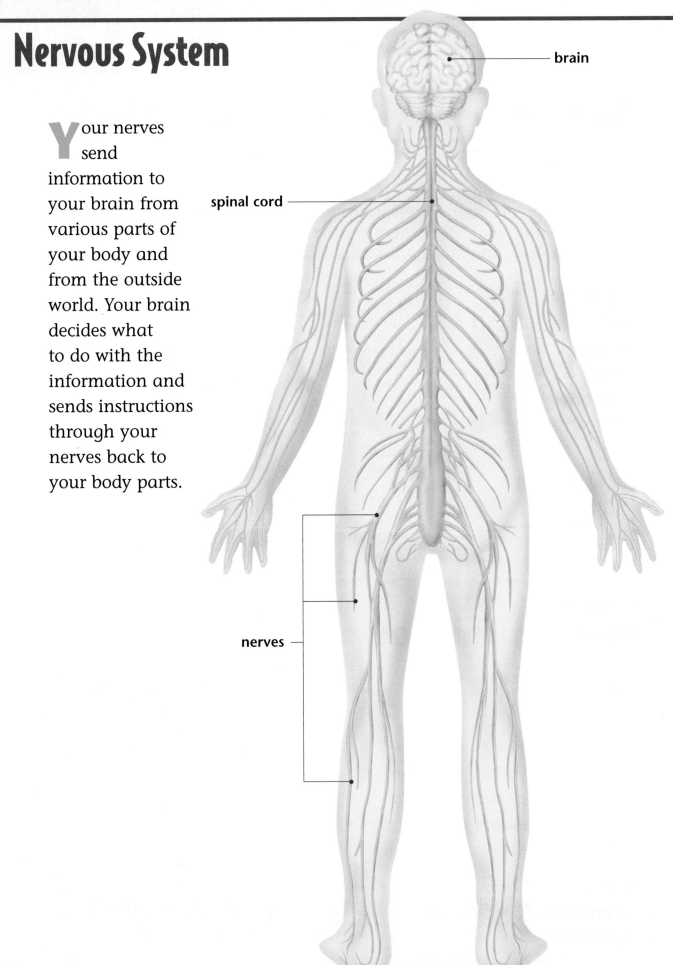

Your nerves send information to your brain from various parts of your body and from the outside world. Your brain decides what to do with the information and sends instructions through your nerves back to your body parts.

brain

spinal cord

nerves

Your Brain

Your brain is about two pounds of wrinkled, pinkish-gray material. It's protected by your skull and cushioned by a thin layer of liquid. The brain's main connection to the body is the spinal cord.

Different parts of the brain send signals to different parts of your body. For example, the part right behind your forehead tells your body how to move. The area near the base of your neck controls your breathing and heartbeat. If you are left-handed, the right half of your brain controls your handwriting.

skull

liquid cushion

brain

Caring for Your Nervous System

- Many injuries to the brain are caused by car crashes. Wear your safety belt and sit in the back seat when you are in the car.

- Always wear a helmet when you ride your bike, skate, or use a skateboard.

Activities

1. Make a list of signals your nerves are sending to your brain right now. Also list instructions your brain is sending to your nerves.

2. Read a paragraph out of a book while the television is on. Do you know what the paragraph was about? Do you know what happened on television?

3. Write your name with your opposite hand ten times. Does your writing improve?

Using Science Reading Strategies

Scientists use reading strategies in their work. They read to find out everything they can about a topic they are investigating. The following are some good strategies to use and how you might use them as you read Harcourt Science.

Weathering is caused by more than the wind. Water also causes weathering. Even plants help break apart rocks on the surface of the Earth.

Water causes weathering when it freezes. Most things take up less space when they freeze. But frozen water takes up more space. Water flows into cracks and holes in rock. As the temperature drops, the water freezes. Since the ice takes up more space, it pushes against the rock around it. The force of the ice widens the cracks and breaks the rock into pieces.

Water also causes weathering when it is not frozen. The movement of water wears rock away. Also, rivers pick up rocks and bounce them around. This wears the rocks down.

Plants cause weathering, too. Roots grow into cracks in rock. As the roots get bigger, they split the rock.

✔ **What is weathering?**

▲ Tree roots grow into cracks in rocks to reach minerals and water. As the roots grow, they split the rocks.

▲ Water breaks rock when it freezes in cracks. Water and ice are important causes of weathering.

◄ After weathering by water, a rock has rounded edges. These rocks tumbled in a river and smashed against other rocks. Their sharp edges were worn away.

C41

When you are reading text like this...

Water causes weathering when it freezes. Most things take up less space when they freeze. But frozen water takes up more space. Water flows into cracks and holes in rock. As the temperature drops, the water freezes. Since the ice takes up more space, it pushes against the rock around it. The force of the ice widens the cracks and breaks the rock into pieces.

page C41

A good strategy to use is...
Use Prior Knowledge

Think about questions like these:

* What new facts are you learning?
* How do the new facts fit in with what you already know about this scientific topic?

Here's what you might say to yourself...

"This passage reminds me of something. One time, my dad left a glass bottle filled with water outside overnight. It was really, really cold that night. In the morning the glass was broken. There were blobs of ice in the cracks. I thought that the cold air had cracked the glass. Now I see it was the water freezing and taking up more space that made the glass break—just like what happens to rock."

When reading text like this...

Activity Purpose

Many places on Earth are hot in summer and cold in winter. In this investigation you will find out why. You will **compare** the way light rays strike a surface. Then you will **infer** how this affects Earth's temperatures.

Materials

- clear tape
- graph paper
- large book
- flashlight
- meter stick
- black marker
- wooden block
- red marker

Activity Procedure

1. Tape the graph paper to the book.

2. Hold the flashlight about 50 cm above the book. Shine the light straight down. The beam will make a circle on the paper. If the circle is bigger than the paper, bring the light closer.

page D66

A good strategy to use is...

Adjust Reading Rate

Think about the kind of science text you are reading and how you should read it.

- Is it an introduction, or a brief description that you can read quickly?

- Does the text have facts or details you'll need to read more than once?

- Are there directions or information you'll need to read slowly so you'll understand what you've read?

Here's what you might say to yourself...

"I see three kinds of text on this page: The first paragraph tells me what the activity is about. The next kind of text is a list. It tells me what I'll need for the investigation. The last kind of text is the beginning of the directions. They tell me what I need to do, step by step.

"I think I can read the description once. I'll read it kind of quickly. I just want to get an idea of what the activity is about.

"I'll look through the list quickly. I might need to look at it more than once, though. I'll want to be sure I have everything I need.

"I'll slow down and read the directions carefully. Then I'll have to reread them a few times. That way, I can make sure I'm doing each step in the investigation the right way."

Today machines are used to sort plastic bottles. Bottles that have a number 1 stamped on them can be used in a new, exciting way, so they are separated from the rest. Their labels and caps are removed. Then the bottles are crushed and chopped into tiny pieces called flake. The flake is melted and pulled into long, thin threads. The threads are stretched and kinked. After that, they look like threads of cotton.

page C106

Create Mental Images

Think about the pictures an artist might draw to go with what you're reading.

- Can you picture each step when you read about a process?
- Can you think of how the process might look in a movie?

Here's what you might say to yourself...

"To get a clear idea of this section, I'm going to picture each of the things described:

First I picture a bunch of big plastic juice bottles with lids and labels. Now I'm seeing the lids and labels coming off. I see the bottles being chopped into tiny chips. Now the chips are melting. I see melted blobs being stretched until they turn into strings, as thin as sewing thread. I see the thread being wound around and pressed into a square."

What Causes Seasons

In most places on Earth, summer and winter are different. Summer is hot. There are many hours of daylight. Sunlight is strong. Winter is cold. The hours of daylight are shorter. Sunlight is weaker. Summer and winter are two seasons.

Earth has seasons because its axis is tilted. This means Earth is tipped to one side, like the book in the investigation was tilted. The tilt changes the way sunlight hits Earth at different times of the year.

page D70

Use Text Structure and Format

What headings are used? How are the paragraphs organized?

- Do the paragraphs tell about causes and effects? sequence?
- Do they compare two or more things or classify concepts?

Here's what you might say to yourself...

"The heading tells me this section is about causes and effects. There are seasons because the axis of the Earth is tilted. As I read on, I'll learn more about how this causes us to have seasons."

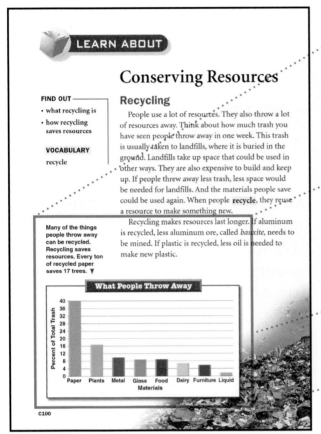

LEARN ABOUT

Conserving Resources

FIND OUT
- what recycling is
- how recycling saves resources

VOCABULARY
recycle

Recycling

People use a lot of resources. They also throw a lot of resources away. Think about how much trash you have seen people throw away in one week. This trash is usually taken to landfills, where it is buried in the ground. Landfills take up space that could be used in other ways. They are also expensive to build and keep up. If people threw away less trash, less space would be needed for landfills. And the materials people save could be used again. When people **recycle**, they reuse a resource to make something new.

Recycling makes resources last longer. If aluminum is recycled, less aluminum ore, called *bauxite*, needs to be mined. If plastic is recycled, less oil is needed to make new plastic.

Many of the things people throw away can be recycled. Recycling saves resources. Every ton of recycled paper saves 17 trees. ▼

What People Throw Away

Percent of Total Trash

Paper Plants Metal Glass Food Materials Dairy Furniture Liquid

C100

When reading text like this...

Many of the things people throw away can be recycled. Recycling saves resources. Every ton of recycled paper saves 17 trees. ▼

What People Throw Away

Percent of Total Trash

| 40 |
| 36 |
| 32 |
| 28 |
| 24 |
| 20 |
| 16 |
| 12 |
| 8 |
| 4 |
| 0 |

Paper   Plants   Metal   Glass   Food   Dairy   Furniture   Liquid
Materials

page C100

A good strategy to use is...
Use Graphic Aids

Think about why the author included a graphic aid. Look at any pictures, graphs, charts, diagrams, or time lines that are included with the text.

- Do they show the same information as the text in a way that's easy to see? Then use them as you read.

- Do they add new information? Then take time to read them carefully, to learn the new information.

Here's what you might say to yourself...

"After reading the paragraph, I see that the graph on this page is adding new information. I need to spend some time reading it carefully.

"I'm going to start by reading the heading. Now I know the graph shows what people throw away. Next I'll read the information along the bottom, to see what kinds of trash people throw away. Then I'll read along the side to see the amounts that are being compared in the graph.

"After that, I'm going to spend a bit of time comparing the types of trash shown in the graph. I want to see what kinds of things are thrown away most and least. Then I'll see if some amounts are about the same. I see two that are almost exactly the same."

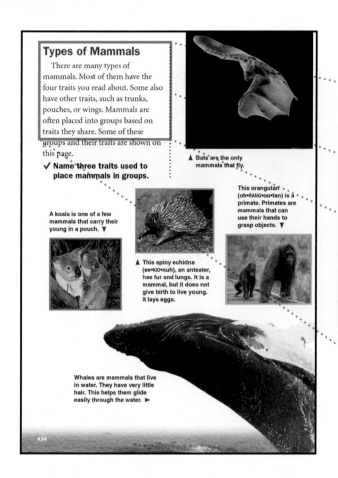

Types of Mammals

There are many types of mammals. Most of them have the four traits you read about. Some also have other traits, such as trunks, pouches, or wings. Mammals are often placed into groups based on traits they share. Some of these groups and their traits are shown on this page.

✓ **Name three traits used to place mammals in groups.**

▲ Bats are the only mammals that fly.

A koala is one of a few mammals that carry their young in a pouch. ▼

▲ This spiny echidna (ee•KID•nuh), an anteater, has fur and lungs. It is a mammal, but it does not give birth to live young. It lays eggs.

This orangutan (oh•RANG•oo•tan) is a primate. Primates are mammals that can use their hands to grasp objects. ▼

Whales are mammals that live in water. They have very little hair. This helps them glide easily through the water. ▶

A54

When reading text like this...

Types of Mammals

There are many types of mammals. Most of them have the four traits you read about. Some also have other traits, such as trunks, pouches, or wings. Mammals are often placed into groups based on traits they share....

page A54

A good strategy to use is...
Reread

Think about whether you are understanding what you're reading. If something doesn't make sense, you might need to reread.

- Does it help to go back and read it again?
- Does the passage mention something you learned in an earlier chapter? You may have to look back at this section to remind yourself of what you learned to understand the passage.

Here's what you might say to yourself...

"Wait. I'm getting confused. I'd better start again.... Oh, I see the problem. The text talks about four traits that were already listed. I don't remember what those four traits are, so I'd better look back to remind myself....

"On the previous two pages, I see that four traits are described: Mammals have fur or hair. They use lungs to breathe. They give birth to live young. Young mammals are sheltered and fed milk by their mothers.

"All right. I'm all set and ready to move on."

Buildings Change Over Time

Long ago, many people lived in simple huts or tents made from wood and animal skins. Most people moved from place to place, following the animals they hunted. As they moved, they took their homes with them. Around 10,000 B.C., clay was first used to weatherproof wooden buildings. Thousands of years later, in Egypt, triangle-shaped stone buildings called pyramids were built. Some pyramids stood as high as 147 meters (about 482 feet). As time passed, building styles changed even more. In the 1300s, for example, the tallest buildings were large towers, domes, and churches made from stone and glass.

Industrial Age

By the late 1800s, cities were springing up throughout the world. Because of growth, more and more tall buildings were being built. Many of these buildings were made of materials such as iron, steel, stone,

1973
The Sears Tower in Chicago was built. At 110 stories and 443 meters (about 1,453 feet), it was now the tallest building in the world.

1900   **2000**

1931
The Empire State Building was built. At that time, it was the tallest building in the world, at 381 meters (1,250 feet) high.

brick, and concrete. Over time, builders used steel frames, which were stronger and lighter than iron rods, to produce even taller buildings. Machines, such as cranes, were used to carry heavy materials to these "high-rise" buildings.

What Keeps Buildings from Falling?

As you know, a force is a push or a pull. Tall buildings experience many different kinds of forces. When a force acts on a building, it is called a load. When wind blows on a structure, for example, it is called the wind load. Wind is a major concern of building designers. They must make buildings sturdy enough to withstand strong winds and other types of dangerous weather.

The dead load is the weight of a building. The live load is a building's weight plus everything in it, such as people, cars, and furniture. If forces such as these loads were powerful enough, buildings could crumble and fall. Builders, however, use materials such as concrete beams and steel bars to make strong buildings.

THINK ABOUT IT

1. What materials did people use to build taller and taller skyscrapers?
2. What is the difference between a live load and a dead load?

F83

When you are reading text like this...

Buildings Change Over Time

Long ago, many people lived in simple huts or tents made from wood and animal skins. Most people moved from place to place, following the animals they hunted. As they moved, they took their homes with them. Around 10,000 B.C., clay was first used to weatherproof wooden buildings. Thousands of years later, in Egypt, triangle-shaped stone buildings called pyramids were built. Some pyramids stood as high as 147 meters (about 482 feet). As time passed, building styles changed even more. In the 1300s, for example, the tallest buildings were large towers, domes, and churches made from stone and glass.

page F83

A good strategy to use is...
Summarize and Paraphrase

Think about how you could shorten a passage without leaving out any key ideas.

- Can you tell the main ideas in your own words when you finish reading a section?
- Is there a chapter summary to help you remember the main points?
- Can you write your own summary?

Here's what you might say to yourself...

"When I summarize this section, my summary should be as brief as it can be. But, I want to be sure to include all the important points. Here is my summary:

Engineers can now design buildings so they will still stand after an earthquake. Some can move with the shaking, like the Transamerica Building that survived a 1989 quake in San Francisco. Smaller buildings that sit on rubber pads are also safe during an earthquake."

Building a Science Vocabulary

Reading and understanding new science words can be a challenge. But you can make it easier if you use what you already know! These ideas will help you to learn and remember the meanings of new science words.

Look for Connections

Have you ever eaten a fruit called a Clementine? If not, you won't know what it tastes like. But what if you found out that a Clementine was a lot like an orange? Then you'd have an idea of what it tasted like. You would know because you made a connection to something you already knew. The two fruits are alike in some way. Knowing about an orange helps you understand what a Clementine might be.

The same kind of thing can happen when you read a chapter in your science book. You often come across words that are connected. You can group these words together. You can learn how they are alike.

Use questions like this to get you started:

Do I see the same word repeated in more than one term?

When you do, you'll know that the terms must be connected in some way. Figure out what the repeated word means. Then you'll already have an idea what the new terms might mean.

Examples
water cycle
rock cycle

In this case, the repeated word is cycle. Think about what it means: A *cycle* is a set of events that happen over and over. One event leads to the next. Once you know *cycle*, you already have some idea of what a water cycle or a rock cycle is. A water cycle is the set of events that happens over and over to water.

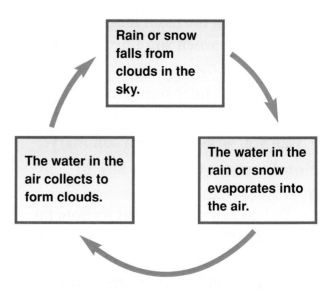

Rain or snow falls from clouds in the sky.

The water in the rain or snow evaporates into the air.

The water in the air collects to form clouds.

A rock cycle is a set of events that happens with rocks. What can you guess about a rock cycle?

Related science terms
yearly cycle
carbon cycle

You can probably figure out the four parts of a yearly cycle. (Hint: One of them is called winter.) You may not know what carbon is. But you can still figure out that a carbon cycle is some set of events that happen over and over. You are already part of the way to knowing what the term means!

Other examples

Look at the words below. What word is repeated in each set of words? Can that repeated word help you understand something about each term?

lunar eclipse **solar eclipse**

renewable resource **nonrenewable resource** **reusable resource**

thermal energy **energy pyramid**

chemical change **physical change**

Here's another question to ask yourself:

Do I see a word I already know in a new term?

You can use the word you know to help you say the new term. You can also use it to help you learn and remember what the new term means.

Example
recycle

Use what you know about the word *cycle*. Put your knowledge to work on *recycle*. Think about it. When people recycle, there must be a set of events or steps that happen over and over.

Related science terms
recycling center
recycling process

Other examples
solar system and *ecosystem*
weather and *weathering*

Compound Words
What familiar words do you see in these terms? Here are words made up of two shorter words:
earthquake
groundwater
topsoil
landform

THINK ABOUT IT
Words like *earthquake*, *groundwater*, *topsoil*, and *landform* are made by making two words into one. Can you make a picture equation to show what one of these terms might mean?

Look for Common Word Parts and "Chunk" Words

You won't always be able to find a whole word that you know when you come to a new science term. Another way to figure out and remember science words is to look for word parts.

- **Look at the beginning of words.** When word parts come at the beginning, they are called prefixes.

- **Look at the end of words.** Word parts called suffixes come at the end of a word.

+ **=** Groundwater

When I come to a new word, do I see any word parts that I know? If so, break the word into chunks. Look for prefixes and suffixes you know. You'll know how to pronounce these chunks already. Now, you only have to figure out how to pronounce the middle of the word. It may turn out to be a word you already know! Below is a chart of scientific words that have been "chunked."

Science Words	Beginning (prefix or prefixes)	Middle	End (suffix or ending)
recycle	re	cycle	
resources	re	source	s
renewable (resource)	re	new	able
nonrenewable (resource)	non + re	new	able
inclined (plane)	in	clin(e)	ed
infected	in	fect	ed
disinfecting	dis + in	fect	ing
loudness		loud	ness
hardness		hard	ness
expandable	ex	pand	able
extraction	ex	trac	tion
reacted	re	act	ed
reinforcement	re + in	force	ment

THINK ABOUT IT

A renewable resource can be replaced. A nonrenewable resource cannot be replaced. What do you think the prefix *non-* means?

re : new : a : ble

Use Sounds and Spellings (Phonics)

It often helps to look for a familiar word or word part. But sometimes you have to try "sounding out" the word. Think about the sounds that the letters in the word might stand for. Here are some things to keep in mind:

Some letters and letter combinations almost always sound the same.

Some letters and letter combinations stand for one sound in most words.

- The letter combination *or* almost always stands for the sound you hear in *store* and *born.* You can see this in the following vocabulary words:

    core
    force
    forest
    land form

- Here are some other science words with *or, oi,* and *oy.*

organ	*alloy*
spore	*coil*
coral reef	*colloid*
tornado	*boiling point*
flora	

    Try sounding them out.

A letter can stand for different sounds.

Use the next letter to decide which sound is right. Some letters may stand for more than one sound.

- The letter *c* can stand for two sounds. The sound to use depends on the letter that follows.

    > Is *c* followed by *a, o,* or *u*? Then it has the *k* sound that you hear in *cat.* This is also true if *c* is followed by most consonants.

    > Is *c* followed by *e, i,* or *y*? Then it probably has the *s* sound that you hear in *city.*

    Here are some vocabulary words. Do the *c*'s in these words follow the rules?

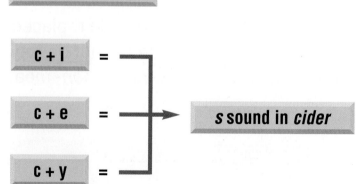

- The letter *g* can also stand for two sounds. Again, the sound depends on the letter that follows.

  > Is *g* followed by the vowels *a, o,* or *u*? Then it sounds like the *g* in *gate.* This is also true if *g* is followed by a consonant.

  > Is *g* followed by *e, i,* or *y*? Then it may sound like the *g* in *gentle.*

  Check out these vocabulary words. Do the *g*'s follow the rules?

  energy, gas, germinate, gravity, igneous

- Here are some more science words to check out. Do they fit the rules for *c* and *g*?

cell	*gauge*
circuit	*gems*
cast	*genus*
trace	*geography*
fungi	*magma*
galaxy	*magnet*

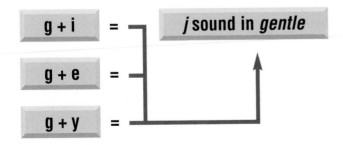

THINK ABOUT IT

There is something unusual about these particular *c* and *g* words: *circuit, recycle, geography, gauge.* What is it?

Some letters and letter combinations don't follow any rules.

A letter or letter combination may stand for different sounds. When you're not sure which sound to use, you need to reach for a glossary or a dictionary.

One example is the letter combination *oo.* It often has the long *u* sound you can hear in the word *school.* But it may stand for the vowel sound you hear in *good.* Sometimes, in a word like *blood,* it has the short *u* sound you hear in *mud.*

Which sound for *oo* does each vocabulary word contain?

flood, food chain, root

Here are some more *oo* science words to think about:

smooth muscle	*sonic boom*
taproot	*cold-blooded*
proof	*tidal pool*

Which sound for *oo* does each of these words contain?

Glossary

As you read your science book, you will see words that may be new to you. The words have phonetic respellings to help you quickly know how to say them. In this Glossary you will see a different kind of respelling. Here, diacritical marks are used, as they are used in dictionaries. *Diacritical respellings* can show more exactly how words should sound.

When you see the ′ mark after a syllable, say that syllable more strongly than the other syllables. The page number after the meaning tells where to find the word in your book. The boldfaced letters in the Pronunciation Key show how each respelling symbol sounds.

PRONUNCIATION KEY

a	add, map	m	move, seem	u	up, done
ā	ace, rate	n	nice, tin	û(r)	burn, term
â(r)	care, air	ng	ring, song	yōo	fuse, few
ä	palm, father	o	odd, hot	v	vain, eve
b	bat, rub	ō	open, so	w	win, away
ch	check, catch	ô	order, jaw	y	yet, yearn
d	dog, rod	oi	oil, boy	z	zest, muse
e	end, pet	ou	pout, now	zh	vision, pleasure
ē	equal, tree	ŏŏ	took, full	ə	the schwa, an
f	fit, half	ōō	pool, food		unstressed vowel
g	go, log	p	pit, stop		representing the
h	hope, hate	r	run, poor		sound spelled
i	it, give	s	see, pass		*a* in *above*
ī	ice, write	sh	sure, rush		*e* in *sicken*
j	joy, ledge	t	talk, sit		*i* in *possible*
k	cool, take	th	thin, both		*o* in *melon*
l	look, rule	th	this, bathe		*u* in *circus*

Other symbols:

- • separates words into syllables
- ′ indicates heavier stress on a syllable
- ′ indicates light stress on a syllable

amphibian [am•fib′ē•ən] An animal that begins life in the water and moves onto land as an adult **(A60)**

anemometer [an′ə•mom′ə•tər] An instrument that measures wind speed **(D40)**

asteroid [as′tər•oid] A chunk of rock that orbits the sun **(D64)**

atmosphere [at′məs•fir′] The air that surrounds Earth **(D30)**

atom [at′əm] The basic building block of matter **(E16)**

axis [ak′sis] An imaginary line that goes through the North Pole and the South Pole of Earth **(D68)**

barrier island [bar′ē•ər i′lənd] A landform; a thin island along a coast **(C35)**

bedrock [bed′rok′] The solid rock that is under soil **(C63)**

bird [bûrd] An animal that has feathers, two legs, and wings **(A55)**

camouflage [kam′ə•fläzh′] A natural disguise some animals have to help them blend in with their surroundings **(A72)**

canyon [kan′yən] A landform; a deep valley with very steep sides **(C35)**

carnivore [kär′nə•vôr′] An animal that eats other animals **(B52)**

cells [selz] The small units that make up all living things **(A8)**

chemical change [kem′i•kəl chānj′] A change that forms different kinds of matter **(E46)**

chlorophyll [klôr′ə•fil′] The substance that gives plants their green color; it helps a plant use energy from the sun to make food **(A28)**

circuit [sûr′kit] The path electricity follows from a battery through a bulb and back to the battery **(F20)**

clay [klā] A type of soil made up of very small grains; it holds water well **(C69)**

coastal forest [kōs′təl fôr′ist] A thick forest with tall trees that gets a lot of rain and does not get very warm or cold **(B17)**

comet [kom′it] A large ball of ice and dust that orbits the sun **(D64)**

community [kə•myoo′nə•tē] All the populations of organisms that live in an ecosystem **(B7)**

condensation [kon′dən•sā′shən] The changing of a gas into a liquid **(D17)**

conduction [kən•duk′shən] The movement of thermal energy from one object to another where they touch **(F46)**

conductor [kən·duk′tər] A material in which thermal energy moves easily **(F47)**

coniferous forest [kō·nif′ər·əs fôr′ist] A forest in which most of the trees are conifers (cone-bearing) and stay green all year **(B18)**

conservation [kon′ser·vā′shən] The saving of resources by using them carefully **(C76)**

consumer [kən·sōōm′ər] A living thing that eats other living things as food **(B51)**

contour plowing [kon′tōor plou′ing] A type of plowing for growing crops; creates rows of crops around the sides of a hill instead of up and down **(C76)**

convection [kən·vek′shən] The movement of thermal energy from one place to another in moving liquids and gases **(F48)**

core [kôr] The center of the Earth **(C8)**

crust [krust] The solid outside layer of the Earth **(C8)**

deciduous forest [dē·sij′ōō·əs fôr′ist] A forest in which most trees lose and regrow their leaves each year **(B15)**

decomposer [dē′kəm·pōz′er] A living thing that breaks down dead organisms for food **(B52)**

desert [dez′ərt] An ecosystem where there is very little rain **(B22)**

earthquake [ûrth′kwāk′] The shaking of Earth's surface caused by movement of the crust and mantle **(C48)**

ecosystem [ek′ō·sis′təm] The living and nonliving things in an environment **(B7)**

electricity [i·lek′tris′ə·tē] A form of energy that people produce from the active energy of wind and moving water and the stored energy in oil and coal **(F7)**

endangered [in·dān′jərd] In danger of becoming extinct **(A76)**

energy [en′ər·jē] The ability to cause change **(F6)**

energy pyramid [en′ər·jē pir′ə·mid] A diagram that shows that the amount of useable energy in an ecosystem is less for each higher animal in the food chain **(B58)**

environment [in·vī′rən·mənt] The things, both living and nonliving, that surround a living thing **(B6)**

erosion [i·rō′zhən] The movement of weathered rock and soil **(C42)**

estuary [es′chōō·er′ē] A place where fresh water from a river mixes with salt water from the ocean **(D12)**

evaporation [ē·vap′ə·rā′shən] The process by which a liquid changes into a gas **(D17, E18)**

extinct [ik·stingkt′] Describes a species that is gone forever because all of its kind have died **(A76)**

fish [fish] An animal that lives its whole life in water and breathes with gills **(A62)**

flood [flud] A large amount of water that covers normally dry land **(C50)**

food chain [fōod′ chān′] The path of food from one living thing to another **(B56)**

food web [fōod′ web′] A model that shows how food chains overlap **(B62)**

force [fôrs] A push or a pull **(F66)**

forest [fôr′ist] An area in which the main plants are trees **(B14)**

fossil [fos′əl] Something that has lasted from a living thing that died long ago **(A77, C20)**

fossil fuel [fos′əl fyōo′əl] Fuel formed from the remains of once-living organisms **(F8)**

fresh water [fresh′ wôt′ər] Water that has very little salt in it **(B34)**

friction [frik′shən] The force between two moving objects that makes it hard for the objects to move **(F41)**

front [frunt] A place where two air masses of different temperatures meet **(D37)**

gas [gas] A form of matter that does not have a definite shape or a definite volume **(E12)**

germinate [jûr′mə•nāt′] When a new plant breaks out of the seed **(A21)**

gills [gilz] A body part found in fish and young amphibians that takes in oxygen from the water **(A61)**

glacier [glā′shər] A huge sheet of ice **(C44)**

grassland [gras′land′] An ecosystem made up of large, flat areas of land that are covered with grass **(B28)**

gravity [grav′i•tē] The force that pulls objects toward each other **(F70)**

groundwater [ground′wôt′ər] A form of fresh water that is found under Earth's surface **(D8)**

habitat [hab′ə•tat′] The place where a population lives in an ecosystem **(B7)**

heat [hēt] The movement of thermal energy from one place to another **(F40)**

herbivore [hûr′bə•vôr′] An animal that eats plants **(B51)**

hibernate [hī′bər•nāt′] To enter a deep sleep in which life activities slow down **(A69)**

humus [hyōo′məs] The part of the soil made up of decayed parts of once-living things **(C62)**

igneous rock [ig′nē•əs rok′] A rock that was once melted rock but has cooled and hardened **(C12)**

inclined plane [in•klīnd′ plān′] A simple machine made of a flat surface set at an angle to another surface **(F79)**

inherit [in•her′it] To receive traits from parents **(A48)**

instinct [in′stingkt] A behavior an animal knows how to do without being taught **(A68)**

insulator [in′sə•lāt′ər] A material in which thermal energy does not move easily **(F47)**

interact [in′tər•akt′] When plants and animals affect one another or the environment to meet their needs **(B50)**

kinetic energy [ki•net′ik en′ər•jē] The energy of motion **(F6)**

landform [land′fôrm′] A natural shape or feature of Earth's surface **(C34)**

leaf [lēf] A plant part that grows out of the stem; it takes in the air and light that a plant needs **(A7)**

lever [lev′ər] A bar that moves on or around a fixed point **(F78)**

liquid [lik′wid] A form of matter that has volume that stays the same, but can change its shape **(E12)**

loam [lōm] A type of topsoil that is rich in minerals and has lots of humus **(C70)**

lunar eclipse [loo′nər i•klips′] The hiding of the moon when it passes through the Earth's shadow **(D78)**

mammal [mam′əl] An animal that has fur or hair and is fed milk from its mother's body **(A52)**

mantle [man′təl] The middle layer of the Earth **(C8)**

mass [mas] The amount of matter in an object **(E24)**

matter [mat′ər] Anything that takes up space **(E6)**

metamorphic rock [met′ə•môr′fik rok′] A rock that has been changed by heat and pressure **(C12)**

migrate [mī′grāt′] To travel as a group from one place to live in another **(A70)**

mimicry [mim′ik•rē] An animal's imitation of another animal or of an object in order to avoid predators **(A72)**

mineral [min′ər•əl] An object that is solid, is formed in nature, and has never been alive **(C6)**

mixture [miks′chər] A substance that contains two or more different types of matter **(E41)**

motion [mō′shən] A change in position **(F67)**

mountain [moun′tən] A landform; a place on Earth's surface that is much higher than the land around it **(C35)**

nonrenewable resource [non′ri•noo̅′ə•bəl rē′sôrs] A resource, such as coal or oil, that will be used up someday **(C96)**

omnivore [om′nə•vôr′] An animal that eats both plants and other animals **(B52)**

orbit [ôr′bit] The path an object takes as it moves around another object in space **(D58)**

phases [fāz•əz] The different shapes the moon seems to have in the sky when observed from Earth **(D76)**

photosynthesis [fōt′ō•sin′thə•sis] The food-making process of plants **(A28)**

physical change [fiz′i•kəl chānj] A change to matter in which no new kinds of matter are formed **(E40)**

physical property [fiz′i•kəl prop′ər•tē] Anything you can observe about an object by using your senses **(E6)**

plain [plān] A landform; a flat area on Earth's surface **(C35)**

planet [plan′it] A large body of rock or gas that orbits the sun **(D58)**

plateau [pla•tō′] A landform; a flat area higher than the land around it **(C35)**

population [pop′yoo̅•lā′shən] A group of the same kind of living thing that all live in one place at the same time **(B7)**

potential energy [pə•ten′chəl en′ər•jē] The energy an object has because of its position or its shape **(F6)**

precipitation [prē•sip′ə•tā′shən] The water that falls to Earth as rain, snow, sleet, or hail **(D18)**

predator [pred′ə•tər] An animal that hunts another animal for food **(B62)**

prey [prā] An animal that is hunted by a predator **(B62)**

producer [prə•doo̅s′ər] A living thing that makes its own food **(B51)**

radiation [rā′dē•ā′shən] The movement of thermal energy without any objects touching or moving **(F48)**

recycle [rē•sī′kəl] To reuse a resource to make something new **(C100)**

renewable resource [ri•noo̅′ə•bəl rē′sôrs] A resource that can be replaced in a human lifetime **(C94)**

reptile [rep′tīl] A land animal that has dry skin covered by scales **(A63)**

resource [rē′sôrs] A material that is found in nature and that is used by living things (**C74, C88**)

reusable resource [rē•yōō′zə•bəl rē•sôrs′] A resource that can be used over and over and can't be used up; examples, air and water (**C94**)

revolution [rev′ə•lōō′shən] The movement of one object around another object (**D68**)

rock [rok] A solid made of minerals (**C8**)

rock cycle [rok′ sī′kəl] The process in which one type of rock changes into another type of rock (**C14**)

root [rōōt] The part of a plant that holds the plant in the ground and takes in water and minerals from the soil (**A7**)

rotation [rō•tā′shən] The spinning of an object on its axis (**D68**)

salt water [sôlt′ wôt′ər] Water that has a lot of salt in it (**B34**)

scales [skālz] The small, thin, flat plates that help protect the bodies of fish and reptiles (**A62**)

sedimentary rock [sed′ə•men′tər•ē rok′] A rock formed from material that has settled into layers and been squeezed until it hardens into rock (**C12**)

seed [sēd] The first stage in the growth of many plants (**A18**)

seedling [sēd′ling] A young plant (**A21**)

simple machine [sim′pəl mə•shēn′] A tool that helps people do work (**F78**)

simple plant [sim′pəl plant′] A plant that has no roots, stems, or leaves (**A14**)

soil [soil] The loose material in which plants can grow in the upper layer of Earth (**C62**)

solar eclipse [sō′lər i•klips′] The hiding of the sun that occurs when the moon passes between the sun and Earth (**D80**)

solar system [sō′lər sis′təm] The sun and the objects that orbit around it (**D58**)

solid [sol′id] A form of matter that takes up a specific amount of space and has a definite shape (**E11**)

solution [sə•lōō′shən] A mixture in which the particles of two different kinds of matter mix together evenly (**E42**)

species [spē′shēz] A name that identifies a specific kind of organism (**A76**)

speed [spēd] The measure of how fast something moves over a certain distance (**F69**)

stem [stem] A plant part that connects the roots with the leaves of a plant and supports the plant above ground; it carries water from the roots to other parts of the plant (**A7**)

strip cropping [strip′ krop′ing] A type of planting that uses strips of thick grass or clover between strips of crops (**C76**)

temperature [tem′pər•ə•chər] The measure of how hot or cold something is **(D36)**

thermal energy [thûr′məl en′ər•jē] The energy that moves the particles in matter **(F39)**

thermometer [thûr•mom′ə•tər] A tool used to measure temperature **(F52)**

threatened [thret′ənd] On the way to becoming endangered or extinct **(A77)**

topsoil [top′soil′] The top layer of soil made up of the smallest grains and the most humus **(C63)**

trait [trāt] A body feature that an animal inherits; it can also be some things that an animal does **(A48)**

tropical rain forest [trop′i•kəl rān′ fôr′ist] A hot, wet forest where the trees grow very tall and their leaves stay green all year **(B16)**

valley [val′ē] A landform; a lowland area between higher lands, such as mountains **(C35)**

vibrate [vī′brāt] To move quickly back and forth, producing sound **(F19)**

volcano [vol•kā′nō] An opening in Earth's surface from which lava flows **(C49)**

volume [vol′yōōm] The amount of space that matter takes up **(E22)**

water cycle [wôt′ər sī′kəl] The movement of water from Earth's surface into the air and back to the surface again **(D18)**

weather [weth′ər] The happenings in the atmosphere at a certain time **(D32)**

weather map [weth′ər map′] A map that shows weather data for a large area **(D46)**

weathering [weth′ər•ing] The process by which rock is worn down and broken apart **(C40)**

weight [wāt] The measure of the pull of gravity on an object **(F70)**

wind [wind] The movement of air **(D40)**

work [wûrk] The measure of force that it takes to move an object a certain distance **(F74)**

Photography Credits–Page Placement Key: (t) top, (b) bottom, (c) center, (l) left, (r) right, (bg) background, (fg) foreground, (i) inset

Cover and Title page: Lynn Stone